Statistical Methods
For
Managers and Administrators

Statistical Methods
For
Managers and Administrators

Isabel S. Patchett

VNR VAN NOSTRAND REINHOLD COMPANY
NEW YORK   CINCINNATI   TORONTO   LONDON   MELBOURNE

519.5
P 294

Copyright © 1982 by Van Nostrand Reinhold Company Inc.

Library of Congress Catalog Card Number: 81-23966
ISBN: 0-442-23124-5

Manufactured in the United States of America

Published by Van Nostrand Reinhold Company Inc.
135 West 50th Street, New York. N.Y. 10020

Van Nostrand Reinhold Limited
1410 Birchmount Road
Scarborough, Ontario MIP 2E7, Canada

Van Nostrand Reinhold Australia Pty. Ltd.
17 Queen Street
Mitcham, Victoria 3132, Australia

Van Nostrand Reinhold Company Limited
Molly Millars Lane
Wokingham, Berkshire, England

15 14 13 12 11 10 9 8 7 6 5 4 3 2 1

Library of Congress Cataloging in Publication Data

Patchett, Isabel S.
  Statistical methods for managers and administra-
tors.

  Includes index.
  1. Commercial statistics. 2. Management—
Statistical methods. 3. Statistics. I. Title.
HF1017.P3   519.5'024658   81-23966
ISBN 0-442-23124-5   AACR2

Preface

The writing of this book was undertaken after a discussion with my former immediate supervisor, who travels around the United States and abroad presenting seminars on sales forecasting. In our discussion, he indicated that many of his seminar attendees expressed a need for some type of review text on basic business statistics. Thus, the idea of the book was born. Of course, it can be used for other purposes as well. It particularly lends itself to usage as a textbook for a beginning college course in statistics.

Within the covers of this book can be found many of the more common everyday statistical problems encountered by a busy managerial person. To help solve those problems, the following are included:

1. Excellent reference sources
2. Construction of Indexes
3. Detailed explanation of the Consumer Price Index. This is particularly important since so many of the people in the United States are directly affected by it in terms of Social Security payments and cost of living adjustments found in union contracts.
4. Time series analysis
5. Seasonal analysis
6. Elements of probability
7. Regression and correlation analysis
8. Statistical tests of significance
9. Analysis of variance
10. Bayes' theorem and decision making

I am grateful to the Literary Executor of the late Sir Ronald A. Fisher, F.R.S., to Dr. Frank Yates, F.R.S., and to Longman Group Ltd. London, for permission to reprint tables from their book *Statistical Tables for Biological, Agricultural and Medical Research.* (6th edition, 1974).

I also wish to thank Pat Mansfield and Joel Stein of Van Nostrand Reinhold, who helped me in editing the manuscript.

ISABEL S. PATCHETT

Contents

Statistical Methods
For
Managers and Administrators

1 Data Sources and Presentation

Finding a particular statistic can be very simple if you know where to look—and very hard if you do not. Often, business executives must obtain data quickly, but have little time to search them out. The purpose of this chapter therefore is to direct readers who need certain statistical and financial information to the proper sources. Data, once collected, must often be displayed in graphic form. This is discussed in the latter part of the chapter.

DATA SOURCES

Statistics are published by both government and private sources. The United States government probably publishes more statistics than any other government in the world. States and cities also prepare statistics. On the international level, there are several data sources. One of the leading suppliers is the Statistical Office of the United Nations, Department of Economic and Social Affairs.

United States Government Publications

Decennial Reports.   Every 10 years the Bureau of the Census conducts a national survey of population and housing. A large number of reports are published as a result. *Current Population Reports* gives information categorized by such characteristics as age, income, and sex. It also gives projections of population trends by state, age, sex, and so on. Table 1.1 shows annual projections of the population of the United States.

In the projection of population trends, assumptions must be made about such factors as future mortality trends, fertility levels, and net immigration (i.e., imigration minus emigration). The Bureau of the Census uses three series, each predicting a different level of future population. For example, Series II predicts that the population of the United States will be 260 million by the year 2000, while Series III projects 246 million. See Figure 1.1.

Table 1.1. Annual Projections of the Population of the United States, by Single Years of Age and Sex: 1970 to 1985 with Quinquennial Extensions to 2020. (In Thousands, Figures relate to July 1 and include armed forces abroad.)

Series, Sex, and Age	1970	1971	1972	1973	1974	1975	1976	1977
Series B, both sexes								
All ages	204,800	207,036	209,484	212,155	215,053	218,177	221,519	225,065
Under 5 years	17,184	17,451	18,054	18,984	19,987	21,321	22,520	23,714
Under 1 year	3,412	3,789	4,021	4,261	4,507	4,753	4,992	5,220
1 year	3,495	3,407	3,782	4,013	4,253	4,498	4,742	4,981
2 years	3,326	3,498	3,410	3,785	4,016	4,255	4,500	4,744
3 years	3,419	3,331	3,503	3,415	3,790	4,021	4,259	4,504
4 years	3,531	3,425	3,337	3,509	3,421	3,796	4,026	4,265
5 to 9 years	19,876	19,278	18,665	18,022	17,629	17,327	17,592	18,193
5 years	3,730	3,537	3,432	3,344	3,516	3,428	3,802	4,033
6 years	3,916	3,737	3,544	3,439	3,351	3,523	3,435	3,809
7 years	4,001	3,923	3,744	3,551	3,446	3,358	3,530	3,442
8 years	4,066	4,008	3,930	3,751	3,558	3,453	3,365	3,537
9 years	4,162	4,073	4,016	3,937	3,758	3,566	3,460	3,373
10 to 14 years	20,805	20,932	20,809	20,651	20,411	20,042	19,446	18,835
10 years	4,134	4,169	4,080	4,022	3,944	3,765	3,572	3,467
11 years	4,190	4,140	4,175	4,086	4,029	3,951	3,772	3,579
12 years	4,194	4,197	4,147	4,182	4,093	4,035	3,957	3,778
13 years	4,222	4,200	4,203	4,153	4,188	4,099	4,041	3,963
14 years	4,065	4,227	4,205	4,208	4,158	4,193	4,104	4,047
15 to 19 years	19,285	19,660	20,167	20,526	20,786	20,930	21,057	20,935
15 years	4,020	4,071	4,232	4,210	4,213	4,164	4,198	4,109
16 years	3,958	4,024	4,075	4,236	4,214	4,218	4,168	4,203
17 years	3,859	3,961	4,028	4,079	4,240	4,218	4,221	4,172
18 years	3,737	3,863	3,965	4,032	4,083	4,244	4,222	4,225
19 years	3,712	3,741	3,867	3,969	4,035	4,086	4,247	4,226
20 to 24 years	17,176	18,097	18,110	18,461	18,886	19,384	19,758	20,263
20 years	3,540	3,716	3,745	3,871	3,973	4,039	4,090	4,251
21 years	3,552	3,544	3,720	3,749	3,875	3,977	4,043	4,094

Age								
22 years	3,528	3,556	3,548	3,724	3,753	3,878	3,981	4,047
23 years	3,744	3,532	3,560	3,553	3,728	3,757	3,883	3,985
24 years	2,812	3,749	3,537	3,565	3,557	3,733	3,762	3,887
25 to 29 years	13,758	14,093	15,162	15,809	16,531	17,302	18,218	18,232
25 years	2,788	2,818	3,754	3,542	3,570	3,562	3,738	3,767
26 years	2,852	2,795	2,825	3,759	3,548	3,576	3,568	3,743
27 years	2,907	2,858	2,801	2,831	3,764	3,553	3,581	3,573
28 years	2,703	2,913	2,864	2,807	2,837	3,769	3,558	3,586
29 years	2,507	2,709	2,918	2,870	2,813	2,842	3,773	3,563
30 to 34 years	11,520	11,822	12,304	12,941	13,468	13,878	14,211	15,273
35 to 39 years	11,208	11,152	11,151	11,225	11,371	11,575	11,875	12,354
40 to 44 years	11,918	11,750	11,576	11,411	11,274	11,176	11,122	11,122
45 to 49 years	12,210	12,212	12,150	12,039	11,902	11,751	11,588	11,420
50 to 54 years	11,059	11,239	11,445	11,640	11,783	11,852	11,855	11,797
55 to 59 years	8,992	10,088	10,174	10,266	10,382	10,529	10,703	10,901
60 to 64 years	8,656	8,806	8,934	9,046	9,150	9,250	9,343	9,427
65 to 69 years	6,831	6,964	7,145	7,344	7,531	7,690	7,827	7,944
70 to 74 years	5,634	5,655	5,635	5,613	5,631	5,704	5,821	5,977
75 to 79 years	3,739	3,881	4,028	4,160	4,257	4,311	4,329	4,316
80 to 84 years	2,341	2,282	2,286	2,331	2,401	2,486	2,582	2,683
85 years and over	1,611	1,672	1,688	1,684	1,674	1,668	1,669	1,680
1 to 4 years	13,771	13,662	14,033	14,723	15,480	16,569	17,528	18,494
5 to 13 years	36,615	35,984	35,270	34,465	33,882	33,177	32,935	32,981
14 to 17 years	15,902	16,283	16,540	16,734	16,826	16,792	16,692	16,531
18 to 21 years	14,540	14,863	15,297	15,620	15,966	16,346	16,603	16,796
14 years and over	151,001	153,601	156,161	158,706	161,185	163,679	166,064	168,370
16 years and over	142,916	145,303	147,723	150,288	152,813	155,323	157,762	160,214
18 years and over	135,100	137,318	139,620	141,973	144,359	146,887	149,372	151,840
21 years and over	124,112	125,998	128,044	130,101	132,267	134,517	136,813	139,138
62 years and over	25,161	25,565	25,975	25,393	26,819	27,249	27,679	28,106
65 years and over	20,156	20,454	20,782	21,133	21,494	21,859	22,228	22,600
Median age (years)	27.9	27.9	27.9	28.0	28.0	27.9	27.9	27.9

Source: *Current Population Reports*, Series P–25, No. 476, U.S. Bureau of Census, p. 13.

3

Year	Series I	Series II	Series III
ESTIMATES			
1930[1].......		123,188	
1935[1].......		127,362	
1940[2].......		132,594	
1945........		140,468	
1950........		152,271	
1955........		165,931	
1960........		180,671	
1965........		194,303	
1970........		204,878	
1975........		213,540	
1976........		215,118	
PROJECTIONS			
1980........	224,066	222,159	220,732
1985........	238,878	232,880	228,879
1990........	254,715	243,513	236,264
1995........	269,384	252,750	241,973
2000........	282,837	260,378	245,876
2005........	297,600	267,603	248,631
2010........	315,248	275,335	250,892
2015........	334,708	283,164	252,548
2020........	354,108	290,115	253,011
2025........	373,053	295,742	251,915

[1]Excludes Alaska and Hawaii.
[2]The figure excluding Alaska and Hawaii is 132,122.

Fig. 1.1 Projections of the population of the U.S. 1977–2050. (in thousands. as of July 1. Includes Armed Forces overseas)

SOURCE: *Current Population Reports—Population Estimates and Projections,* Series P-25, #704, p. 6, U.S. Dept. of Commerce, Bureau of the Census.

Annual Publications. The *Statistical Abstract of the United States* has been published annually since 1878 by the U.S. Department of Commerce. It is a summary of statistics on the social, political, and economic organization of the United States. The volume is designed to serve as a convenient statistical reference. Its data are selected from many publications, both government and private. It also assists readers in locating additional sources of information. Subjects listed in the index include among others agriculture, education, energy, foreign aid, foreign commerce, law enforcement, national defense, population, and veterans affairs.

The Bureau of Labor Statistics (BLS) publishes a *Handbook of Labor Statistics* that includes information on labor force, employment, unemployment, hours, productivity and unit labor costs, comprehensive price and living conditions, unions and industrial relations, occupational injuries and illnesses, foreign labor statistics, and general economic data. It is published annually, with monthly updatings.

A good source reference for data on industries in the United States is the *U.S. Industrial Outlook* published annually by the Industrial Economic Bureau of the U.S. Department of Commerce. The 1981 edition lists 200 industries with projections to 1985. Industries, which are arranged by Standard Industrial Classifica-

agriculture

Subject	Tabular Detail	Areas to Which Data Apply	Frequency	Sources (See Bibliography, pp. 329-339.)
AGRICULTURE[1]				
Farms	All farms; farms with sales of $1,000 or more: 1969; 1974 Acreage: Land in farms; average size Farms with sales less than $2,500 Cropland: Farms; acreage Farm production expenses Value of agricultural products sold Average per farm; crops, including nursery products and hay; forest products; livestock, poultry, and their products Animals on place: Cattle and calves, hogs and pigs; chickens, 3 months or older	Counties	Every 5 years[2]	24. *Agriculture Census, 1974 Preliminary Reports*,[3, 4] table 1. Census Bureau.
	Farms with sales of $2,500 or more: 1969; 1974: By sales, in 6 dollar ranges Organization: Individual or family; partnership; corporation, including family owned; other Farms; value: Farm-related income Related expenses Off-farm income Farms with grain storage facilities of 1,000 bushels or more Farms; animals on place: Heifers and heifer calves For beef and beef cow replacement For milk cow replacement Steers and bulls, including calves Lambs under 1 year old Ewes, 1 year or older Sheep and lambs shorn	Counties	Every 5 years	*Ibid.*, table 7.

[1] The Department of Agriculture, in cooperation with various State statistical or crop and livestock reporting services, assists in the release of numerous annual summaries covering specific crop production, livestock and poultry operations, and characteristics of farming enterprises within individual States. Since subjects vary widely according to State, these reports are not described in this directory.

[2] In years ending in 2 and 7 after the next census, to be taken for 1978.

[3] As this directory went to print, final reports from the 1974 Census of Agriculture were being released; they are essentially similar to the 1969 census final reports and the 1974 preliminary reports described in this directory, but some differences occur, and table numbers are not identical. For further information about final reports from the 1974 census, consult the Bureau of the Census Catalog (Bibliography No. 176) or write to the Chief, Agriculture Division, Bureau of the Census, Washington, D.C. 20233.

[4] Data vary in individual reports.

Fig. 1.2 Directory of Federal Statistics for Local Areas—Agriculture.

SOURCE: *The Directory of Federal Statistics for Local Areas*, Bureau of the Census.

tion (SIC) code, range from basic mining to services such as banks. Each industry description is authored by the Department of Commerce's industry expert in that field.

The *Directory of Federal Statistics for Local Areas,* published by the Bureau of the Census, presents information on areas ranging in size from Standard Metropolitan Statistical Areas (SMSAs) and counties to city blocks. The more than 100 areas include fishery districts, harbors, low-income neighborhoods, oil and gas districts, and rural areas. The reports, which include information published from 1966 through 1976, cover the entire United States broken down by area. The information is arranged by subject headings: Tabular Detail, Areas to Which Data Apply, Frequency, and Sources. See Figure 1.2.

Another helpful publication is the quarterly *Bureau of the Census Catalog.* Its contents are summarized in an annual volume that is updated monthly. It lists publications, data files, special tabulations, material on microfiche, summary tapes, and processing centers. Subjects covered include housing and construction, geography, agriculture, manufacturing, population, retail and wholesale trade, and transportation.

Monthly Publications. The *Survey of Current Business,* published monthly by the U.S. Department of Commerce, comes in two sections. The first gives current business statistics on some 2500 series such as gross national product, new plant and equipment expenditures, United States international transactions, personal income by source, commodity prices received by farmers, and producer prices. The second section discusses the current business situation, presents articles written by experts, and gives information on such timely topics as plant equipment expenditures, national income and product tables, and United States international transactions.

Historical data on the series shown in *The Survey of Current Business* are published every 2 years in *Business Statistics.* The 1977 issue (the latest as of fall 1981), the twenty-first biennial edition, presents data for most series on an annual basis for 1947–76 and monthly for 1973–76. The appendix provides monthly or quarterly data for earlier periods for over 400 of the more important series.

Publications of Private Organizations

There are many good statistical sources published by private organizations. Those mentioned here are but a few of those available.

The *Financial Market Place* (R.R. Bowker Co., 1972) is a directory of major corporations, institutions, services, and publications.

The seventh edition of the *Directory of Business and Financial Services* (Special Libraries Association, 1976) deals exclusively with information services that provide continuous coverage of some facet of business activity.

Business Information Sources (University of California Press, 1976) includes such subjects as methods of locating facts; basic time-saving sources; locating information on companies, organizations, and individuals; basic United States statistical sources; industry statistics; foreign statistics and economic trends; investment sources; United States business and economic trends; and business in American society.

The *Dow Jones-Irwin Business Almanac, Nineteen Eighty-One* (Dow Jones-Irwin, 1980) contains information on major legislation enacted, regulatory agencies, finance and accounting, largest corporations, executive recruiting organizations, stock market, commodities market, money and financial institutions, banks and other financial institutions, and advertising and the media.

Information on international data bases may be obtained from the *Information Market Place, 1978-79* (R.R. Bowker Co., 1978). It provides quick reference to major products and services comprising the international information industry, as well as a trade directory of suppliers and services directed to the industry.

Encyclopedia of Business Information Sources (Gale Research Co., 1980) is a detailed list of primary subjects of interest to management personnel including record source books, periodicals, organizations, directories, handbooks, and bibliographies.

Sales & Marketing Management produces a two-volume *Annual Survey of Buying Power.* It is helpful to management personnel seeking information on retail sales and effective buying power for American and Canadian geographic markets. Part I, which is published each summer, gives information on annual changes in geographic markets such as American metropolitan areas, counties, cities, and states. It also gives a survey of Canadian buying power. Part II, published in the fall, presents an analysis of change in United States metropolitan markets and a 5-year projection of American and Canadian markets. An analysis of American newspaper and television markets is also presented.

Newsletters

Several major national banks issue newsletters on economic and business affairs. Chase Manhattan Bank, N.A. publishes *Business In Brief* bimonthly. *Morgan Guaranty Survey* is produced monthly by Morgan Guaranty Trust Co. of New York, and First National Bank of Chicago produces the bimonthly *First Chicago World Report.* Regional banks also publish similar information; for example, Hartford National Bank & Trust Co. publishes *Comments,* a quarterly newsletter about the Connecticut scene. The newsletters can be found in the business section of most large city libraries. In addition, in most cases they can be obtained by writing directly to the bank.

PRESENTATION OF DATA

Many functional areas of a business enterprise employ statistics in organizing and controlling various activities. Production is concerned with meeting requirements set by management, such as scheduling. Market research needs to know what consumers will buy in order to project sales for a product. Accounting is concerned with sales, income, taxes, profit, etc. All of the areas can reach meaningful conclusion from data if it is properly presented.

Data may be presented either graphically or in a table.

Table Format

In preparing data in tabular form, certain rules should be followed:

1. Number tables in sequence—Table 1, Table 2, etc. When a work is divided into chapters, number tables according to chapter number—Table 1.1 in Chapter 1, Table 2.1 in Chapter 2, etc.
2. Label heading of table clearly.
3. Label columns with proper descriptions (see Table 1.2).
4. If figures are in millions, instead of indicating "1,000,000," for example, it is often easier to drop the last six digits and use "1." Under the column heading or in a footnote, indicate how numbers are reported, i.e., "(Millions of Dollars)."
5. When information is taken from a source, be certain to give proper credit.

Graphic Format

Data may be presented graphically, using the arithmetic scale, in several ways including line graphs, bar charts (simple, component, and two-directional), and pie charts. The semilog scale is used mainly for line charts.

Arithmetic Scale

The arithmetic scale has the following characteristics:

1. Divisions on arithmetic scale are equidistant on both Y (vertical) and X (horizontal) axis.
2. Equal distances represent equal amounts.
3. Data plotted on the Y axis increase or decrease in magnitude from origin of zero.
4. Years progress from left to right on the X-axis.

One series of data (simple line chart) or several related series (multiple line chart) may be produced.

**Table 1.2. Manufacturing and Trade Inventories, Book Value,
End of Selected Years 1948-76.**

Selected Years	Inventories, Book Value, End of Period ($ Millions)
1948	$ 51,985
1956	86,183
1963	104,382
1971	187,087
1976	306,412

Source: *Business Statistics*, 1977 Edition, p. 27.

Line Graph. Arithmetic graph paper is used when it is desired to show an absolute amount of change (as opposed to percent change) from period to period (See Table 1.3). Figure 1.3, net exports of United States goods and services in actual dollars, illustrates the use of arithmetic graph paper and a simple line chart. This time series measures the exports less imports of goods and services. Exports of goods and services are included in the gross national product (GNP) because they are produced by the nation's economy. The GNP is the market value of goods and services produced by labor and property supplied by the residents of the United States before the deduction of depreciation charges and other allowances for business and institutional consumption of capital goods. Other business products used up by business are deducted. Since imports of foreign goods and services are included in the purchases of the various market groups (consumer, government, etc.) distinguished in the GNP breakdown, they must be deducted from the sum of these purchases to derive a measure of output attributable to the nations's economy.

**Table 1.3. XYZ Co., Arithmetic Progression of Sales
(Thousands of Dollars)**

Year	Sales	% Change
1968	$200	–
1969	220	10.0
1970	240	9.1
1971	260	8.3
1972	280	7.7
1973	300	7.1
1974	320	6.7
1975	340	6.3
1976	360	5.9
1977	380	5.6
1978	400	5.4

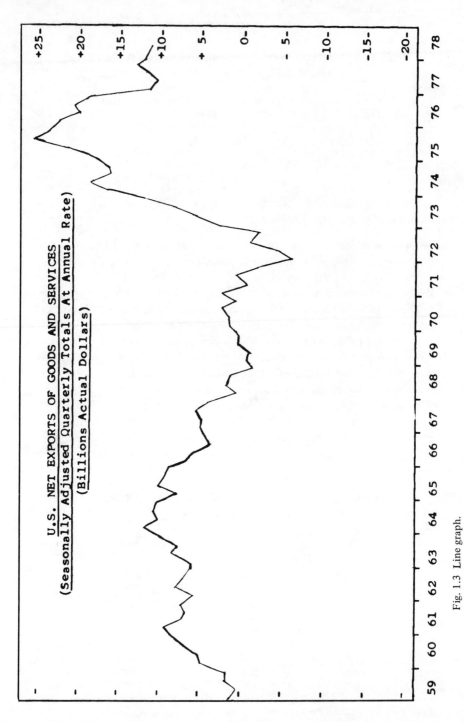

Fig. 1.3 Line graph.

SOURCE: *Monthly Labor Review*, U.S. Dept. of Labor, Bureau of Labor Statistics, Jan. 1980, p. 41.

10

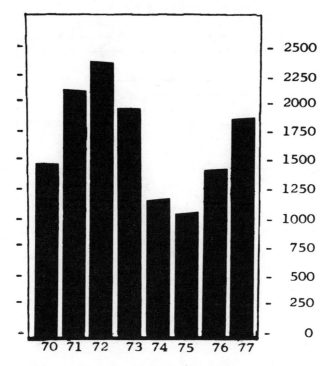

Fig. 1.4 Vertical bar chart.

Bar Chart. Bar charts may be simple (showing one series) or multiple (showing more than one series). They may be vertical or horizontal.

Vertical bar chart. The data to be presented are shown on the Y-axis and the identifying characteristic, such as years or percent change, are shown on the X-axis. Figure 1.4 is a vertical bar chart showing the number of building permits issued in the United States from 1970 through 1977. Building permits provide some indication of the activity in residential building in advance of actual construction.

Horizontal bar chart. A horizontal bar chart shows several classes of a particular group with a common characteristic (unit measure). See Figure 1.5.

Multiple bar chart. A multiple bar chart shows more than one series. See Figure 1.6.

Pie Chart. If relative sizes of components of a total are to be emphasized, a pie chart is useful. The total area of the pie equals 100%. The pie chart in Figure 1.7 shows the estimated United States government budget receipts by source for fis-

Industries With Gains . . .

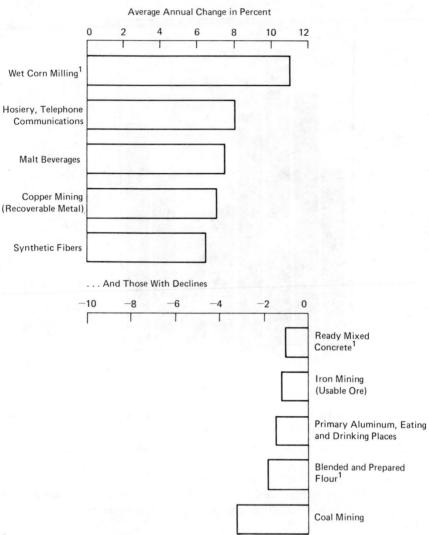

Average Annual Change in Percent

Wet Corn Milling[1]

Hosiery, Telephone Communications

Malt Beverages

Copper Mining (Recoverable Metal)

Synthetic Fibers

. . . And Those With Declines

Ready Mixed Concrete[1]

Iron Mining (Usable Ore)

Primary Aluminum, Eating and Drinking Places

Blended and Prepared Flour[1]

Coal Mining

[1] Rate of Change is For 1973-77

Fig. 1.5 Horizontal bar chart.

SOURCE: *Monthly Labor Review,* U.S. Dept. of Labor, Bureau of Labor Statistics, Jan. 1980, p. 41.

cal 1979. A total of 43.3% came from individual income taxes, 32.2% from social insurance taxes and contributions, 14.2% from corporate income taxes, 5.8% from excise taxes, and 4.5% from miscellaneous taxes including estate and gift taxes, custom duties, and miscellaneous receipts. When these figures are added up, they total 100.0%. See Figure 1.7.

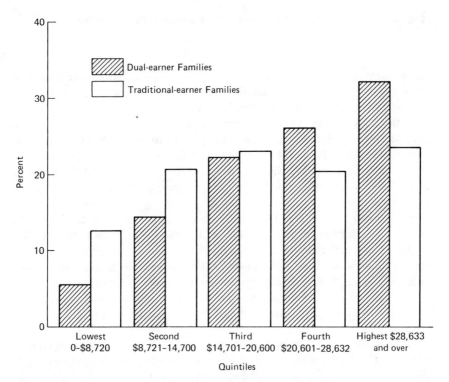

Fig. 1.6 Multiple bar chart.

SOURCE: *Monthly Labor Review,* U.S. Dept. of Labor, Bureau of Labor Statistics, April 1981, p. 61.

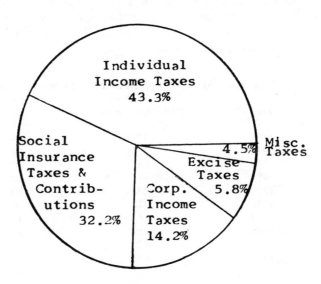

Fig. 1.7 Pie chart.

Ratio (Semilog) Scaling

Management personnel are often interested in the percentage change from year to year of a particular time series. When it is desired to show the percent change in a time series, the ratio (semilog) scale is used.

If the sales of ABC Co. are growing at 10% per year, then in 10 years will sales be 100% greater than at the beginning of the first year? No! Compounding is involved. From Table 1.4, it can be seen that sales increase approximately 160% due to compounding. Looking back at Table 1.3, sales of XYZ Co., we see that sales increased 100% due to the same *constant dollar* amount being added each year.

If a company with $200,000 in sales were to build a plant today that could handle a 10% increase in sales for the next 10 years, its sales would be $518,000 at the end of that time. Using a simple arithmetic progression and neglecting compounding would have yielded $400,000, an underestimate of capacity. Look at XYZ Co. sales. This error is plotted on semilog paper in Figure 1.8.

A straight line on semilog paper means a constant rate of growth, such as 10% per year. On arithmetic paper, a straight line implies a constant dollar amount per year.

Semilog paper has a y- and an x-axis. The x-axis has arithmetic scaling. In addition it is evenly spaced. The y-axis is constructed using logarithms. Equal distance on the ratio paper represents equal percent changes. To illustrate the use of semilog paper, Figure 1.9 is shown with the United States GNP plotted in actual dollars from the first quarter of 1967 to the first quarter of 1978. Note that the distances from $800 billion to $1600 billion and from $1600 billion to $3200 billion are the same, thus representing equal percent changes. From the first quarter of 1967 to the fourth quarter of 1975, GNP increases 100% from about $800 billion to $1600 billion.

Table 1.4. ABC Co., Logarithmic Progression of Sales.

Year	($ Thousands) Sales	% Change
1968	$200	–
1969	220	10.0
1970	242	10.0
1971	266	10.0
1972	293	10.0
1973	322	10.0
1974	354	10.0
1975	389	10.0
1976	428	10.0
1977	471	10.0
1978	518	10.0

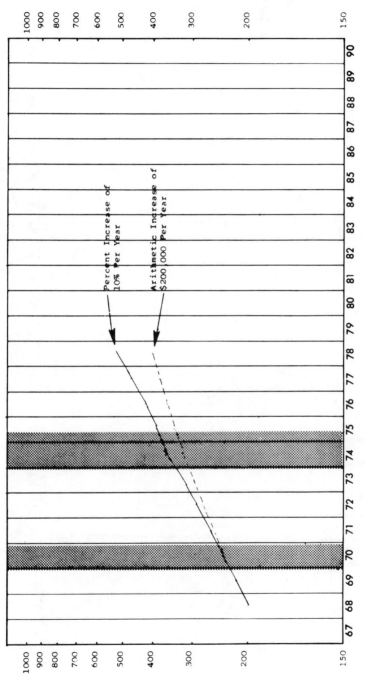

Fig. 1.8 Increase in sales per year 10% vs. $200,000 on semi-log paper.

15

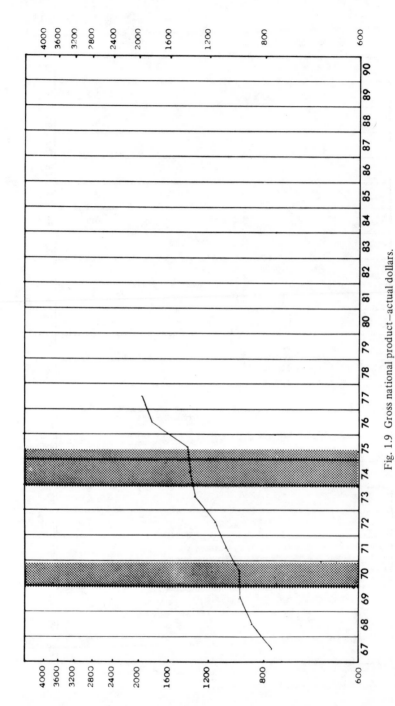

Fig. 1.9 Gross national product—actual dollars.

16

2 Indexes and Their Uses

"Consumer Price Index for October Sends Annual Inflation Rate to 12%!" This type of headline is seen very often these days.

An index measures some current activity in relation to some base period (i.e., the period from which the activity is referenced). There are indexes measuring help wanted, wholesale prices, construction costs, prices received by farmers for their produce, and magazine costs. Consider Figure 2.1, which gives the value of retail sales in the United States as an index for which the base period is 1967 = 100. Note that 1977 is 115% higher than 1968 (225 - 110 = 115). Currently, many of the federal government indexes use 1972 as the base period.

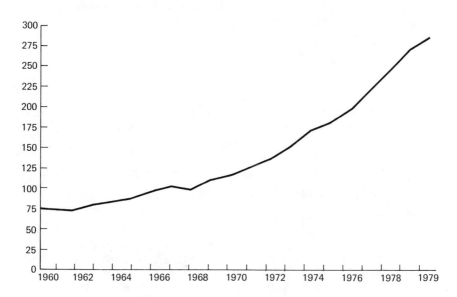

Fig. 2.1 Value of retail sales in the United States.

Indexes have the following characteristics:

1. The base number of most indexes is 100. However, there is no hard and fast rule about this. Any other number, such as 20, 200, and 2000, may be used.
2. Each index has its own base period. For example, the consumer price index (CPI) uses 1967.
3. An index can be used to measure changes in a group of dissimilar (heterogeneous) items. For example, the consumer price index contains about 400 items including such things as expenditures for housing, clothing, entertainment, and medical care.
4. Normally, indexes do not use the percent sign.
5. Most indexes are rounded to the nearest whole number or tenth of a percent.

TYPES OF INDEXES

Simple Index

In the simple or unweighted index, each item has the same weight. To see how a simple index is constructed, look at Table 2.1, which gives the price of widgets for selected years from 1967 to 1978. The formula for computing a simple index—in this case, the price—where p_n is the price in the year other than the base period and p_o is the price in the base period, is:

$$p = \frac{p_n}{p_o} \ (100)$$

From Table 2.1, we can conclude that a widget cost 115% more (215 - 100 = 115) in 1978 than it did in 1967. Two or more years may be used as the base period, i.e., 1967-68 = 100. In that case, the mean of both years would be used as the base.

Table 2.1. Price Index for Widgets, Selected Years (1967 = 100).

Year	Price of Widget	Index
1967	$1.00	($1.00/1.00) × 100 = 100
1970	1.35	(1.35/1.00) × 100 = 135
1972	1.50	(1.50/1.00) × 100 = 150
1975	1.80	(1.80/1.00) × 100 = 180
1977	2.10	(2.10/1.00) × 100 = 210
1978	2.15	(2.15/1.00) × 100 = 215

Table 2.2. Price Index for Sledgehammers, Selected Years (1967-68 = 100).

Year	Price of Sledgehammer	Index
1965	$5.00	($5.00/6.60) × 100 = 75.8
1966	5.50	(5.50/6.60) × 100 = 83.3
1967	6.20	(6.20/6.60) × 100 = 93.9
1968	7.00	(7.00/6.60) × 100 = 106.1
1969	7.15	(7.15/6.60) × 100 = 108.3
1970	8.00	(8.00/6.60) × 100 = 121.2
1971	8.25	(8.25/6.60) × 100 = 125.0
1972	8.75	(8.75/6.60) × 100 = 132.6
1973	9.15	(9.15/6.60) × 100 = 138.6
1974	9.60	(9.60/6.60) × 100 = 145.5
1975	10.00	(10.00/6.60) × 100 = 151.5
1976	10.15	(10.15/6.60) × 100 = 153.8
1977	11.00	(11.00/6.60) × 100 = 166.6
1978	11.75	(11.75/6.60) × 100 = 178.0

Table 2.2 shows the price of sledgehammers where 1967-68 was selected as the base period. The base period price of $6.60 was derived by taking the 1967 price of $6.20, adding the 1968 price of $7.00, and dividing by 2; that is, ($6.20 + $7.00)/2 = $6.60.

Quantity may be used in place of price. The formula is the same as the for-

Table 2.3. Quantity Index for Factory Sales Room Air Conditioners, 1960-76 (1971 = 100).

Year	Quantity (in Thousands)[a]	Index
1960	1580	1580/5438 × 100 = 29.1
1961	1500	1500/5438 × 100 = 27.6
1962	1580	1580/5438 × 100 = 29.1
1963	1945	1945/5438 × 100 = 35.8
1964	2755	2755/5438 × 100 = 50.7
1965	2960	2960/5438 × 100 = 54.4
1966	3345	3345/5438 × 100 = 61.5
1967	4129	4129/5438 × 100 = 75.9
1968	4026	4026/5438 × 100 = 74.0
1969	5459	5459/5438 × 100 = 100.4
1970	5886	5886/5438 × 100 = 108.2
1971	5438	5438/5438 × 100 = 100.0
1972	4508	4508/5438 × 100 = 82.9
1973	5346	5346/5438 × 100 = 98.3
1974	4564	4564/5438 × 100 = 83.9
1975	2670	2670/5438 × 100 = 49.1
1976	2962	2962/5438 × 100 = 54.5

[a]Source: *Business Statistics,* 1977 Biennial Edition, p. 156.

mula for price, except q_1 equals quantity in other than the base period and q_o equals quantity in the base period:

$$q_1 = \frac{q_n}{q_o}(100)$$

Table 2.3 shows the index for factory sales of room air conditioners where 1971 is the base year.

Weighted Index

In a weighted index, each component is given its own relative value. As with the simple index, price or quantity may be measured.

Price Index. The formula for the weighted price index is:

$$p = \frac{p_n q_d}{p_o q_d}(100)$$

where

$$p_n = \text{price in other than base period}$$

$$q_o = \text{quantity in the base period}$$

$$p_o = \text{price in the base period}$$

Table 2.4, a simple weighted price index, shows prices paid by the Smith family for weekly groceries in 1967 and 1978. The base period is 1967. The weighted method in the table uses the amounts consumed in the base period as the con-

Table 2.4. Price Index, 1978 Weekly Grocery Prices Paid by the Smith Family (1967 = 100).

| Items | 1967 | | | 1978 | |
	Price (p_q)	Quantity Consumed (q_o)	$p_o q_o$	Price (p_n)	$p_n q_o$
Meat, poultry, fish (lb)	$0.50	10	$5.00	$1.00	$10.00
Milk (qts)	0.25	8	2.00	0.50	4.00
Fruits and vegetables (lb)	0.10	15	1.50	0.25	3.75
			$8.50		$17.75

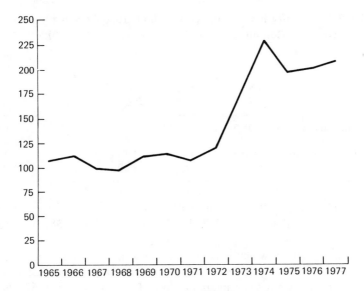

Fig. 2.2 Spot price index.

stant. Only price fluctuated. The Smiths paid 109% more for groceries in 1978 than in 1967; that is, ($17.75 ÷ $8.50) × 100 = 208.8% - 100% = 109%.

An example of a weighted price index is the *Wholesale Spot Market Price Index, Commodities* published monthly by the U.S. Department of Labor, Bureau of Labor Statistics. The index lists the Tuesday price movement of 22 sensitive basic commodities whose markets are presumed to be the first influenced by actual or anticipated changes in economic conditions. The commodities used are either raw materials or products close to the initial production stage, which are traded through organized markets or through markets whose activities are recorded in trade or other government publications. Of the 22 commodities, 9 are foodstuffs (butter, corn, etc.) and 13 are raw industrials (burlap, copper, scrap, etc.). The base year is 1967. Figure 2.2 shows the spot price index plotted from 1965 through 1977.

Quantity Index

Quantity may be used in place of price in computing an index. Base-year prices are held constant in place of quantities. The method of weighting used, the *Laspeyres method,* was developed in the latter part of the eighteenth century. Using the index developed in Table 2.4 and keeping prices constant (Laspeyres method), the quantity index shown in Table 2.5 is developed. The weighted method in the table uses prices that were in effect in the base year (1967) as the

Table 2.5. Quantity Index, Laspeyres Method: 1978 Weighted Index of Groceries Consumed by the Smith Family (1967 = 100).

| | 1967 | | | 1978 | |
| | Price | Quantity Consumed | | Quantity Consumed | |
Items	P_o	q_o	$P_o Q_o$	Q_n	$P_o Q_n$
Meats, poultry, and fish (lb)	$0.50	10	$5.00	12	$6.00
Milk (qt)	0.25	8	2.00	10	2.50
Fruits and vegetables (lb)	0.10	15	1.50	15	1.50
			$8.50		$10.00

constant. Only the quantity consumed fluctuated. The Smiths consumed 18% more food in 1978 than they did in 1967; that is ($10.00 ÷ $8.50) $\times$ 100 = 117.6% - 100% = 18%.

The Paasche method, which uses present-year weights, may be used in place of the Laspeyres method (see Table 2.6). It cost the Smiths more than twice as much in 1978 to buy the same amount of food they consumed in 1967—that is, ($20.75 ÷ $10.00) $\times$ (100) 207.5% - 100% = 108%. A drawback to the Paasche method is that current consumption figures must be computed each year. Therefore, the Laspeyres method is more commonly used.

Value Index

A value index is constructed by multiplying price times quantity. In this instance, price and value are needed in the base year and present year according to the following formula:

$$V = \frac{p_n q_n}{p_o q_o} (100)$$

Table 2.6. Quantity Index, Paasche Method: 1978 Weighted Index of Quantity Consumed by the Smith Family (1967 = 100).

Item	1967 Price (p_o)	1978 Price (p_n)	1978 Quantity Consumed (q_n)	$(p_o q_n)$	$(p_n q_n)$
Meats, poultry, and fish (lb)	$0.50	$1.00	12	$ 6.00	$12.00
Milk (qt)	0.25	0.50	10	2.50	5.00
Fruits and vegetables (lb)	0.10	0.25	15	1.50	3.75
				$10.00	$20.75

Table 2.7. Weekly Grocery Bill, Smith Family, 1978 Value Index (1967 = 100).

| | 1967 | | | 1978 | | |
| | Price | Quantity Consumed | Value | Price | Quantity Consumed | Value |
Item	p_o	q_o	$p_o q_o$	p_n	q_n	$p_n q_n$
Meats, Poultry, Fish (lb)	$0.50	10	$5.00	$0.75	15	$11.25
Milk (qt)	0.25	8	2.00	0.35	12	4.20
Fruits and Vegetables (lb)	0.10	15	1.50	0.20	17	3.40
			$8.50			$18.85

where p_n and q_n are price and quantity in other than the base period and p_o and q_o are price and quantity in the base period. Table 2.7 shows the construction of a value index for the Smith family's weekly grocery bill. The food the Smiths consumed in 1978 cost more than twice as much as the food they consumed in 1967; that is, ($18.85 ÷ $8.50) × 100 = 222%

Special-Purpose Index

Special-purpose indexes are generally a combination of business and economic indicators. For example, suppose a city that wishes to measure general business activity via a special-purpose index finds its three best barometers are department-store sales, employment, and rate of money turnover. It could assign weights to each of the three variables and find their values for a given number of years. Table 2.8 shows the construction of such an index for City X.

To compute the special-purpose index for 1978, each 1978 value is expressed as a relative of the base period and then weighted by the appropriate weights.

$$\text{Department stores sales} \quad \frac{(\$250)}{(100)} \quad (100 \times 0.50) = 125.0$$

$$\text{Employment} \quad \frac{(150)}{(100)} \quad (100 \times 0.30) = 45.0$$

$$\text{Money turnover} \quad \frac{(125)}{(100)} \quad (100 \times 0.20) = \underline{25.0}$$
$$195.0$$

Using 1967 as the base period, business activity in City X increased 95% from 1967 through 1978; i.e., 195% – 100% = 95%.

Table 2.8. Special-Purpose Index City X (1967 = 100).

| | Weight | | |
Year	Department-Store Sales ($ Millions)	Index of Employment	Index Rate Money Turnover
	50	30	20
1967	100	100	100
1976	200	125	115
1978	250	150	125

SHIFTING THE BASE PERIOD

If two indexes have the same base period, they may be directly compared. However, if they do not, the base period must be shifted. Table 2.9 shows the Auto and Parts Manufactured portion of the Industrial Production Index published by the Federal Reserve Board for selected years (1967 = 100) as well as the Motor Vehicles and Parts sector of Personal Consumption Expenditures Index, which is one of the GNP accounts.

Personal Consumption Expenditures represent the goods and services purchased by individuals and nonprofit institutions and the value of food, clothing, rental of dwellings, and financial services received in kind by individuals. Motor Vehicles and Parts are a division of the Durable Goods portion of Personal Consumption Expenditures. Table 2.9 coverts both indexes to the 1971 = 100 base.

The Industrial Production Index of 124.4 becomes the base number for the new series. The 1977 index of 174.2 is converted to the new 1971 base by dividing by 124.4. The Personal Consumption Expenditures Index was developed by using the absolute amounts found in *The Survey of Current Business* using 1972 = 100. The Personal Consumption Expenditures Index is converted to the 1971 base by dividing the 1977 index of 161.1 by 86.6, that is $(161.1 \div 86.6)(100) = 186.0$.

SPLICING AN INDEX

Sometimes the base period of an index will change. The series on the old base must then be updated to a new base. For example, the Help-Wanted Index published by The Conference Board is made up of 51 individual city indexes that have been constructed from The Conference Board's monthly survey of help-wanted advertisements. A weight based on nonagricultural employment is developed for each city. For example, New York City has a weight of 12.2%, Los Angeles 8.1%, and Boston 3.4% (using 1974 city weights).

Table 2.9. Shifting Index Base.

Auto and Parts Manufactured[a] (Industrial Production Index)				Motor Vehicles and Parts (Durable Goods, Personal Consumption Expenditures Index)			
Year	1967 = 100	Calculations	1971 = 100	Year	1972 = 100	Calculations	1971 = 100
1977	174.2	$\frac{174.2}{124.4}$ (100) =	140.0	1977	161.1	$\frac{161.1}{86.6}$ (100) =	186.0
1975	125.8	$\frac{125.8}{124.4}$ (100) =	101.1	1975	106.5	$\frac{106.5}{86.6}$ (100) =	123.0
1972	141.4	$\frac{127.7}{124.4}$ (100) =	102.7	1972	100.0	$\frac{100.0}{86.6}$ (100) =	115.5
1971	124.4	$\frac{124.4}{124\ 4}$ (100) =	100.0	1971	86.6	$\frac{86.6}{86.6}$ (100) =	100.0
1970	98.8	$\frac{98.8}{124.4}$ (100) =	79.4	1970	69.0	$\frac{69.0}{86.6}$ (100) =	79.7
1969	118.1	$\frac{118.1}{124.4}$ (100) =	94.9	1969	74.5	$\frac{74.5}{86.6}$ (100) =	86.0
1968	119.4	$\frac{119.4}{124.4}$ (100) =	96.0	1968	70.8	$\frac{70.8}{86.6}$ (100) =	81.8
1967	100.0	$\frac{100.0}{124.4}$ (100) =	80.3	1967	58.7	$\frac{58.7}{86.6}$ (100) =	67.8

[a] Business Statistics, 1977 Biennial Edition, p. 20.
[b] Survey of Current Business, Vol 56, Part II, Jan., 1976, p. 45.

Table 2.10. National Help-Wanted Index on 1957–1959 Base and 1967 Base.

Year	National Help-Wanted Index	
	(1957–59 = 100) Old Series	(1967 = 100) New Series
1965		
January	137	73
February	145	76
March	148	77
April	143	78
May	145	81
June	146	82
July	145	82
August	157	85
September	160	88
October	168	91
November	181	97
December	186	99
1966		
January	184	100
February	191	102
March	201	108
April	189	104
May	185	105
June	184	106
July	186	106
August	189	105
September	189	103
October	193	103
November	194	103
December	193	102

Sources: United States Department of Commerce, *1969 Business Statistics,* p. 84. The Conference Board, *The Help-Wanted Index,* p. 38, 1977.

In 1971 the base year of the Help-Wanted Index was changed, from 1957–59 = 100, to 1967 = 100. Monthly adjusted advertising volume was divided by the 1967 average monthly adjusted advertising volume. However, the national index was subject to distortion using this method. The national index was converted using a link-relative method. The link is shown in the following formula:

$$\frac{\text{January 1967 (1967 = 100)}}{\text{January 1967 (1957–59 = 100)}} = \frac{103}{189} = 0.54497 = \text{Link}$$

The value for the national Help-Wanted Index for January 1967 (1967 = 100) was 103. The corresponding figure when 1957–59 = 100 was 189. Dividing 103 by 189 yields a factor of 0.54497. In Table 2.10, the figures for January 1965 to December 1976 are shown on the old and new base.

When converting the old series (1957-59 = 100) to the new by multiplying by the factor 0.54497, the results are slightly different than those published for the new series. For example, January 1965 is 137 × 0.54497 = 74.66. The published index figure for the new series is 73. This is due to rounding and seasonal adjustment of the data.

3 Consumer Price Index

We now turn our attention to one of the most important indexes in use today, the monthly consumer price index (CPI). The incomes of many Americans are directly tied to this statistic.

The CPI measures the price change of a constant market basket of goods over time. It also serves as an economic indicator to measure success or failure of government economic policy. For example, during periods of price rise, the CPI is an index of inflation.

Another function of the CPI is to deflate other series including retail sales, hourly and weekly earnings, and some regional personal consumption expenditures used to calculate the gross national product (GNP).

The CPI is also used to escalate income payments. Approximately 8.5 million American workers are covered by collective bargaining contracts, that provide for increases in wages based on increases in the CPI. As of June 1979, such escalator clauses covered about 71% of workers (6 million) in major bargaining units (e.g., United Auto Workers). The remaining 2.5 million covered workers included about 0.6 million postal workers, 1.2 million workers in manufacturing establishments of 1000 employees and less, and some 1.0 million in the nonmanufacturing sector.

In addition, another 57.0 million Americans have their income affected largely as a result of statutory action. Some 34.8 million of these are Social Security beneficiaries, another 2.5 million are retired military and federal civil service employees and survivors, and about 20 million are food-stamp recipients.

In total, about one half of the population of the United States may be directly affected by changes in the CPI. An increase of even 1% in the CPI could increase income payments by $1 billion. However, because most of the income payments go to the lower end of the income distribution, (e.g., social security and food stamp recipients), only about 10% to 15% of total income payments are affected.

CPI CONCEPTS

When the CPI is used as a measure of inflation and as a deflator, it should reflect changes in the price of a fixed market basket of goods. As an escalator for income payments, it should reflect changes in the cost of living. To be able to adequately explain the difference between a price index and a cost-of-living index, one must know what the CPI does not measure.

The CPI compares the cost of a market basket of goods and services for a given month with its cost a month ago, a year ago, or 10 years ago. These goods and services include food and beverages, housing, apparel, medical care, and entertainment. The base period is 1967. In August 1979, the CPI was 221.1; that is, the market basket that cost $100 in 1967, cost $221.10 in August 1979 (more than double the 1967 price).

The contents of the market basket change over time because consumer purchases vary with changes in prices. For example, if beef prices are high and pork prices low, people will tend to buy pork. However, the CPI does not take such behavior into account. It is based on a fixed market basket of goods and services that are purchased in the same proportions month after month. For this reason, it is a price index rather than a cost-of-living index. For example, the CPI does not include income and Social Security taxes, whereas a true cost-of-living index would account for all taxes. The public, however, often refers to the CPI as a cost-of-living index.

The CPI simply measures the price changes for a scientifically selected sample of goods and services based on the average experience of certain population groups. The index has never been limited to the price changes of so-called necessities. Rather, it has also included the cost, for instance, of bread and butter, television, bowling, obstetrical care, funeral services, popular paperbacks, and college textbooks.

Expenditures by a cross section of consumers living in a representative selection of urban places provide the basis both for the selection of items to be priced and the importance, or weight, of each of these items in the index structure. Since the CPI is based on expenditures, it does not reflect noncash consumption, such as fringe benefits received as part of a job.

HISTORY OF CPI

The first CPI, called a *cost-of-living index,* grew out of a decision of the Shipbuilding Labor Adjustment Board during World War I. In November 1917, the board determined that wages in shipbuilding yards should be adjusted when the cost of living had generally increased. In 1919, the Bureau of Labor Statistics began publishing complete cost-of-living indexes twice a year for 32 large shipbuilding and industrial centers. A weighting structure based on data collected in the expenditure survey of wage-earner and clerical-worker families in 1917 through 1919 was used. In February 1921, regular, periodic publication of the National Consumer Price Index was established. In October 1940, at the request of the National Defense Advisory Commission, some monthly indexes were begun. Although changes have occurred over the years in scope, coverage, frequency, and format, the index has continued to measure changes in the price of a fixed market basket of goods and services.

REVISIONS

1940

In 1940 a comprehensive revision of the CPI was completed. The reference base was shifted to 1935–39 on the advice of the Central Statistical Board. The board was the predecessor of the present Statistical Policy Division of the Office of Management and Budget.

During World War II, weights for foods, fuels, transportation, and other items were adjusted temporarily for rationing and wartime shortages. Prewar weight patterns were restored in 1946, when wartime restrictions were removed. A number of changes also took place in the calculation of food prices. Chain and independent stores had separate average prices computed, which were subsequently combined using fixed weights. Food outlet samples were revised for type of store, sales volume, and location.

1953

Surveys of expenditures in a few cities during 1947 through 1949 indicated a serious need for revisions in index weights and market-basket items because of significant postwar changes in consumption, patterns of wage-earner and clerical-worker families. As a result, Congress in 1949 authorized a large-scale, three-year program to modernize the CPI. By the time the revision was completed in 1953, surveys of consumer expenditures had been conducted in 91 cities and the index concept completely reexamined. Also, the reference base had been changed from 1935–39 to 1947–49. For the first time, the purchase of a home was included in the weighting pattern. A new sample of 47 index cities, selected from the 91 in the consumer expenditures survey, included for the first time large cities and small urban places (including areas with as few as 2500 inhabitants). The 1950 weights were revised to 1952.

1964

By the late 1950s, it became apparent that index weights should be revised every decade. Factors upon which the CPI is based, such as composition of urban population, kinds of goods and services available to consumers, and the net income of urban workers had changed dramatically. While the concept of the CPI measuring changes in the price of a fixed market basket for urban wage earners and clerical workers did not change, other things happened. The index was expanded to include persons living alone. In addition, an urban-wage-earner or clerical-worker family was included if 50% or more of the family income came from wage and clerical occupations and if at least one member of the family worked for a minimum of 37 weeks of the year. (Previously, the working member had to be the head of household.) Finally, in 1950 a family income limitation of $10,000 after taxes was dropped because of the increased number of families with more than one worker. As a result, population coverage was increased to include about half of the urban population and under 45% of the total population.

1978

The 1978 revision was begun in 1970. It was a large-scale effort to update the following:

1. Weights assigned to various spending categories such as food, clothing, shelter, and medical care.
2. Sample of items priced each month in the ongoing CPI.
3. Sample of retail stores.
4. Conceptual basis and statistical methods employed in the CPI.

Revisions Visible in Final Published Indexes

CPI-U. The index for urban wage earners and clerical workers (CPI-W) covers about 45% of the population. It was necessary to devise a more comprehensive index, based on a broader population coverage because of the following factors:

1. Migration of middle-income groups to the suburbs due to improved economic status.
2. Large increase in the number of two-earner families, which brought many wage earners and clerical workers into the middle-income group.
3. Shift toward a service economy.
4. Increasing unionization of salaried white-collar wage earners and clerical-workers, providing them with improved living standards comparable with those of the middle-income urban population.

On May 24, 1974, the commissioner of the Bureau of Labor Statistics announced a decision to develop two indexes. Thus, the CPI-U, which covers about 80% of the population, was born.

The movements of the two indexes are being compared. It will be determined whether one index is adequate or both are needed, whether one index can represent the difference between them, or whether a whole family of indexes is needed.

The comprehensive index covers all consumer households in a representative number of SMSAs and of small urban areas outside SMSAs. Broadening the population base to include all urban consumers in the CPI-U, the average annual income has dropped from $12,200 to about $11,700.

No one can tell which of the components of the index will rise more rapidly in the future. Nor can anyone say whether the CPI-U will rise more rapidly than the CPI-W. Some students of the index believe that the two will closely parallel each other. However, no one can be certain until the statistics are reviewed.

How the movements of CPI-U and CPI-W relate in 1977–80 depends on the expenditure weights assigned to the various items in the separate market baskets for the two indexes, as well as the items priced and kinds of outlets sampled.

Expanded City Coverage. A total of 28 cities now have monthly or bimonthly indexes published, compared with 24 previously. Prices are collected in 85 areas based on the 1970 census. The 85-area probability sample can be expanded to at least 152 probability sample areas if it is believed that such expansion would increase the accuracy of the sample.

The increase in the number of areas sampled has made the following possible:

1. Publication of indexes for an additional four cities
2. Improved reliability of national CPI
3. Regional indexes for cities of different population sizes

There are four regions and population classes. Table 3.1 shows areas, population weights, and pricing schedule for CPI-U (established in 1978) and CPI-W (established prior to 1978).

Improved Item Selection. Previously, CPI agents were given detailed descriptions of market-basket items to be priced. Since 1978, however, an improved process called *disaggregation* has been used in selecting the detailed items to be priced. Agents now have more general descriptions to choose from. For example, milk, which was formerly described as "vitamin D, grade A, homogenized in half-gallon containers" is now simply "whole fresh milk." In the disaggregation process, the specific kind of fresh whole milk that will be priced continuously in each outlet is chosen. Therefore, each kind of whole milk is assigned a probability or weight based on the quantity the store sells. If vitamin D, homogenized milk in half-gallon containers makes up 70% of sales of fresh whole milk and the same milk in quart containers accounts for 10% of fresh whole milk sales, then

Table 3.1. Areas, Population Weights, and Pricing Schedule for New and Revised Consumer Price Indexes.

Region, size class, area	Population weight CPI–U	Population weight CPI–W	Pricing schedule		
			Monthly	Jan., Mar., May, July, Sept., Nov.	Feb., Apr., June Aug., Oct., Dec.
Total, all regions	100.000	100.000			
*Northeastern Region.........	26.521	27.468			
*Class A areas:[1]					
*New York, N.Y. —Northeastern N.J	10.006	10.401	X		
* Philadelphia, Pa.—N.J	2.825	3.023	X		
* Boston, Mass	1.737	1.658		X	
* Pittsburgh, Pa	1.403	1.510			X
* Buffalo, N.Y	.772	.860			X
*Class B areas:[2]					
*Northeast Pa. (Scranton).....	.372	.392		X	
Providence, R.I.-Mass	1.015	1.026		X	
Rochester, N.Y	.967	.988			X
Allentown, Pa.-N.J	.955	1.041		X	
Springfield, Mass	1.022	1.026			X
*Class C areas:[3]					
Norwalk, Conn	.884	.816			X
Binghamton, N.Y.-Pa	.924	.983		X	
Portland, Maine	.948	1.065		X	
Johnstown, Pa...........	.932	.936			X
*Class D areas:[4]					
Cape Cod, Mass	.437	.400		X	
Ansonia, Conn	.448	.444			X

See footnotes at end of table.

Table 3.1. Areas, Population Weights, and Pricing Schedule for New and Revised Consumer Price Indexes. (continued)

Region, size class, area	Population weight CPI–U	Population weight CPI–W	Pricing schedule		
			Monthly	Jan., Mar., May, July, Sept., Nov.	Feb., Apr., June Aug., Oct., Dec.
St. Lawrence County, N.Y...	.438	.453			X
Lawrence County, Pa ...	.436	.446		X	
*North Central Region	26.508	28.663			
*Class A areas:					
*Chicago, Ill.–Ind	4.436	5.180	X		
*Detroit, Mich	2.497	2.833	X		
*St. Louis, Mo.–Ill	1.376	1.511		X	
*Cleveland, Ohio	1.208	1.391			X
*Minneapolis-St. Paul, Minn.–Wis	1.118	1.148			X
*Milwaukee, Wis	.803	.918		X	
*Cincinnati, Ohio–Ky.–Ind	.787	.865		X	
*Kansas City, Mo.–Kans	.757	.845			X
*Class B areas:					
Columbus, Ohio	1.101	1.133		X	
Grand Rapids, Mich	1.075	1.189		X	
Indianapolis, Ind	.628	.735			X
Toledo, Ohio–Mich	1.108	1.263		X	
*Class C areas:					
Racine, Wis	.934	.853		X	
Saginaw, Mich	.855	.925			X
Rock Island, Ill.,–Iowa	.873	.916		X	
Canton, Ohio	.896	.984			X
Decatur, Ill	.901	.952		X	

Area						
Terre Haute, Ind	.901	.891			X	X
*Class D areas:						
Mexico, Mo	1.048	.983	X			X
Grand Island, Nebr	1.051	1.079	X		X	
Detroit Lakes, Minn	1.069	1.079	X		X	X
Fort Dodge, Iowa	1.086	.990			X	X
*Southern Region	27.794	26.289				
*Class A areas:						
*Washington, D.C.—Md.–Va	1.786	1.621			X	X
*Dallas—Ft. Worth, Tex	1.405	1.538	X		X	
*Baltimore, Md	1.201	1.316	X		X	
*Houston, Tex	1.147	1.277	X		X	
*Atlanta, Ga	.928	.942	X		X	
*Miami, Fla	.831	.783	X		X	
*Class B areas:						
Tampa, Fla	1.156	.870	X		X	
Raleigh, N.C	.961	.903	X		X	
New Orleans, La	.964	.938	X		X	
Richmond, Va	1.017	.989	X	X	X	X
San Antonio, Tex	.882	.875				
Nashville, Tenn	.989	.990	X		X	
Louisville, Ky.—Ind	.944	1.032	X			
Memphis, Tenn.–Ark.—Miss	.970	.942			X	
*Class C areas:						
Huntsville, Ala	1.009	.785	X	X	X	
West Palm Beach, Fla	.993	.753	X	X	X	
Albany, Ga	.977	.838	X		X	
Baton Rouge, La	.950	.777				
Pine Bluff, Ark	.950	.894	X		X	
Corpus Christi, Tex	.926	.842	X		X	

See footnotes at end of table.

Table 3.1. Areas, Population Weights, and Pricing Schedule for New and Revised Consumer Price Indexes. (continued)

Region, size class, area	Population weight CPI—U	Population weight CPI—W	Pricing schedule		
			Monthly	Jan., Mar., May, July, Sept., Nov.	Feb., Apr., June Aug., Oct., Dec.
Huntington, W.Va.—Ky. —Ohio	.965	.881			x
Brownsville, Tex	.930	.892		x	
*Class D areas:					
Pascagoula, Miss	1.247	1.112		x	
Beaufort, S.C	1.245	1.189			x
Smithfield, Va	1.224	1.161		x	
Rockingham, N.C	1.197	1.149			x
*Western Region	19.177	17.580			
*Class A areas:					
*Los Angeles—Long Beach —Anaheim, Calif	5.443	5.362			x
*San Francisco—Oakland, Calif	2.131	1.984	x		
*Seattle—Everett, Wash	.890	.893		x	
*San Diego, Calif	.855	.638		x	
*Class B areas:					
*Portland, Oreg.—Wash	.627	.625		x	
*Honolulu, Hawaii	.344	.327			x
*Denver-Boulder, Colo	.750	.725		x	
San Jose, Calif	1.189	1.103			x
San Bernardino, Calif	1.163	1.004		x	
Fresno, Calif	.842	.777			x

*Class C areas:				
*Anchorage, Alaska		.037	×	×
Colorado Springs, Colo		.673	×	×
Tucson, Ariz		.582		×
Salinas, Calif		.622	×	×
Bakersfield, Calif		.592		×
*Class D areas:				
Corvallis, Oreg	.469	.382	×	×
Alamogordo, N. Mex	.497	.389	×	×
Logan, Utah	.478	.434	×	
Butte, Mont	.471	.431	×	

* Indicates areas for which separate indexes are published. Indexes are also published for 4 geographic regions by population size class.

[1] Areas with an urban population of 1,250,000 or more (Class A).

[2] Areas with an urban population of 385,000 to 1,250,000 (Class B).

[3] Areas with an urban population of 75,000 to 385,000 (Class C).

[4] Areas with an urban population of 2,500 to 75,000 (Class D).

Source: *The Consumer Price Index: Concepts and Content Over the Years*, U.S. Department of Labor, Bureau of Labor Statistics, Report 517, 19–21 (Revised May 1978).

the half-gallon will have a seven times greater chance of being chosen than the quart container. Once probabilities are assigned, one kind of milk is chosen by random sampling. This insures that the type of milk selected by disaggregation will continue to be priced each month at that outlet.

All high-volume items are represented in proportion to their share of total expenditures. For example, frequently purchased items such as eggs and milk are given more weight than seldom-bought items such as strawberries.

The commodity table indexes in the 1978 revision are different. Market-basket item indexes have been changed. Those formerly published by commodity group, such as "food" and "nonfood" are now published by general household categories of consumption such as "housing" and "transportation." Table 3.2 shows the CPI for all urban consumers (CPI-U) by United States city average and expenditure category.

Less Visible Innovations

Determining what people buy requires data collection from a series of population samples. The CPI-U is based on the following surveys:

1. The *consumer expenditure survey* was undertaken from 1972 through 1974 by the Bureau of Labor Statistics and the Bureau of the Census. The household sample representing rural as well as urban sectors covered 216 areas of the country. Interviews involving about 20,000 families were held quarterly. Table 3.3 indicates changes by major expenditure groups between the CPI-U and the CPI-W.

2. In the *small, frequent purchase survey,* 20,000 families participated in a diary survey from July 1972 through June 1974. They recorded expenditures for small, frequent purchases such as food and personal care items that are difficult to recall over a period of more than 2 weeks.

3. In the *rent survey,* a new rent index designed to be more accurate and current was initiated in 1974. It employs an overall sample within cities that is smaller than the sample of the previous survey. Each sample is divided into six subsamples for semiannual pricing. Rent information is collected from different subsamples each month rather than bimonthly or quarterly as previously.

4. A *point-of-purchase survey* was conducted to select, for each index population, a representative sample of retail stores, mail-order houses, bowling alleys, doctors' offices, and other places where goods and services are brought. Information was obtained directly from consumers regarding where they make their purchases. The survey also provided the only known technique for identifying market-basket outlets frequented by specific population groups such as urban wage earners and clerical workers and all urban consumers.

For the last revision of the CPI-U, data permitting a scientific selection of outlets was unavailable. Although areas and types of outlets were selected on a

Table 3.2. Consumer Price Index for All Urban Consumers: U.S. City Average by Expenditure Category and Commodity and Service Group.

Group	Relative importance December	Unadjusted indexes 1967=100 unless otherwise noted	Unadjusted percent change to— from—		Seasonally adjusted percent change from previous month	
		Expenditure category				
All items						
All items (1957-59=100)						
Food and beverages						
Food						
Food at home						
Cereals and bakery products ...						
Meats, poultry, fish, and eggs.						
Dairy products.............						
Fruits and vegetables						
Sugar and sweets						
Fats and oils..............						
Nonalcoholic beverages[1]						
Other prepared foods[2].						
Food away from home.......						
Alcoholic beverages						
Housing[2]						
Shelter						
Rent, residential...........						
Other rental costs[2]						
Homeownership.............						
Home purchase.............						
Financing, taxes, and insurance[2] .						
Maintenance and repairs.....						
Services						
Commodities						
Fuel and other utilities[2]						
Fuels						
Fuel oil, coal, and bottled gas.						
Gas (piped) and electricity[2] .						
Other utilities and public services[2] .						
Household furnishings and operation[2] .						
Housefurnishings[2]						
Housekeeping supplies						
Housekeeping services[2]						

See footnotes at end of table.

Table 3.2. Consumer Price Index for All Urban Consumers: U.S. City Average by Expenditure Category and Commodity and Service Group. (continued)

Group	Relative importance December	Unadjusted indexes 1967=100 unless otherwise noted	Unadjusted percent change to— from—		Seasonally adjusted percent change from previous month	
		Expenditure category				
Apparel and upkeep.						
Apparel commodities.						
Men's and boys' apparel.						
Women's and girls' apparel						
Infants' and toddlers' apparel.[2]						
Footwear						
Other apparel commodities.[2]						
Apparel services[1]						
Transportation						
Private transportation.						
New cars						
Used cars						
Gasoline[2]						
Maintenance and repair[2]						
Other private transportation.[2]						
Commodities[2]						
Services[2]						
Public transportation.						
Medical care.						
Medical care commodities[2]						
Medical care services[2]						
Professional services [1,2]						
Other medical care services[2]						
Entertainment.[2]						
Entertainment commodities.[2]						
Entertainment services[2].						
Other goods and services.[2]						
Tobacco products						
Personal care[1]						
Toilet goods and personal care appliances [1,2]						
Personal care services[1]						
Personal and educational expenses[2] . . .						
School books and supplies[2]						
Personal and educational services[2]						

Commodity and service group

All items ....

Commodities ....
  Food and beverages ....
  Commodities less food and beverages ....
  Nondurables less food and beverages ....
    Apparel commodities ....
    Nondurables less food, beverages, and
      apparel [1] ....
    Durables ....

Services ....
  Rent, residential ....
  Household services less rent [2] ....
  Transportation services ....
  Medical care services ....
  Other services [2] ....

Special indexes:
  All items less food ....
  All items less mortgage interest costs [1] ....
  Commodities less food ....
  Nondurables less food ....
  Nondurables less food and apparel [1] ....
  Nondurables [1] ....
  Services less rent ....
  Services less medical care [1] ....
  Domestically produced farm foods ....
  Selected beef cuts ....
  Energy [1] ....
  All items less energy ....
  All items less food and energy ....
    Commodities less food and energy ....
    Energy commodities [1] ....
    Services less energy ....

Purchasing power of the consumer dollar:
  1967=$1.00 [1] ....
  1957-59=$1.00 [1] ....

[1] Not seasonally adjusted.

[2] Index series has undergone a change in title or definition. See table 6 for details.

Source: *The Consumer Price Index: Concepts and Content over the Years*, United States Department of Labor, Bureau of Labor Statistics, Report 517, 23–24 (Revised May 1978).

Table 3.3. Percent Distribution of the Consumer Price Index Market Basket by Major Expenditure Group, Benchmark Years.

Major group	Wage earners and clerical workers				All urban consumers 1972-73 [4]
	1935-39 [1]	1952 [2]	1963 [3]	1972-73 [4]	
Food and alcoholic beverages	35.4	32.2	25.2	20.4	18.8
Housing	33.7	33.5	34.9	39.8	42.9
Apparel	11.0	9.4	10.6	7.0	7.0
Transportation	8.1	11.3	14.0	19.8	17.7
Medical care	4.1	4.8	5.7	4.2	4.6
Entertainment	2.8	4.0	3.9	4.3	4.5
Personal care	2.5	2.1	2.8	1.8	1.7
Other goods and services	2.4	2.7	2.9	2.7	2.8

[1] Relative importance for the survey period 1934-36 (updated for price change).
[2] Relative importance for the survey period 1947-49 (updated for price change).
[3] Relative importance for the survey period 1960-61 (updated for price change).
[4] Relative importance for the survey period 1972-73. Revised indexes which require expenditure weights updated for price change between the survey period and the link date will differ from those shown. See table 4 for relative importance as of December 1977.

Source: *The Consumer Price Index: Concepts and Content over the Years* United States Department of Labor, Bureau of Labor Statistics, Report 517, 8 (Revised May 1978).

probability basis, the outlets themselves were not. Outlets that dropped out of the sample were replaced on a judgment basis, and no provision was made for reflecting shifts in merchandising techniques or for the development of new stores and shopping areas.

Improved Statistical Techniques

Statistical techniques used to improve the 1978 revision include:

1. Development of 40 separate area market baskets from which regional and national market baskets were compiled.
2. Design of a more sophisticated procedure to more accurately measure sampling errors.
3. Price collection frequency was increased so that about 53% of the items in the market basket are priced every month compared with 48% in the 1964 revision.

About 41% of goods and services previously priced quarterly are now priced every other month.

CONCEPTUAL PROBLEMS

Population Coverage

In earlier periods, wage earners and clerical workers could be described as "low income." However, with the advent of the two-earner families since World War II, many incomes have been raised. This has put many previously low-income families into the middle-income group. In addition, with the shift toward a service-oriented economy and the increasing unionization of salaried white-collar employees, the standard of living of wage earners and clerical workers has been raised to a level similar to that of the middle-income urban population. As a result, questions were raised about the population coverage of the CPI. For instance, labor representatives argued that 30 years of experience had been built up with the CPI-W, so that they understood its strengths and weaknesses. On the other hand, they did not know how a new index would behave.

However, other users, such as the Interagency Subcommittee on Economic Statistics of the Council on Economic Policy, favored the expansion of population coverages. In response to general support for the new index, in 1975 Congress determined that the CPI revision program should include both the CPI-U and the CPI-W. It thus requested—and was granted—a $3 million increase in the fiscal 1976 budget to fund the preparation of the new index.

Because the CPI is so widely used, the Bureau of Labor Statistics has difficulty finding a segment of the population that is both large enough to encompass most current uses of the index and narrow enough to be considered homogeneous in reflecting price experience. Therefore, combining several indexes into one to produce a family of indexes becomes quite natural. The indexes would represent not only the price experience of all consumer units but also the separate experiences of particular subgroups, such as aged, poor, and rural populations. In practice, such a family of indexes was not feasible in the 1978 revision, given the restraints of time and funds. The family of indexes is roughly analogous to the unemployment data released by the Bureau of Labor Statistics. U-1, for example, covers persons unemployed 15 weeks or longer as a percent of the total labor force, while U-2 through U-6 cover varying restrictions to reflect economic hardship or potential labor supply.

Quality Changes

In compiling a price index, it is difficult to accurately measure and treat quality changes. Products and consumption patterns are constantly changing. Quality changes in a new model of an item should not be reflected as a price change in the CPI since the index measures the cost to consumers of purchasing a constant market basket of goods and services of constant quality through time. The Bureau of Labor Statistics uses an indirect method to measure quality change by evaluating the additional cost associated with producing the change.

For example, attempts are made to adjust for change in the quality of new cars. Here, structural and engineering changes affecting safety, environment, reliability, performance, durability, economy, carrying capacity, maneuverability, comfort, and convenience are considered. Quality adjustments exclude changes in style or appearance, such as chrome trim, unless these features have been offered as options and purchased by a large proportion of customers.

Homeownership

The treatment of owner-occupied housing in the CPI presents a two-tiered problem:

1. Under which concept is housing to be priced?
2. What is the most accurate and efficient way to measure prices and price changes under that concept?

There are two ways to handle the problem:

1. *Asset approach.* A house is not a frequent purchase for consumption. Durable goods provide service to consumers over a substantial period of time.

The previous index of housing implied that house purchasers consumed the total value of the house purchase price plus total financing costs in the survey year. People living in previously purchased homes were assumed to have spent nothing on housing in that year. In the previous index, prices of houses were classified by age and size and converted to a price per square foot. Shelter costs reflected the monthly price per square foot, along with other components of housing and rent.

2. *Flow-of-Services Approach.* The flow-of-services approach assumes housing is consumed by the owner living in a house. However, homeowners do not consume all services, such as shelter and accommodation for eating, playing, and entertaining, in the year in which they buy homes. Rather, they consume them over the years that they live in their houses.

Two methods are are used to estimate the price of homeownership:

a. Rental equivalence. What would you charge if you rented your house to yourself?

b. User-cost function. Major cost components owners incur in providing themselves housing, such as price of house and capital gains and equity costs.

Problems arise in data collection in both approaches. In the rental-equivalent approach, a sample of rental units must be developed to measure changes in owner-occupied housing costs as well as to measure the increasing share of owner-occupied apartments and townhouses in condominium developments. Under the user-cost approach, measurement problems would include (1) source of house prices, (2) capital gains and equity cost, and (3) adjust prices for quality change.

The Bureau of Labor Statistics staff developed an alternative to the previous approach to measuring shelter costs by assembling in a different way the major cost items that homehowners generally face. One major difference under the alternative approach was that a home purchase no longer carried a specific weight. Also, the new approach reflected equity costs and appreciation by adjusting house prices by these two elements in the base year and by allowing for future variations in the elements.

Much debate followed the new Bureau of Labor Statistics proposal. In April 1977, then Commissioner Julius Shiskin decided the previous treatment of owner-occupied housing would continue to be used for computing the housing component of the 1978 revised CPI. His decision was based on:

1. The difficulties faced in developing a method of providing stable estimates of housing costs.
2. The diversity of views concerning the approaches held by the various advisory groups to the bureau.

FUTURE REVISIONS

Continuing Consumer Expenditure Survey

In the past, data on consumer income and expenditures have been collected every 10 to 15 years as a major component of large-scale programs to update and revise the CPI. More than $20 million was spent on the 1972–73 Consumer Expenditure Survey, which was the base for the first release of the revised 1978 CPI. This represents a 5-year lag. A smaller, continuing consumer expenditure survey has been adopted to reduce the lag and eliminate periodic start-up costs. The Reagan administration has approved the budget plan for the continuing consumer expenditure survey to collect data on an ongoing basis in 102 primary sampling units. A total of 85 of the 102 have been selected for ongoing price-data collection. The project will consist of both quarterly interview and diary survey panels. Approximately 6000 households will be interviewed quarterly for five calendar quarters. The first interviews were conducted in October 1979.

Continuing Point-of-Purchase Survey

In the 1978 CPI revision program, modern scientific sampling procedures were developed for the selection of the CPI outlet sample. A point-of-purchase survey is conducted in one-fifth of the 85 primary sampling units in the index outlet sample each year. From these surveys, a new outlet sample for each pricing area covered could be selected.

4 Time Series Analysis

WHY FORECASTING?

Most companies wish to know where they are headed. Is business going up, down, or sideways? What about company sales in relation to industry sales? In making such an analysis, some companies even consider the general course of the national economy.

Out of such reviews come forecasts of future sales. Generally, forecasts are prepared at regular intervals—monthly, quarterly, or annually. However, forecasts of 10 to 20 years into the future may also be prepared. Critical decisions based on these forecasts permeate many areas of a company: the purchasing department wants to have the right inventory on hand at the right time; the accounting department wants to be able to predict cash flow and profits; and the general manager wants to optimize profits.

Operating (Short-Term) Forecast

An *operating* or *short-term forecast* is based on monthly or quarterly data, extending out over the next few months or quarters. It gives management a guide to operating in the short term. Because most companies deal with monthly data (weekly data can also be used), seasonal and random short-term elements are significant. In all, the operating forecast depends to some degree on a company's delivery cycle.

Budget (Medium-Term) Forecast

A *budget* or *medium-term* forecast is generally made 12 months in advance. The forecast, which may be broken down into quarters or months, is generally correlated with the national economy. The critical element affecting the budget forecast is the business cycle.

Capacity (Long-Term) Forecast

Over the long term, a company must estimate its capacity. The *capacity* or *long-term forecast* is designed to predict the long course of the future. It is normally done annually for a 5-, 10-, or 20-year period, with the time interval usually in years. One of the main elements in the capacity forecast is secular trend, i.e., the long-term movement of a time series. Secular trend is longer than a business cycle. In secular trend, a particular year's sales may be above or below the trend line. However, over the long run, annual fluctuations will average out and fit the trend line fairly closely. In recent years, econometric forecasting has been used in long-range forecasting.

Business conditions are not static. Employment, national income, and production decline. Unemployment increases. This scenario continues until a bottom (*trough of cycle*) is reached. Then, either slowly or rapidly, the economy begins to recover. Jobs increase, production goes up, and the employment picture brightens. This continues until the economy reaches its height (*peak of cycle*). Then the downward turn begins again, starting another recession. Such is the description of a business cycle. No business cycle is the same as another. Yet they all have something in common: the fall, rise, and fall again of the economy.

Table 4.1 presents a sales forecast for widgets over the short-term, mid-term, and long-term. The budget forecast is shown from January 1978 through 1983.

TIME SERIES—ONE METHOD OF FORECASTING

If there were no fluctuations in economic data, forecasting would be very simple. Sales, for example, would become a horizontal line, and the past would be a good indicator of the future. However, time series are subject to fluctuations caused by many different events, which may be positive or negative. Thus, the series may be positive at one point in time and negative in another.

In an attempt to analyze fluctuations, a method of forecasting known as time-series analysis has evolved. Basically, there are five components to a time series: trend, seasonality, cyclical, trading-day factors, and irregular fluctuations.

Secular Trend

The secular trend measures the long-term trend in a time series. Secular trend is attributable to factors that affect the long-term movement of a series, such as population shifts or the industrialization of a nation. Time series and the inherent secular trend can fall as well as rise. In declining industries such as anthracite coal mining and rail-passenger miles, secular trends are falling. On the other hand, it is possible for a declining industry to be part of a time series that is rising; for

Table 4.1. Sales Forecast of Widgets (in Thousands).

Month	No. Trading Days	No. Widgets	
1978			
January	19		1236
February	17		1142
March	18		1201
		Quarterly Total	3579
April	20		1352
May	21		1407
June	21		1502
		Quarterly Total	4261
July	21		2000
August	23		2500
September	19		1750
		Quarterly Total	6250
October	22		2200
November	21		2100
December	19		1900
		Quarterly Total	6200
		1978 Total	20,290
1979			
January	20		1100
February	18		1000
March	20		1050
		Quarterly Total	3150
April	20		1200
May	20		1300
June	20		1350
		Quarterly Total	3850
July	20		2100
August	21		2400
September	19		2000
		Quarterly Total	6500
October	21		2200
November	18		2000
December	19		1850
		Quarterly Total	6050
		1979 Total	19,550
1980			21,000
1981			18,050
1982			19,000
1983			22,000

Actual — Short-Term — Mid-Term — Mid-Term — Long-Term

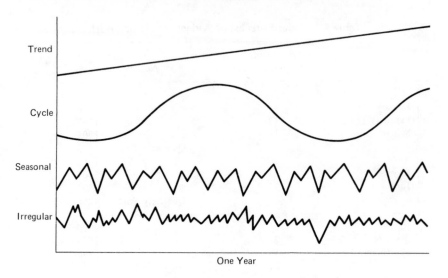

Fig. 4.1 Components of a time series.

example, anthracite coal consumption is falling while total power consumed is rising. A secular trend can change—it can fall, stage a comeback, and rise. The monthly fluctuations of secular trend in a time series are small compared to those of the other components (Figure 4.1). Figure 4.2 shows the long-term trend of United States agricultural products from 1947 through 1976.

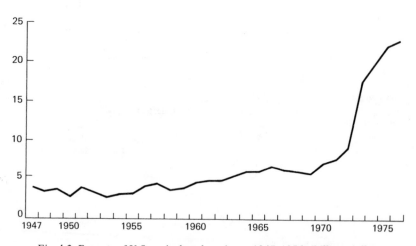

Fig. 4.2 Exports of U.S. agricultural products, 1947–1976. (*billions dollars*)

Several methods may be used to approximate the long-term trend in a time series. These methods vary from freehand estimation to sophisticated computer methods.

Linear Trend

Table 4.2 shows the retail sales of the Jones & Brown Co. for 1972 through 1978. The sales increased by a constant amount of $200,000 per year. To measure the long-term trend of the time series given in the table (assuming it approximates a straight line as many time series do), the formula used to describe the growth is

$$\overline{Y}_p = a + bX$$

where

Y_p = predicted value of Y based on the selected value of X

a = estimated value of Y where $X = 0$

b = measures the average change in Y for each change of $+1$ or -1 in X (or b = slope of line)

X = any chosen value of X

Figure 4.3 shows the straight-line trend for Jones & Brown Co. for 1972 through 1978. The slope of the line, b is 0.2. For 1972, the initial year, $X = 0$ and $Y = \$2.2$ million; the point where the line crosses the Y-axis is a. The long-term trend may be measured using the freehand method or the least squares method which employs the preceding trend equation.

Table 4.2. Retail Sales, Jones & Brown Co., 1972–78.

Year	Sales (in $ Millions)
1972	$2.2
1973	2.4
1974	2.6
1975	2.8
1976	3.0
1977	3.2
1978	3.4

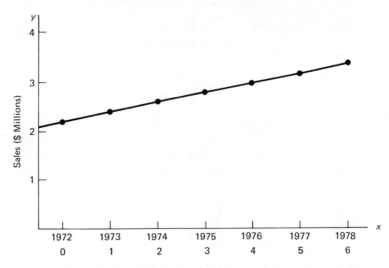

Fig. 4.3 Straight line trend for Jones and Brown Co. based on Table 4.1.

Freehand Method. In the freehand method, a linear trend line is approximated by drawing a line through the middle of the data. This is done by "eyeballing" the data. Then, with a straightedge such as a ruler, the trend line is drawn so that an equal number of observations are above and below the trend line. In Figure 4.4, which shows factory sales of household dishwashers from 1956-76, a trend line

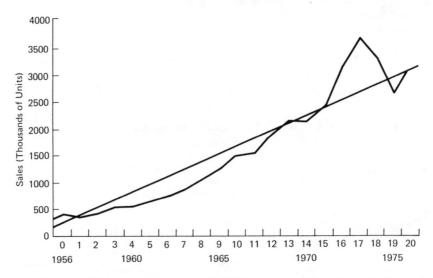

Fig. 4.4 Freehand linear trend line of U.S. factory unit sales of dishwashers. (*in thousands units*)

Table 4.3. Trend Equation—Least Squares Method, Jones & Brown Co.,
Retail Sales.

Year		Y (Sales in $ Millions)	X (Point of Origin)	XY	x^2
1972		2.2	0	0	0
1973		2.4	1	2.4	1
1974		2.6	2	5.2	4
1975		2.8	3	8.4	9
1976		3.0	4	12.0	16
1977		3.2	5	16.0	25
1978		3.4	6	20.4	36
	Total	$19.6	21	64.4	91

has been drawn. X represents time, with the initial year of 1956 equaling the zero year. The year 1976 is designated as year 20. Where the line intercepts the Y-axis (a in the linear equation) in 1956 (zero year), the value is 200,000 units. The freehand line estimates the average sales to be about 3 million units in 1976. Sales have increased about 140,000 units per year (b or slope of line). This increase is determined as follows: 3 million units shipped in 1976, minus 200,000 units shipped in 1956, divided by 20.

The straight-line equation is $\overline{Y}_p = 20 + 140X$ where sales are in thousands of units, the zero year is 1956, and X or time increases by one for each year. To forecast sales for 1986 (year 26), we would use the equation $\overline{Y}_p = a + bX$ or $200,000 + 140,000\,(26) = 3,840,000$ units.

The freehand method is subjective and is used only when a quick approximation is desired.

Least Squares Method. If a more exact procedure is desired, the least squares method may be used. The direct or coded method is used to compute the equation for the linear trend line.

In the *direct method,* the point of origin is the initial year. Two equations are solved simultaneously as follows:

1. $\Sigma Y = Na + b\Sigma X$
2. $\Sigma XY = a\Sigma X + b\Sigma X^2$

Using the retail sales figures for Jones & Brown Co. (Table 4.2), and using the numbers from Table 4.3 in the preceding equations, we get:

$$19.6 = 7a + 21b \tag{4.1}$$

$$64.4 = 21a + 91b \tag{4.2}$$

Multiply Equation 4.1 by 21 and Equation 4.2 by 7:

$$411.6 = 147a + 441b \qquad (4.1)$$

$$450.8 = 147a + 637b \qquad (4.2)$$

Equation 4.2 is subtracted from Equation 4.1 to eliminate a:

$$411.6 = 147a + 441b \qquad (4.1)$$

$$\frac{-450.8 = -147a + -637b}{-39.2 = \qquad 196b} \qquad (4.2)$$

$$b = 0.2$$

The b value of 0.20 is used in Equation 4.1 to solve for a.

$$19.6 = 7a + 21\,(0.20) \qquad (4.1)$$

$$-7a = 21\,(0.20) - 19.6$$

$$-7a = -15.4$$

$$a = 2.2$$

The least squares equation is $\overline{Y}_p = a + bX$. If the preceding values for a and b are substituted, $\overline{Y}_p = 2.2 + 0.2X$. To forecast sales for 1990, $\overline{Y}_p = 2.2 + 0.2(44) = 11.0$ million where

1. Sales are in millions.
2. The zero time period is July 1, 1946.
3. X increases by one unit each year.

The direct method can prove cumbersome if the numbers are large and there are many time periods. In such cases, therefore, the *coded method* is used. With an odd number of years, the zero year (point of origin) is the center year. If months are used, the zero month is the center month. (Table 4.4 presents an odd time period.)

Table 4.4. Trend Equation—Coded Method, Least Squares, Jones & Brown Co., Retail Sales.

Year	Y (Sales in $ Millions)	X (Point of Origin)	XY	x^2
1972	2.2	-3	- 6.6	9
1973	2.4	-2	- 4.8	4
1974	2.6	-1	- 2.6	1
1975	2.8	0	0	0
1976	3.0	+1	3.0	1
1977	3.2	+2	6.4	4
1978	3.4	+3	10.2	9
Total	$19.6		+ 5.6	28

The formulas for a and b are as follows:

$$a = \frac{\Sigma Y}{n} = \frac{19.6}{7} = 2.8$$

$$b = \frac{\Sigma XY}{\Sigma x^2} = \frac{5.6}{28} = 0.2$$

Lower case x is used in these formulas to distinguish from the direct method.

Using the sales data in Table 4.3, the trend equations are determined using an even number of time periods. Note that the zero point falls between 1974 and 1975 (see Table 4.5). a and b then become:

$$a = \frac{\Sigma Y}{n} = \frac{16.2}{6} = 2.7$$

$$b = \frac{\Sigma XY}{\Sigma x^2} = \frac{7.0}{70.0} = 0.1$$

The trend equation would then be $\bar{Y}_p = a + bX$, or $\bar{Y}_p = 2.7 + 0.1X$. In 1985, X would be +21. The forecast for 1985 would be $4.8 millions, i.e., ($\bar{Y}_p = 2.7 + 0.1(21)$.

The b values are the same for both the coded and direct methods. This is another way of showing the value of a:

Direct method = $Y_p = 2.2 + 0.2X$ (origin 1972)

Coded method = $Y_p = 2.8 + 0.2X$ (origin 1975)

Table 4.5. Trend Equation—Coded Method, Least Squares, Jones & Brown Co., Retail Sales.

Year	Y (Sales in $ Millions)	X (Point of Origin)	XY	x^2
1972	2.2	-5	-11.0	25
1973	2.4	-3	- 7.2	9
1974	2.6	-1	- 2.6	1
1975	2.8	+1	+ 2.8	1
1976	3.0	+3	+ 9.0	9
1977	3.2	+5	+16.0	25
	$16.2	0	+ 7.0	70

Both equations yield the same forecast for a given year—for example, 1986. When the direct method is used, 1986 is year 15; with the coded method, it is year 12. The results are:

$$\text{Direct method} \quad \overline{Y}_p = 2.2 + 0.2(15) = \$5.2 \text{ million}$$

$$\text{Coded method} \quad \overline{Y}_p = 2.8 + 0.2(12) = \$5.2 \text{ million}$$

The preceding discussion applies to time series that are increasing or decreasing by equal *amounts*. When plotted on graph paper with an arithmetic scale, the data will produce a straight line. Hence, *linear* trend. On the other hand, a time series increasing or decreasing by equal *percents* will appear curvilinear when plotted on graph paper with an arithmetic scale. The same time series when plotted on graph paper with a semilogarithmic scale will appear as a straight line. Logarithms of the data are used to produce the trend equation. Also, the least

Table 4.6. Adams Co., Household Toaster Sales.

Year	Household Toaster Sales (Thousands of Units)
1970	1.10
1971	1.22
1972	1.34
1973	1.47
1974	1.62
1975	1.78
1976	1.96
1977	2.16
1978	2.38

squares method may be used. Table 4.6 shows the 1970–78 unit sales of household toasters for the Adams Co. which are increasing at 10% per year.

Adams Co. sales are plotted on arithmetic paper in Figure 4.5 and on semilog paper in Figure 4.6.

The trend equation used here is the same as that used in linear trend. However, logarithms of numbers are used. The coded method equation is:

$$\log \overline{Y}_p = \log a + b(X)$$

then $\log a$ and $\log b$ are:

$$\log a = \frac{\Sigma \log Y}{n}$$

$$\log b = \frac{\Sigma (x \log Y)}{\Sigma x^2}$$

The information needed to complete these equations is found in Table 4.7.

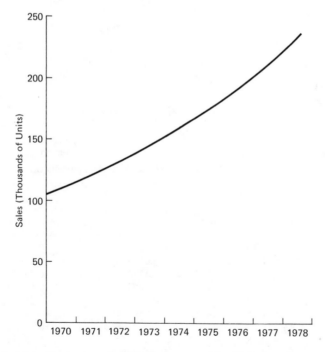

Fig. 4.5 Adams Co. toaster sales plotted on paper with arithmetic scale, 1970–1978.

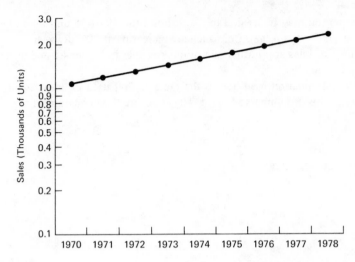

Fig. 4.6 Adams Co. toaster sales plotted on paper with ratio (semilogarithmic) scale.

Taking the necessary information and placing it in the preceding equations, we get:

$$\log a = \frac{1.88540}{9} = 0.2095$$

$$\log b = \frac{2.49845}{60} = 0.04164$$

$$\log \overline{Y}_p = 0.2095 + 0.04164X$$

Table 4.7. Trend Equation—Coded Method Logarithmic, Straight-Line Equation, for Sales of Household Toasters, Adams Co.

Year	Y (Household Toaster Sales in Thousands of Units)	log Y	X	X(log Y)	x^2
1970	1.10	0.04139	−4	−0.16556	16
1971	1.22	0.08636	−3	−0.25908	9
1972	1.34	0.12710	−2	−0.25420	4
1973	1.47	0.16732	−1	−0.16732	1
1974	1.62	0.20952	0	−	0
1975	1.78	0.25042	+1	+0.25042	1
1976	1.96	0.29226	+2	+0.58452	4
1977	2.16	0.33445	+3	+1.00335	9
1978	2.38	0.37658	+4	+1.50632	16
		1.88540		2.49845	60

Table 4.8. Coordinates for 1970 and 1978.

Year	X	$\log \overline{Y}_p$	Antilog	Coordinates X	Y
1970	−4	0.04139	1.10	−4	1.10
1978	+4	0.37658	2.38	+4	2.38

where sales of household toasters (Y) are in thousands of units; the origin, or zero year, is 1974 (July 1, 1974); and x increases 1 unit for each year. If $x = 0$, then the log of $\overline{Y}_p$ is 0.2095 and its antilog is 1.62; This gives the coordinates of one point on the trend line: $X = 0$ and $Y = 1.62$. The coordinates for 1970 and 1978 are shown in Table 4.8.

Figure 4.7 illustrates the use of trend equations to forecast toasters to 1985. The slope on the line, or the percent change in Y for every increase of one X, is represented by b. Hence, the average increase in sales per year from 1970 to 1978 can be determined by using antilogs. The log of b is 0.04164. The antilog is 1.1006. Subtracting 1 from this number leaves 0.1006 or 10%, which is the average percent increase for each year from 1970 through 1978.

To forecast Adams Co. sales of household toasters in 1985, for which $X = 11$, the following formula would be used:

$$\log \overline{Y}_p = 0.2095 + 0.04164(11)$$

$$= 0.66754$$

The antilog of 0.66754 is 4.6509. Hence, estimated sales of household toasters by the Adams Co. in 1985 is 465,090 units.

Seasonality

When a time series changes in volume from month to month, a seasonal pattern occurs. Such a change is predictable; it is recurrent and occurs in the same month from year to year. For example, sales of electric appliances such as toasters and electric knives are higher in December because of Christmas sales. Fluctuations in seasonality vary widely from one series to another. Within a particular series, there normally is little change in seasonal factors from year to year. Seasonality is explained in depth in Chapter 5.

Cyclical Variations

Another component of a time series is cyclical variation. While the trend line may be moving slowly upward or downward over a long period of time, the line

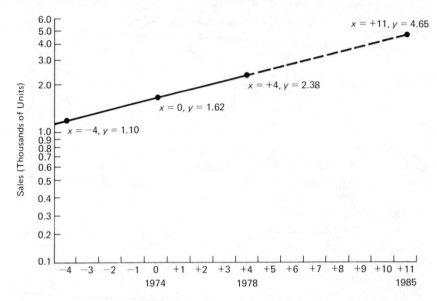

Fig. 4.7 Forecast Adams Co. toaster sales to 1985 using logarithmic trend line (semilog scale).

representing the business cycle may be moving above and below it on a recurring basis. Such movement is generally related to the business cycle, which is recurrent but not periodic and therefore hard to forecast. Since World War II, the United States has had several business cycles. Those ending in a recession occured in 1949, 1954, 1958, 1961, 1970, and 1973. Most economic time series of the United States are affected by business cycles. They last from 1 to 10 years, with the average length being 4 years. The amplitude measured from peak to trough varies widely.

Orders for new metal-cutting machine tools are closely tied to capital expenditures and the business cycle. Figure 4.8 shows new orders from 1947 through 1976. Notice the dip in orders in 1949, 1954, 1958, 1970, and 1975.

Trading-Day Factors

Trading days are an important component of a time series. Many fluctuations that occur repeatedly are related to calendar variations, which cause the number of trading days to differ for two given months in the same year, as well as for the same month in different years. For example, December is longer than November simply because it has more days. However, certain other variations are not repetitive—for example, the month in which Easter falls and the number of Saturdays in a month. Saturday is particularly important for retail stores since it is usually the day with the largest amount of sales. These calendar variations are special because they vary from year to year.

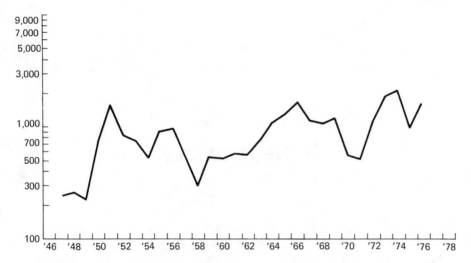

Fig. 4.8 New orders for U.S. machine tools (metal-cutting type), 1947–1976. (*millions of dollars*)

Variations are important to forecasters for they must know how many trading days there are going to be from one year to the next.

Irregular Fluctuations

The fluctuations remaining in a time series after the removal of seasonal calendar variations, trend, and cycle are lumped together as the "irregular components." Some irregular components, such as war and strikes, cannot be predicted—but they can be identified. Some forecasters call these *episodic fluctuations*. After these have been removed from the time series, residual variations are left (i.e., those that are due to chance, that are unpredictable, or that cannot be identified).

5 Seasonality

As discussed in Chapter 4, seasonality is predictable. A seasonable pattern is recurrent and occurs in the same month from year to year. Being able to predict changes in retail sales volume, for example, helps department store managers to determine levels of inventory and personnel needed, as well as cash flow.

Analysis of seasonal variation can be used to eliminate it from, or at least reduce it in, a company's sales. A sporting-goods company can offer a different product for each of the four seasons, thereby obviating a slack season with subsequent layoffs. ABC Toy Co., a manufacturer of games, whose sales occur largely in November and December due to the Christmas season, uses "anticipation stocking." It lays in stock in the early part of the year, when sales are slow, in anticipation of higher than normal volume in November and December. A trade show held in the normally slow first quarter of the year gives ABC Toy ideas about what type of products will be in demand during the Christmas season. In addition, during the slow period, ABC Toy sales representatives call on customers with prototypes of new games, and state that orders will be filled during the summer. The company also has a four-step plan wherein sales are analyzed by quarter. Should one quarter deviate from the plan, the following quarter can be adjusted accordingly. In this manner, ABC Toy does not spend its money too soon and can better control its cash flow.

XYZ Electric Co., a large manufacturer of electric housewares with seasonal products, operates much like ABC Toy. It spends the first half of the year gearing up for production in the last half. Trade shows are held in January and in July. Also, company sales representatives ask customers what items they believe will be in demand at Christmas. XYZ Electric then uses this feedback in planning its production schedules.

Studying seasonal variations over a period of years can also be helpful in spotting trends. Figure 5.1 shows total monthly United States retail sales from January 1969 through July 1979. The solid line shows sales after being adjusted for seasonal, holiday, and trading-day differences.

Dividing an economic time series by a set of seasonal indexes yields a desea-

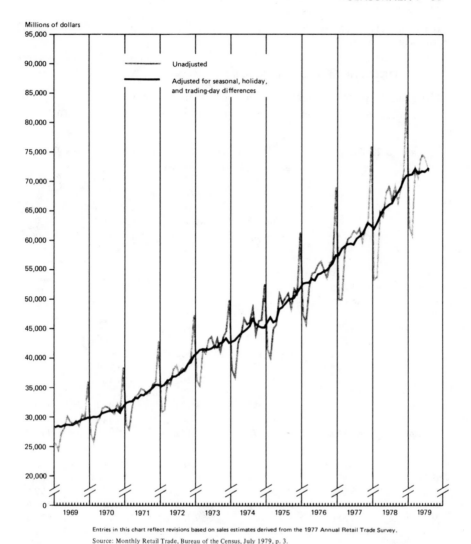

Millions of dollars

Unadjusted

Adjusted for seasonal, holiday, and trading-day differences

Entries in this chart reflect revisions based on sales estimates derived from the 1977 Annual Retail Trade Survey.
Source: Monthly Retail Trade, Bureau of the Census, July 1979, p. 3.

Fig. 5.1 Estimated monthly retail sales for the United States: Jan. 1969–July 1979.

sonalized or seasonally adjusted series. This leaves the trend and cycle to be studied.

An economic time series contains the five factors mentioned in Chapter 4—namely, trend, seasonal, cyclical, irregular, and trading-day variation, or T, S, C, I, CV. (Calender variation may be considered part of the irregular variation.) Dividing by the seasonal factor removes the seasonality, that is, $(T, S, C, I, CV) \div S = T, S, C, CV$. Then the remaining components may be studied. Looking at Figure 5.1, we can see the upward trend of sales after the seasonality has been removed.

COMPUTING THE SEASONAL INDEX

The seasonal pattern is recurrent and occurs in the same month from year to year. There are 12 seasonal factors in a monthly series and four factors in a

Table 5.1. Ratio-to-Moving, Average Seasonal Method, United States Total Retail Sales (in $ Millions).

Raw Data	(1) Retail Sales	(2) 12-Month Moving Total	(3) 12-Month Moving Average	(4) Centered 12-Month Moving Average	(5) Seasonal Factor
1976					
January	47,275	-	-	-	-
February	45,608	-	-	-	-
March	51,836	-	-	-	-
April	54,281	-	-	-	-
May	54,503	-	-	-	-
June	55,711	655,163 √	54,597 √	-	-
July	56,323	657,727 √	54,810	54,704	103.0
August	54,815	661,949 √	55,162	54,987	99.7
September	53,377	668,459 √	55,705	55,434	96.3
October	55,998	674,292	56,191	55,948	100.1
November	56,485	680,267	56,689	56,440	100.1
December	68,951	686,075	57,172	56,931	121.2
1977					
January	49,839	690,784	57,565	57,369	86.9
February	49,830	697,901	58,159	57,862	86.1
March	58,346	704,094	58,675	58,417	99.9
April	60,114	710,198	59,183	58,929	102.0
May	60,480	717,034	59,753	59,468	101.7
June	61,519	724,020	60,335	60,044	102.5
July	61,032	727,390	60,616	60,476	100.9
August	61,930	731,172	60,931	60,774	101.9
September	59,570	737,590	61,466	61,199	97.3
October	62,102	741,314	61,776	61,621	100.8
November	63,321	748,786	62,399	62,088	102.0
December	75,937	756,323	63,027	62,713	121.1
1978					
January	53,209	761,848	63,487	63,257	84.1
February	53,612	769,020	64,085	63,786	84.0
March	64,764	775,669	64,639	64,362	100.6
April	63,838	782,182	65,182	64,911	98.3
May	67,952	790,158	65,847	65,515	103.7

quarterly series. However, not all 12 indexes will equal 100. Suppose October had an index of 75% and February had one of 110%; this would mean October was 25% below average and that February was 10% above average. Several methods ranging from simple hand calculations to sophisticated computer programs have been used to compute seasonal indexes. However, the manual methods are prone to human error and are much more time-consuming.

Ratio-to-Moving-Average Method

The ratio-to-moving-average method assumes that there are five causes of change; trend-cycle, seasonal, trading-day effects, calendar variation, and irregular (all the others lumped together). This method of seasonal adjustment removes the trend-cycle from the original data. The best way to explain this method is with a step-by-step example. Total retail sales for the United States, a time series with a good seasonal pattern, is used in the calculation in Table 5.1.

12-MONTH MOVING TOTAL

The 12-month moving total is calculated by adding up sales for each month of 1976. Because the number of months is even, the moving total is centered between June and July. The next 12 months (February 1976 through January 1977) is obtained by dropping January 1976 sales of $47,275 million and adding January 1977 sales of $49,389 million. The total ($657,727 million) is placed between July and August. This procedure is followed until all possible 12-month moving totals have been computed.

It is necessary to insure the accuracy of the calculations. Turn to Table 5.1. Start with the first figure, cross it out when subtracted, and place a check mark next to the figures added. Continue until all figures have been used. Next, totals for 12 months should be checked. For example, the total retail sales of $655,163 million placed between June and July 1976 equal the sum of the sales for 1976. Figure 5.2 is an adding-machine tape showing total sales from January to December 1976 of $655,163 million.

UNCENTERED AND CENTERED 12-MONTH MOVING AVERAGES

Multiply the 12-month moving total by 0.083 (the reciprocal of 1/12), or divide each figure by 12. Note that each figure is still centered between the 2 months; for example, $655,163 \div 12 = 54,597$, which is positioned between June and July 1976. Then, make a 2-month moving average from the uncentered 12-month figures by adding two figures and dividing by 2. For example:

$ 54,597 million   (centered between June and July)

$54,810 million   (centered between July and August)
_____

$109,407 million $\div 2 = $54,704 million (centered for July)

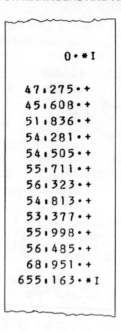

Fig. 5.2 Total sales from January to December 1976.

The 12-month moving average has eliminated the seasonal and irregular components. It contains trading day variations, trend and cycle.

ESTIMATED SEASONAL FACTORS

The next step is to divide retail sales (raw data, Column 1 in Table 5.1) by the centered 12-month moving average. The raw data contains trend, cyclical, seasonal, irregular, and trading-day variations. The seasonal and irregular components have been removed, leaving only the trend, cycle, and trading-day variations in the 12-month moving average. The formula for conversion is:

$$(TSCICV)\ 100 = SI$$

July–September 1976 seasonals are computed as follows:

July 1976	$(56,323/54,704)\ 100 = 103.0$
August 1976	$(54,813/54,987)\ 100 = 99.7$
September 1976	$(53,377/55,434)\ 100 = 96.3$

Table 5.2. Computation of Seasonal Index.

Year	January	February	March	April	May	June	July	August	September	October	November	December	Total
1976	-	-	-	-	-	-	~~103.0~~	~~99.7~~	~~96.3~~	~~100.1~~	100.1	121.1	
1977	~~86.9~~	~~86.1~~	~~99.9~~	~~102.0~~	~~101.7~~	~~102.5~~	100.9	~~101.9~~	97.3	~~100.8~~	~~102.0~~	121.1	
1978	84.1	84.0	100.6	98.3	103.7	~~100.5~~	100.1	101.8	~~98.8~~	100.7	101.5	~~122.9~~	
1979	83.8	83.4	100.2	98.0	103.8	101.0	100.0	101.8	98.6	100.5	100.0	119.8	
1980	82.9	~~83.0~~	100.4	97.8	104.0	100.8	~~98.8~~	101.6	98.4	100.3	~~99.7~~	~~118.6~~	
1981	~~81.8~~	84.0	~~100.9~~	~~97.5~~	~~106.0~~	100.6	-	-	-	-	-	-	
Total After Taking Out													
High and Low	250.8	251.4	301.2	294.1	311.5	302.4	301.0	305.2	294.3	301.5	301.6	362.0	*Total* 1192.2
Modified Mean	83.6	83.8	100.4	98.0	103.8	100.8	100.3	101.7	98.1	100.5	100.5	120.7	1192.2
Typical Factor	84.1	84.4	101.0	98.6	104.5	101.4	101.0	102.4	98.7	101.2	101.2	121.5	1200.0

REMOVAL OF IRREGULAR FACTOR

The seasonal indexes just computed contain the irregular factor as well as the seasonal. To remove the irregular factor, the seasonal factors are placed in an array, as shown in Table 5.2. Hypothetical seasonal factors from July 1978 to June 1981 are used for illustrative purposes. To obtain the modified mean, the highest and lowest seasonal factors are removed. A modified mean of the remaining seasonal factors is then computed. For example, look at the month of June in Table 5.2. The highest seasonal is 102.5 and the lowest is 100.5. The modified mean of the remaining three factors is 100.8. A modified median may be used in place of the modified mean.

TYPICAL INDEX

The sum of 12 monthly indexes equals 1200 with an average of 100. However, the sum of the seasonal indexes produced by the modified mean may not add up to 1200 due to rounding and the removal of highs and lows. In Table 5.2, we see the modified mean totals 1192.2. A factor of 1.0065 is produced by dividing 1200 by 1192.2. The modified mean for all 12 months is multiplied by this factor to produce the typical seasonal factors (Table 5.3). The seasonal factors in the table are plotted in Figure 5.3.

SEASONALLY ADJUSTED SALES

Once the typical seasonal factors (see Figure 5.3) have been produced, the seasonally adjusted sales can be computed. This is done by dividing the raw data by the seasonal factor (see Table 5.4). These data are plotted in Figure 5.4.

Table 5.3. Typical Seasonal Indexes for Total Retail Sales in the United States

Month	Index
January	84.1
February	84.4
March	101.0
April	98.6
May	104.5
June	101.4
July	101.0
August	102.4
September	98.7
October	101.2
November	101.2
December	121.5

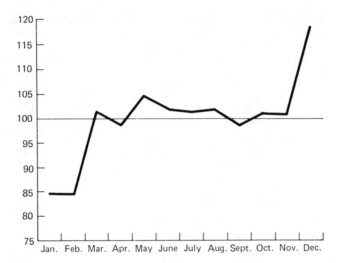

Fig. 5.3 Typical seasonal factors.

The ratio-to-moving average is not without its shortcomings. Due to the need for centering, 6 months are lost at the beginning and at the end. Also, the ratio-to-moving average flattens the peaks and troughs because it covers so long a time span.

COMPUTER METHODS

X-11 Variant, Census Method II Program

The Census Method II uses the ratio-to-moving-average method, which was developed by Frederick R. Macaulay of the National Bureau of Economic Research during the 1920s. In 1954 the Bureau of the Census introduced the first electronic computer program for seasonally adjusting economic time series. Thus, for the first time, the ratio-to-moving-average method could be employed on a large-scale basis. Today, variants of the census method are used throughout the world to adjust series at the company, industry, and national-aggregate levels.

In 1955, the Bureau of the Census replaced its original program with a revised procedure called *Census Method II*. From time to time, experimental versions of Method II have been introduced. The first version, made available to the public in 1960, was the X-3. It differed from the original Method II in the replacing of extreme values and the computing of the seasonal factors for the most recent years. In 1961, the X-9, which was used as the standard program, and the X-10, which was used to adjust more erratic series, were introduced.

In October 1965, the X-11 version of Method II replaced the X-9 and X-10 versions as the standard program for the Bureau of the Census. Now widely used,

Table 5.4. United States Total Retail Sales, 1976–78, Seasonally Adjusted

Month	Unadjusted (in $ Millions) Sales	Seasonal Index	Seasonally (in $ Millions) Adjusted Sales
1976			
July	$56,323	101.0	$55,765
August	54,813	102.4	53,528
September	53,377	98.7	54,080
October	55,998	101.2	55,333
November	56,485	101.2	55,815
December	68,951	121.5	56,750
1977			
January	49,839	84.1	59,262
February	49,830	84.4	59,040
March	58,346	101.0	57,768
April	60,114	98.6	60,967
May	60,480	104.5	57,875
June	61,519	101.4	60,670
July	61,032	101.0	60,427
August	61,930	102.4	60,479
September	59,570	98.7	60,345
October	62,102	101.2	61,365
November	63,321	101.2	62,570
December	75,737	121.5	62,335
1978			
January	53,209	84.1	63,270
February	53,612	84.4	63,521
March	64,764	101.0	64,123
April	63,838	98.6	64,744
May	67,952	104.5	65,025
June	69,056	101.4	68,102

it includes several improvements over earlier versions and offers several options to time-series analysts. For example, they may specify the moving averages to be used in estimating the trend-cycle and seasonal components.

X-11 Computer Program Printouts

In the United States and many foreign countries, the X-11 program has become the standard program for seasonally adjusting a time series. Figure 5.5a shows the first page of a computer printout of an X-11 run. It gives the title of the series run. At the bottom, the X-11 program options are listed. The date at the top (October 1, 1966) indicates the last time the X-11 program was changed. The time series used in the printout is from *U.S. Total Retail Sales* as reported by the Bureau of the Census. The "standard program," which eliminates many of the tables and charts, has been used.

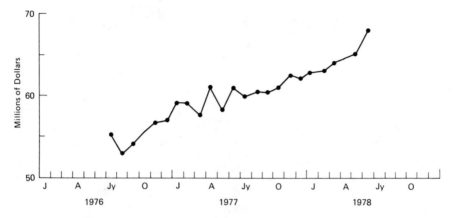

Fig. 5.4 U.S. total retail sales: July 1976–June 1978, seasonally adjusted.

A user's manual, *X-11 Information for the User,* is available from the Bureau of the Census. Also available is *The X-11 Variant of the Census Method II Seasonal Adjustment Program* (Technical Paper No. 15), giving formulas, equations, a picture of every table, and many other details. In addition, *Estimating Trading Day Variations in Monthly Economic Time Series* (Technical Paper No. 12) is available for those interested in the special aspects of trading-day adjustment.

Options

The standard program will satisfy the needs of most users. Nevertheless, Technical Paper No. 15 lists the options available, should the analyst wish to use them. These include:

1. *Multiplicative or additive version.* The multiplicative process should be used unless negative numbers are present in the time series. In the additive process, seasonal factors are presented in terms of units rather than index numbers.

2. *Standard or long printout.* The long version is necessary only where seasonal adjustment is controversial and the tables must be studied in great detail. The standard printout produces 17 to 27 tables (depending on the options chosen).

3. *Prior daily weights.* See Prior Trading-Day Factors.

4. *Length-of-month allowance.* The length-of-month allowance is necessitated by the fact that some months of the year have 30 days, others have 31, and February has at least 28.

5. *Trading-day options.*

Several other options are available including the adjustment of trend-cycle for strikes, the use of moving averages for seasonal factors, the choice of moving

X-11 SEASONAL ADJUSTMENT PROGRAM
U.S. BUREAU OF THE CENSUS
ECONOMIC RESEARCH AND ANALYSIS DIVISION
OCTOBER 1, 1966

THE X-11 PROGRAM IS DIVIDED INTO SEVEN MAJOR PARTS—
PART   DESCRIPTION
A. PRIOR ADJUSTMENTS, IF ANY
B. PRELIMINARY ESTIMATES OF IRREGULAR COMPONENT WEIGHTS
     AND REGRESSION TRADING DAY FACTORS
C. FINAL ESTIMATES OF ABOVE
D. FINAL ESTIMATES OF SEASONAL, TREND-CYCLE AND IRREGULAR COMPONENTS
E. ANALYTICAL TABLES
F. SUMMARY MEASURES
G. CHARTS

TABLES ARE IDENTIFIED BY THEIR PART LETTER AND SEQUENCE WITHIN THE PART. A GIVEN TABLE HAS THE SAME
IDENTIFICATION IN THE STANDARD, LONG AND FULL PRINTOUTS. THE SAME NUMBER IS GIVEN TO CORRESPONDING
TABLES IN PARTS B, C AND D. THUS, TABLES B10., C10. AND D10. ARE ALL TABLES OF SEASONAL FACTORS.
WHERE NO CORRESPONDING TABLE EXISTS THE SEQUENCE NO. IS NOT USED IN THE PART. THUS, B8. AND D8. ARE
TABLES OF UNMODIFIED SI RATIOS BUT THERE IS NO C8.

SERIES TITLE— U.S. TOTAL RETAIL SALES   THIS SERIES RUN   JAN. 1979
                              PERIOD COVERED— 1/67 TO 12/79   SERIES NO. RSALES   MILLIONS OF DOLLARS

TYPE OF RUN - MULTIPLICATIVE SEASONAL ADJUSTMENT
STANDARD PRINTOUT. STANDARD CHARTS.
PRIOR TRADING DAY ADJUSTMENT WITHOUT LENGTH OF MONTH ADJUSTMENT.
TRADING DAY REGRESSION COMPUTED STARTING 1967 EXCLUDING IRREGULAR VALUES OUTSIDE 2.5-SIGMA LIMITS.
TRADING DAY REGRESSION ESTIMATES NOT APPLIED.
SIGMA LIMITS FOR GRADUATING EXTREME VALUES ARE 1.5 AND 2.5

Fig. 5.5a Title series of an X-11 run.

averages for the trend-cycle portion of series, and the exclusion of extreme values so that they will not be picked up as irregular.

Pre-Computer Adjustments

The X-11 program allows the analyst to alter the input. This can be done in the following ways:

1. *Prior Monthly Adjustment Factors.* The user may feel it necessary to adjust the original series for one reason or another. He or she might wish to adjust for the effect of certain holidays. Suppose more retail sales occur in December than in November. The user might believe that December should produce 15% more sales than November and November 5% more than the other 10 months. The user would estimate an index of 120 for December and 105 for November, with the remaining 10 months at 97.5%. These factors would then be divided into the original series.

In Figure 5.5b, the original series appears just as it was fed into the computer. In addition, the yearly sales total and the average monthly sales are shown. It is most important to proofread such tables. Mistakes made here will spoil almost every subsequent table.

Prior Trading-Day Factors

In some states, retail stores are open 7 days a week. At the top of Figure 5.5c, prior daily weights are shown, which assume that all 7 days of the week have an equal influence on the dollar value of retail sales. For example, Table 5.5 indicates that in December 1972, there were five Fridays, Saturdays, and Sundays, and four of each of the other days.

Thus, the factor for December 1972 is computed as follows: $(31.000 \div 31) \times 100 = 100.0$. Factors for the other months are computed in the same way and printed in Figure 5.5c. Trading-day factors for 1980 (one year ahead) are shown at the bottom.

Trading-Day Adjustments

The computer takes the original data (Figure 5.5b) and divides it by the prior trading-day adjustment factors (Figure 5.5c) to produce the prior adjusted original series (Figure 5.5d).

Extreme irregular values are excluded from the calculations by the establishment of sigma limits. In the retail sales time series in Figure 5.5a, sigma limits outside 2.5 were excluded. This is normally satisfactory; however, it is adjustable. The lower the sigma limit, the greater the number of extreme irregular components that will be eliminated. This is true for a highly irregular series of a series substantially affected by strikes, where a greater portion of the series may be re-

A 1. ORIGINAL SERIES   JAN. 1979 U.S. TOTAL RETAIL SALES   MILLIONS OF DOLLARS   P. 1, SERIES RSALES

YEAR	JAN	FEB	MAR	APR	MAY	JUN	JUL	AUG	SEP	OCT	NOV	DEC	TOTAL
1967	21064.	20107.	23631.	23030.	24513.	25591.	24154.	24597.	24591.	24546.	25852.	31280.	292956.
1968	22726.	22813.	25469.	25935.	27660.	27482.	27262.	28297.	25913.	28210.	29197.	33394.	324358.
1969	25564.	24224.	27260.	27935.	30069.	29104.	28742.	29222.	28363.	30714.	29738.	36072.	346717.
1970	27107.	25548.	28776.	29608.	31399.	31680.	31534.	30918.	30361.	32232.	30794.	38446.	368403.
1971	28642.	27714.	31739.	33359.	33787.	34702.	34460.	33796.	33921.	35395.	35893.	42826.	406234.
1972	30730.	31035.	36065.	35254.	38005.	38729.	37157.	38246.	37656.	38940.	39966.	47286.	449069.
1973	35952.	35118.	41305.	40693.	43009.	43560.	41684.	43270.	40885.	43489.	44450.	49917.	503332.
1974	37859.	36506.	42424.	43844.	46664.	45587.	46004.	48530.	43788.	46218.	46342.	52543.	536309.
1975	41388.	39896.	44906.	45593.	50860.	49191.	50103.	50915.	48213.	51694.	50736.	61281.	584776.
1976	47275.	45608.	51836.	54281.	54505.	55711.	56323.	54813.	53377.	55998.	56485.	68951.	655163.
1977	49839.	49830.	58346.	60114.	60480.	61519.	61032.	61930.	59570.	62102.	63321.	75937.	724020.
1978	53209.	53612.	64764.	63838.	67952.	69056.	66557.	69102.	66219.	68615.	71297.	84597.	798818.
1979	61878.	60653.	72198.	70540.	74981.	74813.	72075.	77801.	72630.	76389.	78658.	92067.	884683.
AVGE	37172.	36359.	42209.	42621.	44914.	45133.	44391.	45495.	43499.	45708.	46364.	54969.	

TABLE TOTAL- 6874838.   MEAN- 44069.   STD. DEVIATION- 16011.

Fig. 5.5b Original series.

A 4. PRIOR TRADING DAY ADJUSTMENT FACTORS   JAN. 1979 U.S. TOTAL RETAIL SALES   P. 2, SERIES RSALES
A4A. PRIOR DAILY WEIGHTS

MON	TUE	WED	THUR	FRI	SAT	SUN
1.000	1.000	1.000	1.000	1.000	1.000	1.000

A4B. PRIOR TRADING DAY ADJUSTMENT FACTORS WITHOUT LENGTH OF MONTH ADJUSTMENT

YEAR	JAN	FEB	MAR	APR	MAY	JUN	JUL	AUG	SEP	OCT	NOV	DEC	AVGE
1967	100.0	99.1	100.0	100.0	100.0	100.0	100.0	100.0	100.0	100.0	100.0	100.0	99.9
1968	100.0	102.7	100.0	100.0	100.0	100.0	100.0	100.0	100.0	100.0	100.0	100.0	100.2
1969	100.0	99.1	100.0	100.0	100.0	100.0	100.0	100.0	100.0	100.0	100.0	100.0	99.9
1970	100.0	99.1	100.0	100.0	100.0	100.0	100.0	100.0	100.0	100.0	100.0	100.0	99.9
1971	100.0	99.1	100.0	100.0	100.0	100.0	100.0	100.0	100.0	100.0	100.0	100.0	99.9
1972	100.0	102.7	100.0	100.0	100.0	100.0	100.0	100.0	100.0	100.0	100.0	100.0	100.2
1973	100.0	99.1	100.0	100.0	100.0	100.0	100.0	100.0	100.0	100.0	100.0	100.0	99.9
1974	100.0	99.1	100.0	100.0	100.0	100.0	100.0	100.0	100.0	100.0	100.0	100.0	99.9
1975	100.0	99.1	100.0	100.0	100.0	100.0	100.0	100.0	100.0	100.0	100.0	100.0	99.9
1976	100.0	102.7	100.0	100.0	100.0	100.0	100.0	100.0	100.0	100.0	100.0	100.0	100.2
1977	100.0	99.1	100.0	100.0	100.0	100.0	100.0	100.0	100.0	100.0	100.0	100.0	99.9
1978	100.0	99.1	100.0	100.0	100.0	100.0	100.0	100.0	100.0	100.0	100.0	100.0	99.9
1979	100.0	99.1	100.0	100.0	100.0	100.0	100.0	100.0	100.0	100.0	100.0	100.0	99.9
AVGE	100.0	99.9	100.0	100.0	100.0	100.0	100.0	100.0	100.0	100.0	100.0	100.0	99.9

TABLE TOTAL- 15599.1

A4C. PRIOR TRADING DAY ADJUSTMENT FACTORS, ONE YEAR AHEAD

YEAR	JAN	FEB	MAR	APR	MAY	JUN	JUL	AUG	SEP	OCT	NOV	DEC	AVGE
1980	100.0	102.7	100.0	100.0	100.0	100.0	100.0	100.0	100.0	100.0	100.0	100.0	100.2

Fig. 5.5c Prior daily weights.

Table 5.5. Number Days Week—December 1972

Day of Week	No. in December 1972	Weight	Total Weight
Sunday	5	1.000	5.000
Saturday	5	1.000	5.000
Friday	5	1.000	5.000
Thursday	4	1.000	4.000
Wednesday	4	1.000	4.000
Tuesday	4	1.000	4.000
Monday	4	1.000	4.000
	31		31.000

garded as extreme. On the other hand, higher limits are sometimes better for a very smooth series. (See Figure 5.5e).

The development of the trading-day adjustment factors is in large part determined by the prior daily weights supplied by the user. However, the X-11 program allows the computer to test via the regression method to determine whether workdays cause more fluctuations than those supplied by the user. The results of such a test are shown in Figure 5.5f. The second column shows the prior daily weights supplied by the user. Regression coefficients are shown in the third column. The combined weights shown in the first column are the sum of the second and third columns.

Figure 5.5g shows trading-day adjustment factors determined by the regression method. Note the difference in the daily weights from those in Figure 5.5c.

The irregular component factors are tested, and weights for this component are chosen. See Figure 5.5h.

The heading at the top of Figure 5.5i states that the trading-day adjustment factors are the same as in Table A4 (see Figure 5.5i). Therefore, the trading-day regression computed from the prior daily weights was not significant. The trading-day weights in Figure 5.5c are now divided into the original series to produce a series adjusted for trading days (Figure 5.5c). Therefore, Figure 5.5j, Adjusted Original Series, is the same as Figure 5.5d. Up to this point, the original data have only gone through a series of preliminary adjustments. Now the seasonal adjustment begins.

Final Adjustments

The following three tables are the most crucial of the X-11 program:

1. *Final unmodified seasonal-irregular ratios.* The computer continues the iterative approach, repeatedly working on the trend-cycle until it has produced an exceedingly smooth trend-cycle average. The seasonal-irregular ratios produced in Figure 5.5k are the result of dividing the original series by the smoothed trend-cycle average. Included in these ratios are fluctuations caused by seasonal trading-day and irregular factors.

B 1. PRIOR ADJUSTED ORIGINAL SERIES

JAN. 1979 U.S. TOTAL RETAIL SALES

MILLIONS OF DOLLARS

YEAR	JAN	FEB	MAR	APR	MAY	JUN	JUL	AUG	SEP	OCT	NOV	DEC	TOTAL
1967	21064.	20287.	23631.	23030.	24513.	25591.	24154.	24597.	24591.	24546.	25852.	31280.	293136.
1968	22726.	22223.	25469.	25935.	27660.	27482.	27262.	28297.	25913.	28210.	29197.	33394.	323768.
1969	25564.	24440.	27260.	27985.	30069.	29104.	28742.	29222.	28363.	30374.	29738.	36072.	346933.
1970	27107.	25776.	28776.	29608.	31399.	31680.	31534.	30918.	30361.	32232.	30794.	38446.	368631.
1971	28642.	27961.	31739.	33359.	33787.	34702.	34460.	33796.	33921.	35395.	35893.	42826.	406481.
1972	30730.	30232.	36065.	35254.	38005.	38729.	37157.	38246.	37656.	38940.	39966.	47286.	448266.
1973	35952.	35432.	41305.	40693.	43009.	43560.	41684.	43270.	40885.	43489.	44450.	49917.	503646.
1974	37859.	36832.	42424.	43844.	46664.	45587.	46004.	48530.	43788.	46218.	46342.	52543.	536635.
1975	41388.	40252.	44906.	45593.	50860.	49191.	50103.	50915.	48213.	51694.	50736.	61281.	585132.
1976	47275.	44428.	51836.	54281.	54505.	55711.	56323.	54813.	53377.	55998.	56485.	68951.	653983.
1977	49839.	50275.	58346.	60114.	60480.	61519.	61032.	61930.	59570.	62102.	63321.	75937.	724465.
1978	53209.	54091.	64764.	63838.	67952.	69056.	66557.	69102.	66219.	68615.	71297.	84597.	799297.
1979	61878.	61195.	72198.	70540.	74981.	74813.	72075.	77801.	72630.	76389.	78658.	92067.	885225.
AVGE	37172.	36417.	42209.	42621.	44914.	45133.	44391.	45495.	43499.	45708.	46364.	54969.	
	TABLE TOTAL-	6875598.				MEAN- 44004.				STD. DEVIATION- 16017.			

Fig. 5.5d Prior adjusted original series.

C14. EXTREME IRREGULAR VALUES EXCLUDED FROM TRADING DAY REGRESSION

JAN. 1979 U.S. TOTAL RETAIL SALES
(OUTSIDE 2.5-SIGMA LIMIT)

YEAR	JAN	FEB	MAR	APR	MAY	JUN	JUL	AUG	SEP	OCT	NOV	DEC	AVGE
1967	*0000.0	*0000.0	*0000.0	*0000.0	*0000.0	*0000.0	*0000.0	*0000.0	*0000.0	95.6	*0000.0	*0000.0	*66674.6
1968	*0000.0	*0000.0	*0000.0	*0000.0	*0000.0	*0000.0	*0000.0	*0000.0	95.9	*0000.0	*0000.0	*0000.0	*66674.7
1969	*0000.0	*0000.0	*0000.0	*0000.0	*0000.0	*0000.0	*0000.0	*0000.0	*0000.0	*0000.0	95.8	*0000.0	*00000.0
1970	*0000.0	*0000.0	*0000.0	*0000.0	*0000.0	*0000.0	*0000.0	*0000.0	*0000.0	*0000.0	*0000.0	*0000.0	*66674.6
1971	*0000.0	*0000.0	*0000.0	*0000.0	*0000.0	*0000.0	*0000.0	*0000.0	*0000.0	*0000.0	*0000.0	*0000.0	*00000.0
1972	*0000.0	*0000.0	*0000.0	*0000.0	*0000.0	*0000.0	*0000.0	*0000.0	*0000.0	*0000.0	*0000.0	*0000.0	*00000.0
1973	*0000.0	*0000.0	*0000.0	*0000.0	*0000.0	*0000.0	*0000.0	*0000.0	*0000.0	*0000.0	*0000.0	*0000.0	*00000.0
1974	*0000.0	*0000.0	*0000.0	*0000.0	*0000.0	*0000.0	*0000.0	104.9	*0000.0	*0000.0	*0000.0	*0000.0	*66675.4
1975	*0000.0	*0000.0	*0000.0	97.8	103.9	*0000.0	*0000.0	*0000.0	*0000.0	*0000.0	*0000.0	*0000.0	*33350.1
1976	*0000.0	*0000.0	*0000.0	*0000.0	*0000.0	*0000.0	*0000.0	*0000.0	*0000.0	*0000.0	*0000.0	*0000.0	*00000.0
1977	*0000.0	*0000.0	*0000.0	*0000.0	*0000.0	*0000.0	*0000.0	*0000.0	*0000.0	*0000.0	*0000.0	*0000.0	*00000.0
1978	*0000.0	*0000.0	*0000.0	*0000.0	*0000.0	*0000.0	*0000.0	*0000.0	*0000.0	*0000.0	*0000.0	*0000.0	*00000.0
1979	*0000.0	*0000.0	*0000.0	*0000.0	*0000.0	99.5	*0000.0	*0000.0	*0000.0	*0000.0	*0000.0	*0000.0	*66675.0

Fig. 5.5e Extreme irregular values excluding trading day regression.

C15. FINAL TRADING DAY REGRESSION

JAN. 1979 U.S. TOTAL RETAIL SALES

	COMBINED WEIGHT	PRIOR WEIGHT	REGRESSION COEFF.	ST.ERROR (COMB.WT.)	T (1)	T (PRIOR WT.)
MONDAY	1.012	1.000	.012	.049	.249	.249
TUESDAY	.905	1.000	-.095	.050	-1.907	-1.907
WEDNESDAY	1.026	1.000	-.026	.049	-.530	-.530
THURSDAY	1.050	1.000	.050	.049	1.018	1.018
FRIDAY	1.404	1.000	.404	.048	8.370*	8.370**
SATURDAY	1.012	1.000	.012	.050	.232	.232
SUNDAY	.590	1.000	-.410	.049	-8.333*	-8.333**

* COMBINED WT. SIGNIFICANTLY DIFFERENT FROM 1 AT 1 PER CENT LEVEL
** COMBINED WT. SIGNIFICANTLY DIFFERENT FROM PRIOR WEIGHT AT 1 PER CENT LEVEL

SOURCE OF VARIANCE	SUM OF SQUARES	DGRS.OF FREEDOM	MEAN SQUARE	F
REGRESSION	15.686	6.	2.614	55.876***
ERROR	6.691	143.	.047	
TOTAL	22.376	149.		

*** RESIDUAL TRADING DAY VARIATION PRESENT AT THE 1 PER CENT LEVEL

STANDARD ERRORS OF TRADING DAY ADJUSTMENT FACTORS DERIVED FROM REGRESSION COEFFICIENTS
31-DAY MONTHS-   .13
30-DAY MONTHS-   .15
29-DAY MONTHS-   .17
28-DAY MONTHS-   .00

Fig. 5.5f Final trading day regression.

C16. TRADING DAY ADJUSTMENT FACTORS DERIVED FROM REGRESSION COEFFICIENTS
JAN. 1979 U.S. TOTAL RETAIL SALES

C16A. REGRESSION COEFFICIENTS

MON	TUE	WED	THUR	FRI	SAT	SUN
1.012	.905	1.026	1.050	1.404	1.012	.590

C16B. REGRESSION TRADING DAY ADJUSTMENT FACTORS

YEAR	JAN	FEB	MAR	APR	MAY	JUN	JUL	AUG	SEP	OCT	NOV	DEC	AVGE
1967	98.4	100.0	101.6	98.7	99.8	101.5	98.8	99.9	101.4	98.4	100.3	100.0	99.9
1968	99.8	100.2	100.0	99.7	101.6	98.7	99.8	101.5	98.7	99.9	101.5	98.4	100.0
1969	101.6	100.0	98.8	99.8	101.5	98.7	99.9	100.0	99.7	101.6	98.7	99.9	100.0
1970	101.5	100.0	98.4	100.3	100.0	99.7	101.6	98.8	99.8	101.5	98.7	99.9	100.1
1971	100.0	100.0	99.8	101.5	98.8	99.8	101.5	98.4	100.3	100.0	99.7	101.6	100.1
1972	98.8	99.7	101.6	98.7	99.8	101.5	98.8	99.9	101.4	98.4	100.3	100.0	99.9
1973	99.8	100.0	100.5	98.7	99.9	101.4	98.4	101.6	98.7	99.8	101.5	98.8	100.0
1974	99.9	100.0	100.0	99.7	101.5	98.7	99.8	101.5	98.7	99.9	101.4	98.4	100.0
1975	101.6	100.0	98.8	101.5	98.7	99.9	100.0	100.0	99.7	101.6	98.7	99.8	100.1
1976	101.5	98.6	99.8	101.5	98.4	99.8	101.5	98.4	100.3	100.0	99.7	101.6	100.1
1977	98.8	100.0	99.9	101.4	98.4	100.3	100.0	99.8	101.5	98.8	99.8	101.5	100.0
1978	98.4	100.0	101.6	98.7	99.8	101.5	98.8	99.9	101.4	98.4	100.3	100.0	99.9
1979	99.8	100.0	101.5	98.7	99.9	101.4	98.4	101.6	98.7	99.8	101.5	98.8	100.0

TABLE TOTAL- 15598.6

C16C. REGRESSION TRADING DAY ADJUSTMENT FACTORS, ONE YEAR AHEAD

YEAR	JAN	FEB	MAR	APR	MAY	JUN	JUL	AUG	SEP	OCT	NOV	DEC	AVGE
1980	99.9	101.4	98.8	99.8	101.5	98.7	99.9	100.0	99.7	101.6	98.7	99.8	100.0

Fig. 5.5g Trading day adjustment factors.

C17. FINAL WEIGHTS FOR IRREGULAR COMPONENT
JAN. 1979 U.S. TOTAL RETAIL SALES
GRADUATION RANGE FROM 1.5 TO 2.5 SIGMA

YEAR	JAN	FEB	MAR	APR	MAY	JUN	JUL	AUG	SEP	OCT	NOV	DEC	S=D.
1967	100.0	100.0	28.4	100.0	100.0	0.0	100.0	100.0	100.0	0.0	100.0	100.0	1.2
1968	100.0	100.0	100.0	100.0	100.0	100.0	100.0	43.9	0.0	100.0	43.5	100.0	1.2
1969	100.0	100.0	100.0	100.0	100.0	100.0	100.0	100.0	100.0	100.0	100.0	100.0	1.2
1970	100.0	100.0	100.0	100.0	100.0	100.0	100.0	100.0	100.0	100.0	0.0	100.0	1.2
1971	100.0	100.0	100.0	2.1	81.9	100.0	100.0	72.0	100.0	100.0	100.0	100.0	1.2
1972	51.2	100.0	3.9	100.0	100.0	100.0	100.0	100.0	100.0	100.0	100.0	100.0	1.3
1973	100.0	100.0	100.0	100.0	100.0	100.0	100.0	100.0	100.0	100.0	60.8	100.0	1.3
1974	100.0	100.0	100.0	100.0	100.0	100.0	100.0	0.0	100.0	100.0	100.0	0.0	1.4
1975	100.0	100.0	100.0	65.2	0.0	100.0	100.0	100.0	100.0	100.0	94.4	100.0	1.2
1976	7.3	100.0	100.0	70.5	103.0	100.0	40.8	86.6	100.0	100.0	100.0	100.0	1.1
1977	100.0	100.0	100.0	100.0	100.0	100.0	100.0	100.0	100.0	100.0	100.0	100.0	1.2
1978	0.0	100.0	100.0	100.0	100.0	100.0	100.0	100.0	100.0	100.0	100.0	100.0	1.2
1979	100.0	100.0	100.0	100.0	100.0	100.0	54.2	74.9	100.0	100.0	100.0	100.0	1.2

Fig. 5.5h Irregular component factors.

JAN. 1979 U.S. TOTAL RETAIL SALES

C18. TRADING-DAY ADJUSTMENT FACTORS FROM COMBINED DAILY WEIGHTS (SAME AS TABLE A 4.)

P. 8, SERIES RSALES

Fig. 5.5i Trading day adjustment factors.

JAN. 1979 U.S. TOTAL RETAIL SALES

C19. ADJUSTED* ORIGINAL SERIES (SAME AS TABLE B 1.)

P. 9, SERIES RSALES

Fig. 5.5j Adjusted original series.

JAN. 1979 U.S. TOTAL RETAIL SALES

D 8. FINAL UNMODIFIED SI RATIOS

P.10. SERIES RSALES

YEAR	JAN	FEB	MAR	APR	MAY	JUN	JUL	AUG	SEP	OCT	NOV	DEC	AVGE
1967	89.4	85.9	99.7	96.8	102.6	106.4	99.5	100.2	99.0	97.9	102.2	122.6	100.2
1968	88.3	85.6	97.2	97.9	103.4	101.7	100.0	103.1	93.9	101.6	104.7	119.1	99.7
1969	90.7	86.2	95.7	97.9	104.9	101.3	99.7	101.0	97.4	103.6	100.7	121.4	100.0
1970	90.8	85.9	95.4	97.6	102.9	103.2	102.1	99.6	97.3	102.7	97.5	120.7	99.6
1971	89.1	86.2	97.0	101.1	101.5	103.4	101.8	98.8	98.3	101.7	102.5	121.7	100.3
1972	86.9	85.0	100.7	97.5	103.9	104.7	99.4	101.3	98.7	100.7	101.8	118.5	99.9
1973	88.7	86.2	99.6	97.6	102.9	104.1	99.4	102.7	96.6	102.4	104.5	117.0	100.1
1974	88.3	85.3	97.3	99.5	104.9	101.7	102.2	107.5	96.6	101.4	101.1	114.1	100.0
1975	89.6	86.9	96.5	97.3	107.3	102.4	102.7	102.9	96.3	102.4	99.7	119.3	100.3
1976	91.2	84.9	98.1	101.9	101.6	103.3	103.8	100.4	97.0	100.8	100.6	121.3	100.4
1977	86.6	86.4	99.3	101.5	101.4	102.5	101.0	101.7	97.0	100.3	101.6	121.1	100.0
1978	84.3	85.0	100.8	98.3	103.5	104.0	99.2	102.1	97.0	99.5	102.5	120.5	99.7
1979	87.4	85.9	100.8	98.0	103.5	102.4	97.6	104.2	96.3	100.4	102.8	119.7	99.9
AVGE	88.6	85.8	98.3	98.7	103.4	103.2	100.6	102.0	97.0	101.2	101.7	119.8	

TABLE TOTAL- 15603.0

STABLE SEASONALITY TEST

	SUM OF SQUARES	DGRS.OF FREEDOM	MEAN SQUARE	F
BETWEEN MONTHS	9973.824	11	906.711	299.282**
RESIDUAL	436.266	144	3.030	
TOTAL	10410.089	155		

**STABLE SEASONALITY PRESENT AT THE 1 PER CENT LEVEL

Fig. 5.5k Final unmodified S–I ratios.

D10. FINAL SEASONAL FACTORS   JAN. 1979 U.S. TOTAL RETAIL SALES   P.12, SERIES RSALES

YEAR	JAN	FEB	MAR	APR	MAY	JUN	JUL	AUG	SEP	OCT	NOV	DEC	AVGE
1967	89.7	85.9	96.7	97.6	103.5	102.1	100.1	100.7	98.0	102.6	102.0	120.9	100.0
1968	89.7	85.9	96.7	97.7	103.4	102.3	100.3	100.6	98.0	102.5	102.0	121.0	100.0
1969	89.6	85.9	96.6	97.7	103.3	102.3	100.5	100.6	98.0	102.4	102.1	120.8	100.0
1970	89.4	85.8	96.7	97.7	103.3	102.9	100.6	100.6	97.9	102.3	102.1	120.4	100.0
1971	89.2	85.8	97.0	97.9	103.3	103.2	100.9	100.9	97.7	102.1	102.1	119.8	100.0
1972	89.0	85.8	97.3	98.0	103.3	103.3	100.9	101.2	97.5	101.9	102.0	119.3	100.0
1973	88.8	85.7	97.6	98.3	103.3	103.3	101.1	101.6	97.3	101.7	101.7	119.0	100.0
1974	88.6	85.8	97.9	98.8	103.2	103.1	101.4	102.0	97.0	101.6	101.4	119.1	100.0
1975	88.4	85.7	98.1	99.4	103.1	102.9	101.4	102.0	96.9	101.3	101.2	119.5	100.0
1976	88.2	85.8	98.6	99.6	102.8	102.8	101.3	102.1	96.7	101.0	101.2	119.9	100.0
1977	87.9	85.7	99.1	99.7	102.7	102.9	100.9	102.1	96.8	100.6	101.5	120.4	100.0
1978	87.6	85.7	99.6	99.5	102.6	103.0	100.3	102.2	96.8	100.4	101.8	120.6	100.0
1979	87.4	85.6	100.0	99.5	102.6	103.0	100.0	102.2	96.8	100.2	102.0	120.6	100.0

TABLE TOTAL- 15598.9

MEAN- 100.0   STD. DEVIATION- 8.1

D10A. SEASONAL FACTORS, ONE YEAR AHEAD

YEAR	JAN	FEB	MAR	APR	MAY	JUN	JUL	AUG	SEP	OCT	NOV	DEC	AVGE
1980	87.2	85.6	100.1	99.5	102.6	103.0	99.9	102.2	96.8	100.1	102.1	120.6	100.0

Fig. 5.5l Final seasonal factors.

D11. FINAL SEASONALLY ADJUSTED SERIES   JAN. 1979 U.S. TOTAL RETAIL SALES   P.13, SERIES RSALES

YEAR	JAN	FEB	MAR	APR	MAY	JUN	JUL	AUG	SEP	OCT	NOV	DEC	TOTAL
1967	23494.	23617.	24441.	23599.	23678.	25054.	24129.	24418.	25094.	23933.	25349.	25863.	292670.
1968	25332.	25857.	26346.	26557.	26749.	26868.	27177.	28132.	26447.	27519.	28624.	27606.	323216.
1969	28523.	28454.	28218.	28635.	29095.	28381.	28588.	29062.	28950.	29662.	29136.	29856.	346558.
1970	30312.	30031.	29751.	30293.	30406.	30790.	31351.	30729.	31019.	31519.	30174.	31932.	368308.
1971	32096.	32599.	32722.	34084.	32698.	33622.	34216.	33508.	34715.	34682.	35164.	35752.	405858.
1972	34513.	35225.	37052.	35980.	36780.	37475.	36839.	37774.	38615.	38198.	39193.	39620.	447264.
1973	40489.	41325.	42326.	41386.	41615.	42159.	41224.	42570.	42018.	42762.	43696.	41937.	503506.
1974	42721.	42918.	43355.	44358.	45216.	44213.	45419.	47594.	45121.	45495.	45682.	44125.	536217.
1975	46809.	46947.	45765.	45881.	49345.	47782.	49402.	49907.	49780.	51034.	50117.	51299.	584065.
1976	53608.	51776.	52594.	54499.	52996.	54179.	55691.	53698.	55185.	55453.	55798.	57510.	652914.
1977	56674.	58651.	58858.	60302.	58862.	59777.	60503.	60669.	61550.	61711.	62391.	63061.	723008.
1978	60755.	63148.	65004.	64129.	66222.	67067.	66257.	67616.	68414.	68335.	70016.	70169.	797203.
1979	70837.	71486.	72234.	70860.	73078.	72637.	72049.	76126.	75042.	76227.	77096.	76363.	884035.
AVGE	42013.	42464.	42974.	43120.	43595.	43846.	44065.	44754.	44765.	45118.	45572.	45776.	

TABLE TOTAL- 6864823.

MEAN- 44005.   STD. DEVIATION- 15296.

Fig. 5.5m Final seasonally adjusted series.

F 2. SUMMARY MEASURES   JAN. 1979 U.S. TOTAL RETAIL SALES

AVERAGE PER CENT CHANGE WITHOUT REGARD TO SIGN OVER INDICATED SPAN

SPAN IN MONTHS	A1 O	D13 I	D11 CI	D12 C	D10 S	A2 P	C1# TD*	F1 MCD	E1 MOD.O	E2 MOD.CI	E3 MOD.I
1	7.39	1.92	2.16	.77	6.46	0.00	.22	.85	7.15	1.75	1.51
2	9.64	1.87	2.33	1.55	8.81	0.00	.21	1.62	9.49	2.06	1.44
3	10.51	1.33	2.58	2.33	9.70	0.00	.21	2.40	10.46	2.45	1.09
4	10.37	1.89	3.60	3.13	9.50	0.00	.21	3.17	10.31	3.35	1.49
5	9.78	1.66	4.07	3.94	8.79	0.00	.22	3.93	9.79	3.97	1.23
6	10.56	1.43	4.77	4.75	8.50	0.00	.22	4.72	10.50	4.76	1.12
7	11.70	1.95	5.68	5.56	8.68	0.00	.22	5.52	11.60	5.58	1.52
9	13.18	1.31	7.18	7.19	9.99	0.00	.22	7.18	13.10	7.20	1.04
11	11.96	1.48	8.87	8.85	7.13	0.00	.22	8.85	11.94	8.85	1.19
12	9.70	1.59	9.70	9.69	.17	0.00	.15	9.69	9.69	9.69	1.30

RELATIVE CONTRIBUTIONS OF COMPONENTS TO VARIANCE IN ORIGINAL SERIES

SPAN IN MONTHS	D13 I	D12 C	D10 S	A2 P	C18 TD*	TOTAL	RATIO (X100)
1	8.04	1.28	90.58	0.00	.10	100.00	84.33
2	4.16	2.86	92.92	0.00	.05	100.00	89.92
3	1.75	5.37	92.83	0.00	.04	100.00	91.77
4	3.44	9.46	87.06	0.00	.04	100.00	96.41
5	2.87	16.22	80.87	0.00	.05	100.00	99.92
6	2.11	23.25	74.59	0.00	.05	100.00	86.85
7	3.45	28.05	68.46	0.00	.04	100.00	80.50
9	1.12	33.74	65.11	0.00	.03	100.00	98.31
11	1.66	59.61	38.70	0.00	.04	100.00	91.91
12	2.62	97.32	.03	0.00	.02	100.00	102.64

AVERAGE DURATION OF RUN   CI 1.76   I 1.41   C 155.00   MCD 5.28

I/C RATIO FOR MONTHS SPAN

1	2	3	4	5	6	7	8	9	10	11	12
2.51	1.21	.57	.60	.42	.30	.35	.24	.18	.23	.17	.16

MONTHS FOR CYCLICAL DOMINANCE   3

AVERAGE PER CENT CHANGE WITH REGARD TO SIGN AND STANDARD DEVIATION OVER INDICATED SPAN

SPAN IN MONTHS	A1 O AVGE	A1 O S.D.	D13 I AVGE	D13 I S.D.	D12 C AVGE	D12 C S.D.	D11 CI AVGE	D11 CI S.D.	D10 S AVGE	D10 S S.D.	F1 MCD AVGE	F1 MCD S.D.
1	1.55	10.60	.03	2.45	.77	.32	.79	2.49	.74	10.14	.77	.66
2	2.67	12.34	.03	2.40	1.55	.63	1.58	2.52	1.06	11.82	1.55	1.03
3	3.46	12.92	-.00	1.71	2.33	.91	2.33	2.03	1.10	12.48	2.34	1.34
4	4.20	12.54	-.02	2.47	3.13	1.15	3.15	2.84	1.02	11.89	3.13	1.53
5	4.92	11.82	.03	2.22	3.94	1.35	3.97	2.72	.92	11.09	3.92	1.69
6	5.67	11.72	-.02	1.88	4.75	1.53	4.72	2.56	.89	10.86	4.72	1.85
7	6.52	11.78	-.01	2.43	5.56	1.69	5.55	3.11	.91	10.73	5.52	1.97
9	8.39	13.77	-.03	1.84	7.19	1.99	7.16	2.88	1.15	12.67	7.16	2.20
11	9.43	13.70	-.01	1.90	8.45	2.26	8.87	3.10	.89	12.22	8.85	2.43
12	9.70	3.30	.00	2.02	9.69	2.37	9.70	3.28	-.00	.22	9.69	2.53

*(TRADING DAY ADJUSTMENT FACTORS WITHOUT LENGTH OF MONTH ADJUSTMENT)

Fig. 5.5n Summary measures.

2. *Final seasonal factors.* The computer takes Figure 5.5k and makes a moving average of each vertical column. The results become the final seasonal trading-day factors shown in Figure 5.5l.

3. *Final seasonally adjusted series.* The final seasonal adjustment factors from Figure 5.5l are divided into the original data. The resulting seasonally adjusted series is given in Figure 5.5m.

Summary Measures

Summary measures shown in Figure 5.5n indicate the relative importance of each of the components of a time series. They represent the monthly percentage change without regard to sign of the various components. For example, in the "relative contributions of components" for a 1-month span, the irregularity accounts for 8.04% of the changes, the trend-cycle 1.28%, and seasonality 90.58%.

6 Frequency Distribution

Large amounts of data are collected by many agencies, particularly those of the United States federal government. In order for these data to be meaningful to users such as city planners, fundraisers, and school boards, they must be organized. For example, in a frequency distribution, the data are placed in classes, with the number in each class recorded.

Data used in a frequency distribution are quantitative. Nonnumeric characteristics, such as occupation, are qualitative. Both may appear in a population. A quantitative frequency distribution is given in Table 6.1, which shows the number of future births by age grouping for women aged 18 through 34 in the United States as of June 1978. Table 6.2 summarizes the occupations of employed men in the United States in 1976. These data are qualitative.

DEVELOPING A FREQUENCY DISTRIBUTION

Suppose an experience rating analyst in the group department of a large insurance company wishes to determine the premium for 1982 for a small risk, i.e., 40 employees of ABC Tool Co. (Table 6.3). Taking the 1980 raw data shown in the table, the analyst then places the employees' ages in an array from lowest to highest (Table 6.4). The analyst then tallies the age of each employee by placing it in its proper slot and marking it with a checkmark according to the number of times it appears in Table 6.3.

Determination of Class Lines

In setting up a frequency distribution, the class limits, i.e., the lower and upper limits for each class, must first be determined. Usually, the lower limit selected is just below the lowest value in the array. In Table 6.4, the lowest age is 17, so there the lower limit of the lowest class interval is 15. A class width is chosen that will result in a manageable number of classes (see Methods, p. 86). In this

Table 6.1. Future Births Expected, Women 18 to 34 Years, All Races, by Births to Date.

Age Group	Thousands of Women
18–19	2,888
20–21	3,036
22–24	4,617
25–29	7,223
30–34	6,714
Total	24,478

Source: United States Bureau of Census, *Current Population Reports,* Series P-20, No. 341.

Table 6.2. Number of Employed Men in the United States in 1976, by Current Occupation Group.

Occupation Group	Thousands of Men
Professional, technical and kindred workers	7,738
Managers and administrators except farmers	7,440
Sales workers	3,141
Clerical and kindred workers	3,289
Craft and kindred workers	10,603
Operatives except transport	6,088
Transport equipment operatives	3,121
Laborers, except farm	3,420
Farmers and farm managers	1,282
Farm laborers and supervisors	765
Service workers, except private household	4,528
Private household workers	22
Total	51,437

Source: United States Bureau of Census, *Current Population Reports,* Series P-23, No. 75.

Table 6.3. Ages of Employees of ABC Tool Co., 1980.

Employee	Age	Employee	Age	Employee	Age
A.J.	25	R.S.	42	P.M.	37
C.J.	25	D.G.	25	P.S.	30
R.R.	18	T.M.	22	W.H.	52
J.P.	55	B.C.	42	A.D.	28
R.A.	34	A.A.	53	R.G.	40
T.H.	28	R.O'N.	21	B.J.	36
M.P.	48	I.O.	55	A.D.	28
S.A.	52	E. McI.	55	I.C.	20
J.S.	26	J.B.	56	M.S.	28
K.K.	19	D.F.	18	J.A.	17
G.K.	52	H.M.	30	E.S.	31
T.O.	54	S.C.	50	M.V.	36
E.V.	50	T.B.	65	L.T.	62
G.D.	45				

Table 6.4. Array and Tallies of Ages of Employees of ABC Tool Co., 1980.

Age	Tally	Age	Tally	Age	Tally
17	/	30	/ /	50	/ /
18	/ /	31	/	52	/ / /
19	/	34	/	53	/
20	/	36	/ /	54	/
21	/	37	/	55	/ / /
22	/	40	/	56	/
25	/ / /	42	/ /	62	/
26	/	45	/	65	/
28	/ / / /	48	/		

case, 10 was chosen. Hence, the first class interval is "15 up to 25," the second "25 up to 35," etc. The "15 up to 25" class interval includes all ages from 15 up to but not including 25; the second class interval includes 25 up to but not including 35.

From Table 6.5, the following can be observed:

1. The width of the class interval is 10.
2. There are seven employees in the class interval 15 up to 25, 12 in the next interval, etc.
3. The largest concentration of ages is 25 up to 35.

The number in each class is called the *frequency*. From this, measures of dispersion can be computed to describe the spread in the data. These measures will be described in Chapters 9 and 12.

The distribution of the ages of employees of ABC Tool Co. has 6 classes. Normally, a frequency distribution has from 5 to 15 classes, depending on the judgment of the statistician.

A discussion of two of the more widely used methods of determining the width of class intervals follows.

Table 6.5. Frequency Distribution of Ages of Employees ABC Tool Co., 1980.

Age Class	No. Employees (Frequency)
15 up to 25	7
25 up to 35	12
35 up to 45	6
45 up to 55	9
55 up to 65	5
65 up to 75	1
	40

Sturges Method. The formula for the Sturges method is:

$$\frac{\text{Highest value} - \text{Lowest value}}{1 + (3.22 \times \log \text{ of total frequencies})}$$

Filling in the formula with figures from Table 6.4 produces:

$$\frac{65 - 17}{1 + 3.322(\log \text{ of } 40)} = \frac{48}{1 + 3.322(1.6021)}$$

$$= \frac{48}{1 + 5.322}$$

$$= \frac{48}{6.322} = 7.60 = \text{Class interval width}$$

The class interval of 7.6 suggested by the formula should not be used. If ages are rounded to the nearest whole number, for example, then the age of 17 years and 4 months is rounded to 17 years, and 17 years and 7 months is rounded to 18 years.

Using Predetermined Number of Classes. A class interval may be determined where the number of classes has previously been set using the highest and lowest value in the frequency distribution. Suppose we decide to have seven classes, as in Table 6.6 which is based on Table 6.4. The formula is:

$$\text{Suggested class width} = \frac{\text{Highest value} - \text{Lowest value}}{\text{No. Classes}}$$

$$X = \frac{65 - 17}{7}$$

$$= \frac{48}{7}$$

$$= 7 \text{ years approximately}$$

Determining Number of Classes

In determining the number of classes, the logarithm of the total frequencies in the distribution is employed. In the age distribution for ABC Tool Co., there were 40 employees. The following formula is used:

Table 6.6. Frequency Distribution of Ages of Employees of ABC Tool Co., 1980, Using an 8-Year Age Interval.

Age Class	No. Employees (Frequency)
15 up to 23	7
23 up to 31	10
31 up to 39	5
39 up to 47	4
47 up to 55	8
55 up to 63	5
63 up to 71	1
	40

$$\text{No. Classes} = 1 + (3.322)\,(\log N)$$

$$= 1 + (3.322)\,(\log 40)$$

$$= 1 + (3.322)\,(1.6021) = 5.322$$

The formula suggests that five classes would be appropriate. If we use too small or too broad a wage class, the information concerning the age distribution of ABC Tool Co. would not be readily discernible. For example, Table 6.7 shows a frequency distribution with too many classes.

Table 6.7. Too Many Classes.

Age Class	No. Employees (Frequency)
17 up to 20	4
20 up to 23	3
23 up to 26	3
26 up to 29	5
29 up to 32	3
32 up to 35	1
35 up to 38	3
38 up to 41	1
41 up to 44	2
44 up to 47	1
47 up to 50	1
50 up to 53	5
53 up to 56	5
56 up to 59	1
59 up to 62	0
62 up to 65	1
65 up to 68	1
	40

Table 6.8. Frequency Distribution with Open-End Class Intervals: Annual Incomes of Employees of Supreme Wiring Co.

Yearly Income	No. Employees (Frequency)
Under $10,000	2
$10,000 up to 15,000	5
15,000 up to 20,000	20
20,000 up to 25,000	10
25,000 up to 30,000	15
30,000 up to 40,000	5
40,000 and over	1

CONSTRUCTING A FREQUENCY DISTRIBUTION

Following are the criteria for constructing a frequency distribution:

1. Open-end class intervals such as "under $5.00," and "over 100,000," should not be used, if at all possible. Statistical measures such as the arithmetic mean and standard deviation cannot be computed from this type of frequency distribution.

There are times, however, when an open-end class interval may be justified. Consider the income frequency distribution shown in Table 6.8 in which two employees of Supreme Wiring Co. earn under $10,000 and one earns over $40,000. The numbers in the smallest and largest class are small in relation to the rest of the frequency distribution.

2. Problems arise when class intervals in a frequency distribution are unequal —i.e., the frequency distribution is harder to graph, and certain statistical measures are difficult to compute. Therefore, the widths of the class interval should be kept equal when possible.

3. Look at Table 6.9, which indicates the prices of a particular brand of cold cereal in several large American cities. Note the prices tend to cluster at the nearest $0.05 or $0.10. Classes of $0.45 up to $0.55, $0.55 up to $0.65, etc., would allow the midpoints of $0.50 and $0.60 to agree with the concentration of per-box prices of Zoomies cereal.

4. The class interval chosen should result in only one point of concentration (peak) of the data. If there are two peaks (bimodal) the following could exist: (1) class interval too small (2) data may be from two distinct and separate populations.

GRAPHING FREQUENCY DISTRIBUTIONS

Data may be depicted graphically from a frequency distribution. Three types of graphs will be discussed here: histogram, frequency polygon, and cumulative frequency polygon.

Table 6.9. Cost of a Box of Zoomies Cereal in Selected United States Cities, April 1980.

City	Per-Box Retail Price
Boston, MA	$0.50
Providence, RI	0.53
Hartford, CT	0.55
Philadelphia, PA	0.60
Washington, DC	0.50
Baltimore, MD	0.65
Miami, FL	0.50
Houston, TX	0.65
Chicago, IL	0.57
Des Moines, IA	0.45
Little Rock, AR	0.52
Portland, OR	0.57
San Francisco, CA	0.60
Los Angeles, CA	0.65
Phoenix, AZ	0.60

Histogram

In histograms, the frequencies are always plotted on the Y-axis and the variable is plotted on the X-axis. Table 6.5, the frequency distribution of ages of employees of ABC Tool Co., is the basis for the histogram shown in Figure 6.1. Notice that seven employees are in the 15-up-to-25-year class interval. To depict this on the histogram, a straight line was drawn vertically from 15 and 25 on the X-axis to 7 on the Y-axis. A bar was then drawn over this area. Another line was then drawn vertically to a frequency of 12 on the Y-axis over the 25-up-to-35-year class interval. This was repeated until all the frequencies were depicted.

Frequencies in the histogram start at zero, whereas the variable starts at the lower limit of the first class (age 15). The lower limits of the class intervals (age 15, 25, etc.) are shown at the base of each bar. Midpoints of the class intervals placed in the middle of the bars are sometimes used instead.

Frequency Polygon

The frequency polygon is a graph showing the variable on the X-axis and the frequency on the Y-axis. In plotting the frequency polygon, the midpoints of each class are used to represent the typical item within that class, ie., age 20 for the 15-to-25-year class interval of employees of ABC Tool Co., age 30 for the next class interval, and so on. After all frequencies are plotted above the midpoints, the points are connected by straight lines. The line in the frequency polygon is normally extended to the midpoint above and below the extremes. The line is

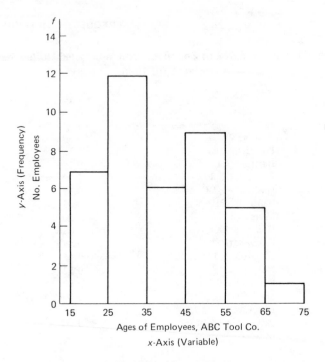

Fig. 6.1 A histogram.

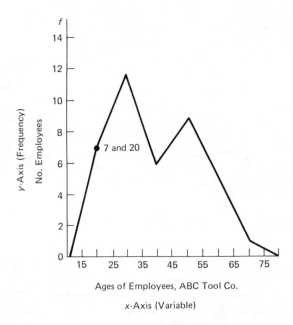

Fig. 6.2 A frequency polygon.

Table 6.10. Number of Defective Parts per 100: Brand X versus Brand Y
Machine Tools

| | Frequency | |
| | No. Machine Tools | |
No. Defective Parts per 100	Brand X	Brand Y
1 up to 5	1	0
5 up to 10	4	2
10 up to 15	11	3
15 up to 20	12	5
20 up to 25	9	4
25 up to 30	3	1
30 up to 35	2	0
	42	15

extended to 10 and 80 in Figure 6.2, which is a frequency polygon based on the
data in Table 6.5.

PERCENTAGE FREQUENCY POLYGON

Where there is a wide disparity in the total numbers of two groups being compared, it is better to use a percentage table and a percentage polygon. Suppose a
quality control engineer wants to compare the number of defective parts per 100
produced with Brand X and Brand Y machine tools (see Table 6.10). From the
table, a percent distribution (Table 6.11) is prepared and a percent frequency
polygon is made (see Figure 6.3).

Table 6.11. Percent Distribution of Defective Parts per 100:
Brand X versus Brand Y Machine Tools.

| | Percent of Total Machine Tools | |
No. Defective Parts per 100	Brand X	Brand Y
1 up to 5	2.4	0
5 up to 10	9.5	13.3
10 up to 15	26.2	20.0
15 up to 20	28.6	33.3
20 up to 25	21.4	26.7
25 up to 30	7.1	6.7
30 up to 35	4.8	0
	100.0	100.0

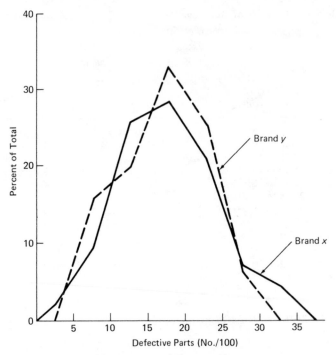

Fig. 6.3 A percentage frequency polygon.

Cumulative Frequency Distributions and Polygons

Suppose the quality control engineer wants to know the percentage of defective parts less than 15 per 100. First, the engineer could establish a less-than-cumulative frequency distribution. In Table 6.12, the frequencies are cumulated from the lowest, to—and including—the highest class. From this, a less-than-cumulative frequency polygon can be constructed (see Figure 6.4). The number of Brand X machine tools is plotted on the Y-axis, and the cumulative number of defective parts is plotted on the X-axis. By drawing a line down vertically to the X-axis and horizontally to the Y-axis it can be seen 16 Brand X machine tools will produce less than 15 defective parts per 100. These defective parts represent less than 38 percent of the total.

A more-than-cumulative frequency distribution may be constructed by starting with the highest class and cumulating frequencies up to the lowest class. Table 6.13 shows the number of defective parts per 100 for all Brand Y machines. The frequency distribution was constructed by starting with the highest defective-part class and cumulating the frequencies up to the lowest class. For example, no parts are defective per 100 for 30 Brand Y machines, 1 part is defective per 100 for 25 Brand Y machines, 5 parts are defective per 100 for 20

Table 6.12. Less-than-Cumulative Frequency Distribution.

Class	Upper Class Limit	Frequency in Class	Cumulative Frequency (No. Brand X Machine Tools Producing More Defective Parts per 100 than Lower Limit Class)
1 up to 5	5	1	1
5 up to 10	10	4	5
10 up to 15	15	11	16
15 up to 20	20	12	28
20 up to 25	25	9	37
25 up to 30	30	3	40
30 up to 35	35	2	42

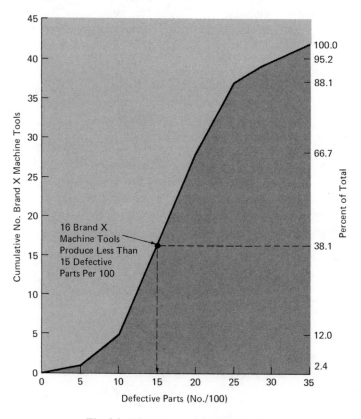

Fig. 6.4 A less-than-cumulative polygon.

Table 6.13. More-than-Cumulative Frequency Distribution.

Class	Lower Limit of Class	Frequency	Cumulative Frequency (No. Brand Y Machine Tools Producing More Defective Parts than Lower Limit of Class)
1 up to 5	1	0	15
5 up to 10	5	2	15
10 up to 15	10	3	13
15 up to 20	15	5	10
20 up to 25	20	4	5
25 up to 30	25	1	1
30 up to 35	30	0	0

Brand Y machines, etc. The cumulative number of Brand Y machine tools are placed on the Y-axis, and the cumulative number of defective parts per 100 for Brand Y machines is placed on the X-axis. This information is then plotted as shown in Figure 6.5. Note that the right side of the more-than-cumulative frequency polygon is labeled "Percent of Total."

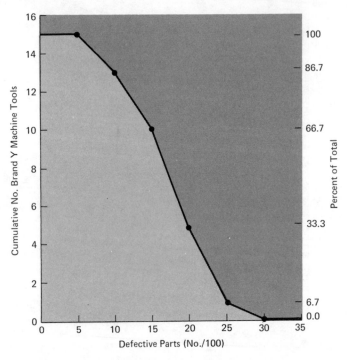

Fig. 6.5 A more-than-cumulative polygon.

7 Probability

In probability, the outcome of an event is forecast based on incomplete information. For example, a population is inferred to have certain attributes based on a sample taken from it. Let's say a company decides to test market a new mint-flavored toothpaste in 10 American cities in order to determine the reaction of the general public. The market research manager decides that a sample of 1000 respondents is adequate. (Sample size is based on several factors including the degree of confidence desired and the amount of money a company wishes to spend for research.) Once the company has gathered the results of the study, the information will be analyzed and predictions will be made for the total market.

Let's take another example. A quality control engineer draws inferences about the total number of units in a particular production run by taking samples from the run. If the samples fall within preset measurements, then the engineer assumes the total population does as well. The engineer then estimates the odds of an event occurring. Thus, probability statements are basically subjective.

Different events have different degrees of probability. A person can predict with relative certainty the odds of picking the queen of hearts from a deck of 52 cards (i.e., 1 in 52). Market researchers, on the other hand, have little knowledge of how their product will sell nationally based on their market study of certain test cities. In both cases, a value is assigned to the occurrence of an event.

PROBABILITY RULES

General Rules

The general rules of probability follow.

1. In probability, a number from zero to one inclusive can be assumed. Assume that there are three goldfish in a bowl of water. In removing a fish from the bowl, the probability of taking out a goldfish is one while the probability of selecting an eel is zero.

2. Events are *mutually exclusive.* For example, suppose we have 2000 carbide cutting tools for which a set of tolerances has been established (see Table 7.1). A cutting tool picked at random from the 2000 will be above, within, or below tolerance. One and only one of the three possible outcomes can happen; the events are mutually exclusive.

Sum of Mutually Exclusive Events Equals 1.00

Since the events in a particular circumstance are mutually exclusive, the sum of all the probabilities must equal 1.00. This is called the *rule of addition.* Thus, in the case of the carbide cutting tools, the probabilities are:

Probability of being within tolerance = 0.900 *(Pa)*
Probability of being under tolerance = 0.025 *(Pb)*
Probability of being over tolerance = 0.075 *(Pc)*
1.000

The formula for addition can be written:

$$\text{Probability of Event } a + \text{Probability of Event } b + \text{Probability of Event } c = 1$$

or

$$P(a) + P(b) + P(c) = 1$$

Thus,

$$0.025 + 0.900 + 0.075 = 1.000$$

Complement Rule

The probability of an event taking place, $P(a)$, plus the probability of it not taking place, $(P{\sim}a)$ is equal to 1. The complement rule can be expressed as:

$$P(a) + P({\sim}a) = 1$$

or, it can be expressed as:

$$P(a) = 1 - P({\sim}a)$$

Suppose we apply the complement rule to the carbide cutting tool situation. We wish to find the probability that a tool selected at random is within tolerance.

Table 7.1. Carbide Cutting Tool Tolerances: Probability of Random Sampling.

Tolerance (in.)	Tolerance Acceptance	Event	No. Carbide Cutting Tools	Probability of Occurrence
0.05 up to 0.25	Above tolerance	a	50	0.025
0.25 up to 0.50	Within tolerance	b	1800	0.900
0.50 and over	Below tolerance	c	150	0.075
			2000	1.000

Taking the probabilities from Table 7.1 and inserting them in the formula above, we find:

$$P(a) = 1 - .025 + 0.075$$

$$= 0.90$$

Addition Rule

The addition rule applies when the outcomes are not mutually exclusive. Suppose we wish to find the probability of drawing either a two or a blue card from a tumbler containing 4 sets of cards; each set is a different color, numbered from 1-100. Here we see the probability of two events happening at the same time (not mutually exclusive) or joint probability, $P(A,B)$. Table 7.2 shows the joint probability of the situation. The formula for joint probability is:

$$P (a \text{ or } b) = P(a) + P(b) - P(a,b)$$

$$= 4/400 + 100/400 - 1/400$$

$$= 103/400$$

$$= 0.2575$$

Table 7.2. Joint Probability.

Card	Probability	Explanation
A two	$P(a) = 4/400$	There are 4 two's in the tumbler of 400.
A blue card	$P(b) = 100/400$	There are 100 blue cards in tumbler of 400.
A blue #2 card	$P(c) = 1/400$	There is one blue #2 cards in the tumbler of 400.

Multiplication Rule

Statistical independence occurs when the outcome of one event in no way affects the outcome of another event. Suppose we want to know the probability of throwing six dies each once and coming up with a one. The probabilities are as follows:

Die No.	Probability	Symbol
1	1/6	$P(a)$
2	1/6	$P(b)$
3	1/6	$P(c)$
4	1/6	$P(d)$
5	1/6	$P(e)$
6	1/6	$P(f)$

Thus, the probability may be expressed as follows:

$$P(a,b,c,d,e,f) = P(a) \times P(b) \times P(c) \times P(d) \times P(e) \times P(f)$$

$$= 1/6 \times 1/6 \times 1/6 \times 1/6 \times 1/6 \times 1/6$$

$$= 1/46,656, \text{ or } 0.00002, \text{ or } 2 \text{ times in } 100,000 \text{ throws to}$$
get a one

Conditional Probabilities

The rule used when probabilities are conditional applies when the outcome of one event depends upon the outcome of another. Suppose that out of every 100 tires inspected, 3 are defective. What is the probability that a tire inspector would select two defective tires at random in two successive inspections? The probability is as follows:

Successive Draws	Probability	Explanation
1	3/100 (Pa)	There are 3 defective tires in 100.
2	2/99 (Pb)	Assuming a defective tire is selected on the first draw, there are 2 defective tires in the remaining 99.

Applying the formula using these figures, we get:

$$P(a+b) = P(a) \times P(b/a)$$

$$= 3/100 \times 2/99$$

$$= 6/9900$$

$$= 0.0006, \text{ or 6 in 10,000 times}$$

The probability of getting a defective tire on the second draw using the conditional probabilities rule depends on the following:

1. The outcome of the first draw: Was the tire defective or not?
2. No replacement has occurred; i.e., after the first defective tire was inspected, it was *not* put back in the lot before the second tire was drawn.

N FACTORIAL: PERMUTATIONS AND COMBINATIONS

It may be difficult to determine the total number of possible outcomes in a situation. Suppose two people are playing cards, and it makes no difference in which order the cards are played. To determine the total number of outcomes, the permutations and combined rules are used.

Permutations

When two persons are playing with one deck of 52 cards, assuming each person has 26 cards, the number of ways the cards can be played are as follows:

$$nPr = \frac{n!}{(n-r)!}$$

where

P = number of ways the cards can be played

n = total number of cards, or 52

r = number of cards in each player's possession, or 26

The $n!$ is "n factorial," the product of

$$n(n-1)(n-2)(n-3)\ldots(n-n-1)$$

Solving the formula for the number of ways the 26 cards in each person's possession can be played yields:

$$nPr = \frac{n!}{(n-r)!}$$

$$= \frac{52}{(52-26)!}$$

$$= \frac{52!}{26!}$$

$$= \frac{52 \times 51 \times 50 \times 49 \ldots 1}{26 \times 25 \times 24 \times 23 \ldots 1}$$

Take another example. Suppose a women's speciality shop wishes to display the latest fashions on 12 mannequins in three display windows. They do not have to be displayed in any particular order. What is the total number of different ways the mannequins can be arranged in the windows? There are 12 possibilities for the first window, 11 for the second window (one has already been used), 10 for the third window, etc. So.,

$$(12)\,(11)\,(10) = 1320 \text{ possibilities}$$

Mathematically expressed, we have:

$$nPr = \frac{n!}{(n-r)!}$$

$$= \frac{12!}{(12-3)!}$$

$$= \frac{12!}{9!}$$

$$= \frac{(12)\,(11)\,(10)\,\cancel{(9)}}{\cancel{(9)}} = 1320$$

In the preceding cases, repetitions were not permitted. In cases where they are allowed, the formula is:

$$nPr = n^2$$

For example, suppose a person is playing checkers with a computer and wants to know the total number of moves possible with 20 checkers. Using the formula

$$P = n^r$$

where

P = number of permutations

n = total number of checkers, or 20

r = number of players per game, or 2

we would have:

$$P = 20^2 = 400 \text{ possibilities}$$

Combinations

In permutations, the order of things is important. For example, 1, 2, 3, 4, 5, 6 is one order, and 1, 3, 4, 5, 6, 2 is another. In combinations, however, order is not important. Suppose the quality control department of an electric appliance manufacturer must design a system of color-coding the wires used on 10 different models of its food processor. Two different colored wires are to be used on each model, but the color combination cannot be repeated. For example, the combination of green and red used for model A cannot be used for model B. Would six colors taken two at a time be sufficient to code 10 different models?

The formula for combinations is:

$$nCr = \frac{n!}{r! \, (n-r)!}$$

where

n = number of different colors (i.e., six)

C = combination

r = number of colors (n) taken at one time

Using this formula, would six colors taken two at a time be enough to code 10 different food-processor models?

$$_6C_2 = \frac{n!}{r! \, (n-r)!} = \frac{6!}{2! \, (6-2)!} = \frac{6!}{2!4!} = \frac{(6 \times 5 \times 4 \times 3 \times 2 \times 1)}{(2 \times 1)(4 \times 3 \times 2 \times 1)} = 15$$

The formula indicates that there are 15 different combinations, which are more than adequate for color-coding the wires of the 10 food processor models.

8 Decisionmaking under Uncertainty

In solving a given problem, decisionmakers must choose from several alternative courses of action. For example, suppose market researchers have been given the assignment of exploring the future United States market for stainless-steel strip. They must forecast sales for 1990. Several factors could have a bearing, such as substitute materials, a union contract to be negotiated in 1982, etc. They know from their research that about 50 million tons were sold in 1980 in the United States. Should they predict that total sales in 1990 will be $60 million, $80 million, or $45 million? In decision theory, under conditions of uncertainty, they have a choice among several different sales projections (i.e., alternative acts).

CASE STUDY—FUTURE DEMAND UNKNOWN

The illustrate the steps employed in decisionmaking under uncertainty, the problems facing the management of the hypothetical Wooden Toy Co. are presented here.

The Wooden Toy Co. is a small manufacturer of wooden toys designed primarily for 2-to-12-year-olds. Each February, right after the national Toy Manufacturers of America (TMA) trade show, Sam Smith, president of The Wooden Toy Co., starts preparing for the following Christmas season when the company's sales are the highest.

Payoff Table

When Sam Smith went to the TMA trade show, he noticed three items among those on display in which there was a great deal of interest—a set of 24 wooden building blocks, a wooden rocking horse, and a wooden dollhouse. In conversations with toy buyers at the show and his own sales representatives, Smith learned that the toy market was expected to be exceptionally good for the Christmas season. However, there was a threat of a lumbermen's strike in April,

Table 8.1. Payoff Table, 1980 Sales, The Wooden Toy Co.

Product	Sales in Exceptionally Good Year	Profit	Profit % Sales	Sales Assuming Lumbermen's Strike	Profit	Profit % Sales
Building blocks	$30,000	$ 3,000	10.0	$10,000	$2,000	20.0
Rocking horse	50,000	5,000	10.0	18,000	3,000	16.7
Dollhouse	60,000	10,000	16.7	15,000	2,000	13.3

which could cut raw material supplies by two-thirds. Smith, being a small manufacturer, decided he would only make one of the three items. To aid in this decision, he developed a payoff table (Table 8.1). Here he assumed two sets of conditions: (1) the exceptionally good year predicted by the trade, and (2) a two-thirds cut in the supply of wood due to the threatened lumbermen's strike. If The Wooden Toy Co. did not start manufacturing in May and June for the Christmas sales, there would be no way it could make up the slack later in the year (July through October).

Expected Payoff

If the payoff table was the only information available, Smith might have chosen to manufacture dollhouses because they produced the greatest profit in an exceptionally good year. For the same reason, if the strike materialized, he would most likely manufacture rocking horses.

Smith however, had additional data—the TMA tally of sales statistics by product category for the last 15 years. He found that sales of wooden toys had risen in 10 years and, mainly due to strikes fallen in 5. He concluded that there is a 0.67 probability of a rise in sales and a 0.33 probability of a sales dropoff.

If it is assumed that these probabilities represent what is likely to happen in 1984, then we can set up an *expected payoff table* for producing dollhouses (Table 8.2). If Smith decided to manufacture dollhouses and the lumbermen's strike took place, sales would only amount to $15,000. However, over the past 15 years, sales have fallen only one-third of the time. In the long run then, falling sales volume would add $5000 to the expected payoff (i.e., $15,000 × 0.33). If the $5000 is added to the $40,000 sales volume to be experienced in an exceptionally good year, the total expected payoff in the long term would be $45,000. The expected payoff for the other two products is also shown in Table 8.2.

Table 8.3 indicates that Smith would probably choose to manufacture the dollhouses if exceptionally good sales materialized. However, he might also give credence to making rocking horses because in event of a lumbermen's strike, the

Table 8.2. Expected Payoff Table, Three Alternative Products, Wooden Toy Co.

	1984 Sales		
Event (A)	Building Blocks (B)	Rocking Horse (C)	Dollhouse (D)
Exceptionally good year	$30,000	$50,000	$60,000
Lumbermen's strike	10,000	18,000	15,000

	Probability of Event P(A)	Expected Value		
		P(A) × B	P(A) × C	P(A) × D
Exceptionally good year	0.67	$20,000	$33,000	$40,000
Lumbermen's strike	0.33	3,000	6,000	5,000
Total expected payoff		$23,000	$39,000	$45,000

Note: Expected values have been rounded to nearest thousands of dollars.

profit would be $1000 more ($3000 on rocking horses and $2000 on dollhouses) as shown in Table 8.1.

Opportunity Regret

Smith can determine which wooden toy will be the most profitable to produce by finding the amount of the lost sales volume. This is due to the fact that the exact condition of the toy market is not known at the time a decision is made to produce a certain product. The potential loss is called *opportunity loss*. If Smith had decided to manufacture rocking horses and an exceptionally good sales year developed, sales volume would have reached $50,000. On the other hand, however, if he *had* manufactured the dollhouses, total sales would have reached $60,000 in a good year. Smith would have missed making an additional $10,000

Table 8.3. Expected Payoff Table, Manufacture of Wooden Dollhouses.

Event A	Sales B	Probability of Event P(A)	Expected Value P(A) × B
Exceptionally good year	$60,000	0.67	$40,000
Lumbermen's strike	15,000	0.33	5,000
		Total	$45,000

Table 8.4. Opportunity Losses, Three Alternative Products, Wooden Toy Co.

Product	Opportunity Loss	
	Exceptionally Good Market	Lumbermen's Strike
Building blocks	$30,000	$8,000
Rocking horse	10,000	0
Dollhouse	0	3,000

in sales, together with an additional $5000 profit (his opportunity loss). If he had decided to make dollhouses, there would have been no opportunity loss. Opportunity losses for all three products, each representing a combination of the decision to manufacture and the movement of the market, are shown in Table 8.4. In a good year, the manufacture of dollhouses (zero opportunity loss) would be the best selection. Conversely, in a poor year, rocking horses would produce the lowest opportunity loss (zero).

Expected Opportunity Loss

The opportunity losses in Table 8.4 do not give credence to past history. TMA's historical figures showed the probability of a rise in sales to be 0.67 and of a loss in sales, mainly due to the lumbermen's strike, to be 0.33. The probabilities, together with the opportunity loss, are shown in Table 8.5. From the table, we see

Table 8.5. Expected Opportunity Loss Table, Three Alternative Products, Wooden Toy Co.

Event A	Building Blocks B	Rocking Horse C	Dollhouse D
Exceptionally good year	$30,000	$10,000	$ 0
Lumbermen's strike	8,000	0	3,000

	Probability of Event P(A)	Expected Opportunity Loss		
		P(A) × B	P(A) × C	P(A) × D
Exceptionally good year	0.67	$20,000	$7.000	0
Lumbermen's strike	0.33	3,000	0	1,000
	Total	$23,000	$7,000	$1,000

Note: Expected opportunity losses have been rounded to nearest thousand dollars.

that in the long run, if Smith decided to make rocking horses, he would lose the chance to make an additional $7000 in sales. He would incur this loss because of his inability to correctly project the market. In an exceptionally good year, he could make an additional $23,000 in sales by manufacturing building blocks. In a market decline caused by a lumbermen's strike, he could earn an additional $1000 in sales by producing dollhouses.

Table 8.5 shows the expected opportunity losses for the three wooden toy products. The decision to make dollhouses in order to produce the lowest opportunity loss is reinforced because ultimately it would have the highest payoff.

Perfect Information

Before deciding on a product, Smith might want to accurately predict the near future movement of the market. What should he do to choose the product that will produce maximum profits? Suppose a management consulting firm had conducted a study that provided good insight into the matter. The company would charge Smith $1500 for a report of the study—how much should he be willing to pay? The value of this information is called the *value of perfect information,* which is the dollar difference between the maximum payoff under conditions of *certainty* minus the maximum payoff under conditions of *uncertainty*. If the actual behavior of the market were unknown, the product to manufacture would be dollhouses (Table 8.2). Therefore, the value of perfect information in this case would be $1000—that is, the difference between $46,000 (Table 8.6) and $45,000 (Table 8.2.).

The management consulting firm's report is only worth up to $1000 to Smith, and thus the firm's price of $1500 is too much under the rule of perfect information. However, if the company lowers the price to $800, then Smith should consider it because the expected payoff is $200 more than the cost of the fee ($1000 minus $800). The value of perfect information ($1000) is the same as the minimum value of opportunity loss shown in Table 8.5.

Table 8.6. Expected Payoff under Conditions of Certainty, Wooden Toy Co.

Event A	Payoff B	Probability of Event P(A)	Expected Payoff P(A) × B
Exceptionally good year	$60,000	0.67	$40,000
Lumbermen's strike	18,000	0.33	6,000
		Total expected payoff	$46,000

In an exceptionally good year, the greatest expected value would come from the manufacture of dollhouses while in a poor year it would pay to produce rocking horses.

Table 8.7. Expected Payoff for Wooden Toy Co., under Three
Sets of Probabilities.

	Expected Payoff		
Product	Historical Experience (67% Good Year, 33% Poor Year)	Toy Industry Analyst's Estimate (50% Good Year, 50% Poor Year)	Economist's Estimate (40% Good Year, 60% Poor Year)
Building blocks	$23,000	$20,000	$18,000
Rocking horse	39,000	34,000	31,000
Dollhouse	45,000	38,000	33,000

For method of calculation of above see Table 8.2.

Changes in Probability within a Plausible Range

In the preceding analysis, the probabilities were based on historical experience. However, suppose that because of certain conditions, history might not repeat itself. Assume that a top financial analyst in the toy industry believes there is a 50% probability of an exceptionally good year and a 50% chance of a poor year with sales cut two-thirds by the lumbermen's strike. Further assume that one of the country's top economists believes there is a 40% chance of an exceptionally good year and a 60% probability of a poor year. Expected payoffs, based on historical experience, the toy industry analyst's estimate, and the economist's estimate, are shown in Table 8.7. An analysis of Table 8.7 indicates that the best alternative is to manufacture dollhouses. (For calculations in Table 8.7 see Table 8.2).

Decision Trees

A *decision tree* shows graphically all of the possible alternatives to a decision and their outcomes. In Figure 8.1, a decision tree is shown depicting the three alternative acts of manufacturing building blocks, rocking horses, or dollhouses.

If Mr. Smith drew the decision tree under conditions of uncertainty, he would start with the premise that he must decide whether to manufacture dollhouses (highest expected payoff of $45,000). To do this, he would draw a box, above which he would place $45,000. From the box, he would draw three branches reflecting the three alternatives open to him and the expected payoffs: $45,000 for dollhouses, $39,000 for rocking horses, and $23,000 for building blocks. Then, from each of the three alternatives, he would draw two branches showing the probability of an exceptionally good year in sales (67%) and of a poor year (33%). At the end of each branch the estimated sales given a good or poor year

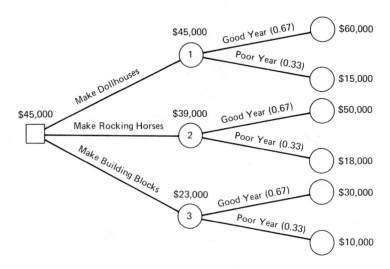

Fig. 8.1 Decision tree for Wooden Toy Co. under conditions of uncertainty.

are shown. For example, the sales for the building blocks would be $30,000 for a good year and $10,000 for a poor year.

Assuming Smith wished to maximize the expected future value of his profits, $45,000 is more than $39,000 and $23,000 (see Figure 8.1). Moving to the left toward the box, Smith would draw a double line across the two alternatives he has rejected (i.e., $39,000 and $23,000). The branch that he selected leads back to the box representing the product to be manufactured, dollhouses.

A decision tree may also be used in *backward induction*. Suppose Smith was seriously thinking of manufacturing sets of building blocks. In the lower right corner of the tree, he would see that the expected sales is $30,000 in a good year and $10,000 in a poor year. Moving backward and applying the probabilities of 0.67 and 0.33, Smith would obtain the expected payoff of $23,000, that is, [(0.67($30,000) + 0.33($10,000)] . He would enter the expected payoff of $23,000 above the appropriate circle.

Decision trees can also be used to portray what is likely to happen under conditions of certainty. In this instance, Smith would manufacture dollhouses with an expected payoff of $46,000. (See Table 8.6).

In constructing a decision tree under conditions of certainty, he would start at the right and draw three circles indicating the sales in a good year from manufacturing dollhouses, rocking horses, and building blocks ($60,000, $50,000, and $30,000, respectively). Below this, Smith would place three more circles showing sales in a poor year ($15,000, $18,000, and $10,000).

The three lines from the three circles showing the sales in a good year converge in a box showing the highest sales, $60,000. Smith would do the same thing

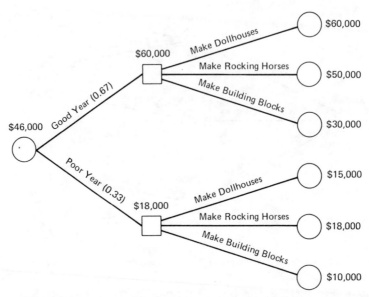

Fig. 8.2   Decision tree for Wooden Toy Co. under conditions of certainty.

for sales in a poor year, showing $18,000 (the highest sales in a poor year) above the box. Smith would then draw one line with the probability for the good year (0.67) and a line for the probability in a poor year (0.33). Both lines would terminate in a circle showing $46,000 for the highest expected payoff under conditions of certainty.

The difference of $1000 in the numbers at the left of Figure 8.1 ($45,000 under conditions of uncertainty) and Figure 8.2 ($46,000 under conditions of certainty) is the value of perfect information.

9 Mean, Median, and Mode: Measures of Central Tendency

In Chapter 6, we discussed how quantitative data are organized into a frequency distribution. These distributions not only call attention to the highlights of the data but also allow for easy handling of central tendencies. The central value of a distribution is represented by a single number. The *mean, median, mode,* and *geometric mean* are the most widely used measures to represent this central value.

ARITHMETIC MEAN

The mean or average is the total of all the figures divided by the number of figures. The result is taken to be representative of that group. It is expressed slightly differently in ungrouped and grouped data. Ungrouped data are data not grouped in a frequency distribution. Grouped data are figures placed in a frequency distribution.

Ungrouped Data

Suppose we wanted to determine the mean average of Sally Jones's grades in the second semester of her freshman year in college. In English, she has a quality point of 3.8, in business mathematics 4.0, in elementary economics 3.6, in French 3.4, and in United States history 3.2. Her quality point average can be determined as follows:

English	3.8
Business mathematics	4.0
Elementary economics	3.6
French	3.4
United States History	3.2
	18.0 ÷ 5 = 3.6 Average grade point

From this, we can develop the formula for the arithmetic mean:

$$Mean = \frac{\text{Sum of all values}}{\text{No. values}}$$

Expressing this in algebraic terms,

$$\bar{X} = \frac{\Sigma x}{n} = \frac{18.0}{5} = 3.6$$

Grouped Data

Let us assume we have eight screwheads with outer diameters (O.D.) of 0.010, 0.015, 0.020, 0.022, 0.023, 0.030, 0.035, and 0.036 in. taken as a sample from a high-volume production run. The following frequency table shows the screwheads grouped into classes of 0.005 up to 0.015, 0.015 up to 0.025, 0.025 up to 0.035, and 0.035 up to 0.045 in.

Screwheads O.D. (in.)	No. Screwheads Frequency
0.005 up to 0.015	1
0.015 up to 0.025	4
0.025 up to 0.035	1
0.035 up to 0.045	2
Total	8

The midpoint of each frequency class is taken to be representative of that class. If this is so, the following table results:

Screwheads O.D. (in.)	Midpoint X	No. Screwheads Frequency	Frequency × Midpoint
0.005 up to 0.015	0.010	1	0.010
0.015 up to 0.025	0.020	4	0.080
0.025 up to 0.035	0.030	1	0.030
0.035 up to 0.045	0.040	2	0.080
		Total	0.200

The average mean O.D. for the eight screwheads in 0.025 in., which is found by dividing 0.200 in. by 8 or:

$$\overline{X} = \frac{\Sigma fx}{n} = \frac{0.200}{8} = 0.025 \text{ in.}$$

where

$\overline{X}$ = average of X

x = midpoint of each class in frequency distribution

f = frequency in each class in frequency distribution

fX = frequency multiplied by midpoint for each class

ΣfX = sum of frequencies times midpoints

n = total number of frequencies

If the mean had been calculated from the ungrouped data, it would have been

$$\frac{(0.010 + 0.015 + 0.020 + 0.022 + 0.023 + 0.030 + 0.035 + 0.036)}{8} = \frac{0.191}{8} = 0.023$$

The difference of 0.002 in. (i.e., 0.025 in. - 0.023 in.) is due to the grouping of the data.

Coded Method

If the frequencies and class midpoints are large, then an alternative method is used—the coded method. Suppose that for tax purposes we were interested in the mean number of miles driven in 1979 by routemen of Good Bread Co. The frequency distribution would be set up as follows:

Miles Driven in 1979	Midpoint	Frequency (f)	Deviation (d)	Frequency × Deviation (fd)
2,000 up to 4,000	3	3	-2	-6
4,000 up to 6,000	5	1	-1	-1
6,000 up to 8,000	7	8	0	0
8,000 up to 10,000	9	6	+1	+6
10,000 up to 12,000	11	2	+2	+4
		20		+3

The formula is:

$$\bar{X} = \bar{X}_o + \frac{i(\Sigma fd)}{n}$$

Using the data from the above frequency distribution in the formula, we get:

$$\bar{X} = 7 + \frac{2(+3)}{20} = 7 + \frac{6}{20} = 7.3$$

In the preceding example, we assume the following:

1. A guessed mean $(\bar{X}_o)$ of 7 is established. A midpoint near the center of the frequency distribution is chosen, in the case above 7.

2. The midpoint of the class interval containing the guessed mean is set equal to zero, the one immediately above to +1, etc., while the one immediately below is set equal to -1, etc.; hence, the coding of midpoints.

3. Class frequency, f, is multiplied by deviation, d, to produce fd. In the above frequency distribution, the sum of the entries in the fd column equals +3.

4. The class interval i—in this case, 2—is then taken and multiplied by the sum of the figures in the fd column. The resulting figure of 6 is divided by n or 20, the sum of the frequencies.

5. The resulting factor of 0.3 is added to the guessed mean $(\bar{X}_o)$ of 7 to develop the average of 7300 miles driven in 1979 by routemen of the Good Bread Co.

MEDIAN

In a group of numbers, the median is that value above and below which exactly half of the values occur. It is a single number used to represent the values of a group of figures.

Ungrouped Data

Suppose we go to a boat show to look at yachts. The prices of five different yachts are $25,000, $40,000, $50,000, $75,000, and $125,000. The median is $50,000, and the arithmetic mean is $63,000. However, the figure of $50,000 (the median) is more representative of the group.

One problem with the mean is that it is influenced by extreme values. To illustrate, take the number of parts per million (ppm) of poison in seven brands of insecticide tested by ABC Laboratory. From lowest to highest, the results are:

Parts per Million
0.0001
0.0025
0.0030
0.0040
0.0060
0.0080
0.0090

If ABC Laboratory has to report the representative figure to the Food and Drug Administration, it will use the median, 0.0040. The arithmetic mean is 0.0047, which is not actually representative of the group.

Grouped Data

It is fairly easy to establish a median for a small number of values in ungrouped data. For grouped data, it can be a different story because they can include a large number of values. To make the computation easier, a median is estimated by interpolation from the class interval with the middle value. Using the frequency distribution for the screwheads, we have:

Screwhead O.D. (in.)	Frequency (f)	Cumulative Frequency (CF)
0.005 up to 0.015	1	1
0.015 up to 0.025	4	5 (1 + 4)
0.025 up to 0.035	1	6 (1 + 4 + 1)
0.035 up to 0.045	2	8 (1 + 4 + 1 + 2)

There are eight screwheads. To locate the median we do the following:

1. Set up a column giving the frequencies for each class interval.
2. Compute cumulative frequencies by adding the frequencies together.
3. Locate the class interval which contains the middle value or 4. Here, it is in the class interval of 0.015 in. up to 0.025 in.
4. We find that the fourth screwhead is 4/5ths of the way between 0.015 in. up to 0.025 in. or 0.008 in. (4/5 of 0.010 in.).
5. Finally, 0.008 in. is added to the 0.015 in. to give a median of 0.023 in.

The median is also computed according to a formula:

$$\text{Median} = L + \frac{(n/2) - CF}{f}$$

where:

L = lower limit of class interval
containing median = 0.015 in.

n = total of frequencies = 8

CF = sum of all frequencies in classes
immediately above class containing
median. The fourth screwhead fell
somewhere in the 0.015-up-to-0.025-in.
class. Cumulative number of
frequencies prior to this class is
one.

f = class frequency containing median

i = width of the class interval where median
falls. The width of the class
containing the median is 0.010 in.

Substituting the values from the frequency distribution in the formula, we get the following:

$$\text{Median} = 0.015 + \frac{(8/2) - 1}{4}\ (0.010)$$

$$= 0.015 + 3/4\ (0.010)$$

$$= 0.023$$

This method assumes that the frequencies in the median class are evenly distributed between 0.015 up to 0.025 in.

Notice the computation in the following frequency distribution. It is both open-ended and uses percents for frequencies. Nevertheless, the median can be computed.

RST Co. Employees Annual Wages	No. Employees as Percent of Total	Cumulative Frequency (CF)
Under $3,000	5.0	5.0
$3,000 up to $7,000	20.0	25.0 (5.0 + 20.0)
$7,000 up to $15,000	45.0	70.0 (5.0 + 20.0 + 45.0)
$15,000 up to $25,000	20.0	90.0 (5.0 + 20.0 + 45.0 + 20.0)
$25,000 and over	10.0	100.0 (5.0 + 20.0 + 45.0 + 20.0 + 10.0)

Using the formula for computing the median in a frequency distribution, we have:

$$\text{Median} = 7000 + \left\{ \frac{[(100.0/2) - 25.0]\ (8000)}{45.0} \right\}$$

$$= \$7,000 + \left[\frac{25.0}{45.0} (\$8,000) \right]$$

$$= \$7,000 + \$4,444$$

$$= \$11,444$$

Therefore, the median wage is $11,444.

MODE

The mode is the number that appears most frequently.

Ungrouped Data

The ages of 10 active employees of BCD Corporation are listed here. From the ungrouped data, we find that the mode is 29.

BCD Corporation Employees' Ages	
21	29
22	30
25	31
29	32
29	33

Grouped Data

Referring again to the frequency distribution of the screwheads, we see that the modal class is 0.015 in. up to 0.020 in. and the mode is 0.020 in. By definition then, the mode in grouped data is the value that is represented by the midpoint of the class with the most frequencies.

O.D. of Screwheads (in.)	Midpoint (X)	No. Screwheads (f)
0.005 up to 0.015	0.010	1
0.015 up to 0.025	0.020	4
0.025 up to 0.035	0.030	1
0.035 up to 0.045	0.040	2

The midpoint of the class interval with the most frequencies is often called the *crude mode*. The midpoint of 0.020 in. is assumed to be representative of the modal class.

A crude mode of 0.020 in. has been selected for this frequency distribution. In so doing, it is assumed that the outer diameters of the screwheads are evenly distributed in the modal class, i.e., 0.015 in. up to 0.025 in. In real life, this is not true. To compensate for this, an *interpolated mode* may be used. In the frequency distribution of screwheads computed using the following formula, the interpolated mode would be 0.020 in. Computation of the interpolated mode is done as follows:

$$L = \frac{F_m - F_{m+1}}{F_m - F_{m-1} + F_{m+1}} \text{ (Class interval)}$$

where

L = lower-limit modal class = 0.015 in.

F_m = frequency of modal class = 4

F_{m-1} = frequency of class immediately preceding modal class = 1

F_{m+1} = frequency of class immediately following modal class = 1

Class interval = size of class interval = 0.010

Using the information in the frequency distribution of screwheads, the interpolated mode would be computed as follows:

$$\text{Interpolated mode} = 0.015 \text{ in.} + \frac{4 - 1}{(4 - 1) + (4 - 1)} (0.010)$$

$$= 0.015 \text{ in.} + 3/6 \, (0.010)$$

$$= 0.015 \text{ in.} + 0.005 \text{ in.}$$

$$= 0.020 \text{ in.}$$

In theory, the true mode of a frequency distribution is not available due to a lack of raw data. Hence both the crude and computed mode are approximations of the true mode.

Bimodal Distribution

A bimodal distribution occurs when samples are taken from populations that are not homogeneous. Suppose running times of 10 runners in a population of 100 in the 100-meter dash in a track meet are clocked at the following times:

Runners' Times (sec)			
9	11	27	30
10	11	27	
11	13	27	

We can see that there are two modes: 11 and 27 sec. If further analysis of the data is undertaken, the bimodal distribution should be broken into two parts.

The bimodal distribution that might result is graphically displayed in Figure 9.1. The two modal peaks are of different heights.

Geometric Mean

The geometric mean is not as greatly influenced by extreme values as is the arithmetic mean. Its two main uses are discussed in the following pages.

Average Percent Increase in a Time Series. Suppose top management of RST Industrial Co. developed a patent that made its sales soar. Two years later, the

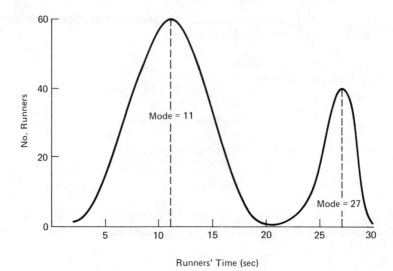

Runners' Time (sec)

Fig. 9.1 Bimodal distribution.

corporate president, Frank Jones, in preparing information for the annual stock-holders' meeting, wanted to know RST's average annual percent increase in sales. The sales 1976 through 1980 were as follows:

Year	Sales
1976	$ 25,000
1977	30,000
1978	300,000
1979	350,000
1980	450,000
	$1,155,000

Using these sales figures, the formula for the geometric mean is:

$$\text{G.M.} = \left((n-1) \sqrt{\frac{\text{Sales at end of period}}{\text{Sales at beginning of period}}} \right) - 1$$

$$= \left((5-1) \sqrt{\frac{450,000}{25,000}} \right) - 1$$

$$= \left(4\sqrt{18} - 1 \right)$$

To find the fourth root of 18, logarithms are used. (See Appendix A for instructions and Appendix B for tables.) The fourth root of 18 is developed according to the following formula:

$$\frac{\text{Log of 18}}{4} = \frac{1.2553}{4}$$

$$= 0.31382$$

The next step is to determine the antilog of 0.31382, which is approximately 1.206. The geometric percent increase is then found by 1.206 - [1(100)] or 20.6%. RST sales therefore increased at a rate of 20.6% per year from 1976 through 1980.

The computation of the arithmetic mean is:

$$\frac{\text{Total sales, 1976–80}}{5}(100)$$

$$\frac{\$1,155,000}{5}(100) = 23.1\%$$

Based on the arithmetic mean, the average percent increase in sales from 1976–1980 is 23.1%. This differs somewhat from the geometric mean of 20.6%. The arithmetic mean produces a higher figure because it is influenced by extremes such as the 1980 sales of $450,000.

Average Percents, Indexes, or Relatives. An investor is looking at Crumbly Cookie Co. as a possible investment. The company's annual report shows a pre-tax profit percent of sales of 5%, 6%, 8%, 9%, and 4% for 1976 through 1980.

The geometric mean can also be found by using logarithms exclusively.

Year	Percent X	Logarithms of X
1976	5	0.6990
1977	6	0.7782
1978	8	0.9031
1979	9	0.9542
1980	4	0.6021
		3.9366

The formula for the log of the geometric mean when logarithms are used is:

$$\text{Log of G.M.} = \frac{\Sigma \text{ Log } X}{n}$$

$$= \frac{3.9366}{5}$$

$$= 0.7873$$

The antilog is 6.13. Therefore, Crumbly Cookie Co.'s annual average pretax profit as percent of sales is 6.1%.

Mean, Median, and Mode

The relationship of the mean, the median, and the mode to one another depends on the distribution of the numbers in the sample taken from a given population. If the numbers are fairly evenly dispersed throughout a sample, going from lowest to highest in value, then the distribution takes the form of a bell-shaped curve. On this curve, the median, mode, and median are equal; thus, if a line were drawn down the middle of the curve, it would be divided into two equal and symmetrical parts. The bell-shaped curve in Figure 9.2 represents a sample of ten ping pong balls taken from a production run. Normally the outside diameters range from 1.80 to 2.20 inches. The mean, median and mode of the sample equals 2.00 inches.

A distribution may also be *positively* or *negatively skewed,* that is, the numbers in the sample are not evenly dispersed ranging from lowest to highest. (See Figures 9.3 and 9.4.)

A description of the properties of negatively and positively skewed distributions follows:

Negatively Skewed Distribution	*Positively Skewed Distribution*
1. Curve is shifted to the right; the mode is more than the median or mean.	1. Curve is shifted to the left. The mode is the smallest of three measures.
2. The mean, greatly influenced by a few extremely low numbers, is the lowest of the three averages.	2. The mean, greatly influenced by a few extremely large numbers, is larger than the mode or median.
3. The median is greater than the mean.	3. The median is the second largest figure.

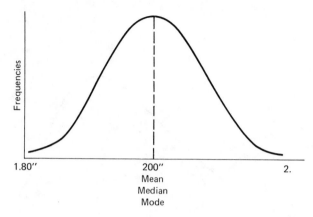

Fig. 9.2 Bell-shaped curve.

In a distribution that is only moderately skewed, the mode is approximately one-third of the distance between the mean and mode.

Hence the following three formulas apply:

$$Mode = Mean - [3(Mean - Median)]$$

$$Median = \frac{2(Mean) + Mode}{3}$$

$$Mean = \frac{3(Median) - Mode}{2}$$

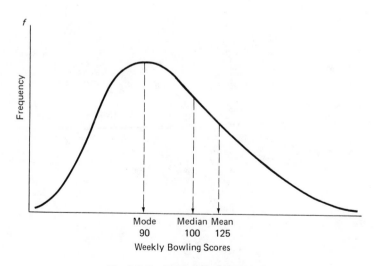

Fig. 9.3 Positively skewed distribution.

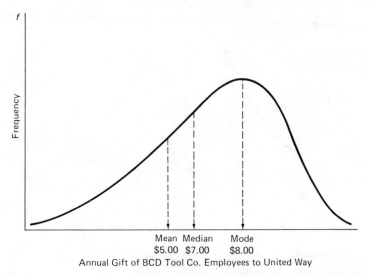

Mean Median   Mode
$5.00 $7.00 $8.00
Annual Gift of BCD Tool Co. Employees to United Way

Fig. 9.4 Negatively skewed distribution.

If we wanted to know the mean deviation from the standard in the shank of a high-volume production part where the mode was 1 in., the median 1.5 in., and the mean 1.75 in. the mode would be found by:

$$\text{Mode} = \text{Mean} - 3(\text{Mean} - \text{Median})$$

$$= 1.75 - 3(1.75 - 1.50)$$

$$= 1.75 - 0.75$$

$$= 1.00$$

To find the mean use the following formula:

$$\text{Mean} = \frac{[3(\text{Median})] - \text{Mode}}{2}$$

$$= \frac{[3(1.5)] - 1}{2}$$

$$= \frac{4.5 - 1}{2}$$

$$= 1.75 \text{ in.}$$

The median can be found by:

$$\text{Median} = \frac{[2(\text{Mean})] + \text{Mode}}{3}$$

$$= \frac{[2(1.75)] + 1}{3}$$

$$= \frac{3.5 + 1}{3}$$

$$= \frac{4.5}{3}$$

$$= 1.5 \text{ in}$$

10 Probability Distributions

A probability distribution must have the following characteristics:

1. Events must be mutually exclusive.
2. All possible events are included.
3. Any given outcome is completely due to chance.

To illustrate, if a card is picked at random from a deck of 52 playing cards, the chance of picking a king of hearts is 1/52 or 0.01923. The event is repeated until all possible outcomes have taken place—that is, until each card has been drawn once. Table 10.1 shows the probabilities.

NORMAL PROBABILITY DISTRIBUTION

The normal curve has the following characteristics:

1. Bell-shaped.
2. A line drawn through the middle of a normal curve divides it in half. One-half of the area under the curve is to the right of the line, and the other half is to the left of the line. Hence, the total area under the bell-shaped curve equals unity or 1.00.
3. To construct a curve, a mean (μ) and standard deviation (δ) are necessary.
4. There is a curve for each separate μ and δ. A normal curve is thus made up of many curves.
5. All of the area under the normal curve is equal to all of the frequencies from which it was taken.
6. The normal curve comes close to but does not touch the X-axis. (It is asymptotic.)
7. Nearly all of the values fall within ±3 δ.

Table 10.1. Chance Selection of Picking a Particular Card from a Deck of 52

Picking Card	No. Times	Probability
King of hearts	1	1/52 = 0.01923
Queen of diamonds	1	1/52 = 0.01923
Ten of clubs	1	1/52 = 0.01923
Ace of spades	1	1/52 = 0.01923
Two of hearts	1	1/52 = 0.01923
Ace of diamonds	1	1/52 = 0.01923
Event is repeated until 52 cards are chosen.		
	$\overline{52}$	$\overline{52/52 = 0.99996^a}$

[a]Does not add to 1.00 due to rounding.

Construction of a Normal Curve

Suppose we wish to construct a normal curve relating to test scores on a national high-school French test. The mean test score is 80, and the standard deviation is 5.

As stated previously, since each normal distribution only requires a mean and standard deviation, there is an infinite number of values for X in the formula for a normal probability distribution shown below:

$$Y = \frac{1}{\delta\sqrt{2\pi}} \; \delta^{-\frac{1}{2}} \; \frac{(X - \mu)^2}{\delta^2}$$

where

$$\mu = \text{mean}$$

$$\delta = \text{standard deviation}$$

$$\pi = 3.14159$$

$$e = 2.71828$$

A table showing the areas and ordinates under a normal curve has been constructed to alleviate the problem of solving for X (see Appendix C). However, before the table can be used, the X values must be changed into z (standard deviation) values. The formula is:

$$z = \frac{X - \mu}{\delta}$$

If we have an X value of 95 in the nationwide high-school French test, then the corresponding Y value is computed as follows:

$$z = \frac{X - \mu}{\delta}$$

$$= \frac{95 - 80}{5}$$

$$= 3.00$$

Looking at the z value of 3.00 in column 1 of Appendix C, we find the corresponding Y value of 0.00443. To complete the construction of a normal curve, several more Y values corresponding to X values are computed. (See Figure 10.1).

1. X value of 85:

$$z = \frac{X - \mu}{\delta}$$

$$= \frac{85 - 80}{5}$$

$$= 1.00$$

Corresponding Y value = 0.24197

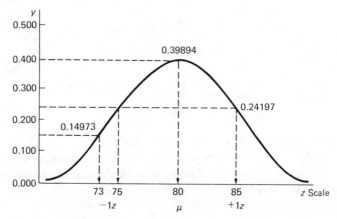

Fig. 10.1 Construction of normal curve using X and Y values.

2. X value of 80:

$$z = \frac{X - \mu}{\delta}$$

$$= \frac{80 - 80}{5}$$

$$= 0.00$$

Corresponding Y value = 0.39894

3. X value of 75:

$$z = \frac{X - \mu}{\delta}$$

$$= \frac{75 - 80}{5}$$

$$= -1.00$$

Corresponding Y value = 0.24197

4. X value of 73:

$$z = \frac{X - \mu}{\delta}$$

$$= \frac{73 - 80}{5}$$

$$= -1.40$$

Corresponding Y value = -0.14973

**Selected Value X and Arithmetic Mean—Total Area
Under Normal Curve**

To find the proportion of total area under the normal curve between a selected
value of X and the arithmetic mean, the z value is used. If a student has a score

of 90.0 (X value) and the mean is 80.0 on the nationwide French test, then:

$$z = \frac{X - \mu}{\delta}$$

$$= \frac{90 - 80}{5}$$

$$= 2.00$$

Using Appendix C and a corresponding z value of 2.00, the proportion of the total area under the curve is 0.47725. If a student has a test score of 70.0 (which produces a z value of -2.00), the proportion of the area under the normal curve would be 0.47725. This is so because a normal curve is symmetrical. So approximately 95.45% of test scores will fall within ±2z. This relationship is shown in Figure 10.2. The area under the normal curve *outside* ±2z is 0.0455 (0.02275 on each side). To determine the percentage of students scoring better than 90 (+2z) on the nationwide French test, take the 0.50000 - 0.47725 = 0.02275. Those students getting less than 70 (-2z) on the test are found in the same manner

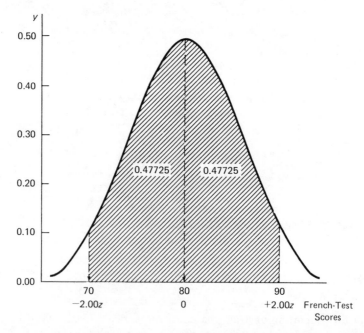

Fig. 10.2 Selected value of X and arithmetic mean, total area under normal curve.

(0.50000 - 0.47725 = 0.02275). In other words, approximately 2% of the students taking the test would score *below* 70 or *above* 90.

Total Area Under Normal Curve: Two Selected Values of X

The proportion of the total area under the normal curve for two selected values of X may be found as follows:

1. Difference between first selected value of X and mean.
2. Difference between second selected value of X and mean.
3. Subtract difference of two proportions.

The proportion of the students scoring between 85 and 90 on the nationwide French test can be determined as follows:

1. Proportion between 80 (mean) and 85:

$$z = \frac{X - \bar{X}}{\delta}$$

where

$$X = \text{selected value test score (85)}$$

$$\bar{X} = \text{mean test score (80)}$$

$$\delta = \text{standard deviation (5)}$$

$$z = \frac{85 - 80}{5}$$

$$z = 1.00$$

$$z = 0.34134$$

2. Proportion between 80 (mean) and 90:

$$z = \frac{X - \bar{X}}{\delta}$$

where

$$X = \text{selected value test score (90)}$$

$$\overline{X} = \text{mean test score (80)}$$

$$\delta = \text{standard deviation (5)}$$

$$z = \frac{90 - 80}{5}$$

$$z = 2.00$$

$$z = 0.47725$$

3. Subtract the difference between the two proportions:

$$0.47725 - 0.34134 = 0.13591$$

Approximately 13.5% of all students taking the French test have a score between 85 and 90, as shown in Figure 10.3.

**Proportion of Total Area under Normal Curve:
Two Tails**

Suppose a written examination to determine eligibility for promotion has been administered to the employees of DEF Insurance Company. From the results, a list of eligible employees is drawn up. Past test scores of employees have been normally distributed with a mean of 120 and a standard deviation of 10. One position available in DEF requires a score in the top 2%. John Jones, president of DEF, wants to know what the minimum test score is. Using the formula for z he makes the following computations:

1. Proportion of total area under one-half of normal curve = 0.50000.
2. Jones interested in top 2%.
3. Corresponding z Value to 0.48000 is about 2.05 (see Appendix C).
4. Solving for X using z formula:

$$z = \frac{X - \mu}{\delta}$$

$$\frac{2.05}{10} = \frac{X - 120}{10}$$

$$X = 140.5$$

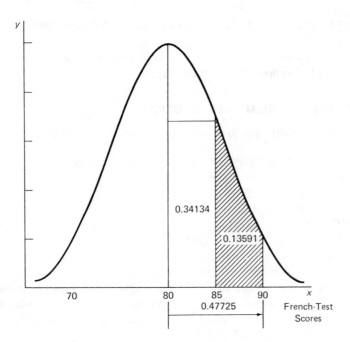

Fig. 10.3 Total area under normal curve, two selected values of X.

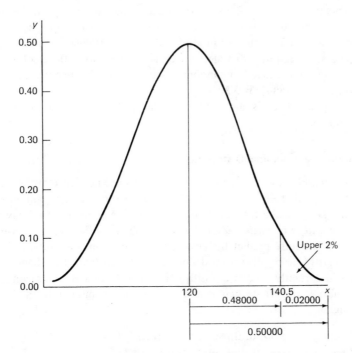

Fig. 10.4 Proportion of total area under normal curve, with score top 2%.

Thus, to be considered for the position, a DEF employee must get a minimum test score of 140.5 (upper 2%). See Figure 10.4.

BINOMINAL PROBABILITY DISTRIBUTION

A binominal probability distribution has the following characteristics:

1. Deals with the attribute (characteristic) of an item where only *two* outcomes are possible. For example:
   a. The electric light is on.
      The electric light is off.
   b. The airplane takes off.
      The airplane stays on the ground.
   c. The part meets inspection requirements.
      The part does not meet inspection requirements.
2. In an event that is repeated over and over again, the outcomes are independent. The results do not follow a predetermined pattern. For example, if a die was tossed in the air many times, the results would not repeatedly be 1,2,3,4,5,6; 1,2,3,4,5,6; 1,2,3,4,5,6.
3. In tossing a true die, the probability of a one resulting is 1/6 time after time. Hence, in a probability distribution, the probability of an outcome stays the same trial after trial. It is conceivable, however, that the probabilities of an outcome do not have to be equal. For example, suppose tests have shown a carburetor in Model 200 of a particular automobile engine passes inspection 800 times out of 1000 and fails 200 out of 1000. If a carburetor is picked at random from a lot, the probability of passing is 0.80 and of failure is 0.20.
4. Outcome of trials are counted. Hence, the binominal distribution is discrete.

Illustration of a Binominal Distribution

Suppose a market research analyst, with no previous knowledge of the outcome, attempts to predict how respondents in three separate markets will answer the question, "Do you like the new Zoomies cereal?" A respondent will say that he or she either *likes* or *dislikes* Zoomies. The probability that the market-research analyst will correctly predict the answer of a respondent in Market A (the first market area) to be positive toward Zoomies is 1/2 or 0.50. The chance that the analyst will correctly predict a positive answer in Market B (the second market area) is also 0.50. What then is the chance of the market research analyst predicting:

- Precisely three out of three markets properly?
- Precisely two out of three markets properly?

- Precisely one out of three markets properly?
- Precisely zero out of three markets properly?

To obtain the probability of three out of three correctly, the calculation would be:

$$1/2 \times 1/2 \times 1/2 = 0.125$$

This can also be expressed as $(1/2)^3$.

The probability of the market-research analyst precisely forecasting two out of three markets correctly would be more difficult due to the number of possible combinations. Instead of listing all of the possible combinations, a formula may be applied in which the number of combinations of two correct and one wrong are multiplied by the probability of having two correct and one wrong in *any* combination. The calculations are:

1. Determining the number of combinations of precisely two correct and one correct: where

$$n = \text{total number combinations}$$

$$r = \text{number correct combinations}$$

$$nC_r = {}_3C_2$$

$$= \frac{n!}{r! \, (n-r)!}$$

$$= \frac{3!}{2! \, (3-2)!}$$

$$= \frac{3!}{2! \, 1!}$$

$$= \frac{3 . \cancel{2} . \cancel{1}}{\cancel{2} . \cancel{1} \times 1}$$

$$= \frac{3}{1}$$

$$= 3$$

Note that ! denotes 3 factorial, i.e., 3.2.1.

2. Determining probability of having precisely two correct and one wrong out of three in *any* combination:

$$(p)^r (q)^{n-r} = (0.50)^2 (1 - 0.50)^{3-2}$$

$$= (0.50)^2 (0.50)^1$$

$$= 0.125$$

where

$p = 0.50$ or probability of answering question purely by chance.

q = probability of a failure = $1 - p$ or 0.50.

n = total number of markets = 3.

r = correct number predictions out of total = 2.

3. Multiplying the number of combinations of precisely two correct and one wrong by the probability of precisely two correct and one wrong in *any* combination.

$$P(2) = {_3}C_2 \, (P)^2 \, (q)^{3-2}$$

$$= \frac{3!}{2! \, 1!} (0.50)^2 (0.50)^1$$

$$= \frac{3 \cdot 2 \cdot 1}{2 \cdot 1 \times 1} (0.50)^2 (0.50)^1$$

$$= 3 \, (0.50)^2 (0.50)^1$$

$$= 0.375$$

The probability of the market-research analyst correctly predicting *three* out of *three* respondents' answers correctly is found by:

$$P(r) = {_n}C_r \, (p)^r \, (q)^{n-r}$$

which may also be written:

$$P(r) = \frac{n!}{r! \, (n - r)!} (p)^r \, (q)^{n-r}$$

$$P(3) = \frac{3!}{3! \, (3-3)!} (0.50)^3 (0.50)^{3-3}$$

$$P(3) = \frac{\cancel{3 \cdot 2 \cdot 1}}{\cancel{3 \cdot 2 \cdot 1} \times 1!} (0.50)^3 (0.50)^0$$

$$P(3) = 1! \, (0.50)^3 (0.50)^0$$

$$P(3) = 1 \, (0.125) \, (1)$$

$$P(3) = 0.125$$

You will note in the above that zero factorial and 0.50^0 both equal 1.
The probability of the market-research analyst forcasting one out of three respondents correctly is found by:

$$P(r) = \frac{n!}{r! \, (n-r)!} \, p^r \, q^{n-r}$$

where

$p = 0.50$

$q = 1 - \text{p or } 0.50$

$n = $ total number of markets $= 3$

$r = $ correct number of predictions out of total $= 1$

$n - r = $ number of incorrect answers out of total $= 3 - 1 = 2$

$$P(1) = \frac{3!}{1! \, (3-1)!} (0.50)^1 (0.50)^{3-1}$$

$$P(1) = \frac{3!}{1! \times 2!} (0.50)^1 (0.50)^{3-1}$$

$$P(1) = \frac{3 \cdot \cancel{2 \cdot 1}}{1 \times \cancel{2 \cdot 1}} (0.50)^1 (0.50)^{3-1}$$

$$P(1) = 3 \, (0.50)^1 (0.50)^2$$

$$P(1) = 0.375$$

Table 10.2. Number of Correct Predictions Where *n* = 3 and *p* = 0.50.

No. Correct Predictions	Probabilities
0	0.125 (1/8)
1	0.375 (3/8)
2	0.375 (3/8)
3	0.125 (1/8)
	1.000

The probabilities of forecasting exactly zero out of three respondents correctly is also computed. The resulting probabilities, together with those computed above, are combined in Table 10.2 to produce a binominal probability distribution where *n* = 3 and *p* = 0.50.

Probability Tables for Use with Bimodal Distribution

A table has been developed that makes the preparation of a bimodal distribution fairly easy (see Appendix D). The table is based on the formula:

$$P(r) = \frac{n!}{r! \, (n-r)!} \, p^r \, q^{n-r}$$

The table is set up with probabilities from 0.05 to 0.50. There is a probability column corresponding to each *n* and *r*, which are shown in the extreme left-hand column.

Suppose the market-research analyst wanted to obtain the probability of predicting zero out of four respondents' answers correctly in the market test on Zoomies. Using Table 10.3,

1. *n* = Number of test markets = 4
   r = Correct number of predictions out of total = 0
   p = Probability of answering question purely by chance
2. The analyst assigns the probability (*p*) that he will answer questions purely by chance of 0.50.

Looking at Table 10.3, where *n* = 4, *r* = 0, and *p* = 0.50, the analyst finds that the probability of getting zero out of four predictions by chance is 0.0625. If the analyst were to change the probability to 0.45, where *n* = 4 and *r* = 0, he

Table 10.3. Binominal Distribution Table (n = 4 and Probability = 0.05 to 0.50).

		Probability				
n = 4	r	0.05	0.10	0.15	0.20	0.25
	0	0.8145	0.6561	0.5220	0.4096	0.3164
	1	0.1715	0.2916	0.3685	0.4096	0.4219
	2	0.0135	0.0486	0.0975	0.1536	0.2109
	3	0.0005	0.0036	0.0115	0.0256	0.0469
	4	0.0000	0.0001	0.0005	0.0016	0.0039
n = 4	r	0.30	0.35	0.40	0.45	0.50
	0	0.2401	0.1785	0.1296	0.0915	0.0625
	1	0.4116	0.3845	0.3456	0.2995	0.2500
	2	0.2646	0.3105	0.3456	0.3675	0.3750
	3	0.0756	0.1115	0.1536	0.2005	0.2500
	4	0.0081	0.0150	0.0256	0.0410	0.0625

would increase the probability of getting zero out of four predictions purely by chance to 0.0915.

Poisson Probability Distribution

Poisson probability distributions are a form of binominal distribution where the probability of success is very small and n is quite large. It is used in quality control and queuing theory. The formula for a Poisson distribution is as follows:

$$P(x) = \frac{\mu^x e^{-\mu}}{x!}$$

where

μ = arithmetic mean of each occurrence

e = constant of 2.71828

$P(x)$ = probability of X number of occurrences

As an example, suppose a company makes ceiling tile and is trying to ascertain the number of tiles where not all of the perforated holes are drilled in the tile. This is a rare occurrence. The quality control manager takes a random sample of 600 tile and finds 240 where all the perforated holes have not been drilled. The arithmetic mean is 240/600 or 0.40. The probability of finding all holes perforated in a tile (no defects) is:

$$P(0) = \frac{0.40^0 \ (2.71828)^{-0.4}}{0!} \quad \text{(when } x = 0,$$
$$\text{denominator} = 1)$$

$$P(0) = \frac{1 \ (2.71828)^{-0.4}}{1}$$

$$P(0) = \frac{1}{(2.71828)^{+0.4}}$$

$$P(0) = \frac{1}{0.4 \ (\text{Log of } 2.71828)}$$

$$P(0) = \frac{1}{0.4 \ (0.4346)}$$

$$P(0) = \frac{1}{0.17384}$$

The antilog of 0.173716 is 1.149 or 1/1.49 = 0.671 or about 67% of the ceiling tile will have all holes perforated (no defects).

Instead of figuring the Poisson probability by hand, probability tables may be used. Appendix E, a probability table for the Poisson distribution showing selected values of mean (μ), is based on the following formula:

$$P(x) = \frac{\mu^x \ e^{-\mu}}{x(x - 1)(x - 2) \cdots 1}$$

Using Appendix E and looking at the column headed $\mu = 0.4$, the probability of no defective ceiling tile (zero successes) is 0.6703. Table 10.4 shows the probability for x occurrences [$P(x)$] where the arithmetic mean of occurrences (μ) = 0.40. (See Figure 10.5.)

Poisson Probability Distribution vs. Normal Probability Distribution

The Poisson distribution approximates a normal distribution as following occurs:

1. Probability of μ becomes larger. Figure 10.6 shows a Poisson probability distribution for $\mu = 6.0$.

Table 10.4. Poisson Probability Distribution (μ = 0.40).

No. Occurrences		Probability Event Will Happen
X		
0		0.6703200
1		0.2681280
2		0.0536256
3		0.0071501
4		0.0007150
5		0.0000572
6		0.0000038
7		0.0000002
	Total	0.9999999

2. As the number n becomes larger, even with a relatively low probability, the Poisson distribution becomes bell-shaped. Figure 10.7 shows four distributions where n becomes larger (n = 3, 11, 15, and 19) and the probability (p) is low, 0.05.

3. As n becomes larger and probability increases, the curve becomes more bell-shaped. Note that the curves in Figure 10.8 are more bell-shaped than in Figure 10.7 because the probability has been increased to 0.40 from 0.05.

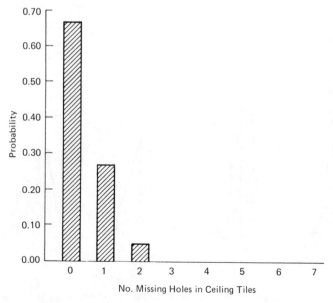

Fig. 10.5 Poisson probability distribution for defective ceiling tile where μ = 0.4.

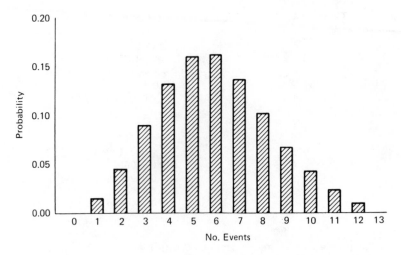

Fig. 10.6 Poisson probability distribution where $\mu = 6.0$.

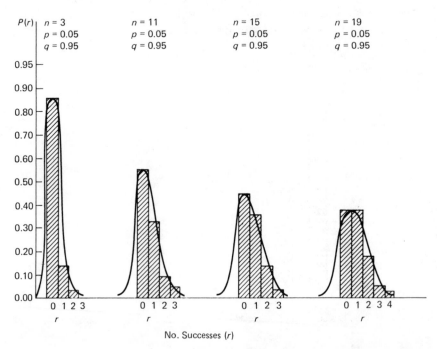

Fig. 10.7 Four Poisson probability distributions where n becomes larger and low p of 0.05.

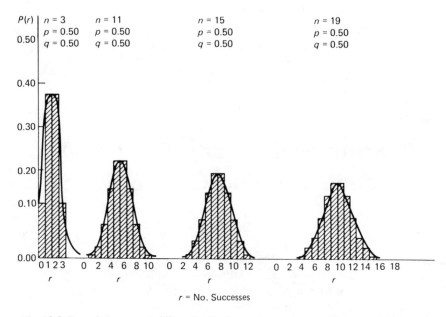

Fig. 10.8 Four Poisson probability distributions where n becomes larger and high p of 0.40.

11 Statistical Quality Control And the Manufacturing Control Process

Prior to 1900, individual workers were considered to be craftsmen who had almost complete control over the items they produced. They selected raw materials themselves and saw to it personally that the final product met their requirements. However, the mechanization of factories in the United States in the early 1900s changed this. Products began to be mass-produced, and the large production lines in factories employed operators who were less skilled than craftsmen. Increased technology caused products and their integral parts to become more complex. The chance of a person's working on a product from start to finish was minimal. Thus, some type of control became necessary in the manufacturing process, and manufacturers began inspecting parts in order to help control quality.

In the early 1930s, a new concept in controlling the quality of a product was introduced: the statistical sampling of the in-process manufacturing of parts. If the items selected at random from a particular run of a manufactured part passed inspection, then, by inference, so did the balance of that run. The concept was introduced by Dr. Walter A. Shewhart of Bell Telephone Laboratories. With the mass production of intricate parts during World War II, the need for statistical quality control increased. The techniques introduced by Dr. Shewhart were refined, and new ones were added. Control charts came into wide use, as did statistical techniques for evaluating production parts. Today, many companies employ quality control engineers. They conduct reliability tests and statistical techniques, including tests of significance such as t-tests and chi-square tests.

STATISTICAL INFERENCE IN QUALITY CONTROL

Parts in a particular manufacturing process are expected to vary—no two are exactly alike. For example, in inspecting two glass bottles taken at random from Run 22 in a glassmaking plant, Bottle 1 is not expected to be precisely the same

**Table 11.1. Variations in Mouths of I.D. Glass Bottles, Run 25,
See-Through Glass Co.**

| I.D. | | No.
Bottles |
|---|---|---|
| 1.05 | | 5 |
| 1.10 | | 10 |
| 1.15 | | 15 |
| 1.20 | | 20 |
| 1.25 | | 60 |
| 1.30 | | 15 |
| 1.35 | | 10 |
| 1.45 | | 5 |
| | Total | 140 |

as Bottle 2. Hence the need for specified tolerances. If the bottle falls within specified limits, it passes inspection; if not, it fails.

Table 11.1 shows the variation in the inside diameter (I.D.) of the mouths of glass bottles taken from Run 22 of the See-Through Glass Co. The company specializes in making glass bottles for manufacturers of salad dressings. The mean I.D. of the bottles is 1.25 in. The I.D.'s can be considered to be normally distributed; hence the use of measures of central tendency (Chapter 9), normal curve (Chapter 10), and dispersion and skewness under a curve (Chapter 12). Note that in Table 11.1 most of the bottles (60/140) fall at the mean of 1.25 in.

Variations in the manufacturing process are either random or not random. Random variations are generally large in number and cannot be entirely eliminated. Examples are small variations in materials used to manufacture a product and the amount of dust in the air in the manufacturing plant. Nonrandom causes, on the other hand, are small in number and can be reduced or eliminated. A malfunctioning machine tool, an inept operator, and raw material not up to specifications are examples of nonrandom, or assignable, causes. Random variations can cause a change in the measures of central tendency in the frequency distribution of the product, whereas nonrandom causes can normally be easily identified and corrected. Figure 11.1 shows a normally distributed curve for the I.D.'s of glass bottles for all salad dressing manufacturers, where the pattern is due to chance variation. It is assumed that the lower and upper limits are the same as those shown in Table 11.1; thus, 99.73% or 997 out of 1000 bottles inspected would be theoretically acceptable. (The arithmetic mean number of occurrences, $\mu \pm 3$ standard deviations $[\sigma]$, represents 99.73% of the area under a normal curve; (see Chapter 12.) If the mean I.D. were to shift upward or downward (such a change could be caused by the temperature of the mold used to make the glass containers), then a considerable portion of the output would

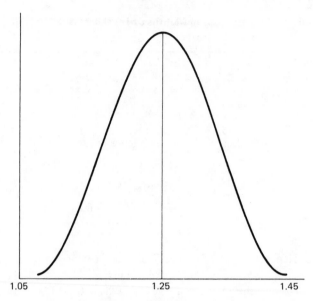

Inside Diameter, Mouths of Glass Bottles, Run No. 26

Fig. 11.1 Normal distribution curve, inner diameters of glass bottles of all salad dressing manufacturers.

be unacceptable. Figures 11.2a and b shows the effects of upward and downward shift in the arithmetic mean. Assignable causes are responsible for the pattern shown in Figure 11.2a and b.

QUALITY CONTROL CHARTS

A quality control chart is a tool that indicates to management just how well the manufacturing process is progressing. It can be compared to a traffic signal. If the light is green—if pieces are within prescribed limits—production keeps going; if the light is red—if parts are not acceptable—then production stops until the cause of the problem is discovered. Variations from the norm, such as a larger-than-normal O.D. and thickness of sheet steel, can be tracked on a quality control chart. Whether a tire fits over a rim, whether a screwdriver works, and so on may also be recorded on quality control charts.

Variable Quality Control Charts

Sampling concepts such as those described in Chapters 9, 10, and 12, are employed in quality control.

As an illustration, suppose a certain number of pieces are taken as a sample

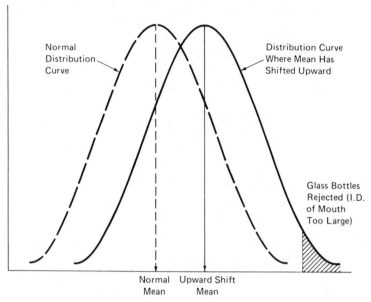

Normal
Distribution
Curve

Distribution Curve
Where Mean Has
Shifted Upward

Glass Bottles
Rejected (I.D.
of Mouth
Too Large)

Normal   Upward Shift
Mean   Mean

Inside Diameter, Mouths of Glass Bottles, Run No. 26

Fig. 11.2a Distribution curve affected by upward shift of mean inner diameters of glass bottles for all salad dressing manufacturers.

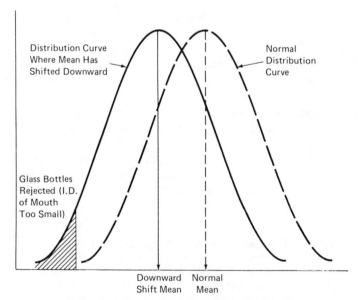

Distribution Curve
Where Mean Has
Shifted Downward

Normal
Distribution
Curve

Glass Bottles
Rejected (I.D.
of Mouth
Too Small)

Downward   Normal
Shift Mean Mean

Inside Diameter, Mouths of Glass Bottles, Run No. 26

Fig. 11.2b Distribution curve affected by downward shift of mean inner diameters of glass bottles for all salad dressing manufacturers.

from Run 30, the same number of pieces from Runs 31 through 39. The arithmetic means of each of these samples are computed and designated as follows:

$$\overline{X}_1 = \text{Run } 30 \quad \overline{X}_6 = \text{Run } 35$$

$$\overline{X}_2 = \text{Run } 31 \quad \overline{X}_7 = \text{Run } 36$$

$$\overline{X}_3 = \text{Run } 32 \quad \overline{X}_8 = \text{Run } 37$$

$$\overline{X}_4 = \text{Run } 33 \quad \overline{X}_9 = \text{Run } 38$$

$$\overline{X}_5 = \text{Run } 34 \quad \overline{X}_{10} = \text{Run } 39$$

The mean of the sample means is calculated by adding all of the arithmetic means of the samples and then dividing the sum by the number of arithmetic means. In the case of parts selected at random from Runs 30 through 39, the mean would be expressed as follows:

$$\overline{X} = \frac{\Sigma \overline{X}_1 - \overline{X}_{10}}{10}$$

Inferences may be drawn regarding the relationship of the frequency distributions of the sample means to that of the population, as follows:

1. The distribution of the sample means will approximate a normal curve.
2. The total dispersion of the population is more than that of the distribution of the sample means by a factor $\sqrt{n}$.
3. If the distribution of the means of a sample is normal, then forecasts can be made of the distribution of the $\overline{X}$ average as shown in Table 11.2.

Table 11.2 shows that if the distribution of the means of samples is normal, then a little more than 68% of the subgroup averages $(\overline{X})$ will fall within $\pm 1\sigma$ of population mean, etc. The upper and lower control limits of subgroup samples of a certain size are based on these relationships.

Table 11.2. Forecasts of the Distribution of Averages (X).

% $\overline{X}$'s	Relationship of Standard Error of Mean (σ) to Population Mean $(\overline{X})$
68.27	$\pm 1\sigma$
95.45	$\pm 2\sigma$
99.73	$\pm 3\sigma$

Mean Charts.   Mean charts employ the use of upper and lower control limits. To illustrate, suppose QST Corporation manufactures hammerheads to be marketed principally to the building trade. Variations in the size can be caused by such factors as the drop forge and quality of raw material. Every hour, a QST quality control inspector selects 10 pieces at random and checks the overall length. From four samples of Run 22 taken a 9 A.M., 10 A.M., 11 A.M., and 12 noon, the information given in Table 11.3 is recorded.

The upper and lower control limits are computed according to the following formulas:

$$\text{Upper control limit} = \overline{X} + A_2 R$$

$$\text{Lower control limit} = \overline{X} - A_2 R$$

where

A_2 = factor for control limits
for samples of various sizes (see Appendix F)

$\overline{X}$ = mean of sample means

$\overline{R} = \pm 3_{\sigma_R}$ (range of samples 997 times out of $1000 \pm 3_{\sigma_R}$)

In the construction of a mean chart, a centerline $(\overline{R})$ must be established. Taking figures from Table 11.3, the centerline is 4.50, determined by dividing $\Sigma \overline{X}$ by the number of samples selected ($17.99 \div 4 = 4.50$). The mean of the range $(\overline{R})$ is found by dividing $\Sigma \overline{R}$ by the number of samples selected (that is $19 \div 4 = 4.75$). Thus,

$$\text{Upper control limit} = \overline{X} + A_2 R$$

$$= 4.50 + 0.308(3)$$

$$= 5.424$$

Conversely,

$$\text{Lower control limit} = \overline{X} - A_2 R$$

$$= 4.50 - 0.308(3)$$

$$= 3.576$$

The data just computed were used to construct the mean chart shown in Figure 11.3.

Table 11.3. Measurements of Length of Hammerheads, Conducted Hourly, 9 A.M. to 12 Noon, March 15, 1979.

	Part A, O.D. Shank (in.)										Arithmetic Mean (X)	Range[a] (R)
Time	1	2	3	4	5	6	7	8	9	10		
9 A.M.	4.50	4.52	4.50	4.54	4.50	4.48	4.48	4.50	4.54	4.52	4.51	6
10 A.M.	4.49	4.50	4.53	4.50	4.52	4.53	4.50	4.54	4.52	4.49	4.51	5
11 A.M.	4.47	4.50	4.51	4.48	4.50	4.50	4.51	4.47	4.49	4.48	4.49	4
12 Noon	4.46	4.50	4.47	4.48	4.50	4.50	4.46	4.48	4.49	4.50	4.48	4
											17.99	19

[a] = Numbers treated as whole numbers.

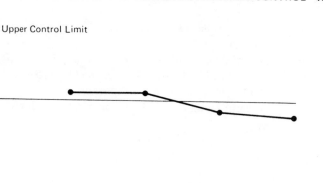

Fig. 11.3 Mean chart, outer diameters, shank of hammerhead.

A total of 997 times out of 1000, the mean length of the hammerhead will fall between 3.576 and 5.424 in. when 10 pieces are picked at random and measured. (Thus, 99.73% of the area under the normal curve is within ±3σ of the mean.) If many 10-piece samples are taken and their arithmetic means calculated, the average of 4.50 in. will appear most frequently.

Range Charts. A range chart depicts the ranges of the samples selected at random from production runs. Only when the values of the randomly selected samples fall *outside* the range limits is production out of control. Using the information gathered on the hammerheads in Table 11.3, a range chart was constructed (Figure 11.4). The figure shows the upper control limit to be 5.31 in.

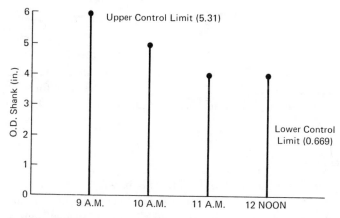

Fig. 11.4 Range chart, outer diameter, shank of hammerheads.

and the lower control limit to be 0.669 in. A total of 997 times out of 1000, the range of samples will fall within these control limits (i.e., 99.73% of the area under the normal curve is within ± 3σ of the mean). If a hammerhead falls outside of the limits, the part is either too short or too long. These are assignable causes. Factors for control limits are found in Appendix F.

The upper control limit of 5.31 in. is computed as follows:

$$\text{Upper control limit} = D_4 \overline{R}$$

where

D_4 = Factor developed for control charts—upper limit = 1.77

$\overline{R} = + 3_{\sigma_R}$ (range of samples falls 997 times out of $1000 \pm 3_{\sigma_R}$)

$\qquad = 1.77\,(3)$

$\qquad = 5.31 \text{ in.}$

The lower control limit of 0.669 in. is computed as follows:

where

D_3 = Factor developed for control charts—lower limit = 0.223

$\overline{R} = - 3_{\sigma_R}$ (range of samples 997 times out of $1000 \pm 3_{\sigma_R}$

$\qquad = 0.223\,(3)$

$\qquad = 0.669 \text{ in.}$

Once the upper and lower control limits have been placed on the range chart, the actual ranges for the sample are shown. For example, the range for 9 A.M., March 15, 1979, is 6. (The decimal is treated as a whole number: 4.54 – 4.48 = 0.06 – 6. See table 11.3).

Attribute Charts

In manufacturing, an attribute is used to describe whether or not a part is defective. Percent defective charts ($\overline{p}$ charts) and number of defects per unit charts ($\overline{c}$ charts) are used in quality control to graphically present such information.

Percent Defective Charts ($\bar{p}$ charts). Suppose a company manufactures gun barrels. An inspector must use a go/no-go gauge on each barrel to see whether the inside diameter is within tolerance limits. At the end of an 8-hour shift, the inspector has recorded the data (see Table 11.4). The mean percent defective is approximately 5.8% (i.e., $0.47 \div 8 = 0.059$).

Quality control personnel define the upper and lower control limits according to the following formula:

$$\text{Upper and lower control limit} = p \pm 3 \sqrt{\frac{\bar{p}(1-\bar{p})}{n}}$$

where

$\bar{p}$ = average percent defective = 0.059

± 3 = assuming 997 times out of 1000, the range of samples will fall within $\pm 3_{\sigma_R}$

$1 - p = 1.00$ minus average percent defective = $1.00 - 0.059 = 0.941$

n = number inspected per hour = 20

So,

$$\bar{p} \pm 3 \sqrt{\frac{\bar{p}(1-\bar{p})}{n}}$$

$$= 0.059 \pm 3 \sqrt{\frac{(0.059)(0.941)}{20}}$$

$$= 0.059 \pm 3 \sqrt{\frac{0.055519}{20}}$$

$$= 0.059 \pm 3 \sqrt{0.0027759}$$

$$= 0.059 \pm 3 (0.05269)$$

$$= 0.21707 \text{ and } -0.09907$$

The lower control limit is zero (no defect below zero), and the upper control limit is 0.217. The quality control manager then sets up a $\bar{p}$ chart with these

Table 11.4. Number of Gun Barrels Not Fitting Go/No-Go Gauge.

Hour	No. Inspected	No. Not Fitting Go/No-Go Gauge	Percent Defective
7:00–8:00 A.M.	100	5	0.05
8:00–9:00 A.M.	100	10	0.10
9:00–10:00 A.M.	100	0	–
10:00–11:00 A.M.	100	0	–
11:00–12:00 Noon	100	10	0.10
12:00 Noon–1:00 P.M.	100	0	–
1:00–2:00 P.M.	100	10	0.10
2:00–3:00 P.M.	100	12	0.12
			0.47

limits and plots the percent defective per hour in an 8-hr day (Figure 11.5). For example, 0.05, 0.10, etc., are plotted (Table 11.4).

Quality control can provide management with the following information:

1. Arithmetic mean defective = 5.9%.
2. For 997 times out of 1000, the percent defective will be between zero and 21.7%.

Figure 11.6 shows an actual $\bar{p}$ chart.

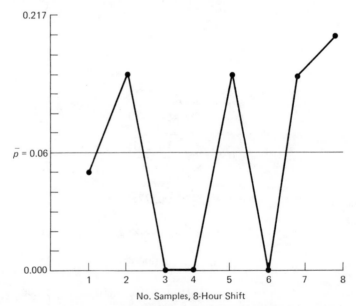

Fig. 11.5 p-chart, number of defective gun barrels.

SPEED SENSOR—100% INSPECTION RESULTS

SCOPE

WEEK ENDING	UNITS INSPECTED	UNITS REJECTED	% REJECTED
7/1/79	25,503	197	0.8%
7/7	24,255	177	0.7%
7/22	25,813	234	0.9%
7/29	30,780	168	0.6%
8/5	14,615	135	0.9%
8/12	2,132	61	2.9%
8/19	8,810	92	1.0%
9/16	13,428	204	1.5%
9/23	9,753	83	0.9%
9/30	10,454	87	0.8%
TOTAL	165,543	1,438	0.9%

Fig. 11.6 Actual *p* chart. (Courtesy Century Brass Products Co., Waterbury, Connecticut)

Reasons for rejection on scope

WEEK ENDING	DUDS	LOW OUTPUT	HIGH OUTPUT	ERRATIC OUTPUT	OTHER
7/1/79	36	161	0	0	0
7/7	57	120	0	0	0
7/22	96	135	0	3	0
7/29	35	133	0	0	0
8/5	32	103	0	0	0
8/12	13	48	0	0	0
8/19	22	70	0	0	0
9/16	57	147	0	0	0
9/23	23	60	0	0	0
9/30	7	80	0	0	0
TOTAL	378	1,057	0	3	0

Fig. 11.6 Actual p chart. (Courtesy Century Brass Products Co., Waterbury, Connecticut) (continued)

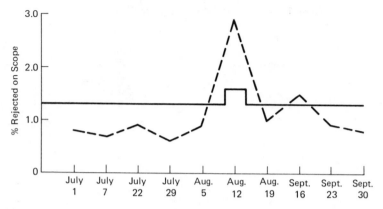

Fig. 11.6 Actual p chart. (Courtesy Century Brass Products Co., Waterbury, Connecticut) (continued)

Defects per Unit Chart. A $\bar{c}$-chart shows the number of defects per unit. It can be valuable in letting management know where the weak spots are in the construction of a particular unit or subassembly.

For example, suppose a bicycle manufacturer inspects the wheels before final assembly. Experience has shown that some of the spokes might not be held in place properly, some might be missing, and some might be bent. Those wheels without defects are sent from inspection to final assembly. On a typical day, quality control records the defects per wheel as shown in Table 11.5. The quality control manager then computes the upper and lower control limits.

The upper control limit of 10.29 defective spokes per bicycle wheel is computed as follows:

$$\text{Upper control limit} = \bar{c} \pm 3\sqrt{\bar{c}}$$

where

$\bar{c}$ = average number of defects per wheel ($25 \div 6 = 4.17$)

+ 3 = 997 times out of 1000, the number of defective spokes per bicycle wheel will be within $\pm 3\sigma_c$

$= 4.17 \pm 3\sqrt{4.17}$

$= 4.17 \pm 3\,(2.04)$

$= 10.29$ defective spokes per bicycle wheel

The lower control limit is zero, since there cannot be less than zero spokes.

Table 11.5. Number of Defects per Bicycle Wheel.

Wheel No.	No. Defects
1	5
2	8
3	10
4	1
5	1
6	0
Total	25

The quality control inspector then prepares a $\bar{c}$ chart showing the lower control limit of 0, the upper control limit of 10.29, and the $\bar{c}$ of 4.17 (Figure 11.7). Subsequently, the inspector plots the number of defects per part (Table 11.5).
Management is then supplied with the following information:

1. The average number of defects per wheel is slightly more than four.
2. Over a long period of time, each wheel inspected would have between zero and four defects during 997 out of 1000 inspections.

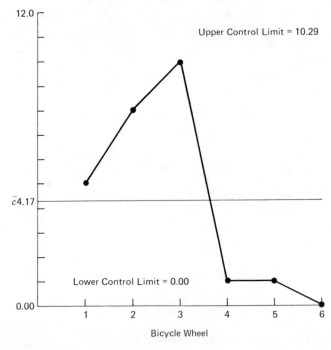

Fig. 11.7 c chart, number of defective spokes per bicycle wheel.

12 Measures of Dispersion and Skewness

We have looked at a frequency distribution and the measures of central tendency—the mean, the median, and the mode. Now we turn our attention to the variation in, or the dispersion of, the data. The dispersion of data gives the reader an idea of how the data are spread out. Absolute and relative measures of dispersion will be presented here, with measures of skewness.

UNGROUPED DATA

Range

Consider the prices Mrs. Smith paid for groceries last week (see Table 12.1). The *range* of prices is from $7.00 - $0.39, or $6.61—very simply, it is the difference between the highest and the lowest values.

Two different sets of data might have the same measure of central tendency but a different spread. Consider, for example, the results of an IQ test given to two separate groups of high-school students. The students at High School A have a mean IQ of 100, as do those at High School B. Further investigation reveals the range in High School A to be 110 - 90.0, or 10.0, while in High School B the range is 120.0 - 70.0, or 50.0. Thus, there is a greater dispersion of scores in High School B. Also, the mean IQ of 100.0 is more representative of High School A.

Average Deviation

The average deviation indicates by how much each value differs from the mean of the sample of the population. Deviations from the median are also used. The formula is:

$$\text{A.D.} = \frac{\Sigma |X - \overline{X}|}{n} \text{ or } \frac{\Sigma |X - \text{median}|}{n}$$

Table 12.1. Prices Mrs. Smith Paid for Groceries.

Item	Price
Butter, lb	$1.49
Coffee, lb	2.99
Roast, 4 lb	7.00
Tomatoes, can	0.39
Chicken, whole	1.85
Milk, half-gallon	1.20
Bread, loaf	0.50
Pizza, frozen	1.69
Eggs, 12	0.89
Dog food, 6 cans	2.00
Ice cream, gallon	1.45

Table 12.2. Average Deviation Based on Mrs. Smith's Grocery Bill.

Price (X)	X = Median
$0.39	−5
0.50	−4
0.89	−3
1.20	−2
1.45	−1
1.49	0
1.69	+1
1.85	+2
2.00	+3
2.99	+4
7.00	+5
	30

Table 12.3. Sample Variance: Weights of Spoonville YMCA Basketball Players.

Weight (X)	Weight–Mean $(X - \bar{X})$	$(Weight - Mean)^2$ $(X - \bar{X})^2$
170	−30	900
170	−30	900
175	−25	625
180	−20	400
200	0	0
200	0	0
200	0	0
210	+10	100
220	+20	400
230	+30	900
245	+45	2025
Total	0	6250

In the above formula, the symbol "/   /" indicates that when the differences from the median are calculated, the plus and minus signs are ignored.

Using the data from Table 12.1, Table 12.2 is constructed. Note that in Table 12.2, the total equals 30. We have disregarded the plus and minus signs. The average deviation is determined as follows:

1. Place the data in ascending order.
2. Locate the median.
3. Calculate the differences from the median.
4. Total the absolute differences, disregarding plus or minus signs.
5. Divide the absolute value by the total number of items to calculate the average deviation:

$$\text{A.D.} = \frac{|X - X|}{n}$$

$$= \frac{30}{11} = 2.7273$$

Suppose Mrs. Smith had chosen a different basket of groceries, for which the average deviation was 1.22. The average price of the second basket of groceries would be more representative than the first basket because the average deviation is smaller. Also, the smaller average deviation indicates that there is less variation of prices in the second basket.

Variance of a Sample. The YMCA in Spoonville recruits male basketball players for its winter league. Each player must undergo a physical examination, which includes being weighed. Table 12.3 shows the weights of 11 of the players. To compute the variance, the mean (in this case, 200) is found and designated as 0. The variances from the mean are then computed and squared. Then the sum of the squares is divided by the number in the sample. This is done according to the following formula for the variance of a sample taken from a population:

$$s^2 = \frac{\Sigma(X - \bar{X})^2}{n}$$

where

$$s^2 = \text{sample variance}$$

$$X = \text{values of sample}$$

$$\bar{X} = \text{arithmetic mean of sample}$$

$$n = \text{number in sample}$$

Table 12.4. Computation Sample Variance: Squaring Values of Weights of Spoonville YMCA Basketball Players.

	Weights (X)	Weights Squared (X^2)
	170	28,900
	170	28,900
	175	30,625
	180	32,400
	200	40,000
	200	40,000
	200	40,000
	210	44,100
	220	48,400
	230	52,900
	245	60,025
Total	2,200	446,250

Taking the information from Table 12.3, the variance would be:

$$s^2 = \frac{6250}{11}$$

$$= 568.18$$

The formula for the variance of a population is as follows:

$$\mu^2 = \frac{(X - \bar{X})^2}{N}$$

where

X = population values

μ = population mean

N = number of observations in the population

This method for the computation of the sample variance is used where the numbers are small as well as where the mean is a whole number. If the observations in the sample are large and the mean is not a whole number, the values for X

(sample values) are squared. (See Table 12.4.) The formula for computing the variance is then:

$$s^2 = \frac{\Sigma X^2}{n} - \left(\frac{\Sigma X}{n}\right)^2$$

$$= \frac{446{,}250}{11} - \left(\frac{2200}{11}\right)^2$$

$$= 40{,}568.18 - 40{,}000.00$$

$$= 568.18$$

Reference to Appendix G, squares and square roots, makes the preceding calculations easier.

GROUPED DATA

Range

Table 12.5 shows a frequency distribution of the incomes of male employees of RSD Company in 1979. The range may be grouped from the frequency distribution as follows:

1. Subtract the value of the lower limit of the lowest class value from the value of the upper limit of the highest class value ($35,000 - $5000 = $30,000).
2. Assume that the midpoint is more representative of the highest and lowest classes. In this case, the range would be $32,500 - $7500 = $25,000.

Table 12.5. Range of Grouped Data, 1979 Annual Income, Male Employees of RSD Company.

Annual Income ($ Thousands)	No. Male Employees
$ 5 up to $10	2
10 up to 15	5
15 up to 20	10
20 up to 25	5
25 up to 30	3
30 up to 35	1

Quartile Deviation

The quartile deviation covers the distance of the middle 50% of the cases in a frequency distribution. It is determined as follows, using data from Table 12.6:

1. Compute the first quartile, the point below which 25% of the frequencies occur:
   a. Locate the first quartile of observations:

$$\frac{26}{4} = 6.5$$

   b. Using the following list, locate the class in the frequency distribution where the first quartile (6.5) is located.

Annual Income ($ Thousands)	Cumulative Frequency
$ 5 up to $10	2
10 up to 15	7

We wish to locate the value of 6.5 for the quartile deviation in the frequency distribution. The second column of Table 12.6 shows the cumulative frequencies to be 7 for the class interval of $10,000 up to $15,000. Since 6.5 is below this, we have to interpolate; 6.5 - 2.0 = 4.5. The class interval is $5,000, so 4.5 × 5000 = $4500. When the $4500 is added to the lower class limit of $10,000, we obtain a first quartile deviation of $14,500.

Table 12.6. Determination Quartile Deviation, 1979 Annual Income of Male Employees of RSD Company.

Annual Income ($ Thousands)	No. Male Employees (f)	Cumulative Frequencies (CF)
$ 5 up to $10	2	2
10 up to 15	5	7
15 up to 20	10	17
20 up to 25	5	22
25 up to 30	3	25
30 up to 35	1	26
	26	

The following formula may also be used to compute the first quartile.

$$Q_1 = \left[\frac{L + (n/4) - CF}{f}(i)\right]$$

where

L = lower limit class containing first quartile

n = total number of frequencies

CF = cumulative frequencies immediately prior to the class containing the first quartile

f = frequency of the class containing the first quartile

i = interval of the class of the first quartile

Taking the following information from Table 12.6,

$$Q_1 = \$10,000 + \left[\frac{26/4 - 2}{5}(\$5000)\right]$$

$$= \$10,000 + \left[\frac{4.5}{5}(\$5000)\right]$$

$$= \$14,500$$

2. Locate the third quartile, the point *above* which 25% of the frequencies occur. Then use the following formula: (26 X .75 = 19.5 located in class $20,000 up to $25,000).

$$Q_3 = L + \frac{(3n/4) - CF}{f}(i)$$

$$= \$20,000 + \left(\frac{\{[(3)\,26]/4\} - 17}{5}(\$5000)\right)$$

$$= \$20,000 + \left[\frac{19.5 - 17}{5}(\$5000)\right]$$

$$= \$20,000 + \$2500$$

$$= \$22,500$$

3. Determine quartile deviation:

$$Q.D. = \frac{Q_3 - Q_1}{2}$$

$$= \frac{\$22,500 - 14,500}{2}$$

$$= \$4000$$

Relationships Between Quartiles

The relationships between quartiles vary depending on the shape of the distribution.

Symmetrical Distribution. If the distribution is symmetrical (normal curve), then the distance between quartiles is as follows:

$$Q_1 - Q_2 = Q_2 - Q_3$$

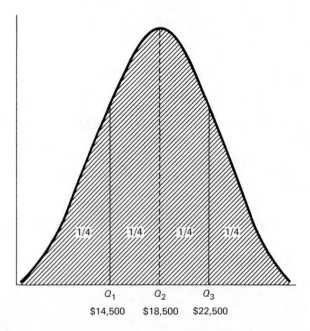

Fig. 12.1 Location of quartiles in a symmetrical distribution of 1979 annual earnings of male employees of RSD Company.

Table 12.7. Determination of Quartiles in a Positively Skewed Distribution.

Miles per Gallon	No. Cars (in Thousands) (f)	Cumulative Frequency (CF)
5 up to 10	2	2
10 up to 15	4	6
15 up to 20	15	21
20 up to 25	7	28
25 up to 30	4	32
30 up to 35	2	34
	34	

If the quartile deviation (Q.D.) is subtracted from the median (Q_2), the first quartile (Q_1) will result. Conversely, if it is added to the median, the answer will be the third quartile (Q_3). So,

$$Q_1 \text{ and } Q_3 = \text{Median} \pm \text{Quartile deviation}$$

or $18,500 - 4000 = 14,500$ while $18,500 + 4000 = 22,500$. Q_1, Q_2, and Q_3 divide a normal curve into four parts (see Figure 12.1).

Positive Skewness.   If the distribution is positively skewed (to the left), then:

$$Q_2 - Q_1 < Q_3 - Q_2$$

Consider a test conducted by a federal agency to determine the fuel efficiency in miles per gallon of a 1981 automobile. (see Table 12.7). The first quartile is:

$$Q = L + \left[\frac{(n/4) - CF}{f} \ (i) \right]$$

$$= 15 + \left[\frac{(34/4) - 6}{15} \ (5) \right]$$

$$= 15 + \left[\frac{8.5 - 6}{15} \ (5) \right]$$

$$= 15 + \left[\frac{2.5}{15} \ (5) \right]$$

$$= 15.8333$$

The median,

$$Q_2 = \left[L + \frac{(n/2) - CF}{f} (i) \right]$$

is

$$\text{Median } (Q_2) = L + \left[\frac{(n/2) - CF}{f} (i) \right]$$

$$= 15 + \left[\frac{(34/2) - 6}{15} (5) \right]$$

$$= 15 + \left[\frac{(11/15)}{15} (5) \right]$$

$$= 18.667$$

$$\text{Third Quartile } (Q_3) = L + \left[\frac{(3n/4) - CF}{f} (i) \right]$$

$$= 20 + \left[\frac{3(34/4) - 21}{7} (5) \right]$$

$$= 20 + \left[\frac{25.5 - 21}{7} (5) \right]$$

$$= 20 + 3.214$$

$$= 23.214$$

$Q_2 - Q_1 = 18.667 - 15.833 = 2.834$, the distance between Q_1 and Q_2

$Q_3 - Q_2 = 23.214 - 18.667 = 4.547$, the distance between Q_2 and Q_3

Negative Skewness. In a negatively skewed distribution (skewed to the left), the distance between Q_1 and Q_2 and between Q_2 and Q_3 is as follows:

$$Q_2 - Q_1 > Q_3 - Q_2$$

Suppose the same federal agency tested 1981 cars for fuel efficiency and obtained the results shown in Table 12.8. It can be seen that the frequencies per class are greater in the last three classes. Hence the distribution is skewed to the right— that is, negatively skewed.

Table 12.8. Determination of Quartiles in a Negatively Skewed Distribution.

Miles per Gallon	No. Cars (in Thousands) (f)	Cumulative Frequency (CF)
5 up to 10	2	2
10 up to 15	4	6
15 up to 20	6	12
20 up to 25	10	22
25 up to 30	15	37
30 up to 35	8	45
	45	

The formulas for the quartiles and the computations in a negatively skewed distribution follow:

$$\text{First quartile } (Q_1) = L + \left[\frac{(n/4) - CF}{f} (i) \right]$$

$$= 15 + \left[\frac{(45/4) - 6}{6} (5) \right]$$

$$= 15 + \left[\frac{11.25 - 6}{6} (5) \right]$$

$$= 15 + 4.375$$

$$= 19.38$$

$$\text{Median } (Q_2) = L + \left[\frac{(n/2) - CF}{f} (i) \right]$$

$$= 25 + \left[\frac{(45/2) - 22}{10} (5) \right]$$

$$= 25 + \left[\frac{22.5 - 22}{10} (5) \right]$$

$$= 25 + 0.25$$

$$= 25.25$$

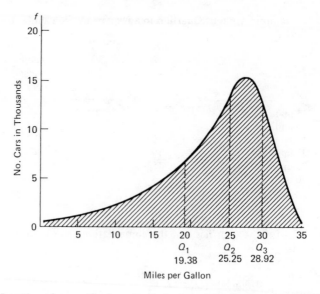

Fig. 12.2 Location of a quartiles in a negatively skewed distribution of 1981 cars tested for fuel efficiency.

$$\text{Third quartile } (Q_3) = L + \frac{(3n/4) - CF}{f} \quad (i)$$

$$= 25 + \left[\frac{[3(45)/4] - 22}{15} \quad (5) \right]$$

$$= 25 + \left[\frac{33.75 - 22}{15} \quad (5) \right]$$

$$= 25 + 3.917$$

$$= 28.917$$

$$Q_2 - Q_1 = 25.25 - 19.38 = 5.87$$

$$Q_3 - Q_2 = 28.92 - 25.25 = 3.67$$

Figure 12.2 shows the three quartiles based on the preceding frequency distribution.

Table 12.9. Determination of a Quartile Deviation in an Open-Distribution.

Miles per Gallon	No. Cars (in Thousands) f
Under 10	2
10 up to 15	4
15 up to 20	6
20 up to 25	10
25 up to 30	15
30 and over	8

The quartile deviation can be used with open-end distributions and with those distributions that have unequal class intervals. However, the quartile deviation has one weakness not affected by extreme variations. Note that Table 12.9 is an open-end distribution. Since the quartile deviation is based on Q_1 and Q_3, (two definite values) it would remain the same whether the miles per gallon were 30 or 300.

Deciles and Percentiles

Deciles and percentiles may be found in the same manner as quartiles. The first quartile is the 25th percentile, the second quartile is the 50th percentile, and the third quartile is the 75th percentile.

Using the data in Table 12.7, the third decile can be computed as follows:

$$D_3 = L + \left[\frac{(3n/10) - CF}{f} (i) \right]$$

$$= 15 + \left[\frac{\{[3(34)]/10\} - 6}{15} (5) \right]$$

$$= 15 + 1.4$$

$$= 16.4$$

Thus, 30% of the cars tested got less than 16.4 mpg.

Using the data in Table 12.7, the 72nd percentile would be computed as follows:

$$P_{72} = L + \left[\frac{\{[72(n)]/100\} - CF}{f} (i) \right]$$

$$= 20 + \left[\frac{\{[72(34)]/100\} - 21}{20} (5) \right]$$

$$= 20 + \left[\frac{24.48 - 21}{20} (5) \right]$$

$$= 20 + 0.87$$

$$= 20.87$$

A total of 72% of the cars tested got less than 20.87 mpg.

Average Deviation

The formula for the average deviation in group data is:

$$\text{A.D.} = \frac{\Sigma f |X - \bar{X}|}{n}$$

where

X = midpoint of each class

$\bar{X}$ = arithmetic mean

f = observations in each class

n = total number of observations

Since it is used infrequently, the calculation will not be shown. Instead, more widely used measures—the variance and standard deviation—will be emphasized.

Variance and Standard Deviation

The standard deviation is a unit of measurement that shows the variation in the population. The variance is based on deviations from the mean. Using data from Table 12.10, the standard deviation is computed as follows:

1. Determine the midpoints (X) of the classes.
2. Square each midpoint (X^2).

Table 12.10. Standard Deviation, Grouped Data.

Miles per Gallon	No. Cars (in Thousands) (f)	Midpoints (X)	Midpoint Squared (X²)	Frequency × Midpoint Squared (fX²)	Frequency × Midpoint (fX)
5 up to 10	2	7.5	56.25	112.50	15.0
10 up to 15	4	12.5	156.25	625.00	50.0
15 up to 20	15	17.5	306.25	4,593.75	262.5
20 up to 25	7	22.5	506.25	3,543.75	157.5
25 up to 30	4	27.5	756.25	3,025.00	110.0
30 up to 35	2	32.5	1,056.25	2,112.50	65.0
	34			14,012.50	660.0

3. Multiply each squared midpoint by the frequency (f) in each class (fX^2).
4. Total all fX^2.
5. Multiply the frequency times the midpoint (fX).
6. Compute the standard deviation using the following formula:

$$s = \sqrt{\frac{\Sigma fX^2}{n} - \left(\frac{fX}{n}\right)^2}$$

$$= \sqrt{\frac{14012.5}{34} - \left(\frac{660}{34}\right)^2}$$

$$= \sqrt{412.1324 - 376.8166}$$

$$= \sqrt{35.3158}$$

$$= 5.942$$

To eliminate some of the calculations, particularly where there are large numbers in each class and the midpoints are large numbers, the *coded* method is used. Steps in the coded method calculation are:

1. Substitute class deviations (d) for midpoints. Normally the class with the greatest number of frequencies (f) is designated zero (class of origin). However, any class may be chosen.
2. Multiply the frequency in each class by the deviation for each class (fd). Add the results.
3. Multiply $f \times fd$, which yields f^2d. Add the results.
4. Apply the formula for the coded method:

$$s = i \sqrt{\frac{\Sigma fd}{n}^2 - \left(\frac{\Sigma fd}{n}\right)^2}$$

Table 12.11 shows the information needed to compute the standard deviation using the coded method and the above formula.

$$s = 5 \sqrt{\frac{53}{34} - \left(\frac{+13}{34}\right)^2}$$

$$= 5 \sqrt{\frac{53}{34} - \frac{169}{1156}}$$

Table 12.11. Standard Deviation of Grouped Data, Coded Method.

Gas (mpg)	f	d	fd	fd(d)
5 up to 10	2	−2	−4	8
10 up to 15	4	−1	−4	4
15 up to 20	15	0	0	0
20 up to 25	7	+1	+7	7
25 up to 30	4	+2	+8	16
30 up to 35	2	+3	+6	18
	34		+13	53

$$= 5 \sqrt{1.5588 - 0.1462}$$

$$= 5 \sqrt{1.4126}$$

$$= 5(1.1885)$$

$$= 5.942$$

Uses of Standard Deviation. The standard deviation is a unit of measurement that shows the variation in a population. It serves as a common denominator for judging the representativeness of two means from samples of two comparable populations. In addition, the standard deviation signifies the homogeneity of a distribution. Thus, if a sample or population has two means about equal with the data expressed in the same units, then the smaller of the two standard deviations comes from the more homogeneous distribution. The larger of the two standard deviations comes from a distribution that is more spread out; therefore, it is not so homogeneous.

Relationship of the Standard Deviation to the Mean in a Normal Distribution. The relationship of the probability distributions was discussed in Chapter 10. However, we will briefly touch on them here.

1. The mean divides the *normal* distribution into two equal parts. Fifty percent of the observations are below the mean and 50% are above the mean.
2. In a normal distribution, there is a definite relationship between the mean and the standard deviation, as shown in the following table.

Observations (%)	No. Standard Deviations from Mean
68.3	$\pm 1 \, \sigma$
95.5	$\pm 2 \, \sigma$
99.7	$\pm 3 \, \sigma$

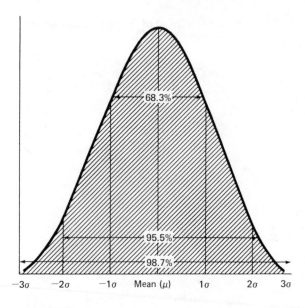

Fig. 12.3 Relationship between mean and standard deviation in a normal distribution.

Figure 12.3 shows this relationship. As can be seen, approximately 68.3% of the observations fall within $\pm1\sigma$ from the mean, 95.5% within $\pm2\sigma$, and 99.7% within $\pm3\sigma$.

Relative Measures of Dispersion. Two standard deviations from *unlike* populations cannot be compared. The absolute measures of dispersion must be changed to percents of relative measures. The following relative measures of dispersion are computed based on the data in Table 12.12.

1. Coefficient of variation

$$\frac{s}{\overline{\overline{X}}}(100)$$

where

$$s = \text{standard deviation of the sample}$$

$$\overline{X} = \text{mean of the sample}$$

2. Average deviation

$$\frac{\text{A.D.}}{\overline{X}}(100)$$

Table 12.12. Relative Measures of Dispersion of 1979 Annual Income of Male Employees of RSD Co.

Annual Income	No. Male Employees (f)	Midpoint of Class (X)	fX	Class Deviation (d)	fd	fd(d)	X - $\bar{X}$
$ 5 up to $10	2	7.5	$ 15.0	-2	-4	8	-10.96
10 up to 15	5	12.5	62.5	-1	-5	5	- 5.96
15 up to 20	10	17.5	175.0	0	0	0	- 0.96
20 up to 25	5	22.5	112.5	+1	+5	5	+ 4.04
25 up to 30	3	27.5	82.5	+2	+6	12	+ 9.04
30 up to 35	1	32.5	32.5	+3	+3	9	+14.04
Total	26		$480.0		+5	39	+ 9.24

where

A.D. = average deviation of the sample

$\overline{X}$ = mean of the sample

3. Range

$$\frac{\text{Range}}{\overline{X}}(100)$$

where

Range = range of the sample

$\overline{X}$ = mean of the sample

4. Quartile Deviation

$$\frac{\text{Q.D.}}{\text{Median}}(100)$$

where

Q.D. = quartile deviation of the sample

Median = median of the sample

5. First and Third Quartile of Sample

$$\frac{Q_3 - Q_1}{Q_3 + Q_1}(100)$$

where

Q_3 = third quartile of the sample

Q_1 = first quartile of the sample

Calculations:

$$1. \text{ Mean} = X = \frac{\Sigma fX}{n} = \frac{480}{26} = \$18.46$$

2. Standard-deviation coded method

$$s = i \sqrt{\frac{\Sigma fd^2}{n} - \left(\frac{\Sigma fd}{n}\right)^2}$$

$$= 5 \sqrt{\left(\frac{39}{26}\right) - \left(\frac{5}{26}\right)^2}$$

$$= 5 \sqrt{\left(\frac{39}{26}\right) - \left(\frac{25}{676}\right)}$$

$$= 5 \sqrt{(1.50 - 0.0369)}$$

$$= 5 \sqrt{(1.4631)}$$

$$= (1.2096)$$

$$= 6.05$$

3. Coefficient of variation

$$= \frac{s}{\overline{X}} (100)$$

$$= \frac{6.05}{18.46} (100)$$

$$= 32.8\%$$

4. Average deviation (A.D.) $= \dfrac{f|X - X|}{n}$

$$= \frac{26|9.24|}{26}$$

$$= \frac{240.24}{26}$$

$$= \$9.24$$

Then,

$$\frac{\text{A.D.}}{\bar{X}}(100)$$

$$= \frac{\$9.24}{18.46}(100)$$

$$= 50.0$$

5. Range (use midpoints of the highest and lowest classes, together with the mean of the sample):

$$= \$32.5 - 7.5 = \frac{\$25.00}{18.46}(100)$$

$$= 135.43$$

6. $\dfrac{\text{Q.D.}}{\text{Median}}(100)$

a. As previously computed under discussion on quartile deviation, the quartile deviation is $4000 and the median is $18,500.

b. $\dfrac{4000}{18,500}(100) = 21.6$

7. $\dfrac{Q_3 - Q_1}{Q_3 + Q_1}(100)$

a. As previously computed, $Q_3 = \$22,500$ and $Q_1 = \$14,500$.

b. $\dfrac{Q_3 - Q_1}{Q_3 + Q_1} = \dfrac{22,500 - 14,500}{22,500 + 14,500}$

$$= \frac{8000}{37,000}(100)$$

$$= 0.2162(100)$$

$$= 21.62$$

Uses of the Coefficient of Variation

Two Unlike Frequency Distributions. Suppose we want to compare the mpg rating of a group of eight-cylinder Cadillacs with the mpg rating of a group of four-cylinder Mazdas that have been tested on the highway under normal driving conditions. Results showed that the mean mpg rating is 10 for the Cadillacs and 36 for the Mazdas. Similarly, the standard deviation is 1 for the Cadillacs and 6 for the Mazdas. The coefficients of variation follow.

$$\text{For Cadillacs, C.V.} = \frac{s}{\overline{X}}(100) = (1/10)(100), \text{ or } 10.0\%$$

$$\text{For Mazdas, C.V.} = \frac{s}{\overline{X}}(100) = (6/36)(100), \text{ or } 16.7\%$$

Since the standard deviation is higher for the Mazdas, there is more dispersion in that distribution. The mean of 10 mpg is more representative of the Cadillacs than is the 36 mpg in the Mazda group.

Comparison of Two Distributions in Unlike Units. Suppose we want to compare the dispersion in a distribution of mpg ratings of Cadillacs to a corresponding distribution of the ages of the vehicles. The mean mpg is again 10, and the standard deviation is 1; the mean age of the Cadillacs is 5 years, and the standard deviation is 1. The coefficients of variation are:

$$\text{Miles per gallon} = \frac{s}{\overline{X}}(100) = (1/10)(100), \text{ or } 10.0\%$$

$$\text{Age of vehicle} = \frac{s}{\overline{X}}(100) = (1/5)(100), \text{ or } 20.0\%$$

There is more dispersion in the vehicle-age distribution since the coefficient of variation (20.0%) is twice as large as the coefficient for mpg rating (10.0%).

COEFFICIENT OF SKEWNESS

In a normal distribution, the mean, the median, and the mode are equal. When extreme observations are added, the mean is influenced more than the median or mode. The distribution is positively skewed if the frequencies are extremely large, thus making the mean larger than the median or the mode. If the values are extremely low, then the mean becomes less than the median and mode, and the distribution is negatively skewed. The coefficient of skewness measures the direction and the amount of skewness according to the following formula:

$$Sk = \frac{3\,(\overline{X} - \text{Median})}{s}$$

In a distribution where the mean is 100, the median is 105, the mode is 107, and the standard deviation is 10, the coefficient of skewness is determined as follows:

$$Sk = \frac{3\,(\overline{X} - \text{Median})}{s}$$

$$= \frac{3\,(100 - 105)}{10}$$

$$= \frac{3\,(-5)}{10}$$

$$= \frac{-15}{10}$$

$$= -1.50$$

The coefficient of skewness falls between ±3. If the preceding distribution was compared with one having a coefficient of skewness of -0.10, it could be concluded that the first distribution was more negatively skewed than the second.

13 Simple Regression and Correlation Analysis

High-school seniors take college entrance examinations, potential insurance sales-people must pass an interest test, tests are given to would-be computer program-mers, and so on. Such tests are supposed to indicate a person's potential for success or failure in a particular endeavor. An attempt is made to predict one dependent variable (i.e., success or failure) on the basis of independent variable (i.e., regression analysis).

SIMPLE REGRESSION

In simple regression analysis, two variables are used—dependent and independent. Suppose the DEF Insurance Company attempts to predict the computer pro-gramming ability of job applicants by giving them a test. In order to check the validity of the test, it randomly selects five members of its present computer pro-gramming staff to take the test and correlates the test scores with annual earn-ings. There are 85 questions, and the passing score is 50 (see Table 13.1).

Scatter Diagram

DEF's personnel director prepares a scatter diagram, which shows graphically the relationships of paired data. The dependent variable (annual earnings) is always placed on the Y-axis, while the independent variable (test scores) is placed on the X-axis (see Figure 13.1). The scatter diagram reveals the following:

1. As computer test scores increase, so do annual earnings.
2. The dots seem to follow a straight line, indicating linear trend.

Table 13.1. Computer Test Scores and Annual Earnings of Five Employees of DEF Insurance Company.

Employee	Test Score	Annual Earnings
A	52	$13,000
B	57	14,000
C	60	16,000
D	65	18,000
E	68	19,000

Regression Equation

To predict the values of Y (dependent variable) based on the values of X (independent variable), one of two methods may be used:

1. *Freehand.* In the freehand method, a ruler or straightedge is used in drawing a line through the middle of the dots. Approximately the same number of dots are above and below the line. The freehand method has one disadvantage—namely, the line is drawn through the middle of the data based on the judgment

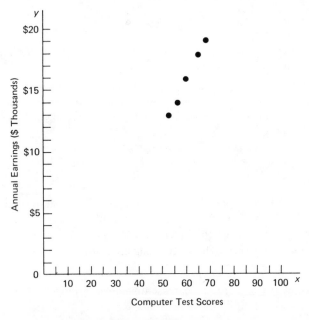

Fig. 13.1 Scatter diagram: relationship between test scores and annual earnings.

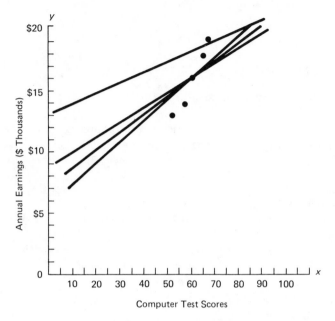

Fig. 13.2 Scatter diagram: freehand lines drawn through dots in regression plane.

of the person drawing it. Four different people could draw four different lines, and each line would give a different prediction (see Figure 13.2).

2. *Least squares method.* The least squares method is a mathematical method designed to produce the "best fitting" straight line, based on the fact that it minimizes the sum of the squares of the vertical deviations about the line.

Table 13.2 shows the necessary steps to solve the regression equation of:

$$\overline{Y}_p = a + bX$$

Table 13.2. Data for Least Squares Regression, DEF Insurance Company.

Employee	Annual Earnings ($ Thousands) (Y)	Test Score (X)	X^2	XY	Y^2
A	13	52	2704	676	169
B	14	57	3249	798	196
C	16	60	3600	960	256
D	18	65	4225	1170	324
E	19	68	4624	1292	361
	80	302	18402	4896	1306

where

$$\overline{Y}_p = \text{average predicted value of } Y \text{ based on given } X \text{ value}$$

$$a = \text{estimated value of } Y \text{ when } X = 0$$

$$X = \text{any value independent variable selected } (X)$$

and b describes the slope of the regression line or the average change that occurs in $\overline{Y}_p$ with each change of ± 1 in the independent variable. Following are the calculations necessary to compute the "best fitting" line per the least squares method:

1. Square independent variable (X) values: X^2.
2. Multiply independent variable (X) by dependent variable (Y): XY.
3. Square dependent variable (Y): Y^2.
4. Determine regression line by:
   a. Solving the following two equations simultaneously:
      (1) Equation 1 = $\Sigma Y = na + b\Sigma X$
          Equation 2 = $\Sigma XY = a\Sigma X + b\Sigma X^2$
      (2) Equation 1 = $80 = 5a + 302b$
          Equation 2 = $4896 = 302a + 18402b$
      (3) Multiply Equation 1 by 60.4: $4832 = 302a + 18240.8b$
          Multiply Equation 2 by 1.0: $4896 - 302a + 18402.0b$
      (4) Subtract Equation 2 from Equation 1:

$$4832 = 302a + 18240.8b$$

$$-4896 = 302a + 18402.0b$$

$$-64 = -161.2b$$

$$b = 0.397 \text{ or } 0.4$$

   (5) Solve for a in Equation 1 by using the value of b.

$$\text{Equation 1: } 80 = 5a + 302b$$

$$80 = 5a + [302\,(0.4)]$$

$$80 = 5a + 120.8$$

$$-40.8 = 5a$$

$$a = -8.16$$

The regression equation becomes $\overline{Y}_p = -8.16 + 0.4X$.

b. Solving for a and b using following formulas, thus avoiding the necessity of solving two equations simultaneously:

$$b = \frac{n\,(\Sigma XY) - [(\Sigma X)\,(\Sigma Y)]}{n\,(\Sigma X^2) - (\Sigma X)^2}$$

$$a = \frac{\Sigma Y}{n} - b\,\frac{\Sigma X}{n} \text{ or } \overline{Y} - b\overline{X}$$

(1) Use the information in Table 13.2, and solve for b and a:

$$b = \frac{n\,(\Sigma XY) - [(\Sigma X)\,(\Sigma Y)]}{\text{n}\,(\Sigma X^2) - (\Sigma X)^2}$$

$$= \frac{5\,(4896) - [(302)\,(80)]}{5\,(18402) - (302)^2}$$

$$= \frac{24480 - 24160}{92010 - 91204}$$

$$= \frac{320}{806}$$

$$= 0.397 \text{ or } 0.4$$

$$a = \overline{Y} - b\overline{X}$$

$$= \frac{80}{5} - \left[(0.4)\,\frac{302}{5}\right]$$

$$= 16 - 24.16$$

$$= -8.16$$

Various values of X can be placed in the least squares equation, $\overline{Y}_p = -8.16 + 0.4X$ to determine points on the regression line (see Table 13.3).

Figure 13.3 shows the predicted annual earnings using the regression line equation. Notice that the regression line goes through the averages of X and Y ($\overline{X} = 60.4$ and $\overline{Y} = 16.0$).

Table 13.3. Predicted Annual Earnings Based on the Regression Equation $\overline{Y}_p = -8.16 + 0.4\,x$.

When Computer Programming Test Score Is	Y_p Predicted Annual Earnings ($ Thousands)	Solution
52	12.64	$\overline{Y}_p = -8.16 + 0.4\ (52)$
57	14.64	$\overline{Y}_p = -8.16 + 0.4\ (57)$
60	15.84	$\overline{Y}_p = -8.16 + 0.4\ (60)$
65	17.84	$\overline{Y}_p = -8.16 + 0.4\ (65)$
68	19.04	$\overline{Y}_p = -8.16 + 0.4\ (68)$

Standard Error of Estimate

From Figure 13.3, it can be seen that there is some error in the regression line estimate because all points do not fall on the line. If they did, we would have had a perfect prediction, which, in the real world, is hard to achieve. The standard error of estimate $(S_{y.x})$ measures the accuracy of the forecasted value of Y based on X.

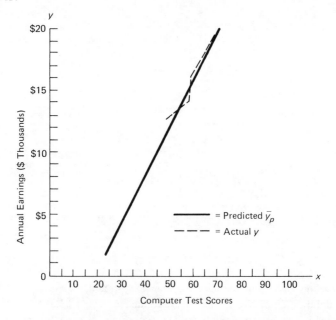

Fig. 13.3 Scatlter diagram: freehand line drawn through dots in regression plane based on regression equation $Y_p = -8.16 + 0.4x$.

The steps used in computing the standard error of estimate are:

1. Use formula for standard error of estimate:

$$S_{y.x} = \sqrt{\frac{\Sigma(Y - \bar{Y}_p)^2}{n - 2}}$$

This is the standard deviation of dependent variable values (Y's) based on independent variable values (X's).
2. Determine each forecasted value of $Y(\bar{Y}_p)$ based on each value of X.
3. Subtract the predicted value of $Y(\bar{Y}_p)$ from the actual Y value.
4. Square $Y - \bar{Y}_p$ and compute the total.

The following computation of $s_{y.x}$ is based on the data in Table 13.4.

$$1 - s_{y.x} \equiv \sqrt{\frac{\Sigma(Y - \bar{Y}_p)^2}{n - 2}}$$

$$= \sqrt{\frac{0.5920}{5 - 2}}$$

$$= \sqrt{0.1973333}$$

$$= 0.44418$$

Annual earnings on Table 13.4 are in thousands of dollars. Thus, 0.44418 becomes $444.

Table 13.4. Standard Error of Estimate Calculation.

| Employee | Test Score (X) | Annual Earnings ($ Thousands) | | $Y - \bar{Y}_p$ | $(Y - \bar{Y}_p)^2$ |
		Actual (Y)	Predicted ($\bar{Y}_p$)		
A	52	13	12.64	+0.36	0.1296
B	57	14	14.64	-0.64	0.4096
C	60	16	15.84	+0.16	0.0256
D	65	18	17.84	+0.16	0.0256
E	68	19	19.04	-0.04	0.0016
	302	$80	$80.00	0	0.5920

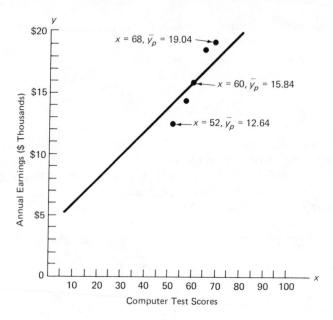

Fig. 13.4 Sum of vertical deviations about regression line.

The values in the column headed $Y - \bar{Y}_p$ in Table 13.4 are actually the vertical deviations from the regression line (see Figure 13.4). A good check on how well the values of Y are being predicted on the basis of X values is if the sum of $Y - \bar{Y}_p$ equals zero.

CONFIDENCE LIMITS—PREDICTED VALUE OF Y_p

1. *Large sample (approximately 1000).* If the dots are normally distributed about the regression line, the standard error of estimate may be used to predict the value of $Y(\bar{Y}_p)$ with the following confidence limits.

$s_{y.x}$	% of Dots Around Regression Line
±1.00	68.0
±1.96	95.0
±3.00	99.7

If $\bar{Y}_p$ (predicted value of Y) = $17,840 and X = 65, then the confidence limits at the 95% level would be $17,840 ± 1.96 ($444) or $16,970 and $18,710.

2. *Small sample.* (Less than 30) The preceding confidence limits are not valid if the sample is small. To alleviate this problem, a correction factor is used. The formula is:

$$\overline{Y}_p \pm t\,(s_{y.x})\sqrt{\frac{1}{n} + \frac{(X - \overline{X})^2}{\Sigma\,(X - \overline{X})^2}}$$

where

$\overline{Y}_p$ = predicted value of Y based on any selected value of X

$s_{y.x}$ = standard error of estimate

t = value of t for three degrees of freedom (df).

n = number of observations in the sample

X = any selected value of X

$\overline{X}$ = mean of X values

The value of t was introduced in the early 1900s by William Gossett (who used the pseudonym Student) to correct for small sample sizes. The larger the size of the sample, the more closely the confidence limits approach $\pm 1.98s$ (where 95% of observations fall). Successively larger samples taken from Appendix H, Student's t Table, show this to be true.

Degrees of Freedom	% (At 5% Level of Significance)
120	1.980
40	2.021
20	2.086
10	2.228
5	2.571
1	12.706

The smaller the size of the sample, the larger the t (correction) factor. Using the information and data concerning the annual earnings predicated on computer-programmer test scores, Table 13.5 has been developed. It should be noted that the column headed $X - \overline{X}$ has been based on $\overline{X}$ value of 60.4 (i.e., $320 \div 5$). Using

Table 13.5. Small Sample—Confidence Limit Calculations.

Employee	Test Score X	Annual Earnings ($ Thousands) Y	$X - \bar{X}$	$(X - \bar{X})^2$
A	52	13	-8.4	70.56
B	57	14	-3.4	11.56
C	60	16	- .4	.16
D	65	18	+4.6	21.16
E	68	19	+7.6	57.76
Total	302		0	161.20

the preceding formula for the predicted value of $Y(\bar{Y}_p) = \$17,840$ (where $X = 65$) with the small sample correction factor, we have:

$$\bar{Y}_p \pm t\,(s_{y.x}) \sqrt{\frac{1}{n} + \frac{(X - \bar{X})^2}{\Sigma\,(X - X)^2}}$$

$$= \$17,840 \pm 3.18\,(\$444) \sqrt{\frac{1}{5} + \frac{(65.0 - 60.4)^2}{161.20}}$$

$$= \$17,840 \pm 3.18\,(\$444) \sqrt{\frac{1}{5} + \frac{21.16}{161.20}}$$

$$= \$17,840 \pm 3.18\,(\$444) \sqrt{0.3312655}$$

$$= \$17,840 \pm 3.18\,(\$444)\,(0.5756)$$

$$+ \$17,027 \text{ and } \$18,653$$

If an applicant scored 65 on the computer-programming test, the company could be 95% certain that his or her annual earnings would be between $17,027 and $18,653.

CONFIDENCE LIMITS: ACTUAL VALUE OF Y

Confidence limits may be set around a particular Y rather than the predicted value of Y. To illustrate, let's take the case of Employee E whose test score is 68 (X value). The formula for the 95% confidence limits would be:

$$\bar{Y}_p \pm t\,(s_{y.x}) \sqrt{1 + \frac{1}{n}\,\frac{(X - \bar{X})^2}{\Sigma\,(X - X)^2}}$$

Note that 1 has been added to the number under the square root. From Table 13.4, we find that actual value of Y to be $19,000:

$$\overline{Y}_p = \$19,040 \pm 3.18\ (\$444)\sqrt{1 + \frac{1}{5} + \frac{(68.0 - 60.4)^2}{161.20}}$$

$$= \$19,040 \pm 3.18\ (\$444)\ \sqrt{1.5583}$$

$$= +19,040 \pm 3.18\ (\$444)\ (1.248)$$

$$+ \$17,278 \text{ and } \$20,802$$

Based on $\overline{Y}_p$ of $19,040 and a test score of 68, it is 95% certain that the annual earnings of Employee E will be between $17,278 and $20,802.

CORRELATION ANALYSIS

The more widely the dots are scattered around the regression line, the less accurate is the predicted value of $Y(\overline{Y}_p)$ based on X. Conversely, the closer the dots cluster around the regression line, the more accurate is the predicted value of $Y(\overline{Y}_p)$ based on the value of X. In fact, if the standard error estimate is zero, then all dots fall on the regression line.

It can therefore be seen that not all of the predicted value of $Y(\overline{Y}_p)$ is due to a change in X. Hence the unexplained variation. Conversely, the amount explained is called the *explained variation*. The explained and unexplained variations are expressed as percents, i.e., 95% of the variation in Y determined by X.

There are three measures used in correlation analysis:

1. The *coefficient of determination* is the proportion of variation in the dependent variable (Y) explained by the independent variable (X). It has a value of zero to one. A coefficient of determination (r^2) of 100 suggests that 100% of the variation in Y is explained by X. An r^2 of 0.10 tells us that X explains little of the variation in Y.

2. The *coefficient of nondetermination* is the proportion of variation in Y that is *not* explained by X.

3. The *coefficient of correlation* measures the degree of relationship between the X and Y variables. Designated by r, it is the square root of the coefficient of determination. It gives a higher degree of correlation between the X and Y variables than does the coefficient of determination. For example, if the coefficient of determination (r^2) is 0.80, then the correlation coefficient ($\sqrt{0.80}$) is 0.89. Therefore, r^2 is more conservative.

The coefficient r can fall between +1.00 and –1.00. There can be perfect positive correlation ($r = +1.00$) between X and Y as well as perfect negative correlation ($r = -1.00$). For example, perfect positive correlation would occur if, as the

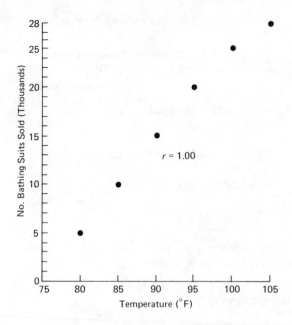

Fig. 13.5 Perfect positive correlation between two variables.

temperature (degrees Fahrenheit) increased, the number of bathing suits sold increased (see Figure 13.5).

Methods of Computation

1. Coefficient of determination
   a. 1 - Coefficient of Nondetermination.
   b. $r^2 = 1 - \dfrac{\text{Unexplained variation}}{\text{Total variation}}$
   c. The coefficient of correlation is squared.
2. Coefficient of nondetermination: $1 - r^2$
3. Coefficient of correlation: $r = \dfrac{n\,(\Sigma XY) - [(\Sigma X)\,(\Sigma Y)]}{\sqrt{[n(\Sigma X^2) - (\Sigma X)^2]\,[n(\Sigma Y^2) - (\Sigma Y)^2]}}$

Computation of Coefficient of Determination. The prior computations on the relationship between the test scores (Y) and annual earnings (X) are used to determine the coefficient of determination below: (See Table 13.2).

$$r = \frac{5\,(4896) - [(302)\,(80)]}{\sqrt{[5\,(18{,}402) - (302)^2]\,[5\,(1306) - (80)^2]}}$$

$$= \frac{24{,}480 - 24{,}160}{\sqrt{[5\,(18{,}402) - (91{,}204)]\,[5\,(1306) - (6400)]}}$$

$$= \frac{320}{\sqrt{[92{,}010 - 91{,}204] \ [6530 - 6400]}}$$

$$= \frac{320}{\sqrt{[806] \ [130]}}$$

$$= \frac{320}{\sqrt{104{,}780}}$$

$$= \frac{320}{323.697}$$

$$= 0.9886$$

Significance of r (Coefficient of Correlation).   The manner in which r is tested for significance depends upon the size of the sample. However, the basic premise of whether or not the paired observations come from a population with zero correlation is the same, regardless of sample size.

Large Samples

Large samples are defined as those where $n = 50$ or more. To test for correlation, the z test is applied. For example, suppose we had a sample with 300 paired observations of X and Y and an r of 0.40. The formula for the z test is:

$$z = \frac{r}{1/\sqrt{n - 1}}$$

$$= \frac{0.40}{1/\sqrt{300 - 1}}$$

$$= \frac{0.40}{1/\sqrt{299}}$$

$$= \frac{0.40}{1/17.29}$$

$$= \frac{0.40}{0.0578}$$

$$= 6.92$$

Two hypotheses are used to determine the significance of the 6.92. The first is called the null hypothesis (H_o) where r in the population is zero. The second is the alternative hypothesis (H_1) where r in the population is significantly different from zero. No statement is made asking if r "more or less than" i.e., direction not stated. Thus, we have a two-tailed test. (Does the value of r fall outside ±1.96 standard deviations at the 0.05 level of significance? This is more fully discussed in Chapter 15.) The null hypothesis is accepted if the computed z value falls within ±1.96 standard deviations at the 0.05 level of significance. The computed value of z is 6.92 which falls outside ±1.96. Therefore, the null hypothesis is rejected. In essence, the relationship between the two sets of variables has a relationship of more than zero at the 0.05 level of significance (see Figure 13.6).

Small Samples

Small samples are those having less than 50 paired observations. The t test is applied to test for the significance of r. Using the computer test scores to predict annual earnings, we have a sample of 5 paired observations with an $r = 0.98$. Is there zero correlation in the population from which the 5 paired observations were taken? The reasoning is:

1. State null (H_o) and alternative (H_1) hypotheses:
   a. H_o = At the 0.05 level of significance, if the computed value of t falls within ±3.182 standard deviations, then r in the population equals zero.
   b. H_1 = At the 0.05 level of significance, if the computed value of t falls outside ±3.182 standard deviations, then r in the population is significantly different from zero.
2. Apply formula for t (again, a two-tailed test), i.e., no direction stated):

$$t = \frac{r\sqrt{n-2}}{\sqrt{1-r^2}} \quad \text{with } n - 2 \text{ degrees of freedom.}$$

$$= \frac{0.98\sqrt{5-2}}{\sqrt{1-(0.98)^2}}$$

$$= \frac{0.98\sqrt{3}}{\sqrt{0.0396}}$$

$$= \frac{1.697}{0.199}$$

$$= 8.528$$

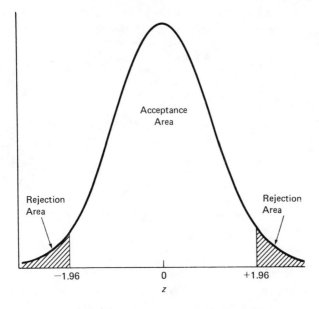

Fig. 13.6 Significance of correlation coefficient, large samples.

3. On the basis of the computed value of t, accept or reject the null hypothesis. Since the computed value of t of 8.528 falls outside the predicted value of 3.182, the null hypothesis is rejected. Therefore, the population from which the five paired observations is drawn is significantly different from zero (see Figure 13.7).

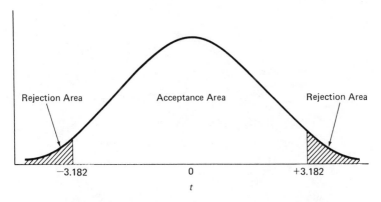

Fig. 13.7 Significance of correlation coefficient, small samples.

Table 13.6. Average Maximum Temperatures and Average Sales of Room Air Conditioners, PQR Distributing Co.

Month	Average Sales Room Air Conditioners 1975-1979 (in Thousands Units) (Y)	Average Maximum Temperatures (°F) (X)
May	3.5	85
June	3.6	88
July	3.8	89
August	4.5	90
September	3.7	88
October	3.6	85

COMPUTER APPLICATION

Suppose PQR Distributing Co. of Miami, Florida, which sells room air conditioners, wants to know if there is any correlation between the average maximum temperature (X) and its average sales (Y). (See Table 13.6). From the computer printout in Figure 13.8, it can be seen that the coefficient of determination (R^2) is 0.5653. Thus, 56.5% of sales of room air conditioners is explained by the temperature variations, and 43.5% is not. The correlation coefficient (the square root of the coefficient of determination) is 0.7518. This is shown in the correlation matrix.

SIMPLE REGRESSION ANALYSIS

```
6 OBSERVATIONS,   2 VARIABLES
RANGE =E/1-E/6

EQUATION:
Y(1)=-7815.503876+132.5581395*X(1)

R-SQUARED              0.5653
ADJUSTED R-SQUARED     0.4566      F-VALUE ( 1,  4) 5.2012
SUM SQUARED RES.   290542.6357     DEGREES OF FREEDOM        4
STD. ERROR OF RES. 269.5100349     DEPENDENT MEAN     3783.3


VARIABLE              COEFFICIENT STD. ERR.  T-STATISTIC    BETA

CONSTANT TERM        -7815.503876 5087.042552-1.536355121
X(1)                  132.5581395 58.12402894 2.280608243   0.75185


CORRELATION MATRIX:

                          1          2

1 X(1)                1.0000
2 Y(1)                0.7518    1.0000
```

Fig. 13.8 Correlation matrix for sales of room air conditioners dependent on average maximum temperatures.

14 Multiple Regression and Correlation Analysis

Annual earnings (the dependent variable) were predicted for computer programmers on the basis of test scores (the independent variable). Using the least squares method to obtain the "best fitting" trend line and the accompanying equation of $\overline{Y}_p = -8.16 + 0.4X$, we were able to forecast the annual earnings based on computer-programming test scores (Table 13.3). To measure the accuracy of the forecasted value of annual earnings (Y-dependent variable) based on test scores (X-independent variable), the standard error of estimate ($s_{y.x}$) of $444 was computed. For example, for Employee A, who scored 52 on the computer-programming test, the predicted annual earnings were $12,640. The significance of the standard error of estimate is that the forecasted annual earnings figure could differ from the actual by either plus or minus $444.

Simple regression uses only one independent variable to predict the dependent variable. However, there can be more than one independent variable that will affect the dependent variable. For example, in addition to using computer-programming test scores to predict annual earnings, we might also use on-the-job performance ratings made by the employees' supervisors. Adding this variable might improve the prediction of annual earnings. The addition of a second independent variable to the computation is called *multiple regression analysis*.

MULTIPLE REGRESSION ANALYSIS

Formula Relationships

In simple regression, the formula is $\overline{Y}_p = a + bX$. Essentially, the predicted value of the dependent variable is based on a given value of the independent variable. The multiple regression formula is merely an extension of the simple regression formula.

Compare:

$$\text{Simple regression} = \overline{Y}_p = a + bX$$

$$\text{Multiple regression} = \overline{Y}_p = a + b_1X_1 + b_2X_2$$

All we have done here is expand the equation to include an additional independent variable. The variable b_1X_1 equates to the first independent variable, while b_2X_2 equates to the second independent variable.

The interpretation of the formula $\overline{Y}_p = a + b_1X_1 + b_2X_2$ is:

1. a is the regression coefficient.
2. b_1X_1 states:
   b_1 = net change in the predicted value of $Y(\overline{Y}_p)$ for each change of one in the first independent variable (X_1), while the second independent variable (X_2) is held constant.
   b_2 = net change in predicted value of $Y(\overline{Y}_p)$ for each change of one in the second independent variable (X_2), while the first independent variable (X_1) is held constant.
3. b_1 and b_2 are normally called *partial regression coefficients* since each one defines the change in the predicted value of $Y(\overline{Y}_p)$ while one of the independent variables is being held constant. For example, b_1 defines the net change in the $\overline{Y}_p$ for each change of one in the first independent variable (X_1) while the second independent variable (X_2) is held constant.

MULTIPLE REGRESSION COMPUTATION

Solving the Equation

In Chapter 13, we found that it was necessary to solve the following two equations simultaneously in simple regression:

$$\Sigma Y = na + b\Sigma X$$

$$\Sigma XY = a\Sigma X + b\Sigma X^2$$

In multiple regression, there are three equations to solve simultaneously:

$$\Sigma Y = na + b_1\Sigma X_1 + b_2\Sigma X_2$$

$$\Sigma X_1 Y = a\Sigma X_1 + b_1\Sigma X_1^2 + b_2 \Sigma X_1 X_2$$

$$\Sigma X_2 Y = a\Sigma X_2 + b_1\Sigma X_1 X_2 + b_2\Sigma X_2^2$$

Table 14.1. Computer Test Scores, Annual Earnings, On-the-Job
Performance Ratings of Five Employees of DEF Insurance Company.

Employee	Annual Earnings ($ Thousands) (Y)	Test Score (X_1)	Performance Rating (X_2)
A	$13	52	85
B	14	57	80
C	16	60	92
D	18	65	90
E	19	68	95
	$80	302	442

Since solving the three normal equations for a, b_1, and b_2 is time-consuming, a shortcut is now used.

Step 1. Eliminate the first equation, which is

$$\Sigma Y = na + b_1 \Sigma X_1 + b_2 \Sigma X_2$$

Step 2. Solve the other two equations (using lower-case letters):

$$\Sigma x_1 y = b_1 \Sigma x_1^2 + b_2 \Sigma x_1 x_2$$

$$\Sigma x_2 y = b_1 \Sigma x_1 x_2 + b_2 \Sigma x_2^2.$$

Step 3. The computer test scores, the annual earnings of five employees of the DEF Insurance Company (Table 13.1), and their on-the-job performance ratings are found in Table 14.1. Table 14.2 gives the information needed to compute the calculations below:

$$n = 5$$

$$\bar{Y} = \$80/5 = \$16$$

$$\bar{X}_1 = 302/5 = 60.4$$

$$\bar{X}_2 = 442/5 = 88.4$$

$$\Sigma x_1 y = \Sigma X_1 Y - n\bar{X}_1 \bar{Y}$$

$$= 4896 - [(5)(60.4)(16)]$$

$$= 4896 - 4832$$

$$= 64$$

$$\Sigma x_1^2 = \Sigma X_1^2 - n\overline{X}_1^2$$

$$= 18{,}402 - [(5)\,(60.4)^2]$$

$$= 18{,}402 - 18{,}240.8$$

$$= 161.2$$

$$\Sigma x_1 x_2 = \Sigma X_1 X_2 - n\overline{X}_1 \overline{X}_2$$

$$= 26{,}810 - [(5)\,(60.4)\,(88.4)]$$

$$= 26{,}810 - 26{,}696.8$$

$$= 113.2$$

$$\Sigma x_2 y = \Sigma X_2 Y - n\overline{X}_2 \overline{Y}$$

$$= 7122 - [(5)\,(88.4)\,(16)]$$

$$= 7122 - 7072$$

$$= 50$$

$$\Sigma x_2^2 = \Sigma X_2^2 - n\overline{X}_2^2$$

$$= 39{,}214 - [(5)\,(88.4)^2]$$

$$= 39{,}214 - 39{,}072.8$$

$$= 141.2$$

$$\Sigma y^2 = \Sigma Y^2 - n\overline{Y}^2$$

$$= 1306 - [(5)\,(16)^2]$$

$$= 1306 - 1280$$

$$= 26$$

Table 14.2. Information for Computing Multiple Regression Equation.

Annual Earnings ($ Thousand) (Y)	Test Score (X_1)	Performance Rating (X_2)
$13	52	85
14	57	80
16	60	92
18	65	90
19	68	95
$80	302	442

X_1Y	X_1^2	X_1X_2
676	2704	4420
798	3249	4560
960	3600	5520
1170	4225	5850
1292	4624	6460
4896	18,402	26,810

X_2Y	X_2^2	Y^2
1105	7225	169
1120	6400	196
1472	8464	256
1620	8100	324
1805	9025	361
7122	39,214	1306

Step 4. Insert the calculations in Step 3 into Equations 1 and 2, and solve for b_2:

Equation 1 = $\Sigma x_1 y = b_1 \Sigma x_1^2 + b_2 \Sigma x_1 x_2$

Equation 2 = $\Sigma x_2 y = b_1 \Sigma x_1 x_2 + b_2 \Sigma x_2^2$

Equation 1 = $64 = 161.2b_1 + 113.2b_2$

Equation 2 = $50 = 113.2b_1 + 141.2b_2$

Multiply Equation 1 by 56.6 and Equation 2 by 80.6:

Equation 1 = $3622.4 = 9123.92b_1 + 6407.12b_2$

Equation 2 = 4030.0 = $9123.92b_1 + 11{,}380.72b_2$

Subtract Equation 1 from Equation 2:

Equation 1 = 3622.4 = $9123.92b_1 + 6407.12b_2$

Equation 2 = -4030.0 = $-9123.92\,b_1 + -11380.72b_2$

$407.6 = 4973.6b_2$

$$b_2 = 0.0819527 \cong 0.08$$

Step 5. Solve for b_1 in Equation 1:

$$64 = 161.2b_1 + 113.2b_2$$

$$64 = 161.2b_1 + 113.2(0.08)$$

$$64 = 161.2b_1 + 9.056$$

$$64 - 9.056 = 161.2b_1$$

$$54.944 = 161.2b_1$$

$$b_1 = 0.34084 \cong 0.34$$

Step 6. Compute constant a.

$$\Sigma Y = na + b_1 \Sigma x_1 + b_2 \Sigma X_2$$

$$80 = 5a + (0.34)(302) + (0.08)(442)$$

$$80 = 5a + 102.68 + 35.36$$

$$80 - 138.04 = 5a$$

$$a = -11.608 \cong -11.61$$

Step 7. Multiple regression equation is:

$$\overline{Y}_p = -11.61 + 0.34\,X_1 + 0.08X_2$$

Alternative Check of b_1 and b_2

To check the calculations of b_1 and b_2, the following alternative method is used:

Step 1.

$$b_1 = \frac{\Sigma x_2^2 \Sigma x_1 y - \Sigma x_1 x_2 \Sigma x_2 y}{\Sigma x_1^2 \Sigma x_2^2 - (\Sigma x_1 x_2)^2}$$

$$= \frac{(141.2)(64) - (113.2)(50)}{(161.2)(141.2) - (113.2)^2}$$

$$= \frac{9036.8 - 5660.0}{22761.44 - 12814.24}$$

$$= \frac{3376.8}{9947.2}$$

$$= 0.33947 = 0.34$$

Step 2.

$$b_2 = \frac{\Sigma x_1^2 \Sigma x_2 y - \Sigma x_1 x_2 \Sigma x_1 y}{\Sigma x_1^2 \Sigma x_2^2 - (\Sigma x_1 x_2)^2}$$

$$= \frac{(161.2)(50) - (113.2)(64)}{(161.2)(141.2) - (113.2)^2}$$

$$= \frac{8060.00 - 7244.8}{22761.44 - 12814.24}$$

$$= \frac{815.2}{9947.2}$$

$$= 0.08195 \cong 0.08$$

Variables b_1 and b_2 are the same as previously computed.

PREDICTING Y

Taking the values for the two independent variables from Table 14.1 and applying the regression equation $\overline{Y}_p = -11.61 + 0.34X_1 + 0.08X_2$, Table 14.3 is developed. Comparing the results of simple and multiple regression in Table 14.4,

Table 14.3. Predicted Annual Earnings of the Employees of DEF Insurance Company Based on the Regression Equation $\overline{Y}_p = -11.61 + 0.34X_1 + 0.08X_2$.

Employee	X_1 When Test Score Is	X_2 When Performance Rating Is	$\overline{Y}_p$ Predicted Annual Earnings ($ Thousands)	Solution
A	52	85	12.87	$\overline{Y}_p = -11.61 + [(0.34)(52)] + [(0.08)(85)]$
B	57	80	14.17	$\overline{Y}_p = -11.61 + [(0.34)(57)] + [(0.08)(80)]$
C	60	92	16.15	$\overline{Y}_p = -11.61 + [(0.34)(60)] + [(0.08)(92)]$
D	65	90	17.69	$\overline{Y}_p = -11.61 + [(0.34)(65)] + [(0.08)(90)]$
E	68	95	19.12	$\overline{Y}_p = -11.61 + [(0.34)(68)] + [(0.08)(95)]$

Table 14.4. Predicted Annual Earnings of Employees of DEF Insurance Company Using Simple and Multiple Regression.

Employee (Y)	Actual	Predicted Simple Regression (Y_p)	Predicted Multiple Regression $(\overline{Y}_p)$	$y - \overline{y}p$	$(y - \overline{y}p)^2$
A	$13,000	$12,640	$12,870	$+0.130	0.0169
B	14,000	14,640	14,170	-0.170	0.0289
C	16,000	15,840	16,150	-0.150	0.0225
D	18,000	17,840	17,690	+0.310	0.0961
E	19,000	19,040	19,120	-0.120	0.0144
				$ 0.000	0.1788

we find that multiple regression was closer to actual earnings for Employees A,B, and C, where simple regression was a little more accurate in the case of Employee D and E.

STANDARD ERROR OF ESTIMATE

The standard error of estimate, as in simple regression, measures the accuracy of the regression equation $\overline{Y}_p = -11.61 + 0.34X_1 + 0.08X_2$. Employee A's predicted salary of $12,870 did not coincide precisely with the actual earnings of $13,000. Not all of the predicted values will fall on the regression line. The standard error of estimates $(S_{y.12})$ measures the variation. The subscript 12 indicates that two independent variables are being used to predict the dependent variable.

The formula for the standard error of estimate is:

$$S_{y.12} = \sqrt{\frac{\Sigma(Y - \overline{Y}_p)^2}{n - k}}$$

where

$$n = \text{number in the sample}$$

$$k = \text{number of variables}$$

Information needed to compute the standard error of estimate is shown in Table 14.4.

$$S_{y.12} = \sqrt{\frac{0.1788}{5 - 3}}$$

$$= \sqrt{0.0894}$$

$$= 0.299 \times \$1000 = \$299$$

The independent variables—the test scores and the performance ratings—produced a standard error of estimate of $299. Simple regression with just one independent variable—test scores—produced a standard error of estimate of $444. The addition of one independent variable cut the error by about one-third ($444 − $299 = $145, or 32.7%).

FORECASTING CONFIDENCE LIMITS

Small and Large Samples

When the sample size is small (less than 30), the formula for the prediction of the confidence limits is:

$$\overline{Y}_p = \pm t\, S_{y.12} \left(\frac{1}{\sqrt{n}} \right)$$

Here we will be using the t value again (Appendix H), as in simple regression. Suppose the management of DEF Insurance Company, using the 95% confidence level, wants to predict the annual earnings $(\overline{Y}_p)$ of prospective employees who have forecasted earnings of $12,870, a computer-programming test score of $52(X_1)$, and a performance rating of $85(X_2)$. The formula used is

$$\text{Confidence limits} = Y_p = \pm \left[t S_{y.12} \left(\frac{1}{\sqrt{n}} \right) \right]$$

$$= 12.87 \pm \left[4.303(0.299) \left(\frac{1}{\sqrt{5}} \right) \right]$$

$$= 12.87 \pm \left[4.303(0.299) \frac{1}{2.236} \right]$$

$$= 12.87 \pm [4.303(0.299)(0.447)]$$

$$= 12.293 \text{ and } 13.446$$

DEF Insurance Company can be 95% certain that an employee with a test score of 52 and a performance rating of 85 will have annual earnings between $12,293 and $13,446. If $n = 30$ or more, the sample is considered large and the same formula is used except the z value is substituted for the t value.

For a Particular Forecasted Value of Y

Suppose we want to be 95% certain of the salary limits for Employee E whose *predicted* annual earnings are $19,120 and who scored 68 on the test and obtained a performance rating of 95.

The formula would be:

$$\text{Confidence limits} = \overline{Y}_p = \pm tS_{y.12}\sqrt{\frac{n+1}{n}}$$

$$= 19.12 \pm \left[4.303\,(0.299)\sqrt{\frac{5+1}{5}}\,\right]$$

$$= 19.12 \pm [4.303\,(0.299)\,(1.095)]$$

$$= 19.12 \pm [4.303\,(0.327)]$$

$$= 17.712 \text{ and } 20.528$$

We can be 95% confident that the annual salary of Employee E will fall between $17,712 and $20,528.

CORRELATION ANALYSIS

In multiple regression, the coefficients used to explain the fact that not all of the predicted value of $Y(\overline{Y}_p)$ is due to changes in X_1 and X_2 are the same as in simple regression.

Multiple Determination Coefficient

The multiple determination coefficient is the proportion of variation in the dependent variable (Y) explained by the independent variables $(X_1, X_2,$ etc.). A coefficient of determination (R^2) of 100 indicates that 100% of the variation in Y is explained by $X_1 + X_2$, etc. An R^2 of 0.10 suggests that the independent variables $(X_1, X_2,$ etc.) explain little of the variation in the dependent variable (Y).

Multiple Nondetermination Coefficient. The coefficient of multiple nondetermination is the proportion of the variation in the dependent variable Y *not* explained by the independent variables $X_1 + X_2$, etc.

Multiple Correlation Coefficient. The multiple correlation coefficient measures the degree of relationship between the dependent and independent variables. Designated by $R_{y.12}$, it is the square root of the coefficient of multiple determination.

Methods of Computation

Multiple Determination Coefficient. The formula is:

$$R_{y.12}^2 = 1 - \frac{S_{y.12}^2}{S_y^2}$$

where

$$R^2 = \text{multiple determination coefficient}$$

$y.12 = Y$ is the dependent variable, and X_1 *and* X_2 are independent variables

$S_{y.12}^2 = $ the standard error of the estimate squared

$s_y^2 = $ total variation in Y

In predicting the salary of Employee A of DEF Insurance Co., the standard error of estimate $(s_{y.12})$ was \$299, or \$0.299 thousand. Therefore, the numerator is simply the standard error of estimate squared, or \$0.299 squared.

The denominator, s_y^2, is the total variation of Y. The formula to calculate it is:

$$s_y^2 = \frac{\Sigma y^2}{n-1}$$

where

$$\Sigma y^2 = \text{total variation in } Y = 26$$

$$n = \text{number in sample} = 5$$

Both the total variation in Y and the number in the sample may be found in the section on the multiple regression computation at the beginning of this chapter. So, the total variation of $Y = s_y^2 = 26 \div 4$, or 6.5.

Thus, in the formula for the multiple determination coefficient of

$$R_{y.12}^2 = 1 - \frac{s_{y.12}^2}{s_y^2}$$

we have

$$R_{y.12}^2 = 1 - \frac{(0.299)^2}{6.5}$$

$$= 1 - \frac{0.0849}{6.5}$$

$$= 1 - 0.0131$$

$$= 0.9869$$

The preceding multiple determination coefficient states that about 98.7% of the variation in annual earnings is explained by the test scores and performance ratings.

Multiple Nondetermination Coefficient

As one would expect from the term *nondetermination,* the multiple coefficient describes the change in the dependent variable not explained by the independent variables. The formula is:

$$1 - R_{y.12}^2$$

or

$$1 - 0.9869 = 0.0131$$

About 1.3% of the variation in annual earnings is not explained by test scores and performance ratings.

Multiple Correlation Coefficient

In the case of the prediction of annual earnings based on test scores and performance ratings, the multiple determination coefficient is 0.9869. The multiple correlation coefficient is the square root of 0.9869 or 0.9934. This indicates a very high degree of relationship between the dependent variable, annual earnings, and the two independent variables, test scores and performance ratings.

COMPUTER APPLICATION

Suppose we add another variable, the consumer price index (CPI), to the computer application shown in Chapter 13. Data for sales of room air conditioners dependent on average maximum temperatures and CPI are shown in Table 14.5. From the information in Table 14.5, a computerized run is made (Figure 14.1). The results follow:

1. Adding the average CPI (all items) for 1975-1979 to the average maximum temperatures increases the coefficient of determination to 0.6055. From 0.5653 (see Figure 13.8). Thus the addition of the CPI explains only an additional 4.1% (60.6 - 56.6) of the change in the sales of room air conditioners.
2. The correlation coefficient is increased to 77.8%, (square root of 0.6055).
3. The correlation matrix at the bottom of Figure 14.1 indicates how the variables are related to each other:
   a. 0.7518 (column 1, row 3) indicates how much X (average maximum temperatures) correlates with Y (sales of room air conditioners).
   b. 0.2871 (column 2, row 3) indicates how much Z (CPI) correlates with Y (sales of room air conditioners).

Table 14.5. **Sales of Room Air Conditioners Dependent on Average Maximum Temperatures and CPI, PQR Distributing Co.**

Month	Average Sales 1975-1979 (in Thousands Units) Y	Average Maximum Temperatures X_1	Average CPI All Items 1975-1979x[a] X_2
May	3.5	85°F	186.6
June	3.6	88	187.8
July	3.8	89	189.0
August	4.5	90	189.9
September	3.7	88	190.6
October	3.6	85	191.5

[a]x = Hypothetical where 1967 = 100.

MULTIPLE REGRESSION ANALYSIS

6 OBSERVATIONS, 3 VARIABLES
RANGE =E/1-E/6

EQUATION:
Y(1)=-15148.33889+128.3960736*X(1)+40.67473554*Z(1)

R-SQUARED	0.6055		
ADJUSTED R-SQUARED	0.3426	F-VALUE (2, 3)	2.3027
SUM SQUARED RES.	263627.942	DEGREES OF FREEDOM	3
STD. ERROR OF RES.	296.4388315	DEPENDENT MEAN	3783.3

VARIABLE	COEFFICIENT	STD. ERR.	T-STATISTIC	BETA
CONSTANT TERM	-15148.33889	14382.88184	-1.053220006	
X(1)	128.3960736	64.37245936	1.994580832	0.72824
Z(1)	40.67473554	73.49623865	0.553426084	0.20206

CORRELATION MATRIX:

	1	2	3
1 X(1)	1.0000		
2 Z(1)	0.1168	1.0000	
3 Y(1)	0.7518	0.2871	1.0000

Fig. 14.1 Computer printout of Table 14.5: sales of room air conditioners dependent on average maximum temperatures and CPI, PQR distributing co.

15 Statistical Inference

Suppose a manufacturing concern wants to know about the quality of a given lot of telephone handsets being assembled in its factory. The quality control inspector could pull handsets at random off the assembly line and inspect them. If the sample passed inspection, he could assume that the lot was alright. The quality control inspector would be applying statistical inference. In saying that the total number of handsets in the inspected group is satisfactory based on the sample he picked at random, he would be making a decision about a population parameter. Thus, statistical inference is the process of drawing conclusions on a population parameter based on a random sample.

WHY SAMPLE?

There are several reasons for sampling:

1. It is too expensive to interview the entire population, and a company may have only a limited budget for market testing.

2. Usually, a market-research study must be completed within a certain amount of time. Time limitations thus make it impossible to interview an entire population.

3. Including 100% of all items in a population may yield no better results than a sample properly selected. For example, if a survey on a particular issue was being taken among voters in the United States, interviewing each and every voter would not greatly increase the accuracy of a projection obtained by surveying a sample population of voters.

SAMPLE SELECTION METHODS

Nonprobability Sampling

In nonprobability sampling, all of the items in a population do not have an equal chance of being selected. Rather, the element of judgment is involved—i.e., someone decides which items in a population will be selected. Nonprobability sampling is widely used in market research for the sake of convenience and to reduce cost. In addition, the results may be as valid as those obtained in probability sampling, where all items in a population have an equal chance of being selected.

Test Marketing. Suppose Eat Ums Inc. is introducing a new brand of cereal, Gulp Ems. It wants to ascertain whether people will like the product. First, the company picks a small test market that has the same attributes as the nationwide market. Gulp Ems is then advertised and placed in the regular channels of distribution. Reception of the cereal is gauged through store audits, questioning buyers about their attitude toward the new product, etc.

Panels. Panels are a good way to conduct market research. They cost less and take less time than probability sampling. For example, suppose Madame Mane, a beauty parlor in a large city, wishes to ascertain the effectiveness of its advertisement in the Yellow Pages. Members for a consumer panel would be chosen using a sampling procedure and asked such questions as:

1. What size ad is best?
2. What type of ad is most representative of an honest and reliable beauty parlor?
3. What information do consumers look for in a Yellow Pages ad?
4. How does the Madame Mane ad compare with those of other beauty parlors in the Yellow Pages?

Once the panel's answers have been summarized, the results would be given to the Madame Mane salon for its use in developing an ad that would attract more customers.

Probability Sampling

In probability sampling, each member of the population has an equal chance of being selected.

Table of Random Numbers. A candidate for political office in East Overshoe hires Anne Reilly, a market researcher, to determine voter opinion on a particular issue. Ms. Reilly first consults *Final Reports: Block Statistics* H.C. #3-36 (Bureau of the Census) based on the 1970 Census of Housing. *Block Statistics* based on the 1980 Census of Housing will be available on microfiche only in late 1982. *Block Statistics* divides cities into sections or cells. Ms. Reilly finds that there are 800 cells in East Overshoe. She proceeds as follows:

1. Ms. Reilly enters the table at any location she desires. Suppose she selects row 1, column 10-12. Located here is 108. It is the first number that she uses because it falls within the assigned numbers of 001 to 800.

Table 15.1. Partial Table of Random Numbers.

Row	1-3	4-6	Column 7-9	10-12	13-15
1	732	609	323	108	188
2	392	379	538	884	409
3	391	298	182	366	136
4	117	432	267	37	470
5	109	574	873	883	405

Row	16-18	19-21	Column 22-24	25-27	28-30
1	62	713	638	49	671
2	800	436	20	134	679
3	686	306	457	369	956
4	362	439	555	747	38
5	665	305	288	352	145

2. Reading to the right, the next number to be used is 188; then 62, 713, and 638.

3. Since she is dealing with three digit numbers, the next number selected would be 627 (combinations of 62 and 7); the next would be 136 (combinations of 13 and 6).

4. Subsequent numbers selected would be 384, 139, 237, 440, 043, 620, 134, and 391. She proceeds from row 1, column 28-30 to row 2, column 1-3, etc., reading any combination of three digits falling between 001 and 800.

5. Ms. Reilly continues until all 100 cells in the sample have been selected. (If there were a total of 80 cells in East Overshoe, Ms. Reilly would assign numbers from 01 to 80 to all cells in the population. If she started at the same place—row 1, column 10-12—in Table 15.1, the first number selected would be 10, the second 39, and the third 23. She would select only two digit numbers.)

Choosing Each nth Item. In certain cases, simple random sampling may become time-consuming. Consider, for example, the vice president of market research in a management consulting firm who wants to obtain a sample of 180 suppliers out of a total population of 1800. To individually number each supplier on the list and then use a table of random numbers to choose 1800 would be time-consuming. Therefore, the vice president takes a table of random numbers to select the first supplier, starting at some arbitrarily chosen point in the table. Each tenth supplier on the list is taken until a total of 180 are picked. This is called *systematic sampling.* It is used when a population is organized in an orderly fashion.

Table 15.2. Shelf Layout, Candy and Gum Section, Fast & Easy Inc.

Item	Shelf No.	Bin No.	Bin No.	Bin No.	Bin No.	Bin No.
Adult	6	1	2	3	4	5
Adult	5	6	7	8	9	10
Older children	4	11	12	13	14	15
Older children	3	16	17	18	19	20
Young children	2	21	22	23	24	25
Young children	1	26	27	28	29	30

Table 15.3. Proportional Stratified Random Sample, Fast & Easy Inc.

Group	National Average Inventory Turns per Year[a]	Total Bins in US[a]
Adult candy and gum	13	14,000
Older children's candy and gum	20	16,000
Small children's candy and gum	26	20,000
		50,000

Group	No. Fast & Easy Bins Sampled	% of Sample
Adult candy and gum	3	28 (14/50)
Older children's candy and gum	3	32 (16/50)
Small children's candy and gum	4	40 (20/50)
	10	100

[a]Hypothetical.

Table 15.4. Carbide Tools Used Annually by United States Manufacturers, Study for Sharp Tool Co.

No. Tools Used Annually (in Thousands)[a]	No. Manufacturers	No. in Sample
10 up to 15	15	2
5 up to 10	30	4
Under 5	155	21
	200	27

[a]Hypothetical.

Systematic sampling should not be used in all cases. Suppose a supermarket, Fast & Easy Inc., stocks the 10 lower bins of the first two shelves of the candy-and-gum section with items for young children; 10 bins on the third and fourth shelves for older children; and 10 bins on the fifth and sixth shelves for adults. Here we have a predetermined pattern in the population—that is, the bins are stocked with candy and gum according to age groupings. See Table 15.2.

Fast & Easy runs an inventory audit of the candy-and-gum section to determine which items have the most rapid turnover. Starting at the upper left-hand corner, it selects every fourth bin. The numbers selected are bin numbers 1, 5, 9, 13, 17, 21, 25, and 29. This gives the adult items three bins (1, 5, and 9), older children's items two bins (13 and 17), and young children's items three bins (21, 25, and 29). The bin selection of 37.5% adult items, 25% older children's items, and 37.5% young children's items does not agree with the actual 33.3%, 33.3%, and 33.3% relationship. Hence the inventory audit results would be biased in favor of the adult and young children's items.

Suppose we wish to correct this problem. Either a proportional or a nonproportional stratified random sample may be used.

Proportional Stratified Random Sample.

1. Applying the rules of proportional random sampling to the supermarket candy-and-gum display, we would break the population into subgroups:
   a. adult items: candy and gum
   b. older children's items: candy and gum
   c. small children's items: candy and gum
2. We would obtain a total sample of 10 bins in three groups from the shelves of Fast & Easy in the same proportion as they occur in the population.

Suppose ABC Company, a national market-research firm, establishes national averages for the number of times in a year that an inventory is sold or turned over for candy-and-gum items on the supermarket shelves. This information is classified by age group as well as by the total number of storage bins for the merchandise in the United States. ABC Company sells this information as a commercialized service. The information is shown in Table 15.3. From the table, we can see that three each of Fast & Easy's adult and older children's bins would be sampled, while four of the young children's bins would be used.

Nonproportional Stratified Random Sample. In a nonproportional stratified random sample, the proportion of each class in the sample is *not* the same as in the population. For example, Sharp Tool Co., a manufacturer of carbide tools, wants to know the market for its product. The company conducts a study that reveals the information shown in Table 15.4. Most likely, the two manufacturers in the sample that use 10,000 to 15,000 carbide tools per year account for more dollar volume than do the 155 firms using less than 5000 carbide tools annually.

Suppose Sharp Tool Co. wants to find out what the manufacturers' needs are. It would save both time and expense to interview the two manufacturers using 10,000 to 15,000 tools annually and to only interview some of the 155 companies using under 5000 per year. However, if a proportional sample is used, the total number in each category will have to be interviewed, most likely increasing the cost to Sharp Tool Co.

CENTRAL LIMIT THEOREM

The statistics kept by an American golf association indicate that the mean score for all 13-to-15-year-old girls in the United States is 76. Then suppose that all 13-to-15-year-old girls playing at the Spoonville Country Club, Knightsville Country Club, and Gopher Gulch Country Club have mean averages of 74, 75, and 77, respectively. It is not expected that the means of the samples (74, 75, and 77) will be exactly the same as the mean of the population (76). Called *sampling variation*, this is the result of each member of a sample being selected by chance.

The central limit theorem, which applies to sampling distributions, has four distinct but related parts:

1. The mean of the sampling distribution $(\overline{X})$ will equal the population mean (μ) when all possible random samples of size n have been drawn from the population.

2. The distribution of sample means is normally distributed when drawn from a population that is normally distributed.

3. If a sampling distribution is established from a skewed population, the more the size of the sample is increased, the nearer the sampling distribution approaches normality.

4. The formula for the standard error of the mean from the sampling distribution is:

$$\sigma_{\overline{x}} = \frac{\sigma}{\sqrt{n}}$$

Sampling Distribution and Population Means Equal

Suppose we have a total population of eight golfers with scores of 72, 73, 74, 75, 76, 77, 78, and 79, and we choose a sample size of two. All possible samples (64) are shown in Table 15.5. Each sample has the possibility of being selected by chance (i.e., replaced) on subsequent selections.

Placing the means in tabular form, a frequency distribution is formed as shown in Table 15.6. The mean of the sample means, 75.5, is determined by dividing 4832.0 by 64; the mean of the population, 75.5, is determined by dividing 604.0 by 8. Note that the means are the same.

Table 15.5. All Possible Samples of Golf Scores
Where n = 2 and Population = $P.$ = 8

Population Sample No.	Sample Scores		Mean Score
	Golfer 1	Golfer 2	
1	72	72	72
2	73	72	72.5
3	74	72	73
4	75	72	73.5
5	76	72	74
6	77	72	74.5
7	78	72	75
8	79	72	75.5
9	72	73	72.5
10	73	73	73
11	74	73	73.5
12	75	73	74
13	76	73	74.5
14	77	73	75
15	78	73	75.5
16	79	73	76
17	72	74	73
18	73	74	73.5
19	74	74	74
20	75	74	74.5
21	76	74	75
22	77	74	75.5
23	78	74	76
24	79	74	76.5
25	72	75	73.5
26	73	75	74
27	74	75	74.5
28	75	75	75
29	76	75	75.5
30	77	75	76
31	78	75	76.5
32	79	75	77
33	72	76	74
34	73	76	74.5
35	74	76	75
36	75	76	75.5
37	76	76	76
38	77	76	76.5
39	78	76	77
40	79	76	77.5
41	72	77	74.5
42	73	77	75
43	74	77	75.5
44	75	77	76
45	76	77	76.5
46	77	77	77

| Population | Sample Scores | | Mean |
Sample No.	Golfer 1	Golfer 2	Score
47	78	77	77.5
48	79	77	78
49	72	78	75
50	73	78	75.5
51	74	78	76
52	75	78	76.5
53	76	78	77
54	77	78	77.5
55	78	78	78
56	79	78	78.5
57	72	79	75.5
58	73	79	76
59	74	79	76.5
60	75	79	77
61	76	79	77.5
62	77	79	78
63	78	79	78.5
64	79	79	79

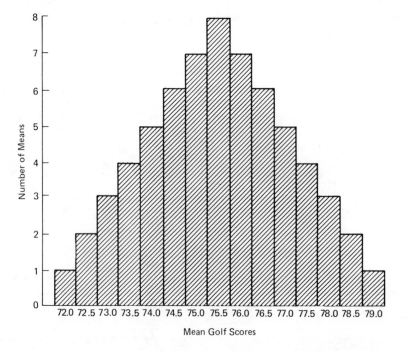

Fig. 15.1 Frequency distribution of means where *n* = 2 and population = *p.* = 8.

Mean	No. Means	Maximum of Sample Means	Population Means
72.0	1	72.0	72.0
72.5	2	145.0	73.0
73.0	3	219.0	74.0
73.5	4	294.0	75.0
74.0	5	370.0	76.0
74.5	6	447.0	77.0
75.0	7	525.0	78.0
75.5	8	604.0	79.0
76.0	7	532.0	604.0
76.5	6	459.0	
77.0	5	385.0	
77.5	4	310.0	
78.0	3	234.0	
78.5	2	157.0	
79.0	1	79.0	
	64	4832.0	

Distribution of Sample Means

Looking at Table 15.6, we see that the distribution of the sample means is normally distributed. Hence, it can be assumed that samples are taken from a population that is normally distributed. Figure 15.1 shows this in graphic form.

Standard Error of Mean

In the preceding example, the standard error of the mean would be computed according to the following steps:

1. Calculate the standard deviation of the population, where golf scores are 72, 73, 74, 75, 76, 77, 78, and 79, according to the formula:

$$\sigma = \sqrt{\frac{\Sigma X^2}{N} - \bar{X}^2}$$

$$\sigma = \sqrt{\frac{45,644}{8} - (75.5)^2}$$

$$\sigma = \sqrt{5705.5 - 5700.25}$$

$$\sigma = \sqrt{5.25}$$

$$\sigma = 2.29$$

(See Table 15.7 for the computation of X^2.)

Table 15.7. Computation of the Standard Deviation of the Population of Eight Golfers.

Golf Score X	X^2
72	5,184
73	5,329
74	5,476
75	5,625
76	5,776
77	5,929
78	6,084
79	6,241
	45,644

2. Calculate the standard error of the mean (σ_x):

$$\sigma_{\bar{x}} = \frac{\sigma}{\sqrt{n}}$$

$$\sigma_{\bar{x}} = \frac{2.29}{\sqrt{2}}$$

$$\frac{2.29}{1.41}$$

$$1.62$$

Here, the standard error of the mean, 1.62, is actually the standard deviation of the sampling distribution of the means of the golf scores. Therefore, ± 1 standard error of the mean (1.62) includes the middle 68% of all total possible means while ± 1.96 standard error of the mean includes 95% of all total possible means. If this is so, then the population mean of 75.5 falls within $\bar{X} \pm 1.96_{\bar{x}}$, or ± 1.96 (1.62), a total of 95% of the time, or between 72.32 and 78.68. This is shown graphically in Figure 15.2.

SAMPLING AND CENTRAL LIMIT THEOREM

Let us return to the case of Eat Ums Co., which is using test marketing to predict the acceptance of Gulp Ems. It is attempting to establish a population figure based on a sample number. Since Matthew Michaels, the market-research man-

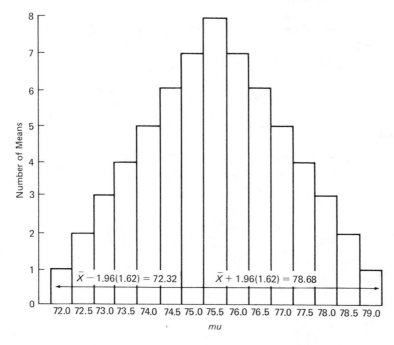

Fig. 15.2 Graphic presentation of population mean of 75 falling within ±1.96 standard deviation.

ager of Eat Ums, is unable to sample the entire United States population, he will not know the standard deviation of the population. It must be estimated from the sample. The formula for estimation (assuming the population standard error of the mean is the same as that of the sample) then becomes:

$$s_{\bar{x}} = \sqrt{\dfrac{s}{n}}$$

where

$s_{\bar{x}}$ = standard error of the mean

s = standard deviation of the sample

n = number in the sample (normally 30 or more)

In the test marketing, Eat Ums Co. interviews a sample of 200 people. Of these 200, a total of 150 say they would buy the cereal when it is available in their supermarkets. The arithmetic mean of those responding affirmatively is

15, and the standard deviation is 2. The standard error of the mean thus becomes:

$$\frac{2}{\sqrt{150}} \text{ or } \frac{2}{12.25} = 0.163$$

Confidence Limits

Now suppose that Mr. Michaels wants to establish 95% confidence limits, based on the sample, for all people desiring to buy Gulp Ems.

He would proceed accordingly:

$$\bar{X} \pm 1.96 \, (s_{\bar{x}})$$

Upper Confidence Limit

$$15 + [1.96(0.163)]$$

$$15 + 0.32 = 15.32$$

Lower Confidence Limit $\quad 15 - [1.96(0.163)]$

$$15 - 0.32 = 14.68$$

Based on the sample statistics, Mr. Michaels can infer with 95% confidence that about 10% (15/150) of the total population of the United States will buy Gulp Ems. Suppose that the breakfast cereal market is highly competitive and the Eat Ums Co. has 3% of the total American market. Based on the test marketing of Gulp Ems, the company could hope to increase its market share somewhat because 15 out of 150 or 10% of the people indicated that they would buy Gulp Ems. Suppose Mr. Michaels wanted to increase the confidence level from 95% to 98%. His computation would be as follows:

$$\bar{X} \pm 2.33 \, (s_{\bar{x}})$$

Upper Confidence Limit

$$15 + [2.33(0.163)]$$

$$15 + 0.38 = 15.38$$

Lower Confidence Limit   15 − [2.33(0.38)]

$$15 - 0.38 = 14.62$$

Based on the sample statistics, Mr. Michaels can infer with 98% confidence that from 9.7% to 10.3% (14.62/150 and 15.38/150) of the total United States population would buy Gulp Ems.

Determinable Population

A determinable (finite) population exists when the total number in the population can be defined—for example, the total employee population of 50 at corporate headquarters of Tuff Co. and the 3500 room air conditioners produced by Kool-Aire Co. in April 1981.

The confidence limits for a finite population are altered by applying a correction factor to the standard error of the mean. In estimating the arithmetic mean of a population, the larger the sample is in relation to the total finite population, the more accurate the estimate, and hence the smaller the correction factor.

Mary Greene is the market-research manager for Kool-Aire Co., a manufacturer of room air conditioners. Ms. Greene wants to ascertain, with 95% confidence, the range within which the true mean life of the 3500 room air conditioners produced by the company in April 1981 falls. After consultation with Mr. Rhodes, the quality control manager, Ms. Greene decides that 7% of the population would be a good sample. Mr. Rhodes tests 245 (7%) of the room air conditioners and finds the mean life to be 38 months. The standard deviation of the mean is found to be 2 months.

Ms. Greene proceeds as follows:

1. Ms. Greene collects the information so she can apply the correction factor to the sample mean life of 38 months at the 95% level of probability:

38 = mean life of sample of 245 room air conditioners

±1.96 = number of standard deviations from mean at the 95% confidence level (area under normal curve)

2 = standard deviation of sample

245 = number in sample (n)

3500 = number in total finite population (N)

2. Ms. Greene applies this information to the following formula:

Correction factor of the sample =

$$\text{Sample Mean Life} \pm 1.96 \left(\frac{\text{Standard deviation of sample}}{\sqrt{\text{Sample size}}} \right) \sqrt{\frac{N - n}{N - 1}}$$

$$38 \pm 1.96 \left(\frac{2}{\sqrt{245}} \sqrt{\frac{3500 - 245}{3500 - 1}} \right)$$

$$38 \pm 1.96 \left(\frac{2}{15.65} \sqrt{\frac{3255}{3499}} \right)$$

$$38 \pm 1.96 [0.1278(0.9645)]$$

$$38 \pm 1.96(0.1233)$$

Upper Confidence Limit

$$38 + 1.96(0.1233)$$

$$38 + 0.2417$$

38.24 months

Lower Confidence Limit

$$38 - 1.96(0.1233)$$

$$38 - 0.2417$$

37.76 months

Ms. Greene can be 95% certain that the true mean length of the life of the 3500 room air conditioners is between 37.76 and 38.24 months.

Suppose Ms. Greene only wanted to apply a correction factor to the standard deviation of the mean in order to better predict the arithmetic mean of the population given a sample size of 7%. She would proceed as follows:

$$\text{Correction factor formula} = \sqrt{\frac{N - n}{N - 1}}$$

where

$$N = \text{total number in finite population}$$

$$n = \text{number in sample}$$

$$= \sqrt{\frac{3500 - 245}{3500 - 1}}$$

$$= \sqrt{\frac{3255}{3499}}$$

$$= \sqrt{0.93}$$

$$= 0.9645$$

Applying the correction factor of 0.9645 to the sample size of 245 with a standard deviation of 2 would reduce the error in predicting the population mean by 0.9645 × 2 = 1.93. This would represent a 3.5% reduction in the prediction; that is:

$$\frac{2.0 - 1.93}{2.0} = \frac{0.07}{2.0} = 3.5\%$$

The correction factor is of some help here since the sample is 7% of the finite population. Where the sample is less than 5% the correction factor is of little use.

SELECTING A SAMPLE SIZE

The following factors affect the size of the sample but have no relationship to the population size.

Degree of Confidence

The higher the degree of confidence required, the greater the size of the sample. Suppose the market research manager for Tell-Time Co., a manufacturer of toy clocks, wants to estimate the arithmetic mean of the population of 2- to 4-year-old children in the United States. He estimates it to be between 0.5 and 1.5 million. Assuming the interval does not change, a sample size with a 90% confidence limit will be smaller than one with a 100% confidence limit (when all children in the population will have to be canvased).

Maximum Error Allowed

What is the maximum error allowed in estimating population mean? Suppose a cable television supplier, CATV Supreme, wants to estimate the market for cable television in the northwest section of Spoonville. CATV Supreme will pay up to $1500 for the survey. How many houses should be sampled? CATV Supreme hires A&B Associates, a market-research company, to do the job. Alice Allan, manager of A&B Associates, does the following:

1. She estimates the mean income of the residents of the northwest section of Spoonville. After looking at homes in the area, Ms. Allan believes that assuming a 99.7% probability, the total error in predicting the mean income should not exceed $100, i.e., $3.00 S_{\bar{x}} = \$100$. She then computes the standard error of mean:

$$s_{\bar{x}} = \frac{\$100}{3.00} = \$33.33 \cong \$33$$

2. She estimates the standard deviation of the sample based on her knowledge of the population. First, Ms. Allan goes to Spoonville Town Hall to obtain income statistics for the northwest section of the town. From this, she estimates that the standard deviation is $1000.

3. She computes the number for the sample:

$$s_{\bar{x}} = \frac{s}{\sqrt{n}}$$

$$\frac{\$100}{3.00} = \frac{\$1000}{n}$$

$$\$33\sqrt{n} = \$1000$$

$$\sqrt{n} = \frac{\$1000}{\$33}$$

$$\sqrt{n} = 30.30$$

$$n = 30.30^2$$

$$n = 918$$

4. Does the sample of 918 give Ms. Allan the information she needs, namely, that the true mean falls within ±$100? The sample of 918 can be correct, too small, or too large. If the cost of interviewing 918 respondents was $5 each, or a total of $4590, CATV Supreme would not conduct the research since it would

exceed its allowable cost of $1500. If CATV Supreme was willing to increase the total error in predicting the mean income for residents of the northwest section of Spoonville from $100 to $500 with a 99.7% level of confidence, the sample size could be reduced to 230. If the same $5 per interview applied, CATV Supreme would most likely have the survey done as it does not exceed the $1500 limit. The total cost would be $1150. If the standard deviation of the sample was $500, then the sample size would have been computed as follows:

$$\frac{\$100}{3.00} = \frac{\$500}{\sqrt{n}}$$

$$\$33\sqrt{n} = \$500$$

$$\sqrt{n} = \frac{\$500}{33}$$

$$\sqrt{n} = 15.15$$

$$n = 15.15^2$$

$$n = 230$$

PROPORTIONS

Population Proportions

Inferences similar to those just described may be related to proportions of the population. Assume, for example, that two-thirds of those polled in a randomly selected sample of 2000 women preferred Gentle Touch dishwashing liquid. Then, the proportion of women favoring Gentle Touch is 0.67 or 67%. This is the best estimate of the real population proportion.

Mr. Black, market research manager at Snow Flake Co., the manufacturer of Gentle Touch, want to establish the true population proportion based on the sample statistic of 0.67. If he takes another sample of 2000 women, he knows it will *not* exactly equal the previous sample of 0.67. However, based on the results of the first sample, he can set up con.idence limits within the true proportion of the population will fall.

1. Determine what level of confidence he wishes to use. Let's say he chose 95% confidence limits.

2. Determine whether the population was of definite size (finite) or of indefinite size (infinite). Here it is assumed that the population of American women is so large as to make it infinite for the manufacturer's purposes.

3. Apply the standard error of proportion formula for infinite populations:

$$\sqrt{\frac{p(1-p)}{n}}$$

where

$$p = \text{proportion}$$

$$n = \text{total number in population}$$

If it had been a finite population (See Finite Populations, in earlier section of this chapter), a correction factor would have been used:

$$\sqrt{\frac{N-n}{N-1}}\sqrt{\frac{p(1-p)}{n}}$$

4. Calculate 95% confidence limits using the following formula:

$$\text{Confidence Limits} = p \pm z \left(s_p\right)$$

$$= p \pm z \sqrt{\frac{p(1-p)}{n}}$$

where

$p =$ the total proportion of the population preferring Gentle Touch

$\pm 1.96 =$ number of standard deviations from the mean at the 95% confidence level (area under normal curves)

$n =$ number in sample (i.e., 2000)

$$= 0.67 \pm 1.96 \sqrt{\frac{0.67\,(1.00 - 0.67)}{2000}}$$

$$= 0.67 \pm 1.96 \sqrt{\frac{0.221}{2000}}$$

$$= 0.67 \pm 1.96 \sqrt{0.0001105}$$

$$= 0.67 \pm 1.96 \, (0.0105)$$

$$= 0.67 + 1.96 \, (0.0105) = 0.69058$$

$$= 0.67 - 1.96 \, (0.0105) = 0.64942$$

Mr. Black concludes that at the 95% confidence level, the best estimate of the total number of women in the United States preferring Gentle Touch is between 65% and 69%.

Proportion of Sample Sizes

The sample size may be estimated when dealing with proportions. Suppse Ms. Johnson, president of a local union, wants to ascertain how many members will ratify a contract that is now before them. In the last ratification vote, 70% voted in favor. Ms. Johnson has said that the true proportion voting for the ratification must be correct within ±5%. She also wants the 95% level of confidence used. Ms. Johnson first states proportions:

1. The degree of confidence is 95%.
2. The proportion estimated from previous knowledge is 0.70.
3. Ms. Johnson solves for the size of the sample using the following formula:

$$p = \pm z \sqrt{\frac{p(1-p)}{n}}$$

$$p = \frac{0.05}{1.96} = \sqrt{\frac{0.70 \, (1 - 0.70)}{n}}$$

$$p = \frac{0.05}{1.96} = \sqrt{\frac{0.21}{n}}$$

$$p = 0.026 \sqrt{n} = \sqrt{0.21}$$

$$p = \sqrt{n} = \sqrt{\frac{0.21}{0.026}}$$

$$p = \sqrt{n} = \left(\frac{0.45825}{0.026}\right)^2$$

$$p = \sqrt{n} = \frac{0.209993}{0.000676}$$

$$n = 311$$

If Ms. Johnson had not known the proportion (in this case, 0.70), she could have estimated 0.50, which produces the largest size of n.

16 Parametric Tests of Significance

WHAT IS HYPOTHESIS TESTING?

In hypothesis testing, a statement concerning a given situation is accepted or rejected. Suppose a student at Spoonville High School tells Sam Sands, the guidance counselor, that high-school graduates earn smaller average salaries than college graduates. Mr. Sands decides to determine whether this statement is true. First, he states the null hypothesis, "The average salaries of high-school graduates are less than those of college graduates." The alternative hypothesis is, "The average salaries of high-school graduates are greater than those of college graduates."

If Sands accepts the null hypothesis (H_0), then the statement is true. If he rejects the null hypothesis, then he is accepting the alternative hypothesis (H_1). To ascertain which statement is correct, Sands does some research. He finds statistics indicating that high-school graduates earn smaller average salaries than do college graduates. Thus, Sands would be correct in accepting the null hypothesis.

RULES OF HYPOTHESIS TESTING

The steps to be taken in hypothesis testing follow.
1. *State the null and alternative hypotheses.*
   a. Null Hypothesis (H_0): Average salaries of high-school graduates are less than those of college graduates.
   b. Alternative Hypothesis (H_1): Average salaries of high-school graduates are greater than those of college graduates.
2. *Determine which statistical test to use.* Sands considers several factors before choosing a statistical test. These include:
   a. How many samples are in the problem? Different tests of significance apply according to the number in the sample.
   b. Are the samples related or unrelated?

Table 16.1. Probability of Zero Through 20 Cities Being a True
Sample of the Population where N = 20 and P = 0.25.

No. Cities Successively Selected	Probability
0	0.0032
1	0.0211
2	0.0669
3	0.1339
4	0.1897
5	0.2023
6	0.1686
7	0.1124
8	0.0609
9	0.0271
10	0.0099
11	0.0030
12	0.0008
13	0.0002
14	0.0000
15	0.0000
16	0.0000
17	0.0000
18	0.0000
19	0.0000
20	0.0000
Total	1.0000

3. *Determine the level of significance to be used.* Sands has a choice of two alternatives:

   a. He can reject the null hypothesis—that average salaries of high-school graduates' are less than those of college graduates—even though it is true. This is called a *Type I* or *alpha error.*

   b. He can accept the null hypothesis—that high-school graduates' average salaries are higher than college graduates' average salaries when in fact it is not true. This is a *Type II* or *beta error.*

Sands must now ask himself what level of risk he wishes to accept, given the possibility of committing a Type I or Type II error. Suppose he accepts the 5% level of significance.

Suppose Mr. Sands takes the average earnings of high-school and college graduates of five cities that were picked at random from a Bureau of Labor Statistics study. Sands is testing the fact that at the 5% level of significance, the randomly selected cities are a true sample of the population of 20 cities in the study. Hence, the null hypothesis (P_h) assumes the random selection of the five cities

Table 16.2. Sampling Distribution: Average Salaries of High-School
Graduates Where N = 202 and n = 3.[a]

Mean Salary (in $ Thousands)	No. Means	Probability
5.00	2	0.0099
6.00	8	0.0396
7.00	24	0.1188
8.00	40	0.1980
9.00	52	0.2574
10.00	40	0.1980
11.00	24	0.1188
12.00	8	0.0396
13.00	2	0.0099
14.00	2	0.0099
Total	202	0.9999[b]

[a]N = population total; n = sample total.
[b]Rounding error.

to be true. Then P_h = 0.25. The alternative hypothesis states that the null hypothesis is not true and $P_h > 0.25$.

The probability of thirteen cities being successfully selected by chance is 0.0002 or 2 in 10,000 (See Table 16.1). This is a very infrequent happening. In this case, if the null hypothesis is rejected, (P_h = 0.25), then the alternative hypothesis ($P_h > 0.25$) is accepted. If this were a true event, i.e., that thirteen cities actually had been selected by chance, then a Type I error had occurred— the null hypothesis was rejected when it should have been accepted.

In a Type II error, the null hypothesis is accepted when it should be rejected. Suppose the thirteen cities were not selected by chance, when it was believed they were. In effect, a Type II error was committed (the probability for the null hypothesis (P_h) is still equal to 0.25 and the alternative hypothesis (P_h) is still > 0.25).

4. *Identify the sampling distribution of the test statistic.* Sands decides to test the average salaries of high-school graduates, using a population of 202 cities with a sample size of three, assuming replacement. (That is, three samples can be put back in the population and have the chance of being selected on the next random selection of a sample from the population.) The symmetrical sampling distribution is shown in Table 16.2.

5. *Formulate the decision rule.* Sands must next establish the conditions under which the null hypothesis is accepted or rejected. He has divided the sampling distribution into two areas, acceptance and rejection. The statistical test used is the z-test since its sampling distribution is normally distributed. If Sands calculates a z-value of 3.765, it is unlikely that the null hypothesis is true because

the z value of 1.645 is the critical value at the 0.05 level of significance, i.e., the boundary line between acceptance and rejection. This is a one-tailed test since the alternative hypothesis states a direction, i.e., average salaries of high-school graduates are more than those of college graduates. (See Figure 16.1.)

A two-tailed test applies when H_1 (alternative hypothesis) does *not* state a direction. In the case of the average salaries of high-school and college graduates, a two-tailed test would apply given the following null and alternative hypotheses:

- H_0: There is no significant differences between the average salaries of high-school and college graduates.
- H_1: There is a significant difference between the average salaries of high-school and college graduates.

LEVELS OF MEASUREMENT

Tests of significance relating to hypothesis testing can be broken into two parts, nonparametric and parametric, depending on levels of measurement.

Nonparametric

Nominal. Suppose we are studying the population statistics of certain cities within Illinois and have gathered the information shown in Table 16.3. From the table, it can be seen that the nominal level of measurement has the following

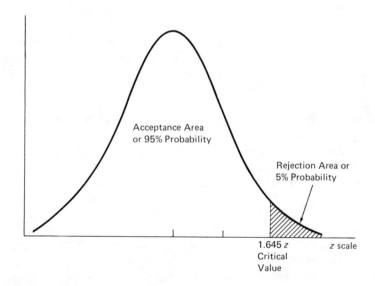

Fig. 16.1 Curve showing areas of acceptance and rejection at a z critical value of 1.645.

Table 16.3. Population of Hypothetical Cities.

City	Population
Spoonville	10,536,238
McCreery	8,410,217
Pond's Crossing	6,242,011
Golden Nugget	4,210,012
Sand's Creek	2,060,211
Total	31,458,689

characteristics:

1. Data can only be classified into categories.
2. Arrangements can be changed. McCreery could have been listed before Spoonville. Therefore, one city can be placed before another—that is, there is no ranking.
3. The categories are mutually exclusive.
4. Numbers cannot be added; that is, the sum of the population of a Spoonville plus that of McCreery does not equal the population of Pond's Crossing.
5. Nonparametric tests are applied to nominal-level types of data. These tests assume nothing about the population distribution from which the sample was taken.

Ordinal. One hundred respondents in a market-research study were asked to compare the taste of XYZ breakfast cereal to that of ABC breakfast cereal. The questionnaire read as follows:

How do you rate the taste of XYZ's brand compared to ABC's brand? (Please place a check mark next to the rating you prefer.)

Much tastier ____
Tastier ____
Just as tasty ____
Not as tasty ____

Upon completion of the study, the statistics were tabulated. The results are shown in Table 16.4. Note that the table has the following characteristics.

1. Data can be ranked.
2. In an ordinal level of measurement, the rankings do state to what degree one ranking is superior to another.

Table 16.4. Respondents' Ratings of the Taste of XYZ versus ABC Breakfast Cereal.

Rating	No.
Much tastier	25
Tastier	20
Just as tasty	30
Not as tasty	25
	100

Tests applied to parametric data assume that the data are either ratio- or interval-scaled.

Interval Levels. The following are characteristics of interval levels:

1. Distances between numbers are of a known, constant size.
2. Each class is mutually exclusive.
3. Categories can be ranked.

HYPOTHESIS TESTING

In hypothesis testing, several sets of circumstances are considered.

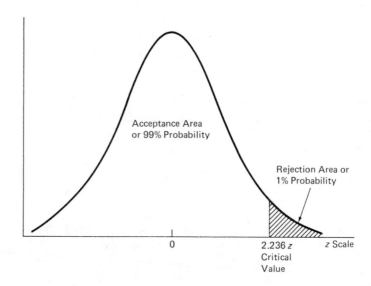

Fig. 16.2 Curve showing areas of acceptance and rejection at a z critical value of 2.236.

Population Mean and Standard Deviation Are Known

Suppose we go back to the case of Mr. Sands, the guidance counselor at Spoonville High School. He has taken some samples of high-school graduates' salaries and found the mean to be $10,000. Further investigation into Bureau of Labor Statistics studies indicates the population mean to be $10,500 with a standard deviation of $420. However, the guidance counselor from Tuftstown High School, Ms. Brown, claims that her study reveals the population mean to be significantly higher than $10,500. In order to test this claim, Sands conducts an investigation of 50 cities based on the following steps:

1. *State the null hypothesis.* According to the null hypothesis, no significant difference exists between the sample mean annual salary of $10,000 ($\overline{X}$) and the population mean (μ). Brown's study shows a significantly higher mean; hence, a direction has been mentioned, which indicates that a one-tailed test should be used. The hypotheses would be expressed as follows:

$$\text{Null hypothesis } (H_0) = \$10,000 \ (\overline{X}) \leqslant \$10,500 \ (\mu)$$

$$\text{Alternative hypothesis } (H_1) = \$10,000 \ (\overline{X}) > \$10,500 \ (\mu)$$

If one accepts the null hypothesis, he accepts that there is no significant difference between the sample and population means. The difference is due to chance. If there is a significant difference, however, the two means came from different populations. Any differences are thus not due to chance.

2. *Apply the z-test.* The z-test is used since it is assumed that the population figures from which the sample was taken are evenly distributed. Sands's sample included at least 30 cities, and the data are scaled.

3. *Select the level of significance.* Sands selected the 0.01 level of significance.

4. *Formulate the decision rule.* Under the set of circumstances previously outlined, we have the following:

   a. A 1% level of significance.
   b. One-tailed test. Brown says the population mean is significantly higher than Sands's population mean of $10,500. Hence, a direction has been mentioned indicating that the area of rejection is the 0.01 area in the right tail of the normal curve (see Figure 16.2). Had Brown found the mean to be significantly less than Sands's $10,500, the area of rejection would have been in the left tail of the curve.
   c. Use of z-test.

The decision rule is thus: Accept the null hypothesis if the computed value of z is less than +2.326 (the z value is equal to 0.4900; see Appendix C). If the z value is $\geqslant 2.326$, the H_1 should be accepted and H_0 rejected.

5. *Accept or reject the null hypothesis.* Each of the 50 cities are studied, and

the mean high-school graduates' salary is found to be $10,725. The z value is calculated as follows:

$$z = \frac{\bar{X} - \mu}{\sigma/\sqrt{n}} = \frac{\$10,725 - \$10,500}{420/\sqrt{50}}$$

$$= \frac{\$225}{420/7.07}$$

$$= \frac{\$225}{59.41}$$

$$= 3.787$$

The computed value of z, 3.787, exceeds the critical value of 2.326; hence, the null hypothesis is not accepted at the 1% level of significance. Stated differently, it is not likely that the difference of $225 between the sample mean and population mean is due to chance. It therefore seems likely that the population mean at the 1% level of significance could exceed $10,000.

Population Mean Is Known But Standard Deviation Is Not

Sometimes the population standard deviation is not known. In such a case, it is estimated using a sample standard deviation s. This is done by using the t-test statistic rather than the z.

A study by Forche, a major automobile manufacturer, indicates that one out of every four of its new luxury model cars has an average total of 65 defects when it comes off the assembly line. Forche considers this average too high and initiates more stringent quality control measures to reduce the number of defects. Two weeks later, 25 luxury model cars are pulled off the assembly line at random. The mean number of defects of the sample X, is 60, and the standard deviation of the sample, s, is 4. Thus the average number of defects has dropped by 10. Are the more stringent measures working, or is the drop due to sampling?

Since a direction has been stated, this is a one-tailed test (i.e., the average number of defects per car has dropped from 65 to 60).

The two hypotheses are stated as follows:

1. Null hypothesis (H_0): The sample mean is equal to or greater than the population mean ($H_0 \geqslant \mu$).
2. Alternative hypothesis (H_1): The sample mean is less than the population mean ($H_0 < \mu$).

Forche's quality control manager, Ted Preston, ascertains whether the more stringent quality control methods are working. He:

1. Uses Student's t-test since the sample number of cars is small (less than 30). The sample number is 25, and the standard deviation is unknown.
2. Selects a 0.05 level of significance.
3. Makes a decision rule as follows:
   a. $n - 1 = 25 - 1 = 24$
   b. One-tailed test. There has been a drop in the average number of defects from 65 to 60. Hence, the area of rejection is in the left tail of the normal curve.
   c. Level of significance = 0.05.
   d. Uses Appendix H to find the t value of 1.711.

Preston will reject the null hypothesis if t as computed is -1.711 or greater.

4. Computes the value of t using the following formula:

$$t = \frac{X - \mu}{s/\sqrt{n - 1}} = \frac{60 - 65}{4/\sqrt{24}}$$

$$= \frac{-5}{4/4.8990}$$

$$= \frac{-5}{0.8165}$$

$$= -6.1237$$

The computed value of t is -6.12, which is greater than -1.711; thus, the null hypothesis is rejected. Apparently the more stringent quality control measures were effective. Since the critical values of t and z become closer as the size of the sample becomes larger, the z statistic may be used where $n \geqslant 30$.

Two Means with Large Samples

Ms. Walker of LMN Equipment Co., a leading supplier of dental equipment, is seeking sources of low-speed dental drills. Walker specifies that the low-speed drills must operate at 7500 rpm. She places invitations to bid in a trade magazine. Eventually, she selects two companies, Sharp Drill and ABC Dental Supply Co., as finalists. Walker invites the two companies to submit drills for the testing. All other factors being equal, the contract will be awarded to the company with the higher rpm. Walker proceeds as follows to reach a decision:

1. Initially, she states that there is no significant difference in the mean rpm

of the low-speed dental drills submitted by Sharp Drill and ABC Dental Supply (null hypothesis). In effect, any difference in the rpm's is due to sampling variation.

The alternative hypothesis states that there is indeed a significant difference between the mean rpm. A two-tailed test will be used because the alternative hypothesis does not state a direction.

2. What statistical test does Walker want? She decides on the z-test, which assumes the following:

    a. Sample will be large (30 or more).

    b. Distances between variables are of a known, constant size. Each class is mutually exclusive, and categories can be ranked (interval level of measurement).

3. Walker selects a level of significance of 0.05.

4. Critical ratio of z. Walker refers to a standard business statistics book and finds that the following conditions apply:

    a. A sufficiently large number of random samples must be selected from two populations.

    b. When a distribution is developed from the differences between means from the two populations, it will resemble a normal curve. The critical ratio (the difference between the two means) is divided by standard error of difference between the two means, or:

$$\frac{\bar{X}_1 - \bar{X}_2}{\dfrac{s_1^{\,2}}{n_1} + \dfrac{s_2^{\,2}}{n_2}}$$

Walker attempts to work out a sample of the formula, so she set up Table 16.5 assuming:

(1) Fifty samples of equal size of low-speed drills were taken from both Sharp Drill and ABC Dental Supply.

(2) The standard deviation was 3 rpm for each sample.

Given that the two population means are equal, if the z values found in Table 16.5 and others are plotted, they should approximate a normal curve.

5. Walker formulates her decision rule based on the following facts:

    a. At the 5% level of significance, 95% of the z values computed will fall within 0 ± 1.96 (see Figure 16.3).

    b. No significant difference exists between the two population means.

    c. A two-tailed test is used since the alternative hypothesis does not state the direction of change.

Table 16.5. Computation of z Value.

Samples	$\bar{X}_1$	Mean rpm ABC Dental Supply Sharp Drill Co. $\bar{X}_2$	$\bar{X}_1 - \bar{X}_2$	Critical Ratio	z
1–10	7504	7510	−6	−6/0.6	−10.0
11–20	7502	7505	−3	−3/0.6	− 5.0
21–30	7510	7510	0	0/0.6	0
31–40	7508	7509	−1	−1/0.6	− 1.7
41–50	7507	7505	+2	+2/0.6	+ 3.3

    d. She will accept the null hypothesis if the z value from her computation falls within ±1.96.

    e. If the z value is greater than ± 1.96, she will accept the alternative hypothesis and reject the null one.

The null hypothesis states that the difference between the two sample rpm of low-speed dental drills is due to chance. The alternative hypothesis states that a z value greater than ±1.96 is not likely to be due to chance.

    6. Walker takes samples from each company and computes the z value.

        a. Samples randomly selected, together with the accompanying statistics, are shown in Table 16.6.

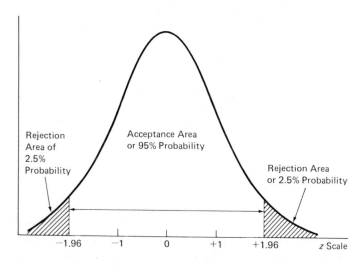

Fig. 16.3 Critical value of z at 0.05 level of significance for two large samples.

Table 16.6. Randomly Selected Samples of Low Speed Dental Drills.

ABC Dental Supply	*Sharp Drill*
$\bar{X}_1 = 7700$ rpm	$\bar{X}_2 = 7200$ rpm
$n_1 = 49$	$n_2 = 64$
$s_1^1 = 462$ rpm	$s_2^2 = 456$ rpm

b. The critical ratio (z value) is computed:

$$z = \frac{\bar{X}_1 - \bar{X}_2}{\sqrt{\left(\dfrac{s_1}{\sqrt{n_1}}\right)^2 + \left(\dfrac{s_2}{\sqrt{n_2}}\right)^2}}$$

$$= \frac{7700 - 7200}{\sqrt{\left(\dfrac{462}{\sqrt{49}}\right)^2 + \left(\dfrac{456}{\sqrt{64}}\right)^2}}$$

$$= \frac{7700 - 7200}{\sqrt{\left(\dfrac{469}{7}\right)^2 + \left(\dfrac{456}{8}\right)^2}}$$

$$= \frac{7700 - 7200}{\sqrt{4489 + 3249}}$$

$$= \frac{500}{\sqrt{7738}}$$

$$= \frac{500}{87.96}$$

$$= +5.684$$

c. The computed value of z (+5.684) falls in the area of rejection because it is beyond +1.96. Therefore, the null hypothesis is rejected at the 0.05 level of significance, and the alternative hypothesis is accepted.

d. Walker determines that there is a significant difference between the

Table 16.7. Time Necessary to Assemble Beaters for Mixettes.

			Assembly Time (sec)			
		Procedure 1			Procedure 2	
Operator	(X_1)	$X_1 - \bar{X}_1{}^a$	$(X_1 - \bar{X}_1)^2$	(X_2)	$X_2 - \bar{X}_2{}^b$	$(X_2 - \bar{X}_2)^2$
1	7	0	0	8	+0.4	0.16
2	6	-1.0	1.00	7	-0.6	0.36
3	7	0	0	7	-0.6	0.36
4	6	-1.0	1.00	8	+0.4	0.16
5	9	+2.0	4.00	8	+0.4	0.16
	35	7.0	6.00	38	7.6	1.20

$a = \bar{X}$ of 7.0
$b = \bar{X}$ of 7.6

    mean rpm of low-speed dental drills submitted by Sharp Drill and ABC Dental Supply.

  e. Since there is a significant difference between the means, Walker decides to buy from Sharp Drill.

  f. Had the z value been 5.684, it would still have fallen in the area of rejection. (This is a two-tailed test since the alternative hypothesis did not state a direction of change.) The null hypothesis would have been rejected; that is, the mean rpm's of the two dental drills would have been reversed, with Sharp Drill equaling 7200 rpm and ABC Dental Equipment equaling 7700 rpm, $(7200 - 7700)/ - 87.96$). Thus the alternative hypothesis would have been accepted.

Two Means with Small Samples

Mr. Snow, quality control manager for Hi-Speed Housewares Co., believes that the operator time limit for assembling the beaters for hand-held mixers (i.e., mixettes) is too long. Two of the operators on the assembly line have each made one suggestion that would reduce assembly-line time. Hi-Speed's industrial engineering department sent two people to the assembly department to independently time the two suggested changes. They timed five assemblers on the procedures; the results are shown in Table 16.7. The mean assembly times for procedures 1 and 2 were 7.0 and 7.6 seconds, respectively.

    Since the samples were small (less than 30), the t statistic was used. Snow went through six steps in testing a hypothesis to reach a decision:

  1. He formulates the null and alternative hypotheses.

    a. Null hypothesis (H_0): No significant difference exists between the mean assembly time of each suggested procedure.

    b. Alternative hypothesis (H_1): There is a significant difference between mean assembly times. This is a two-tailed test because the alternative hypothesis does not state the direction of change.

2. Snow decides to use the t-test since the sample is less than 30.
3. Snow decides on a 0.01 level of significance and 8 degrees of freedom $(10 - 2)$.
4. The critical ratio of t is completed.

$$t = \frac{\bar{X}_1 - \bar{X}_2}{\sqrt{\dfrac{\dfrac{\Sigma (X_1 - \bar{X}_1)^2 + \Sigma (X_2 - \bar{X}_2)^2}{(n_1 + n_2 - 2)} (n_1 + n_2)}{n_1 n_2}}}$$

$$= \frac{7.0 - 7.6}{\sqrt{\dfrac{\dfrac{6.00 + 1.20}{5 + 5 - 2}(5 + 5)}{(5)(5)}}}$$

$$= \frac{-0.6}{\sqrt{\dfrac{\dfrac{7.20}{8}(10)}{25}}}$$

$$= \frac{-0.6}{\sqrt{\dfrac{0.9(10)}{25}}}$$

$$= \frac{-0.6}{\sqrt{0.36}}$$

$$= \frac{-0.6}{0.6}$$

$$= -1.00$$

The critical value of t at the 0.01 level is 3.355 (see Appendix H).

5. Snow formulates his decision rule:
   a. At a 1% level of significance, 99% of t values must fall within ± 3.355 (see Figure 16.4).

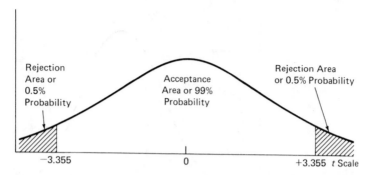

Fig. 16.4 Critical value of t at 0.01 level of significance at 8° of freedom for two small samples.

   b. There is no significant difference between the two population means.
   c. A two-tailed test is used. The alternative hypothesis does not state a direction of change.
   d. The null hypothesis is accepted if the t value falls within ±3.355.
   e. The alternative hypothesis is accepted if the t value is greater than 0 ± 3.355.

The null hypothesis states that the difference between the two sample means in assembly time is due to chance. The alternative hypothesis says that there is a significant difference between mean assembly times.

   6. Based on the computed value of t, Snow accepts or rejects the null hypothesis.
   a. The t value is computed to be -1.00.
   b. Snow accepts the null hypothesis since the critical value of t falls within ±3.355 at the 1% level of significance.

The null hypothesis states that there is no significant difference between the two means. The difference of 0.6 sec (i.e., X_1 = 7.0 and X_2 = 7.6) is probably due to sampling.

TYPE II ERROR

In the discussion of hypothesis testing with one sample where the population mean and standard deviation are known, it was stated that Mr. Sands, the guidance counselor, at Spoonville High, found the population mean to be $10,000 (average annual salary).

   If the population mean (μ) is $9500 at the 5% level of significance with the standard error of the mean (σ_x) equal to 38, the confidence limits would be $9500 ± [1.96 ($38)] . Thus, if the mean salary is between $9426 and $10,074, it will be accepted.

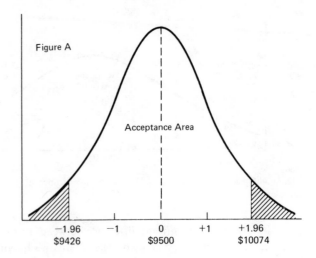

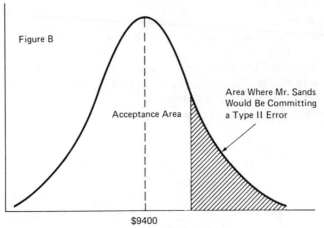

Fig. 16.5A&B Possibility of committing a Type II error at the 0.05 level of significance where the population mean is $9500 and the actual mean is $9400.

Let us examine how Sands could commit a Type II error under three conditions.

1. Assume that the actual mean is $9400 when Sands thought it was $9500 (see Figure 16.5A). Sands will accept any average annual salary above $9426 as being within the confidence limits based on the information in the previous paragraph. However he should reject it. What is the probability of committing a type II error under such circumstances?

   a. Determine the area under the normal curve falling between $9426 and $9400.

(1) Find the z value using the following formula:

$$z = \frac{X - \mu}{\sigma_{\bar{x}}}$$

$$= \frac{9426 - 9400}{38}$$

$$= 26/38$$

$$= 0.6842$$

(2) Using Appendix C, the area under the normal curve is determined to be 0.25175.

c. The area under the normal curve beyond the limit of $9426 is 0.50000 - 0.25175, or 0.24825. (The area under the normal curve from the mean to the upper tail is 0.50000.)

d. We can thus conclude that if Sands assumed the mean annual salary of high-school graduates to be $9500 when in fact it was $9400, then 25% of the time he will accept the mean of $9500 as being correct when in essence it should be rejected (See Figure 16.5B.)

2. The population mean (μ) is $9500. Suppose in reality it is $10,100. What is the probability that Sands will accept a mean annual salary of $9500 as being correct? (See Figure 16.6A.)

a. Determine area under the normal curve between $10,074 (upper limit where population mean equals $9500) and $10,100.

(1) Compute the z value.

$$z = \frac{X - \mu}{\sigma_{\bar{x}}}$$

$$= 10,074 - 10,100$$

$$= -26/38$$

$$= -0.68$$

(2) Find the area under the normal curve corresponding to 0.68. Looking at Appendix C, we find it to be 0.25175. The area under the normal curve between $10,074 and $10,100 is therefore 0.50000 - 0.25175, or 0.24825.

The probability of Sands accepting a population mean of $9500 when it is actually $10,100 is 25%. (See Figure 16.6B.)

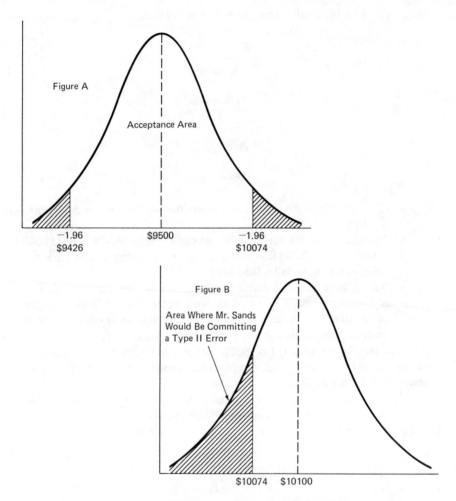

Fig. 16.6A&B Possibility of committing a Type II error at a 0.05 level of significance where the population mean is $9500 and the actual mean is $10,100.

Table 16.8 shows the probability of committing a Type II error for various high-school graduates' mean salaries.

CURVES

Operating Characteristic Curve

Suppose Sands was called upon to present his findings on the average salaries of high-school graduates to the Professional Society for Vocational Guidance Counselors. He decides to present his data graphically. One graph he uses is the oper-

Table 16.8. Probability of Committing a Type II Error Where the Population Mean Is $9500 at the 0.05 Level of Significance.

	Probability	
Means of High-School Graduates' Salaries	*Accepting Hypothesis As True when Not True (Committing Type II Error)*	*Rejecting Hypothesis When True (Not Committing Type II Error)*
$9300	0.0008	0.9992
9350	0.0228	0.9772
9400	0.2482	0.7518
9500	0.9500	0.0500
9550	0.7351	0.2649
9600	0.2483	0.7517
9650	0.0228	0.9972
9700	0.0008	0.9992

ating characteristic curves shown in Figure 16.7. In describing the operating characteristic curve to the society, Sands makes the following comments:

● If I believe the population mean to be $9500 when it is actually $9400, then the probability of my accepting a false hypothesis when I should have rejected it is 24.8% at the 5% level of significance.

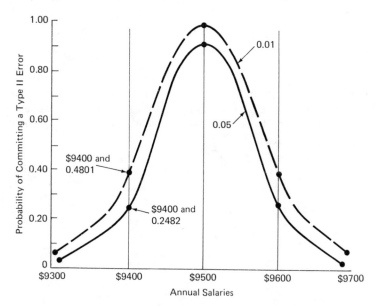

Fig. 16.7 Operating characteristic curves at the 0.05 and the 0.01 levels of significance.

Table 16.9. Probability of Committing a Type II Error where the
Population Mean Is $9500 at a 0.01 Level of Significance.

Means of High-School Graduates' Salaries	Probability	
	Accepting Hypothesis As True When Not (Committing Type II Error)	Rejecting Hypothesis When True (Not Committing Type II Error)
$9300	0.0037	0.9963
9350	0.0853	0.9147
9400	0.4801	0.5199
9500	0.9900	0.0100
9550	0.8961	0.1039
9600	0.4801	0.5199
9650	0.0869	0.9131
9700	0.0037	0.9963

● Note that the operating characteristic curve at the 1% level of significance is spread out more than the one at the 5% level. This indicates that the probability of committing a Type II error is greater at the 1% level. For example, if I believe the mean to be $9500 when actually it is $9400, the probability of my accepting a false hypothesis when it should have been rejected is 48.0% at the 1% level of significance. (See Table 16.9.)

● Sample size and the standard error of the mean affect the operating characteristic curve.

Power Curve

Sands also wished to graphically present the probability of *not* committing a Type II error. He took the appropriate data from Tables 16.8 and 16.9 and constructed a graph (Figure 16.8). Comparing Figures 16.7 and 16.8, we see one is the inverse of the other. Hence, the power curve is $(1 - \beta)$ or the probability of not committing a Type II error.

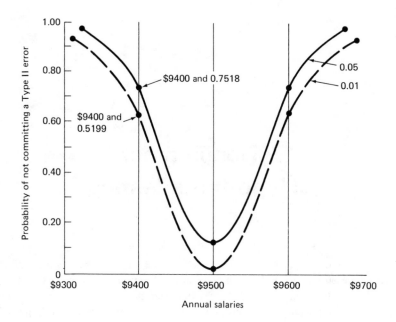

Fig. 16.8 Power curves at the 0.05 and the 0.01 levels of significance.

17 Nonparametric
Hypothesis Testing

In Chapter 16, we learned the difference between parametric and nonparametric levels of measurement. With parametric levels of measurement, it is assumed that the data can be ranked, the distances between the numbers are of a constant known size, and each class is mutually exclusive. Nonparametric levels are either nominal or ordinal, with the following characteristics:

Nominal	Ordinal
• Data cannot be classified into categories.	• One category is higher than another.
• Data cannot be ranked, and there is no particular order for groupings.	• Unequal distances exist between categories.
• Categories are mutually exclusive.	

This chapter will deal with nonparametric tests used for one or more samples.

NOMINAL LEVEL TESTS: ONE SAMPLE

Chi-Square

In a chi-square test, the idea is to see how well the observed set of data fit the expected set.

Mr. Squeaker runs DEF Amusement Co. of Tuftstown. DEF rented equipment, including a mechanical hare game, to the Tuftstown Volunteer Fire Department to use in a fundraising event. In the game, one of DEF's most popular, a player must shoot down one of ten moving mechanical hares. Each hare is numbered. The value of the prize won depends upon the number of the hare

**Table 17.1. Results of 100 Observations of Shots
Taken by Chief Brown at Mechanical Hare.**

Rabbit No.	No. Appearances
1	15
2	5
3	15
4	10
5	15
6	10
7	5
8	7
9	10
10	8
	100

that is shot. One player complained to the Tuftstown chief of police, Harriet Brown, that the game is fixed. The player contended that there are many more opportunities to shoot the hares worth lower value prizes than there are to shoot the hares worth higher value prizes. Of course, Squeaker claims that the game is not fixed. Chief Brown says she will take 100 shots at the mechanical hare while Squeaker records how many times each numbered hare appears.

Chief Brown tests the hypothesis as follows:

1. She states null hypothesis (H_0) and alternative hypothesis (H_1).
   a. Null hypothesis: After Chief Brown fires 100 shots, there will be no significant difference between the *observed* frequencies with which each numbered hare appears and the *expected* frequencies—in effect, indicating that the game has not been tampered with.
   b. Alternative hypothesis: The game has been tampered with—that is, there is a significant difference between the two frequencies.

2. She selects the level of significance equal to 0.01.

3. She determines the areas of acceptance and rejection based on the chi-square test of significance (X^2). The formula for X^2 is:

$$X^2 = \frac{(f_o - f_e)^2}{f_e} \text{ with } k - 1 \text{ degrees of freedom}$$

where k = number in the sample. The results of Chief Brown's 100 shots at the mechanical hare are shown in Table 17.1. There are 9 degrees of freedom (10 − 1). The areas of acceptance and rejection are determined by the critical value. This is determined by referring to Appendix J. With a 0.01 level of significance and 9 degrees of freedom, the critical value is 21.67. Chief Brown reasons that if

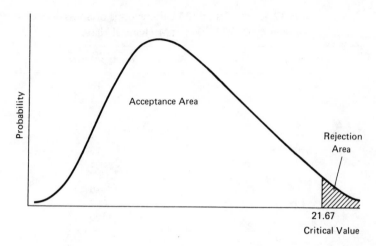

Fig. 17.1 Areas of acceptance and rejection based on critical values of chi-square for a probability distribution at the 0.01 level of significance and with 9 degrees of freedom.

the critical value is less than 21.67, she will assume that the mechanical hare game has not been tampered with (i.e., she will accept the null hypothesis). If, however, the critical value is equal to 21.67, she will reject the null hypothesis and assume that the game has been tampered with (i.e., she will accept the alternative hypothesis). Figure 17.1 shows these areas of acceptance and rejection graphically, based on the critical values of chi square.

4. Chief Brown compares observed and expected frequencies for 100 observed shots at the mechanical hares (Table 17.2). If the game has not been tampered

Table 17.2. Comparison of Observed and Expected Frequencies of Chief Brown's 100 Shots at the Mechanical Hare.

Rabbit No.	Observed Frequency (f_o)	Expected Frequency (f_e)
1	15	10
2	5	10
3	15	10
4	10	10
5	15	10
6	10	10
7	5	10
8	7	10
9	10	10
10	8	10
	100	100

Table 17.3. Computation of Chi-Square.

Rabbit No.	f_o	f_e	$f_o - f_e$	$(f_o - f_e)^2$	$(f_e - f_o)^2 / f_e$
1	15	10	+5	25	2.5
2	5	10	-5	25	2.5
3	15	10	+5	25	2.5
4	10	10	0	0	0
5	15	10	+5	25	2.5
6	10	10	0	0	0
7	5	10	-5	25	2.5
8	7	10	-3	9	0.9
9	10	10	0	0	0
10	8	10	-2	4	0.4
	100	100	0		13.8

with, each rabbit would be expected to appear 10 times in a total of 100 observed shots. In comparing the two sets of data, Chief Brown notices that hares 1, 3, and 5 appear more frequently than do the expected frequencies. Hares 2, 4, 6, 7, 8, 9 and 10 appear less frequently. Are these differences due to chance, or has Squeaker altered the mechanism?

5. Chief Brown computes the chi-square statistic, as shown in Table 17.3. The computed value of the chi-square, 13.8, falls below the critical level of 21.67. Therefore, Chief Brown accepts Squeaker's statement that the game has not been altered. In essence, Chief Brown accepts the null hypothesis at the 0.01 level of significance.

It is possible that Chief Brown committed a Type I error by rejecting the null hypothesis when it should have been accepted.

Chi-Square Test When Expected Frequencies Are Not Equal. Frequently, a company will compare its market share with that of other companies in the same industry. Suppose that for 30 days, Shiny Brass Mills, a major brass producer, is going to reduce the price of brass strip by 20% in order to increase sales. Mr. Greene, the company's market-research analyst, projects what its market share will be as a result of the price reduction. He proceeds as follows:

1. Greene examines the market-research department's files on industry sales of brass strip for 1980 and prepares Table 17.4.

2. Greene expects Tuftstown Brass Mills and Spoonville Rolling Mills to follow suit and drop its brass-sheet prices by 20%.

3. Greene prepares Table 17.5 showing the computation of the chi-square.

4. Greene determines whether to accept or rejct the null hypothesis (i.e., that the price deduction causes no change in the market share).

    a. Sets the level of significance at 0.10.

    b. Refers to Appendix J for the critical value of the chi-square based on

Table 17.4.   Industry Market Shares of Brass Strip in 1980
(Sales in $ Millions).

| Company | Brass Strip | |
	Estimated 1980 Sales	Market Share
Tuftstown Brass Mills	$ 5.6	29.8%
Spoonville Rolling Mills	4.5	23.9
Shiny Brass Mills	3.2	17.0
Rolling Stone Brass Co.	3.0	16.0
Canton Rolling Mills	2.5	13.3
Total	$18.8	100.0%

$K - 1$ or 4 degrees of freedom and a 0.10 level of significance. The critical value of the chi-square equals 7.78.

5. Greene accepts the null hypothesis that the price reduction will cause no change in the market shares of brass-strip sales of the five companies shown in Table 17.4 at a 0.10 level of significance.

Limitations of Chi-Square Tests. If there are only two categories (cells), then the expected frequency in both cells should be at least five. If the *expected* frequency in more than 20% of the cases (with three or more cells) is five or less, the chi-square test should not be used.

Long & Long Inc. is doing a marketing consulting job for a large company that produces blenders. Long & Long develops a questionnaire concerning blenders, which asks the respondents, for example, to check the color they prefer in a blender. The results of the color question are shown in Table 17.6.

There are 10 categories in Table 17.6, of which three (30%) have expected frequencies less than 5. If some of the categories were combined as in Table 17.7, the chi-square could be used. Assuming a 0.10 level of significance with 5 degrees of freedom, the critical value of the chi-square is 9.24. The null hypothesis—there is no significant difference between the expected and observed (sample) results—is accepted at the 10% level of significance, because the computed value (7.59) is less than the critical value of the chi-square.

Population Proportion Known

Suppose ABC Drug Co. has developed a new measles vaccine. Suppose further that federal law requires such a vaccine to be proven 85% or more effective before it is placed on the market. Jane Bond, ABC's market-research manager, must develop statistical procedures to determine if the sample of preschool children to

Table 17.5. Computation of Chi-Square.

| Company | 1980 Market Share | One Month's Sales After Price Reduction (in $ Millions) | | $f_o - f_e$ | $(f_o - f_e)^2$ | $(f_o - f_e)^2/f_e$ |
		f_o	f_e			
Tuftstown Brass Mills	29.8	$0.46	$0.49[a]	−0.03	0.09	0.09/0.49 = 0.18
Spoonville Rolling Mills	23.9	0.41	0.39	+0.02	0.04	0.04/0.39 = 0.10
Shiny Brass Mills	17.0	0.31	0.28	+0.03	0.09	0.09/0.28 = 0.32
Rolling Stone Brass Co.	16.0	0.25	0.26	−0.01	0.01	0.01/0.26 = 0.04
Canton Rolling Mills	13.3	0.21	0.22	−0.01	0.01	0.01/0.22 = 0.05
Total $	100.0	$1.64	$1.64	0		0.69

[a] Assumes no change in market share from price reduction, i.e., Tuftstown = 29.8% × $1.64 = $0.49, etc.

Table 17.6. Color Preferences for Blenders.

Color	Times Chosen f_o	f_e
Bright yellow	5	7
Sunshine yellow	10	15
Off-white	20	18
Eggshell white	4	4
Light green	11	12
Light blue	12	10
Sky blue	9	3
Dark green	12	12
Almond	5	3
Light tan	12	16
Total	100	100

be tested is in the same proportion as that required by federal law. She proceeds as follows:

1. She states the null and alternative hypotheses:

   a. Null hypothesis: The proportion in sample (p) of preschool children to be tested is no different from proportion (0.85) required in population (P).

   b. Alternative hypothesis: The population proportion (P) is less than 0.85.

2. Bond realizes she is working with nominal-level data since all that is required is a yes or no answer (i.e., the vaccine is or is not effective).

3. The level of significance selected is 0.01.

4. A one-tailed test is used since the alternative hypothesis states a direction (P is less than 0.85).

5. Bond selects the z statistic test. A total of 3000 preschool children were given the vaccine. After adequate time had passed, ABC Drug conducted a survey

Table 17.7. Color Preference for Blenders, Categories Revised.

Color	No. Times Chosen f_o	f_e	$f_o - f_e$	$(f_o - f_e)^2$	$(f_o - f_e)^2/f_e$
Bright yellow	15	22	−7	49	49/22 = 2.23
Off-white	24	22	+2	4	4/22 = 0.18
Light green	11	12	−1	1	1/22 = 0.05
Light blue	21	13	+8	64	64/13 = 4.92
Dark green	12	12	0	0	0 = 0
Almond	17	19	−2	4	4/19 = 0.21
Total	100	100	0		7.59

to determine the results. A total of 2225 preschool children did *not* contract the measles, while 775 did.

$$z = \frac{p - P}{\delta_p}$$

where

$P = 0.85$ (known population proportion)

$p = 0.74$ (sample proportion)

$\delta_p = 0.0065$ (standard error of population proportion)

The formula for δ_p is:

$$\delta_p = \sqrt{\frac{P(1 - P)}{n}}$$

$$= \sqrt{\frac{0.85(1 - 0.85)}{3000}}$$

$$= \sqrt{\frac{0.1275}{3000}}$$

$$= \sqrt{0.0000425}$$

$$= 0.0065$$

$$z = \frac{0.74 - 0.85}{0.0065}$$

$$= \frac{-0.11}{0.0065}$$

$$= -16.92$$

6. Bond determines the area of acceptance and rejection by finding the critical value of z (Appendix C).
   a. The critical value of z (from Appendix C) is 1.65.
   b. The area of rejection is 0.0500.
   c. Area of acceptance = 0.5000 – 0.0500 = 0.4500.

    d. The alternative hypothesis stated that the population proportion is less than 0.85. Therefore, a one-tailed test ($P < 0.85$) left-hand half of normal curve is used.

7. Bond accepts or rejects the null hypothesis:
    a. The null hypothesis is accepted if the computed value of z is 0 to -1.65.
    b. The alternative hypothesis is accepted if the computed value of z is more than -1.65.
    c. The computed value of z is -16.92.
    d. The null hypothesis is rejected. The difference between the sample proportion of 0.74 and the required population proportion of 0.85 is significant. This difference is not due to sampling. Therefore, ABC Drug must improve the vaccine in order to meet federal government standards.

NOMINAL LEVEL: TWO SAMPLE TESTS

Two Proportions: Large Samples ($n > 30$)

The Yummy Dog Biscuit Co. considers marketing a new cheese-flavored burger for dogs, Cheesies. It must determine whether Cheesies appeal more to puppies (dogs under 12 months of age) or to dogs who are 12 months of age or older (adults). Here we have two populations, puppies and adult dogs.

    Mr. Golden, the market-research manager, searches the Tuftstown dog-license records and randomly picks 150 dogs under 12 months of age and 150 dogs over 12 months of age. He makes sure that no two dogs have the same owner. Golden then sends samples of Cheesies, along with samples of Goodies, the leading competitor, to the 300 dog owners. He asks the recipients to feed Cheesies to their dogs one day, followed by Goodies the next day, for a 30-day period. At the end of that time, Golden plans to send each owner a questionnaire asking which burger the dogs preferred.

    Golden develops the following procedure:
1. He states the null and alternative hypotheses:
    a. Null hypothesis: No difference exists between the number of younger (P_1) and older dogs (P_2) preferring Cheesies. Hence, $P_1 = P_2$.
    b. Alternative hypotheses: There is a significant difference between the number of younger dogs (P_1) and older dogs (P_2) desiring Cheesies. Hence, $P_1 \neq P_2$.
2. He uses the z-test. One hundred owners of puppies and 100 owners of older dogs responded to Golden's questionnaire. This resulted in a 67% response rate because initially 150 owners in each of the two categories were chosen.
3. Golden selects a 0.05 level of significance.
4. Golden computes the population proportion. He asks the data-processing

department to compile statistics on the 200 questionnaires returned. 60 puppies preferred Cheesies. 75 adult dogs wanted Cheesies in preference to Goodies.

a. The proportions are computed in order to calculate a weighed mean.

(2) P_2 = number of adults dogs preferring Cheesies over Goodies (100)
n_2 = number of adult dogs in sample (100)

$$75/100 = 0.75$$

b. The weighted mean is calculated.

$$\bar{P} = \frac{P_1 + P_2}{n_1 + n_2}$$

$$= \frac{60}{100} + \frac{75}{100} = \frac{135}{200} = 0.675$$

5. The critical value of z is computed.

$$z = \frac{P_1 - P_2}{\sqrt{\dfrac{\bar{P}(1 - \bar{P})}{n_1} + \dfrac{\bar{P}(1 - \bar{P})}{n_2}}}$$

$$= \frac{0.60 - 0.75}{\sqrt{\dfrac{0.675(1 - 0.675)}{100} + \dfrac{0.675(1 - 0.675)}{100}}}$$

$$= \frac{0.60 - 0.75}{\sqrt{\dfrac{0.2194}{100} + \dfrac{0.2194}{100}}}$$

$$= \frac{-0.15}{\sqrt{0.002194 + 0.002194}}$$

$$= \frac{-0.15}{\sqrt{0.004388}}$$

$$= \frac{-0.15}{0.0662419}$$

$$= -2.26$$

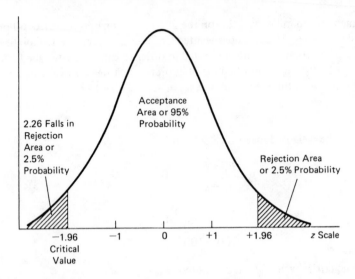

Fig. 17.2 Areas of acceptance and rejection at the 0.05 level of significance of a two-tailed test.

6. The null hypothesis is accepted or rejected.
   a. The null and alternative hypotheses are restated:
      (1) The null hypothesis is $P_1 = P_2$.
      (2) The alternative hypothesis is $P_1 \neq P_2$.
   b. The alternative hypothesis does not indicate that population 1 is more or less than population 2. Hence, no direction is named so we have a two-tailed test.
   c. The critical value of z at 0.05 level of significance = ± 1.96.
   d. Critical and computed values of z are compared:

   Critical value = –1.96

   Computed value = – 2.26

   e. The null hypothesis is rejected at the 0.05 level of significance because –2.26 falls in the area of rejection (see Figure 17.2). There is a significant difference between the proportion of puppies and the proportion of adult dogs preferring Cheesies to Goodies (at the 0.05 level of significance). The difference between the two sampling proportions (0.60 and 0.75) is not due to errors in sampling.
7. Golden concludes that
   a. More research needs to be done on the ingredients of Cheesies.
   b. There is the possibility of a Type I error in that the null hypothesis is rejected when it should have been accepted.

Two Proportions: Small Samples

When samples are small ($n < 30$), the t-test is used instead of the z value. Suppose the city council of Tuftstown has 11 members. Six are Republicans, and five are Democrats. An ordinance requiring alternate-side-of-the-street parking has been proposed to the council. Patricia White, a reporter for the *Tuftstown Times,* finds that three Republicans and four Democrats favor the ordinance.

Ms. White conducts the following investigation:

1. She states the null and alternative hypotheses:
   a. Null hypothesis: No difference exists between the proportion of Republicans (P_1) and the proportion of Democrats (P_2) favoring the ordinance (i.e., $P_1 = P_2$).
   b. Alternative hypothesis: There is a significant difference between the two proportions. Hence, $P_1 \neq P_2$.
2. The t-test is used.
3. The level of significance is 0.05.
4. The ratio of t is computed:

    a.
$$t = \frac{P_1 - P_2}{\sqrt{\dfrac{\bar{P}(1 - \bar{P})}{n_1} + \dfrac{\bar{P}(1 - \bar{P})}{n_2}}}$$

    b. P = weighted value = $3/6 + 4/5 = 7/11 = 0.64$

    c.
$$t = \frac{0.50 - 0.80}{\sqrt{\dfrac{0.64\,(0.36)}{6} + \dfrac{(0.64)(0.36)}{5}}}$$

$$= \frac{0.50 - 0.80}{\sqrt{\dfrac{0.23}{6} + \dfrac{0.23}{5}}}$$

$$= \frac{-0.30}{\sqrt{0.0383 + 0.0460}}$$

$$= \frac{-0.30}{\sqrt{0.0843}}$$

$$= \frac{-0.30}{0.2903}$$

$$= -1.0334$$

5. The null hypothesis is accepted or rejected:
   a. The critical value of t is determined.
      (1) There are 9 degrees of freedom (5 + 6 – 2).
      (2) The level of significance is 0.05.
      (3) Alternative hypothesis does not state direction. Therefore, a two-tailed test is used.
      (4) Referring to Appendix H, the critical value of t = 2.262.
   b. The computed value and the critical value of t are compared.
      (1) The computed value is –1.0334.
      (2) The critical value from Appendix H is –2.262.
   c. The null hypothesis is accepted at the 0.05 level of significance because the computed value of t falls in the acceptance area (below –2.262). Therefore, the difference between the two proportions can be due to sampling error.
6. Ms. White concludes that:
   a. On the basis of her finding that three Republicans and four Democrats are in favor of alternate-side-of-the-street parking, the ordinance will be passed.
   b. There is a 0.05 chance of a Type I error (i.e., the null hypothesis is accepted when it should be rejected).

ORDINAL LEVEL

Remember, in ordinal-level tests it must be possible to rank the data from high to low or vice versa. There are several ways to test two samples of ordinal-level data. The test chosen depends on the relationship of the two samples: Are they independent and from the same population? Are they independent and from two populations? Are the two samples related?

Two Samples from Same Population and Independent

Mann-Whitney U Test. The Mann-Whitney U test is used for small and large samples. In a small sample, $n \leqslant 20$ in the larger of two samples. In a large sample, $n \geqslant 20$ in the larger of two samples.

Small Samples.   Ms. Gonzalez teaches fifth grade in Tuftstown Grammar School. She wants to know if there is a significant difference in IQ test scores of fifth-grade students living in Tuftstown and those bused in from Spoonville. So, she randomly selects six pupils from Tuftstown and seven from Spoonville and gives them an IQ test. Then, Ms. Gonzalez proceeds as follows:

1. She states the null and alternative hypotheses:
   a. Null hypothesis: There is no significant difference in IQ test scores between the two sets of children.
   b. Alternative hypothesis: There is a significant difference in IQ test scores between the two sets of children. If no direction is stated (for example, that children from Tuftstown have higher IQs) then a two-tailed test is used. If a direction is stated, a one-tailed test is used. Assume here that a two-tailed test is used.

2. The statistical test is selected: the Mann-Whitney U Test. In this test, data can be ranked and come from two independent samples.

3. A level of significance of 0.05 is selected.

4. The areas of acceptance and rejection are determined.
   a. n_1 = 6 (children from Tuftstown)
      n_2 = 5 (children from Spoonville)
   b. A two-tailed test is used.
   c. The level of significance is 0.05.
   d. Referring to Appendix K, Mann-Whitney Critical Value U. Look at the top half of the table applying to a two-tailed test at 0.05 and a one-tailed test at 0.025. Go down the column where n_2 equals 5. The critical value U is 3.
   e. If $U \leqslant 3$, the null hypothesis is rejected. If $U > 3$, the null hypothesis is accepted.

5. U is computed. The scores for six students from Tuftstown and five from Spoonville are shown in Table 17.8.

Table 17.8. IQ Test Scores of Students from Tuftstown and Spoonville.

Tuftstown		Spoonville	
IQ Score	Rank	IQ Score	Rank
200	5	210	3
155	11	165	10
250	1	195	6
175	9	205	4
190	7	185	8
225	2		
	35		31

The values of U and U' are then computed using the following values:

n = size of one sample (six students Tuftstown High School)

n' = size of second sample (five students at Spoonville High School)

ΣR_1 = sum of ranks for first sample (35 for students at Tuftstown)

ΣR_2 = sum of ranks for second sample (31 for students at Spoonville)

Thus,

$$U = n_1 n_2 + \frac{n_1(n_1 + 1)}{2} - \Sigma R_1 \qquad\qquad U' = n_1 n_2 + \frac{n_2(n_2 + 1)}{2} - \Sigma R_2$$

$$= (6)(5) + \frac{6(6 + 1)}{2} - 35 \qquad\qquad = (6)(5) + \frac{5(5 + 1)}{2} - 31$$

$$= 30 + (42/2) - 35 \qquad\qquad\qquad = 30 + (30/2) - 31$$

$$= 30 + 21 - 35 \qquad\qquad\qquad\quad = 30 + 15 - 31$$

$$= 16 \qquad\qquad\qquad\qquad\qquad\quad = 14$$

Gonzalez checks U' using the following formula:

$$U' = n_1 n_2 - U$$

$$= (6)(5) - 16$$

$$= 30 - 16$$

$$= 14$$

6. She accepts or rejects the null hypothesis.
   a. Gonzalez uses the smaller of two computed U values, which is 14.
   b. The computed value of 14 is compared to the critical value of 3 at a 0.5 level of significance.
   c. The null hypothesis is accepted since $U > 3$. There is no significant difference between the IQs of children from Tuftstown and those from Spoonville.

Table 17.9. Test Scores, French I Students, Silver Creek and Jones Crossing.

Silver Creek (Sample 1)		Jones Crossing (Sample 2)	
Test Scores	Rank	Test Scores	Rank
200	19	201	18
165	27	204	17
135	38	134	39
145	33	214	12
140	36	193	21
190	22	136	37
185	24	120	40
210	15	155	29
205	16	219	7
150	31	230	3
215	10	187	23
212	14	153	30
160	28	228	4
220	6	148	32
217	9	198	20
213	13	250	1
142	35	168	25
218	8	240	2
215	11		
223	5		
144	34		
167	26		
	460		360

Large Samples. A large sample is $n > 20$ in the larger of the two independent samples. Suppose that 22 students enrolled in French I at Silver Creek High School (Sample 1) were competing against 18 students in French I from Jones Crossing High School (Sample 2) for a trip to Paris. The students from each high school took a written test; the scores are shown in Table 17.9.

　1. Null and alternative hypotheses are stated.

　　a. Null hypothesis: There is no significant difference between the test scores of the French I students at Silver Creek and those at Jones Crossing.

　　b. Alternative hypothesis: There is a significant difference between the test scores of French I students at Silver Creek and those at Jones Crossing.

　2. The statistical test, the modified z test, is selected because $n > 20$ in the larger of the two independent samples. The larger the sample size, the closer the distribution of the statistic becomes.

　3. The level of significance is 0.05.

4. The modified statistic is computed based on the following formula:

$$z = \frac{\Sigma R_1 - \Sigma R_2 - (n_1 - n_2)\left(\dfrac{n_1 + n_2 + 1}{2}\right)}{\sqrt{n_1 n_2 \left(\dfrac{n_1 + n_2 + 1}{3}\right)}}$$

where

n_1 = 22 number in sample 1

n_2 = 18 = number in sample 2

R_1 = 460 = sum ranks sample 1

R_2 = 360 = sum ranks sample 2

Thus,

$$z = \frac{(460 - 360) - \left[(22 - 18)\left(\dfrac{22 + 18 + 1}{2}\right)\right]}{\sqrt{(22)(18)\,\dfrac{22 + 18 + 1}{3}}}$$

$$= \frac{(100 - [(4)(20.5)]}{\sqrt{396(13.67)}}$$

$$= \frac{100 - 82}{\sqrt{5413.32}}$$

$$= \frac{18}{73.58}$$

$$= 0.24463 \cong 0.2446$$

5. The critical and computed values of z are compared.
   a. The critical value at the 0.05 level of significance is ± 1.96.
   b. The computed value at the 0.05 level of significance is 0.25.

Table 17.10 Comparison of the Flavor of Flavor Buds and Frez-Dri Coffee Ratings among Respondents in City A and City B.

Rating Scale	Respondents Preferring Flavor Buds		Cumulative Frequency	
	City A	City B	City A	City B
0 up to 5	2	30	2	30
5 up to 10	7	10	9	40
10 up to 15	15	7	24	47
15 up to 20	20	2	44	49
20 up to 25	6	11	50	60

6. The null hypothesis is accepted or rejected. The computed value of z falls outside ± 1.96 at the 0.05 level of significance so that the null hypothesis is rejected. There is no significant difference between the test scores of French I students at Silver Creek and Jones Crossing.

The Mann-Whitney U Test is designed primarily to determine whether two independent samples come from the same population.

Kolmogorov-Smirnov Test.
One-Tailed Test. The Kolmogorov-Smirnov test of significance is used where there are two independent samples taken from separate populations. Data sample must be at ordinal level i.e., capable of being ranked.

Flavor Brands, a food-processing firm, wants to place a new freeze-dried coffee, Flavor Buds, on the market. The company decides to test market it against the leading brand, Frez-Dri. The market-research manager, Mr. Terry, sends out samples of each coffee along with a questionnaire to 50 people in City A and 60 in City B. Their names were selected at random from a mailing list supplied by a large mailing house. The questionnaire asks "How does the flavor of Flavor Buds compare with the flavor of Frez-Dri? Please rate on a scale of 0 to 25." The results are shown in Table 17.10. Terry proceeds as follows:

1. He states the null and alternative hypotheses.
   a. Null hypothesis: Respondents in Cities A and B exhibit no preference when comparing the flavor of Flavor Buds with that of Frez-Dri.
   b. Alternative hypothesis: Respondents in City A prefer the flavor of Flavor Buds over that of Frez-Dri. The alternative hypothesis states a direction. Thus, a one-tailed test is used.
2. Terry selects a 0.05 level of significance.
3. Terry computes the largest absolute difference between city A and city B (see Table 17.11).

Table 17.11 Computation of the Largest Absolute Difference (D) Between City A and City B.

| | | | Flavor Preference Rating | | | | |
| | Frequency | | Cumulative Frequency | | Cumulative Frequency in Decimals | | |
Rating	City A	City B	City A	City B	City A	City B	Absolute Difference
0 up to 5	2/50	30/60	2/50	30/60	0.040	0.500	0.460
5 up to 10	7/50	10/60	9/50	40/60	0.180	0.667	0.487
10 up to 15	15/50	7/60	24/50	47/60	0.480	0.783	0.303
15 up to 20	20/50	2/60	44/50	49/60	0.880	0.817	0.063
20 up to 25	6/50	11/60	50/50	60/60	1.000	1.000	0.000

4. He uses modified chi-square formula to compute X^2:

$$X^2 = 4D^2 \, \frac{n_1 n_2}{n_1 + n_2} \text{ with 2 degrees of freedom}$$

where

$D = 0.487 = $ largest absolute difference between cumulative frequencies

$n_1 = 50 = $ size of sample 1, city A

$n_2 = 60 = $ size of sample 2, city B

5. X^2 is computed.

$$X^2 = 4(0.487^2)\left(\frac{(50)(60)}{50 + 60}\right)$$

$$= 4(0.487^2)\left(\frac{3000}{110}\right)$$

$$= 4(0.487^2)\,(27.27)$$

$$= 4(0.237)\,(27.27)$$

$$= (0.948)\,(27.27)$$

$$= 25.85$$

6. The critical and computed values of D are compared.
   a. The computed value of X^2 is 25.85.
   b. The critical value of X^2 is 5.99.
Since the distribution of the sample is like that of chi-square, Terry refers to Appendix J.

7. Terry accepts or rejects the null hypothesis. After comparing the critical and computed values of X^2, Terry accepts the alternative hypothesis based on the following facts:
   a. The computed value of X^2 falls outside the area of acceptance for a one-tailed test at the 0.05 level of significance (see Figure 17.3).
   b. Terry therefore accepts that there is a difference between respondents in City A and City B concerning their flavor preference for the two brands of freeze-dried coffee.

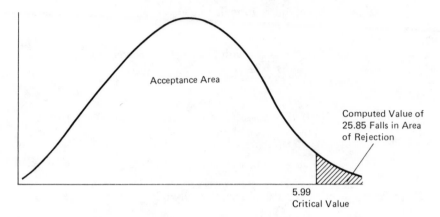

Fig. 17.3 Comparison of computed and critical values of D chi-square probability distribution at the 0.05 level of significance and with 2 degrees of freedom.

Two-Tailed Test. In the previous example, suppose Terry had merely wanted to know the computed value of X^2 necessary to reject the null hypothesis. He would have used the Kolmogorov-Smirnov test of significance. (The alternative hypothesis does not state a direction—two-tailed test, and $n \geqslant 40$ in both sample populations.) Terry would proceed as follows:

1. State values of n_1 and n_2, $n_1 = 50$ and $n_2 = 60$.
2. Select largest value of D from table 17.11.
3. State level of significance = 0.05.
4. Compute critical value of D using a two-tailed test at 0.05 level of significance (from Appendix L, we see $D = 1.36$).

$$D = 1.36 \sqrt{\frac{n_1 + n_2}{n_1 n_2}}$$

$$= 1.36 \sqrt{\frac{50 + 60}{(50)(60)}}$$

$$= 1.36 \sqrt{\frac{110}{3000}}$$

$$= 1.36 \sqrt{0.03667}$$

$$= 1.36(0.1915)$$

$$= 0.26$$

3. In order to accept the alternative hypothesis that there is a difference between two sample populations, the critical value of D must be $\geqslant 0.26$. Conversely, when the critical value of $D < 0.26$, the null hypothesis is accepted.

Signed Ram/Test: Wilcoxon. The Wilcoxon test is used to see if there is a significant difference in paired data from the same population. Suppose a new IQ test has been developed by the IQ Testing Corp. The company wishes to see how the new test compares with its old one. The marketing vice president, Ms. Johnson, randomly selects 35 students from a mailing list for City A. She believes the city is a good test market with a fairly good cross section of student populations.

The students take the old IQ test. A week later, the new IQ test is administered to the same group. The results of both tests are recorded (Table 17.12). Johnson then performs the following steps:

1. She states the null and alternative hypotheses:
   a. Null hypothesis: If the sum of the positive and negative ranks does not differ greatly from zero, the results are most likely due to sampling fluctutations.
   b. Alternative hypothesis: If there is a significance difference between the two IQ tests (see Table 17.12), then it is assumed that the differences are too great to be attributed to chance fluctuations in paired data from the same population.
2. The value of T is computed.
   a. Johnson records the old and new IQ test scores of each student (Table 17.12).
   b. Johnson computes the absolute difference between the old and new IQ test scores. She considers only the positive and negative differences. Zero differences are ignored.
   c. Next, the absolute differences are ranked. In this case, $n = 30$ (i.e., five of the differences equaled zero (see Table 17.13).
   d. Ranks are correctly signed. There are three students with an absolute difference of ± 2. To correctly rank students with the same absolute difference, the average is calculated. Since two of the three absolute differences are -2, each is given a rank of -2.0. The one student with $+2$ is assigned a $+2.0$. Hence, two is computed by $(1 + 2 + 3)/3 = 6/3 = 2$. The averages for the ranks 4 to 14 where the absolute difference is 5 is computed by

$$\frac{4 + 5 + 6 + 7 + 8 + 9 + 10 + 11 + 12 + 13 + 14}{11} = \frac{99}{11} = 9.0$$

Table 17.12. Comparison of Scores Achieved on Old and New IQ Tests by 35 Students in City A.

1	2	3	4
	IQ Test Score		Absolute Difference
Student No.	Old	New	(Column 3 - Column 2)
1	90	95	5
2	115	115	–
3	115	110	-5
4	210	205	-5
5	200	225	25
6	195	184	-11
7	100	100	–
8	205	190	-15
9	175	180	5
10	165	170	5
11	160	160	–
12	95	100	5
13	98	110	12
14	125	115	-10
15	140	150	10
16	150	150	–
17	175	190	15
18	225	230	5
19	215	220	5
20	195	190	-5
21	185	170	-15
22	130	130	–
23	140	190	50
24	165	190	25
25	110	140	30
26	112	110	-2
27	202	190	-12
28	198	200	2
29	175	180	5
30	170	160	-10
31	201	180	-21
32	145	155	10
33	175	160	-5
34	98	110	12
35	102	100	-2

Notice that the sign of the original difference is given to the assigned rank. For example, rank 19 is negative because the value of rank 11 is negative.

e. Johnson adds the negative and positive ranks (column 3, Table 17.13) without regard to sign which equals 465.

f. The sum of the negative figures is -118, while the sum of the positive

Table 17.13. Scores Achieved on Old and New IQ Tests by 35 Students in City A, Ranked According to Sign

1 Absolute Difference According to Sign	2 Column 1 Ranked	3 Column 2 Ranked According to Sign[a]
2	1	−2.0
2	2	−2.0
2	3	+2.0
5	4	−9.0
5	5	−9.0
5	6	−9.0
5	7	−9.0
5	8	+9.0
5	9	+9.0
5	10	+9.0
5	11	+9.0
5	12	+9.0
5	13	+9.0
5	14	+9.0
10	15	−16.5
10	16	−16.5
10	17	+16.5
10	18	+16.5
11	19	−19.0
12	20	−21.0
12	21	+21.0
12	22	+21.0
15	23	−24.0
15	24	−24.0
15	25	+24.0
21	26	−26.0
25	27	+27.5
25	28	+27.5
30	29	+29.0
50	30	+30.0
	Total 465	465.0

[a]Calculation is correct since the total of column 2 equals the total column of 3 without regard to sign.

is +226. The smaller of the two figures without regard to the sign is 118. Therefore, the computed value of T is 118.

3. The ctitical value of T is computed by referring to Appendix M where
   a. $n = 30$
   b. The level of significance = 0.05.
   c. The critical value of $T = 137$.
   d. The sum of the positive and negative numbers if 465 without regard to sign. If any increase in IQ scores were offset exactly by a decrease in

scores, then the figure would be approximately 232.5 (465 ÷ 2). As a result, a computed T value from 137 to 232.5 could occur by chance. This assumes that when the positive and negative ranks are added, they are approximately zero.

4. Johnson compares the critical and computed values of T.
   a. The computed value of T is 118.
   b. The critical value of T is 137.
   c. The computed value of T is less than the critical value.
5. Johnson accepts or rejects the null hypothesis.
   a. Since the computed value is less than the critical value of T at the 0.05 level, Johnson rejects the null hypothesis that the results in the test scores are due to sampling fluctuations.

That the positive differences of 226 exceed the negative differences of 118 suggests that the new IQ test is an improvement over the old one. To measure the improvement, a *one-tailed test* is used. Appendix M indicates a critical value of 151 when $n = 30$ at the 0.05 level of significance. The computed value of T was 118. Since 118 is less than 151, it proves the point. The probability of rejecting the null hypothesis when it should have been accepted (Type I error) is 0.05.

THREE AND MORE SAMPLES

In nominal-level tests, the data cannot be ranked. In an ordinal-level test, the data can be ranked. Statistical tests used for three or more samples are designed to determine whether they came from the same identical populations.

Cochran Q Test

This test uses nominal level information where there are at least three sets of data that are related. Assume four members must be selected to the Board of Regents of Spoonville State College. A randomly selected sample of 25 alumni are invited to hear the four proposed members speak. After hearing the speeches, 25 alumni are asked to indicate whether they will or will not vote for each candidate. The results are shown in Table 17.14. A 1 signifies that a respondent will vote for a certain candidate. A 0 signifies that a respondent will not vote for a certain candidate.

Mr. Daly of the Board of Regents Office analyzes the answers of the 25 respondents. He proceeds as follows:

1. He states the null and alternative hypotheses.
   a. Null hypothesis. There is no difference in the affirmative reactions of the 25 alumni to the speeches of the four candidates.
   b. Alternative hypothesis. There is a significant difference in the affirmative reactions of the 25 alumni to the speeches of the four candidates.
2. The arbitrarily chosen level of significance is 0.05.

Table 17.14. Tabulation of Voting Decisions of 25 Alumni for Four
Candidates for Spoonville State College Board of Regents.

Respondent No.	Proposed Member				Positive Responses (L)	L^2
	1	2	3	4		
1	0	1	1	0	2	4
2	1	0	1	1	3	9
3	1	1	1	1	4	16
4	0	0	1	0	1	1
5	1	0	1	1	3	9
6	1	1	0	1	3	9
7	1	0	0	1	2	4
8	0	1	1	0	2	4
9	1	1	1	1	4	16
10	1	1	1	1	4	16
11	0	0	0	1	1	1
12	1	1	0	1	3	9
13	0	0	1	0	1	1
14	1	1	0	1	3	9
15	0	1	1	1	3	9
16	1	0	0	1	2	4
17	1	1	1	1	4	16
18	0	0	0	1	1	1
19	1	0	1	1	3	9
20	0	1	1	0	2	4
21	1	1	1	0	3	9
22	0	1	1	0	2	4
23	0	0	1	0	1	1
24	1	1	1	0	3	9
25	0	1	0	1	2	4
Total	14	15	17	16	62	179
Sum =	S_1	S_2	S_3	S_4	L	L

3. The Cochran Q test is computed.
   a. The general formula is:

$$Q = \frac{(k - 1)\ [k\Sigma S_j^2 - (\Sigma S_j)^2]}{k\ (\Sigma L) - \Sigma L^2}$$

where

k = number of samples

S_j^2 = sum of responses to one of k samples

L = total number of positive responses

b. Equation particular example:

$$Q = \frac{(k - 1) [k (\Sigma s_1^2 + \Sigma s_2^2 + \Sigma s_3^2 + \Sigma s_4^2)] - (\Sigma L)^2}{k (\Sigma L) - \Sigma L^2}$$

where

k = number of samples = 4

$\Sigma s_1^2 = 14$ = total positive reactions for member 1

$\Sigma s_2^2 = 15$ = total positive reactions for member 2

$\Sigma s_3^2 = 17$ = total positive reactions for member 3

$\Sigma s_4^2 = 16$ = total positive reactions for member 4

$\Sigma L = 62$ = sum of the positive reactions for all of the prospective board members

Thus,

$$Q = \frac{(4 - 1) [4(14^2 + 15^2 + 17^2 + 16^2)] - 62^2}{4(62)^2 - 179}$$

$$= \frac{3 [4(196 + 225 + 289 + 256)] - 3844}{4(3844) - 179}$$

$$= \frac{3(4)(966) - 3844}{15{,}376 - 179}$$

$$= \frac{11{,}592 - 3844}{15{,}197}$$

$$= 0.51$$

4. The critical value of Q is ascertained.
   a. There are three degrees of freedom—$(K - 1) = (4 - 1) = 3$.
   b. The arbitrarily chosen level of significance is 0.05.
   c. Referring to Appendix J, critical value is found to be 7.81.
5. The critical and computed values of Q are compared.
   a. The computed value = 0.51.
   b. The critical value is 7.81.

6. The null hypothesis is accepted or rejected. Since the computed value of Q is below the critical value, the null hypothesis is accepted and the alternative hypothesis is rejected. Hence, results indicate that there is no significant difference in the reaction of the affirmative responses for the four Board of Regents candidates.

7. Use of t-test. If Mr. Daly wants to now whether the proportion of voters favoring member 1 for the Board of Regents was greater than for member 2, he would have to use the t-test. Although the Q-test indicates that there are overall differences in the opinions of two voters, it does not compare proportions between the various samples (in this case, four).

Ordinal-Level Tests of Significance

Data at the ordinal level must be rankable (one category higher than another). A test of significance employing ordinal level data and three or more related k samples is the Friedman two-way analysis of variance test.

Friedman Two-Way Analysis of Variance. Let us return to the case of Flavor Brands, which is test marketing its new freeze-dried coffee, Flavor Buds. Mr. Terry, the market-research manager, wanted to determine consumer reaction to specific characteristics of Flavor Buds including the color of the coffee in the jar, aroma, flavor, and strength. Terry selected City F as the test market because it is a "typical" American city. He sent questionnaires to 35 people selected at random from a mailing list. The questionnaire asked them to rate the four characteristics on a scale of 1 to 10, with 1 being poor and 10 being excellent. He also sent each respondent a jar of Flavor Buds. As an incentive to return the questionnaire he included $0.25 in coin. At the end of two weeks, 25 forms has been returned. The results of Terry's study are found in Table 17.15, and his analysis of the results are as follows:

1. He states the null and alternative hypotheses:
    a. Null hypothesis: There is no overall difference in the preference ratings among the 25 respondents for each of the four coffee characteristics being tested.
    b. Alternative hypothesis: There is a difference among the 25 respondents for each of the four coffee characteristics being tested.
2. He arbitrarily selects a 0.05 level of significance.
3. He computes the value of X_R^2 (Friedman's two-way analysis of variance formula).
    a. The general formula is:

$$X^2_r = \frac{12}{NK(K+1)} \; T^2_1 + T^2_2 + T^2_3 \cdots T^2_k - 3N(K+!)$$

Table 17.15. Preference Ratings for Four Characteristics of Flavor Buds.

Respondent No.	Preference Rating			
	Aroma	Flavor	Strength	Color
1	8	6	4	5
2	2	8	9	10
3	9	8	7	6
4	4	5	2	3
5	8	6	9	10
6	7	10	5	4
7	4	5	8	9
8	10	9	6	4
9	2	5	10	8
10	9	7	4	5
11	8	4	9	10
12	5	2	7	8
13	9	8	5	7
14	4	7	9	5
15	1	4	3	5
16	2	4	10	8
17	8	7	6	2
18	9	6	5	8
19	6	7	5	9
20	7	8	5	10
21	4	1	8	2
22	3	8	6	2
23	4	7	6	2
24	9	1	2	8
25	8	7	5	6

where

N = number in sample

K = number of related samples

T = technique

T_{11}^2, etc. = total of ranks for a specific column

Looking at table 17.16, we see that a respondent's answers are ranked according to rating values. For example, respondent No. 1 gave numeric ratings of 8, 6, 4 and 5. Corresponding rankings would be 1, 2, 4, and 3.

$$N = 25$$

$$T_1^2 = 61^2 \text{ (total of aroma column)}$$

$$T_2^2 = 61^2 \text{ (total of flavor column)}$$

$$T_3^2 = 68^2 \text{ (total of strength column)}$$

$$T_4^2 = 60^2 \text{ (total of color column)}$$

b. Solve for X_r^2.

$$X_r^2 = \frac{12}{(25)(4)(4 + 1)} \{[(61)^2 + (61)^2 + (68)^2 + (60)^2] - [3\,(25)\,(4 + 1)]\}$$

$$= \frac{12}{(25)(4)(5)} [(3721 + 3721 + 4624 + 3600)] - [3(25)(5)]$$

$$= \frac{12}{500}(15666) - (375)$$

$$= 0.024\,(15666) - (375)$$

$$= 375.98 - 375.00$$

$$= 0.98$$

4. Terry determined the critical value of X_r^2.
   a. The number of degrees of freedom is 3 (i.e., $K - 1 = 4 - 1$).
   b. The level of significance is 0.05.
   c. Using Appendix J, the critical value of X_r^2 is 7.81.
5. Terry compared the critical and computed value of X_r^2.
   a. The computed value is 0.98.
   b. The critical value is 7.81.
6. Terry then decided whether to accept or reject the null hypothesis.
   a. The computed value falls inside the area of acceptance i.e., the computed value is below the critical value. Therefore, Terry accepted the null hypothesis that there is no overall difference in preference rating among the 25 respondents for each of the four coffee characteristics being tested.

Table 17.16. Coffee Characteristics Ranked from High to Low by Respondent.

Respondent No.	Ranked by Respondent			
	Aroma	Flavor	Richness	Color
1	1	2	4	3
2	4	3	2	1
3	1	2	3	4
4	2	1	4	3
5	3	4	2	1
6	2	1	3	4
7	4	3	2	1
8	1	2	3	4
9	4	3	1	2
10	1	2	4	3
11	3	4	2	1
12	3	4	2	1
13	1	2	4	3
14	4	2	1	3
15	4	2	3	1
16	4	3	1	2
17	1	2	3	4
18	1	3	4	2
19	3	2	4	1
20	3	2	4	1
21	2	4	1	3
22	4	1	2	3
23	3	1	2	4
24	1	4	3	2
25	1	2	4	3
Total	61	61	68	60

Chi-Square. The chi-square test may be used where there are K independent samples (as well as when there are one and two). Rift Raft Sailboat Co., a large national manufacturer of sailboats, has a problem finding salespeople who can meet the company's sales quotas. Mr. Harris, Rift Raft's president, wonders if a sales aptitude test would give any indication of an employee's propensity to produce, indicated by actual annual earnings. Harris goes to a management consulting firm, Know-All Consultants, which specializes in testing and training personnel. Mr. Appleby, Know-All's president, believes there might be some relationship between annual earnings and the score on a salesman's aptitude test. Appleby agrees to test Rift Raft's employees on a nationwide basis. Aptitude test results are shown in Table 17.17.

If no relationship exists between the annual earnings of Rift Raft employees and the scores achieved on the sales aptitude test, it would be expected that 10%

Table 17.17. Sales Aptitude Test Scores for Rift Raft Sailboat Co. Employees.

Test Score	Annual Earnings $10,000 to $19,999	$20,000 to $29,999	$30,000 to $39,000	$40,000 to $49,999	Total	% Total
91 to 100	5	7	15	10	37	10
81 to 90	7	10	20	15	52	14
71 to 80	15	17	25	20	77	21
61 to 70	20	25	30	22	97	26
52 to 60	15	15	17	6	53	15
51 and under	15	17	16	4	52	14
Total	77	91	123	77	368	100

(37/368) of the 77 employees with actual earnings of $10,000 to $19,999 would have scored 91 to 100. This is called the *expected frequency*. In addition, if there is no relationship between annual income and sales aptitude test scores, it can be expected that 10% of the 91 employees earning between $20,000 to $29,999 would achieve a sales aptitude test score of 91 to 100. Thus, the expected frequency is 9. Appleby then computes the remaining expected frequencies (see Table 17.18). He proceeds as follows in his computation of the value of chi-square based on the following analysis:

1. He states the null and alternative hypotheses:
   a. Null hypothesis: There is no relationship between the sales aptitude test scores of salespeople and their actual earnings.
   b. Alternative hypothesis: There is a relationship between the sales aptitude test scores of salespeople and their earnings.

Table 17.18. Expected and Observed Frequencies of Sales Aptitude Test Scores.

Test Score	Anticipated Earnings $10,000 to $19,999 f_o	f_e	$20,000 to $29,999 f_o	f_e	$30,000 to $39,999 f_o	f_e	$40,000 to $49,999 f_o	f_e
91 to 100	5	8	7	9	15	12	10	8
81 to 90	7	11	10	13	20	17	15	11
71 to 80	15	16	17	19	25	26	20	16
61 to 70	20	20	25	24	30	32	22	20
52 to 60	15	12	15	14	17	19	6	12
51 and under	15	10	17	12	16	17	4	10
Total	77	77	91	91	123	123	77	77

Table 17.19. Computation of Chi-Square.

Test Score	Actual Earnings	f_o	f_e	$f_o - f_e$	$(f_o - f_e)^2$	$(f_o - f_e)^2/f_e$
91 to 100	$10,000 to 19,999	5	8	−3	9	9/8 = 1.1250
	20,000 to 29,999	7	9	−2	4	4/9 = 0.4444
	30,000 to 39,999	15	12	+3	9	9/12 = 0.7500
	40,000 to 49,999	10	8	+2	4	4/8 = 0.5000
81 to 90	10,000 to 19,999	7	11	−4	16	16/11 = 1.4545
	20,000 to 29,999	10	13	−3	9	9/13 = 0.6923
	30,000 to 39,999	20	17	+3	9	9/17 = 0.5294
	40,000 to 49,999	15	11	+4	16	16/11 = 1.4545
71 to 80	10,000 to 19,999	15	16	−1	1	1/16 = 0.0625
	20,000 to 29,999	17	19	−2	4	4/19 = 0.2105
	30,000 to 39,999	25	26	−1	1	1/26 = 0.0385
	40,000 to 49,999	20	16	+4	16	16/16 = 1.0000
61 to 70	10,000 to 19,999	20	20	−	−	−
	20,000 to 29,999	25	24	+1	1	1/24 = 0.0417
	30,000 to 39,999	30	32	−2	4	4/32 = 0.1250
	40,000 to 49,999	22	20	+2	4	4/20 = 0.2000
52 to 60	10,000 to 19,999	15	12	+3	9	9/12 = 0.7500
	20,000 to 29,999	15	14	+1	1	1/14 = 0.0714
	30,000 to 39,999	17	19	−2	4	4/19 = 0.2105
	40,000 to 49,999	6	12	−6	36	36/12 = 3.0000
51 and under	10,000 to 19,999	15	10	+5	25	25/10 = 2.5000
	20,000 to 29,999	17	12	+5	25	25/12 = 2.0833
	30,000 to 39,999	16	17	−1	1	1/17 = 0.0588
	40,000 to 49,999	4	10	−6	36	36/10 = 3.6000
		368	368	0		20.9023

2. He selectes a 0.05 level of significance.
3. He computes the chi-square using the formula:

$$X^2 = \frac{(f_o - f_e)^2}{f_e}$$

where

$$f_o = \text{observed frequencies}$$

$$f_e = \text{expected frequencies}$$

The computed value is 20.9023 (see Table 17.19).
    4. He computes the critical value of the chi-square.
        a. From Table 17.17, it can be observed that there are six rows and four columns of data. Appleby calculates the degrees of freedom as follows:

$$(\text{Row count} - 1)(\text{Column count} - 1)$$

or

$$(6 - 1)(4 - 1) = 15 \text{ degrees of freedom}$$

        b. The level of significance is 0.05
        c. Using Appendix J, the critical value is 25.00.
    5. He compares the critical and computed value of the chi-square.
        a. computed value = 20.9023
        b. critical value = 25.00
    6. He accepts or rejects the null hypothesis. The computed value falls in the area of acceptance (i.e., 20.9023 is less than 25.00). Therefore, Appleby accepts the null hypothesis. There is no relationship between the test scores achieved on the sales aptitude test and the earnings of Rift Raft employees.

    Based on the preceding information, Mr. Harris decides to try a program in which an employee's sales are reviewed quarterly. If the employee's sales fall in two consecutive quarters, he has an interview with the district supervisor to get at the root of the problem.

18 Analysis of Variance

The difference between two populations can be determined by taking a sample from each and calculating the mean and standard deviation. However, if more than two means from two separate populations are being compared, the process can be time-consuming. Suppose it must be determined whether there are any differences among 25 populations, with eight observations drawn from each population. A mean and standard deviation, based upon a random sample of eight, would be drawn from the first population and then be computed. Then a sample of eight would be taken from the second population and its mean and standard deviation computed. This procedure would be repeated for the remaining 23 populations. The z values (where $n \geqslant 30$) and t values (where $n < 30$) would then be calculated to ascertain whether a difference existed between any two populations.

To avoid this problem, a statistical technique called *analysis of variance* (*ANOVA*) is used. ANOVA has two main advantages. First, all populations can be compared at the same time to ascertain if their means are identical. Secondly, sample data can be combined to avoid fluctuations (greater stability). In the case of the 25 populations and eight samples, if a z test were used, only 25 items (observations) could be studied at one time. Contrast that with ANOVA where $25 \times 8 = 300$ observations can be reviewed simultaneously.

APPLICATION

ANOVA employs *samples* to determine whether there is a difference between three or more populations (i.e., whether their means differ). To determine this, three or more conditions are applied to the same situation. Samples are then taken from each condition to determine the differences, if any.

Suppose a drug manufacturer, Diet-Time, wants to place a new weight-reducing aid on the market but is not certain whether one, two or three tablets should be taken daily for maximum results. To find-out, Diet-Time did some pre-market testing using three control groups of eight people each. Over a 30-day

Table 18.1. Weight-Loss Results of Three Groups on 30-Day Trial Using Diet-Time Tablets.

No. Tablets per Day	No. Pounds Lost	
	Sample 1	Sample 2
1	2.3	2.1
2	2.8	2.4
3	3.0	2.6

period, one group was given one tablet per day, the second two per day, and the third group three per day. Weights of each person in each control group were recorded at the beginning and end of the test period. Sample weight losses were recorded for each group (see Table 18.1).

Are the populations from which the recorded sample weight losses were taken identical? If they are not identical, u_1, u_2, and u_3 would be different. If the populations are identical, then $u_1 = u_2 = u_3$.

USES OF ANOVA

One-Way ANOVA with Samples of Equal Size

Suppose the Nice & Fresh Baking Co. wants to increase the shelf life of its basic white bread. An antispoilage ingredient is added to its basic recipe in three different dosage levels; i.e., 1 gram of additive for each 100 grams of basic recipe weight, 2 grams per 100, and finally 3 grams per 100. Sample loaves of the new type bread are then placed in five different cities. Sample shelf lives are recorded over a 6-week period; the results are shown in Table 18.2 (p. 295).

Mr. Price, the head baker at Nice & Fresh, hires a marketing consultant, Analysis Inc., to make the statistical computations. Mr. Owens of Analysis Inc. proceeds as follows:

1. He states the null and alternative hypotheses:
   a. Null hypothesis: There is no significant difference between the mean shelf lives of the three groups.
   b. Alternative hypothesis: At least one mean shelf life of the three groups is different.
2. Based upon the following considerations, Owens ascertains that the F test (see below) is the proper statistical technique to use.
   a. Variance's between the three populations (groups) are equal.
   b. Loaves of bread for which shelf life is recorded must be selected on the basis of probability.

    c. Normal distributions occur for the shelf life of each of the groups (populations) under consideration.

    d. The data accumulated are at least of interval level.

Owens realizes that these considerations apply only if there is no significant difference between the mean shelf lives of the three groups, i.e., only if the null hypothesis applies.

  3. The level of significance is 0.05.

  4. Owens calculates the critical value of F.

    a. Owens applies the F test, which is the ratio of two variances using the following ratio.

$$F = \frac{\sigma_B^2 \text{ with } k - 1 \text{ degrees of freedom (df)}}{\sigma_W^2 \text{ with } N - k \text{ degrees of freedom (df)}}$$

where

$$\sigma_B^2 = \text{population variance estimated between means of squares}$$

$$\sigma_W^2 = \text{population variance computed on variation within samples}$$

$$k = \text{number of considerations} = \text{number of control groups} = 3$$

$$N = \text{number of observations} = 3 \times 5 = 15$$

$$k - 1 = 3 - 1, \text{ or } 2 \text{ degrees of freedom in numerator}$$

$$N - k = 15 - 3, = 12 \text{ degrees of freedom in denominator}$$

    b. Referring to Appendix N, Owens finds the critical value of F.

      (1) A 0.05 level of significance is used.

      (2) The F ratio is 2/12.

      (3) The critical value of F is 3.89. (If the computed value of F is less than 3.89, the null hypothesis is accepted. If it is 3.89 or greater, the alternative is accepted and the null hypothesis is rejected.)

    c. Owens knows that the F value cannot be negative but must either be equal to zero or positive; that it has a positively skewed distribution curve; and that there is one distribution and curve for each separate F ratio. (See Figures 18.1a, b, and c.)

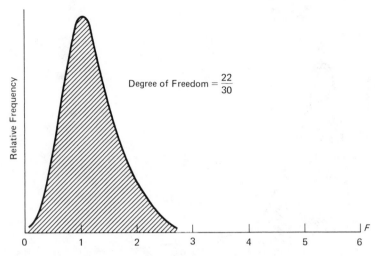

Fig. 18.1a F probability distribution for the ratio of 22/30 degrees of freedom.

d. F will equal:

(1) 1.00 when many techniques (populations) are the same and the ratio of the variation between sample means and the variation within samples is equal.

(2) If technique means are *not* the same, then the variation *between* the sample means will be *greater* than the variation *within* the samples.

(3) If the variation *between* the samples is greater than the variation *within* the samples, then the computed value of $F \geqslant$ critical value of F and the null hypothesis is rejected.

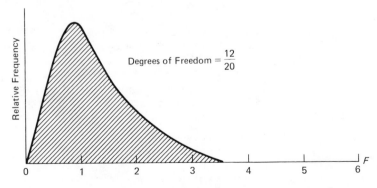

Fig. 18.1b F probability distribution for the ratio of 12/20 degrees of freedom.

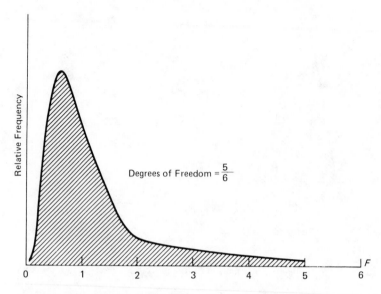

Fig. 18.1c F probability distribution for the ratio of 5/6 degrees of freedom.

5. Owens calculates the value of F.

   a. With population variances unknown, sample variances must be used. Therefore, the F ratio is

$$\frac{s_B^2}{s_W^2}$$

   b. The variation between the sample means is equal to the numerator of the F ratio

   (1)

$$s_B^2 = \frac{n_r \, [\Sigma(\overline{X}_c - \overline{\overline{X}}_c)^2]}{k - 1}$$

where

$$n_r = 5 = \text{number of rows}$$

$$\overline{X}_c = \text{mean of each column}$$

$$= \overline{X}_{c_1} = 4.10$$

$$= \overline{X}_{c_2} = 4.19$$

Table 18.2. Average Shelf Life over 6-Week Period.

Sample City		Group 1[a]	Group 2[a]	Group 3[a]	
			Average Shelf Life (Days)		
A		4.25	4.40	4.30	
B		4.16	4.21	4.25	
C		3.95	4.12	4.15	
D		4.13	4.22	4.30	
E		4.01	3.98	4.15	Σ
Σ_c	Total	20.50	20.93	21.15	62.58
$\overline{X}_c$	Mean	4.10	4.186	4.23	4.172^b

[a]Group 1 had 1 gram of additive per 100 grams of weight; group 2, 2 grams; group 3, 3 grams.
[b]Note: $62.58 \div 15 = 4.172 = \overline{\overline{X}}_c$.

$$= \overline{X}_{c_3} = 4.23$$

$$\overline{\overline{X}}_c = \text{grand mean} = \frac{\overline{X}_{c_1} + \overline{X}_{c_2} + \overline{X}_{c_3}}{k}$$

$$k = \text{number of columns}$$

See Table 18.2 for $\overline{X}_{c_1}, \overline{X}_{c_2}, \overline{X}_{c_3}$, and $\overline{\overline{X}}_c$.

(2)

$$s_B^2 = \frac{5[4.10 - 4.172)^2 + (4.186 - 4.172)^2 + (4.23 - 4.172)^2]}{3 - 1}$$

$$= \frac{5[-(0.072)^2 (+0.014)^2 + (+0.058)^2]}{2}$$

$$= \frac{5[(0.005184) + (0.000196) + (0.003364)]}{2}$$

$$= \frac{5(0.008744)}{2}$$

$$= \frac{0.04372}{2}$$

$$= 0.02186$$

c. The variation *within* samples is equal to the denominator of the F Ratio

(1)

$$s_W^2 = \frac{\Sigma (X_{rc} - \overline{X}_c)^2}{N - k}$$

where

X_{rc} = the value of each observation in the sample

r = row

c = column

$\overline{X}_c$ = mean of each column

N = total number of observations = 15

k = number of columns = 3

Table 18.3 gives the calculations necessary to compute the variance within samples.

$$s_W^2 = \frac{0.0576 + 0.094320 + 0.0230}{15 - 3}$$

$$= \frac{0.17492}{12}$$

$$= 0.0145766$$

d. The F value is computed.

$$\frac{s_B^2}{s_W^2} = \frac{0.02186}{0.0145766}$$

$$= 1.499664 = 1.50$$

Table 18.3. Deviations from the Mean and Squared Deviations
for Variance within Samples.[a]

Sample City	Deviation from Column Mean Consideration No.			Square of Deviations from Column Mean Consideration No.		
	1	2	3	1	2	3
A	+0.150	+0.214	+0.070	0.0225	0.045796	0.0049
B	+0.060	+0.024	+0.020	0.0036	0.000576	0.0004
C	-0.150	-0.066	-0.080	0.0225	0.004356	0.0064
D	+0.030	+0.034	+0.070	0.0009	0.001156	0.0049
E	-0.090	-0.206	-0.080	0.0081	0.042436	0.0064
Totals	0	0	0	0.0576	0.094320	0.0230

[a]Means = 4.10, 4.186 and 4.23.

6. The critical and computed values of F are compared.
   a. The critical value is 3.89.
   b. The computed value is 1.50.
7. The null hypothesis is accepted or rejected. The computed F value of 1.50 is less than the critical value of 3.89. Therefore, the *null* hypothesis is accepted and the *alternative* hypothesis rejected. The differences between the means is due to chance.

Shortcut Method for Computing F Ratio. The F ratio can be computed by a shortcut method when lengthy computations are involved or it is desired to avoid rounding errors. If Owens were to use the shortcut method in his calculations, he would proceed as follows:

1. He would set up an ANOVA table (see Table 18.4).
2. He would compute the sum of the squares consideration by the following formula:

$$SSC = \sum \frac{T_c^2}{n_c} - \frac{(\Sigma X)^2}{N}$$

where

$$T_c^2 = \frac{\text{column total squared}}{\text{number of observations in column}}$$

X = total of all columns

N = total of all observations

Table 18.4. ANOVA F Ratio Calculations, Shortcut Method.

Sample City	Group 1		Group 2		Group 3	
	1 Average Shelf Life *(Days)*	*2* Average Shelf Life Squared	*3* Average Shelf Life *(Days)*	*4* Average Shelf Life Squared	*5* Average Shelf Life *(Days)*	*6* Average Shelf Life Squared
A	4.25	18.0625	4.40	19.3600	4.30	18.4900
B	4.16	17.3056	4.21	17.7241	4.25	18.0625
C	3.95	15.6025	4.12	16.9744	4.15	17.2225
D	4.13	17.0569	4.22	17.8084	4.30	18.4900
E	4.01	16.0801	3.98	15.8404	4.15	17.2225
	20.50	84.1076	20.93	87.7073	21.15	89.4875

$T_c = \Sigma$ Columns 1, 3, 5

n_c = Number of observations in each column 1, 3, 5   5   5   5

$X^2 = \Sigma$ Columns 2, 4, 6

Total 62.58

15

261.3024

Therefore, in this example,

$$SSC = \frac{(20.50)^2}{5} + \frac{(20.93)^2}{5} + \frac{(21.15)^2}{5} - \frac{(62.58)^2}{15}$$

$$= \frac{420.2500}{5} + \frac{438.0649}{5} + \frac{447.3225}{5} - \frac{3916.2564}{15}$$

$$= 84.0500 + 87.61298 + 89.46450 - 261.08376$$

$$= 261.12748 - 261.08376$$

$$= 0.04372$$

3. Owens would compute the error of the sum of the squares using the following formula:

$$SSE = \Sigma(X^2) - \sum \frac{T_c^2}{n_c}$$

where

$\Sigma(X^2) =$ (see table 18.4).

T_c^2 = total of a column squared

n_c = number of observations in each column

Therefore in this example.

$$SSE = 261.3024 - \left[\frac{(20.5)^2}{5} + \frac{(20.93)^2}{5} + \frac{(21.15)^2}{5}\right]$$

$$= 261.3024 - [84.05000 + 87.61298 + 89.46450]$$

$$= 261.3024 - 261.12748$$

$$= 0.17492$$

4. He would compute the total variation (SS total).

$$SS \text{ total} = \Sigma(X^2) - \frac{(\Sigma X)^2}{N}$$

$$= 261.3024 - \frac{(62.58)^2}{15}$$

$$= 261.3024 - 261.08376$$

$$= 0.21864$$

5. He would compute the F value.
   a. First, he would set up an ANOVA table (see Table 18.5).
   b. The formula for the F value is:

$$F = \frac{SSC \div (k - 1)}{SSE \div (N - k)}$$

$$= \frac{0.02186}{0.0145766}$$

$$= 1.4996638 \cong 1.50$$

The F value is the same as previously computed.

Table 18.5. Shelf Life, One-Way ANOVA Table.

Variation	Sum of Squares 1	df 2	Mean Square (Column 1/ Column 2) 3
Considerations (between columns)	$SSC = 0.04372$	$3 - 1 = 2^a$	0.02186
Mistake (between rows)	$SSE = 0.17492$	$15 - 3 = 12^b$	0.0145766
Sum of squares total	0.21864		

[a] No. columns − 1.
[b] No. observations − No. columns.

ONE-WAY ANOVA WITH SAMPLES OF UNEQUAL SIZE

The F value can also be used with samples of unequal size. Suppose Sure-Flo Petroleum Co. produces a new gasoline, Sure-Flo Supreme, designed to give less "ping" in the engine. Before offering it to the public, the firm's vice president of marketing asks company engineers to ascertain how many miles per gallon can be obtained with Sure-Flo Supreme in a four-cylinder car. Carol Carlson, the chief test engineer, ran 40 tests with four minicars from four different countries. The results are shown in Table 18.6.

After recording the results, Carlson proceeds as follows:
1. She states the null and alternative hypotheses.
   a. Null hypothesis: No significant difference between the arithmetic means of the four groups.
   b. Alternative hypothesis: At least one of the means of the four groups is different.
2. The level of significance is 0.05.
3. Carlson calculates the critical value of F.
   a. Formula for F is

$$F = \frac{\text{No. considerations} - 1 \ df}{\text{No. observations} - 4 \ df}$$

where

$$k = \text{number of considerations} = 4$$

$$N = \text{number of observations} = 40$$

$$df = \text{degrees of freedom} - \text{numerator} = 1$$
$$\text{denominator} = K - 1 \ (4 - 1)$$

Table 18.6. Miles per Gallon Obtained Using Sure-Flo Supreme Gasoline.

	Poor (25.0 up to 27.5 mpg)		Fair (27.5 up to 30.0 mpg)		Good (30.0 up to 32.5 mpg)		Excellent (32.5 up to 35.0)	
	X_1	X_1^2	X_2	X_2^2	X_3	X_3^2	X_4	X_4^2
	25.1	630.01	27.5	756.25	30.0	900.00	32.5	1056.25
	27.2	739.84	28.0	784.00	31.0	961.00	34.0	1156.00
	26.3	691.69	29.1	846.81	32.3	1043.29	34.4	1183.36
	25.5	650.25	28.5	812.25	30.7	942.49	33.1	1095.61
	27.0	729.00	29.6	876.16	31.5	992.25	32.7	1069.29
	26.5	702.25	27.8	772.84	32.4	1049.76	34.5	1190.25
			29.9	894.01	30.1	906.01		
			28.3	800.89	32.2	1036.84		
					30.4	924.16		
					31.8	1011.24		
					30.9	954.81		
					31.6	998.56		
					32.3	1043.29		
					30.8	948.64		
					30.6	936.36		
					30.5	930.25		
					31.1	967.21		
					32.0	1024.00		
					30.4	924.16		
					30.6	936.36		
Column Totals	157.6		228.7		623.2		201.2	**Total** 1210.7
No. Observations	6		8		20		6	40
Sum of Column Totals Squared	4143.04		6543.21		19,430.68		6750.76	

Sum of X^2 = 36,867.45

301

Therefore, in this example,

$$F = \frac{4-1}{40-4} = \frac{3}{36} = 0.0833$$

b. Referring to Appendix N, Carlson locates the critical value of F.
   (1) She uses the 0.05 level of significance.
   (2) The F ratio is 3/36.
   (3) The critical value is 2.84. (If the computed value of F is less than 2.84, the null hypothesis is accepted. If $F \geq 2.84$, the *alternative* hypothesis is accepted and the null hypothesis rejected.) See Figure 18.2.
   (4) The computed value of F is calculated using the shortcut method.
       (a) Carlson sets up an ANOVA table (see Table 18.6).
       (b) She computes the sum of squares considerations according to the formula:

$$SSC = \sum \frac{T_c^2}{n_c} - \frac{(\Sigma X)^2}{N}$$

$$= \frac{(157.6)^2}{6} + \frac{(228.7)^2}{8} + \frac{(623.2)^2}{20} + \frac{(201.2)^2}{6} - \frac{(1210.7)^2}{40}$$

$$= 4139.6266 + 6537.9612 + 19{,}418.9120 + 6746.9066 - 36{,}644.8600$$

$$= 198.545$$

(c) She computes the error of the sum of squares using the formula:

$$SSE = \Sigma(X^2) - \sum \frac{T_c^2}{n_c}$$

$$= 36{,}867.45 \left[-\frac{(157.6)^2}{6} + \frac{(228.7)^2}{8} + \frac{(623.2)^2}{20} + \frac{(201.2)^2}{6} \right]$$

$$= 36{,}867.45 - 4{,}139.63 + 6{,}537.96 + 19{,}418.91 + 6{,}746.91$$

$$= 36{,}867.45 - 36{,}843.41$$

$$= 24.04$$

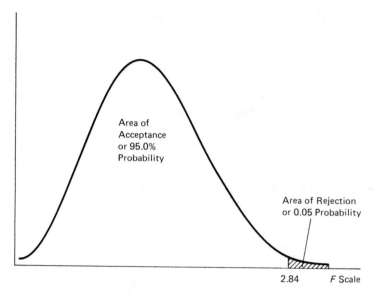

Fig. 18.2 Areas of acceptance and rejection for F distribution at the 0.05 level of significance.

(d) She computes the SS total: $SSC + SSE = 198.545 + 24.04 = 222.59$.

(e) Carlson checks on accuracy of SS total as follows:

$$SS = (X^2) - \frac{(X)^2}{N}$$

$$= 36{,}867.45 - \frac{(1210.7)^2}{40}$$

$$= 36{,}867.45 - 36{,}644.86$$

$$= 222.59$$

(f) She sets up the ANOVA table (see Table 18.7).

(g) She computes the F statistic using the following formula:

$$F = \frac{SSC}{k-1} \div \frac{SSE}{N-k}$$

Table 18.7. Miles per Gallon from Road Test, ANOVA Table.

Variation Source	*1* *Sum of Squares*	*2* *df**	*3* *Mean Square[a]*
Considerations (between columns)	$SSC = 198.545$	$4 - 1 = 3$[b]	66.1817
Mistake (between rows)	$SSE = 24.04$	$40 - 4 = 36$[c]	0.6678
Total of sum of squares	222.59		

[a]Mean square = (column 1 ÷ column 2).
[b]No. columns – 1.
[c]No. observations – No. columns.

where

$$SSC = 198.545$$

$$k = 4 - 1 = 3$$

$$SSE = 24.04$$

$$N = 40 - 4 = 36$$

$$= \frac{198.545/3}{24.04/36}$$

$$= \frac{66.1817}{0.6678}$$

$$= 99.104$$

5. Carlson compares the critical and computed value of F.
   a. The critical value is 2.84.
   b. The computed value is 99.104.

6. Carlson accepts or rejects the null hypothesis. The computed value is more than the critical value at the 0.05 level of significance. Therefore, the null hypothesis is rejected and the alternative hypothesis is accepted. At least one of the four means in the test groups is different. The differences between means is due to more than chance.

Two-Way ANOVA

In two-way ANOVA, two sets of circumstances are tested instead of one. Suppose Super Dog Food Co. markets a new dog food. Mr. Jones, the head researcher is undecided whether an ingredient he proposes to add to Super Dog Food should be used by itself or with a vitamin additive. Jones sets up three control groups; the first group of puppies receives 2 oz of ingredient X per day, the second 3 oz per day, and the third 4 oz per day. In addition, the three groups of puppies receive varying amounts of the vitamin additive. The puppies' weights were recorded at the start of the 6-week period and once per week thereafter. (See Table 18.8 for results.)

Jones then makes the following analysis.

1. He states the null and alternative hypotheses. Since there are two sets of circumstances—ingredient X and vitamin additive—two sets of hypotheses are used.

    a. Ingredient X

        (1) Null hypothesis: The mean weight increases for the three control groups of puppies are equal.

        (2) Alternative hypothesis: The mean weight increases are not all equal.

    b. Vitamin additive

        (1) Null hypothesis: The mean weight increases for all five vitamin additive considerations are equal.

        (2) Alternative hypothesis: The mean weight increases for all five vitamin additive considerations are not equal.

2. Jones selects the 0.05 level of significance.

3. He computes the various components of the sum square total (SS), (SS = SSC + SSB + SSE).

    a. Component 1 = The sum of squares consideration using the following formula:

$$SSC = \frac{T_c^2}{n_c} \frac{(X)^2}{N}$$

$$= \frac{(75)^2}{5} + \frac{(98)^2}{5} + \frac{(97)^2}{5} - \frac{(270)^2}{15}$$

$$= 1125.0 + 1920.8 + 1881.8 - 4860.0$$

$$= 67.6$$

Table 18.8. Mean Weight Increases of Puppies Fed Ingredient X with a Vitamin Additive.

Daily Dosage Vitamin Additive (gram)	2 Oz./Day X		3 Oz./Day X		4 Oz./Day X		Total Cols. 1 + 3 + 5
	1 Weight Increase	2 Col. 1 Squared	3 Weight Increase	4 Col. 3 Squared	5 Weight Increase	6 Col. 5 Squared	
1	15	225	16	256	17	289	48
2	17	289	19	361	20	400	56
3	18	324	21	441	22	484	61
4	14	196	22	484	20	400	56
5	11	121	20	400	18	324	49
$T_c = \Sigma$ Cols. 1, 3, 5	75		98		97		270
$n_c = \Sigma n$ Cols. 1, 3, 5	5		5		5		15
$X^2 = \Sigma$ Cols. 2, 4, 6		1155		1942		1897	4994

b. Component 2 = The Sum of the Rows (SSB). The formula for the sum of the rows is:

$$SSB = \frac{(B_r^2)}{k} - \frac{(X)^2}{N}$$

where

$$B_r^2 = \text{sum of row squares}$$

$$k = \text{number of columns}$$

$$X = \text{sum of column totals}$$

$$N = \text{number of observations}$$

$$SSB = \frac{(48)^2 + (56)^2 + (61)^2 + (56)^2 + (49)^2}{3} - \frac{(270)^2}{15}$$

$$= \frac{2304 + 3136 + 3721 + 3136 + 2401}{3} - \frac{72900}{15}$$

$$= 4899.33 - 4860.00$$

$$= 39.33$$

c. Component 3 = The sum of the squares (SS). The formula for the sum of the squares is

$$SS = (X^2) - \frac{(X)^2}{N}$$

where

$$X^2 = \text{sum of squares}$$

$$X = \text{sum of column totals}$$

$$N = \text{number of observations}$$

Table 18.9. Weight Increases of Puppies Fed Ingredient X with a Vitamin Additive: Two-Way ANOVA Table.

Variation Source	1 Sum of Squares	2 df	3 Mean Square (Col. 1/2)
Considerations Between Columns			
Ingredient X	$SSC = 67.60$	$3 - 1 = 2^a$	33.80000
Considerations Between Rows			
Vitamin additive	$SSB = 39.33$	$5 - 1 = 4^b$	9.83250
Error	$SSE = \underline{27.07}$	$(2)(4) = 8^c$	3.38375
Total	134.00		

[a]No. columns – 1.
[b]No. rows – 1.
[c](No. columns – 1) (No. rows – 1).

Thus,

$$SS = 4994 - \frac{(270)^2}{15}$$

$$= 4994 - 4860$$

$$= 134$$

d. Component 4 = Sum Squares

$$SSE = \text{Total } SS - SSC - SSB$$

$$SSE = 134.00 - 67.60 - 39.33$$

$$SSE = 27.07$$

4. Jones sets up a two-way ANOVA table (see Table 18.9).
5. Jones computes the F value.
   a. For ingredient X consideration,

$$F_{2.8} = \frac{\text{Mean square considerations between columns}}{\text{Total error mean square}}$$

Thus,

$$F_{2.8} = 2 = \text{number of degrees of freedom (df) in numerator}$$

$$8 = \text{number of degrees of freedom (df) in denominator}$$

The mean square consideration between columns is 33.80, and the total error mean square is 3.3875. Therefore,

$$F_{2.8} = \frac{33.80}{3.38375} = 9.99$$

b. For vitamin additive consideration,

$$F_{4.8} = \frac{9.83250}{3.38375}$$

$$= 2.9058 = 2.91$$

6. Jones locates the critical values of F.
   a. For ingredient X consideration,
      (1) The level of significance is 0.05.
      (2) There are two degrees of freedom in the numerator and eight in the denominator.
      (3) Referring to Appendix N, the critical value is 4.46.
   b. For vitamin additive consideration,
      (1) The level of significance is 0.05.
      (2) There are four degrees of freedom in the numerator and eight in the denominator.
      (3) Referring to Appendix N, the critical value is 3.84.
7. Jones compares the computed and critical value of F.
   a. For ingredient X consideration,
      (1) The computed value is 9.99.
      (2) The critical value is 4.46.
   b. For vitamin additive consideration,
      (1) The computed value is 2.91.
      (2) The critical value is 3.84.
8. Jones accepts or rejects the null hypothesis.
   a. For ingredient X, Jones rejects the null hypothesis. The computed value

of F is 9.99, which is greater than the critical value, 4.46. This signifies that all of the means are not equal. Therefore, the amount of ingredient X in Super Dog Food matters.

b. For the vitamin additive, Jones accepts the null hypothesis. The computed value of F is 2.91, which is smaller than the critical F value of 3.84. Therefore, the amount of vitamin additive in Super Dog Food does not matter.

19 Bayes' Theorem

Bayes' theorem allows the decisionmaker to choose the best course of action from several alternatives. Suppose you are planning to drive to Florida from one of the northern states. You would first examine a road map and look at the various routes. If you decided that the best route was the most direct one, you would have chosen the best action from several alternatives. Hence, you would have used Bayes' theorem.

Mr. Jolly works for XYZ Plastics Corp., which manufactures flashcubes. Each cube is color-coded to indicate which camera model it is compatible with; for example, red signifies that a cube is to be used with Model X Superflash cameras. Jolly paints the proper color code on the bottom of each cube, allows it to dry, and places it in a box for shipment to a customer. The box holds 20 cubes.

One day, Jolly realizes that he forgot to color-code one cube in the last box of red-coded cubes he packed. He retrieves the box, knowing that it contains an uncoded cube. What is the probability Jolly will pick out the uncoded cube on the first try? It is 1/20 or 0.05.

Suppose that after opening the box, Jolly sees that none of the visible sides of the cubes are coded red. He decides to conduct an experiment. He will toss each cube in the air 50 times. If it lands with the red side up, he will know that it is not the uncoded one. However, if an uncolored end appears, he will not know it if is the uncoded cube. Jolly wants to know what the probability is that a cube that lands with an uncolored side up is the uncoded cube. If a cube is correctly color-coded, an uncolored side will appear five times out of six. If a cube is uncoded, an uncolored side will appear six times in six. Table 19.1 shows the probability of the number of times an uncoded side would turn up when 20 cubes are tossed in the air 50 times each, assuming cube 20 is the uncoded one.

The probability that cube 20 is the uncoded one is 300/500 or 0.059. This is called the *posterior* probability.

APPLICATION OF BAYES' THEOREM TO ILLUSTRATION

Bayes' theorem may be applied to the problem of determining the probability that cube 20, after being tossed in the air 50 times, is the uncoded one. Certain abbreviations will be used in the discussion that follows:

Uncolo = uncolored side of cube

Colo = colored side of cube

OK = cube uncolored on five sides, colored on one

Not OK = cube uncolored on six sides, hence uncoded

So in this example, the formula for Bayes' theorem is:

P(Not OK1Uncolo) =

$$\frac{\text{P(Not OK)} \times \text{P(Uncolo1Not OK)}}{\text{P(Not OK)} \times \text{P(Uncolo1Not OK)} + \text{P(OK)} \times \text{P(Uncolo1OK)}}$$

where

P (Not OK1Uncolo) is the determined probability. It is the probability that cube 20 is uncoded given the results of the experiment in which Jolly tossed the 20 cubes in the air. It is determined *after* the results of the experiment are known. Hence posterior probability.

P (Not OK) is *prior* probability or the probability of selecting one of 20 cubes before tossing it in the air and finding it defective. P (Not OK) = 1/20 or 0.05.

P(Uncolo1Not OK) is the probability that an uncolored (Uncolo) side will appear face up after the cube has been tossed in the air. This assumes that the cube that is not OK is being tossed. (There is no color on any side of defective cube.) In other words, the probability of getting an uncolored side on a cube that is not OK is 1.00.

P(OK) is the probability of selecting one of the 20 cubes *prior* to its being tossed in the air and finding it OK. P(OK) = 19/20 or 0.950. Here, 19 out of 20 cubes are known to be OK.

Table 19.1. Probability of Uncoded Side Showing in a Total of 20 Six-Sided Cubes Tossed 50 Times Each.

Cube No.	Cube OK or Not OK?	No. Tosses	No. Uncolored Sides
1	OK	50	5 × 50 = 250
2	OK	50	5 × 50 = 250
3	OK	50	5 × 50 = 250
4	OK	50	5 × 50 = 250
5	OK	50	5 × 50 = 250
6	OK	50	5 × 50 = 250
7	OK	50	5 × 50 = 250
8	OK	50	5 × 50 = 250
9	OK	50	5 × 50 = 250
10	OK	50	5 × 50 = 250
11	OK	50	5 × 50 = 250
12	OK	50	5 × 50 = 250
13	OK	50	5 × 50 = 250
14	OK	50	5 × 50 = 250
15	OK	50	5 × 50 = 250
16	OK	50	5 × 50 = 250
17	OK	50	5 × 50 = 250
18	OK	50	5 × 50 = 250
19	OK	50	5 × 50 = 250
20	Not OK	50	6 × 50 = 300
		Total	5050

P *(Uncolo1OK)* is the probability of an uncolored (Uncolo) face appearing, assuming a nondefective cube which is 5/6 or 0.833 because five sides are uncolored while the sixth is color-coded.

Inserting probabilities discussed above in Bayes' formula, we get:

$$P(\text{Not OK1Uncolo}) = \frac{(0.05)\,(1.00)}{[(0.05)\,(1.00)] + [(0.95)\,(0.833)]}$$

$$= \frac{0.05}{0.05 + 0.7914}$$

$$= \frac{0.05}{0.8414}$$

$$= 0.059 \text{ or } 5.9\%$$

If we wish to apply a general formula in place of the specific one used in the illustration, then:

$$A_1 = \text{Not OK (uncoded cube)}$$

$$A_2 = \text{OK (coded cube)}$$

$$B = \text{Uncolo (uncolored side of cube)}$$

Replacing the above letters (A_1, etc.) in the formula previously used:

$P(A_1/B)$ = determined probability replacing P(Not OK|Uncolo)

$P(A_1)$ = prior probability replacing P(Not OK)

$P(B|A_1)$ = probability of selecting a cube—prior to its being tossed in the air—and not finding it OK

$P(B|A_2)$ = probability of an uncolored face showing after cube 20 has been tossed in air, assuming it is coded

So, formula would be:

$$P(A_1/B) = \frac{P(A_1)P(B|A_1)}{[P(A_1)P(B|A_1)] + [P(A_2)P(B|A_2)]}$$

Bayes' theorem and formula as applied here covers two mutually exclusive events (A_1 Not OK and A_2 OK) for a given result B in the preceding formula.

$$P(A_1|B) =$$

$$\frac{P(A_1)P(B/A_1)}{[P(A_1)(P(B/A_1)] + [P(A_2)P(B/A_2)] + [P(A_3)P(B/A_3)\ldots] + [P(A_z)P(B/A_z)]}$$

Here, all possible outcomes of a group of mutually exclusive events are covered for any given result B. In other words, the *posterior* probability of mutually exclusive events are being determined for a particular outcome B.

The formula for the *posterior* probability of mutually exclusive events $A_2 \ldots A_z$ on a given result B would do the same for A_1 except $A_2 \ldots A_z$ would replace A_1 in formula. So the formula for A_z would be:

Table 19.2. Payoff Table for Super X Widget at Various Production Levels (profit in $ thousands).

Level of Production	Estimated Selling Price	Estimated Manu-facturing Cost	Profit/ Unit	Total Profit at Various Production Levels			
				20,000	25,000	30,000	35,000
20,000	$10.00	$4.00	$6.00	$120	$120	$120	$120
25,000	10.00	4.00	6.00	100	150	150	150
30,000	10.00	4.00	6.00	80	130	180	180
35,000	10.00	4.00	6.00	60	110	160	210

$$P(A_z/B) = \frac{P(A_z)P(B/A_z)}{P(A_1)P(B/A_1) + P(A_2)P(B/A_2) + P(A_3)P(B/A_3) \ldots + P(A_z)P(B/A_z)}$$

BAYES' THEOREM APPLIED TO DECISIONMAKING

The ABC Widget Co. has developed a new widget, Super X Widget, with a special patent. The company's management information specialist, Laura Smith, is asked to develop some decisionmaking techniques. She decides to use Bayes' theorem. Ms. Smith's analysis is as follows:

1. She reviews the various manufacturing levels of Super X Widget, its estimated cost of manufacture, and estimated selling price. From this review, Smith sets up a payoff (profit) table (Table 19.2). If ABC Widget manufactures and sells 20,000 Super X Widgets, it will make a profit of $120,000 (20,000 × $6.00). However, should the company manufacture 30,000 and only sell 20,000, then the profit would be (20,000 × $10.00) - (30,000 × 4), or only $80,000.

2. Smith, after discussions with top management of ABC Widget, assigns probabilities of sales to the four levels of production (Table 19.3).

Table 19.3. Sales Probabilities for Four Levels of Production of Super X Widget.

Levels of Production (Units)	Assigned Probabilities to Levels of Production
20,000	0.20
25,000	0.30
30,000	0.45
35,000	0.05
	1.00

Table 19.4. Profit Expected from Manufacturing 20,000 Super X Widgets (in $ Thousands).

Level of Production	Column 1 Profit	Column 2 Probabilities	Expected Profits (Col. 1 × Col. 2)
20,000	$120	0.20	$ 24.0
25,000	120	0.30	36.0
30,000	120	0.45	54.0
35,000	120	0.05	6.0
		Total	$120.0

Table 19.5. Profit Expected from Manufacturing 25,000 Super X Widgets (in $ Thousands).

Level of Production	Column 1 Profit	Column 2 Probability	Expected Profits (Col. 1 × Col. 2)
20,000	$100	0.20	$ 20.0
25,000	150	0.30	45.0
30,000	150	0.45	67.5
35,000	150	0.05	7.5
		Total	$140.0

Table 19.6. Profit Expected from Manufacturing 30,000 Super X Widgets (in $ Thousands).

Level of Production	Column 1 Profit	Column 2 Probability	Expected Profits (Col. 1 × Col. 2)
20,000	$ 80	0.20	$ 16.0
25,000	130	0.30	39.0
30,000	180	0.45	81.0
35,000	180	0.05	9.0
		Total	$145.0

Table 19.7. Profit Expected from Manufacturing 35,000 Super X Widgets (in $ Thousands).

Level of Production	Column 1 Profit	Column 2 Probability	Expected Profits (Col. 1 × Col. 2)
20,000	$ 60	0.20	$ 12.0
25,000	110	0.30	33.0
30,000	160	0.45	72.0
35,000	210	0.05	10.5
		Total	$127.5

Table 19.8. Profit Expected from Four Levels of Production of Super X Widget (in $ Thousands).

Level of Production	Expected Profit
20,000	$120.0
25,000	140.0
30,000	145.0
35,000	127.5

3. Smith sets up expected payoff tables for various levels of production using the assumed probabilities (Tables 19.4 through 19.7).

4. Smith combines all expected payoffs of production of Super X Widget into one table (Table 19.8). Based on a $10.00 selling price and a $4.00 manufacturing cost, the level of production that would yield the best profit would be 30,000 units of Super X Widgets.

5. Smith proceeds to gather *additional* information that could be used to revise *prior probabilities of management*. She does this in two ways:

    a. She questions key customers. First, she has some samples of the Super X Widget made up and given to ABC Widget's salespeople to show 300 key customers. The salespeople show the Super X Widget to the customer. The customer is then asked to evaluate the demand in terms of units for the Super X Widget on a questionnaire. The demand for the product is rated from 1 to 10, with 1 being poor and 10 excellent.

    b. The key customer's evaluation of widgets is compared with those of ABC management (prior relationship). Over a 3-year period, Smith has made it a practice to compare ratings given by key customers on new types of widgets marketed by ABC. (There are 16 in all.) These ratings have been compared with the expectations of management at ABC Widget. This was done to establish a prior relationship. After looking over the various levels of production open to it, ABC Widget chose the level producing the most expected profit.

6. Smith then sets up a table matching the key customers' evaluation of sales demand for 16 different widgets introduced in the last 3 years against ABC Widget's management's assessment of expected level of production (Table 19.9). In Table 19.9, the higher the subscript, the higher the level of production or anticipated demand. (P.L.$_1$ is less than P.L.$_4$, and E.D.$_4$ is more than E.D.$_1$.)

7. Smith converts the absolute units in Table 19.9 into probabilities for use in Bayes' theorem (Table 19.10). For example, for P.L.$_1$ and E.D.$_1$, it would be 100/340 or 0.30; for P.L.$_2$ and E.D.$_1$, it would be 200/500 or 0.40.

8. On the basis of *additional* information secured in step 6, Smith is in a position to revise ABC Widget management's *prior* estimates of the production levels

Table 19.9. Comparison of Key Customers' Evaluation of Demand vs. ABC Management's Suggested Production of 16 New Widgets (Number of Widgets in Thousands).

Suggested Production Level (P.L.)	Evaluation of Demand (E.D.)				
	$E.D._1$	$E.D._2$	$E.D._3$	$E.D._4$	Total
$P.L._1$	100	75	150	15	340
$P.L._2$	200	150	100	50	500
$P.L._3$	150	200	175	125	650
$P.L._4$	50	75	125	175	425
	500	500	550	365	1915

of Super X Widget. Here we have a judgment sample totaling about 4800 (number of key customers (300) multiplied by number of products (16) developed over the 3 past years including the Super X Widget).

9. Smith analyzes the questionnaires filled out by the 300 key customers who were shown the Super X Widget and who had rated it on a scale of 1 to 10. Smith concluded that the sales of the Super X Widget would be about 10,000 units. This figure is lower than the 30,000 units estimated by ABC Widget management. (See Table 19.3.)

After looking over the returned questionnaires, Smith discovered that some of the 300 key customers objected to part of the design of the Super X Widget. Hence, the lower overall rating.

10. Smith revises the prior probability of the 0.45 suggested production level (P.L.$_3$) of ABC Widget management. This is due to the lower demand schedules of the 300 key customers who estimated demand to be 10,000 units (E.D.$_1$).

    a. Bayes' theorem is applied.

        (1) $P(P.L._3/E.D._1)$ = conditional probability to P.L.$_3$ given evaluation demand of E.D.$_1$

        (2) P.L.$_3$ = prior probability given by ABC Widget management with a sales level of 30,000 Super X Widgets

Table 19.10. Probabilities for Suggested Production Levels and Evaluations of Demand.

Suggested Production Level (P.L.)	Evaluation of Demand				
	$E.D._1$	$E.D._2$	$E.D._3$	$E.D._4$	Total
$P.L._1$	0.30	0.22	0.44	0.04	1.00
$P.L._2$	0.40	0.30	0.20	0.10	1.00
$P.L._3$	0.23	0.31	0.27	0.19	1.00
$P.L._4$	0.12	0.18	0.29	0.41	1.00

(3) $P(E.D._1/P.L._3)$ = conditional probability found by the ratio of 10,000/30,000.

b. Only probabilities connected with $E.D._1$ will be used in this example. This is the evaluated demand for the Super X Widget suggested by the key customers.

c. Bayes' theorem then becomes for production level $(P.L._3)$ and evaluated demand $(E.D._1)$:

$$P(P.L._3/E.D._1) =$$

$$\frac{P(PL_3) \, P(ED_1/PL_3)}{P(PL_1)P(ED_1/PL_1) + P(PL_2)P(ED_1)/PL_2) + P(PL_3)P(ED_1/PL_3) + P(PL_4)P(ED_1/PL_4)}$$

$$= \frac{(0.45)(0.23)}{[(0.20)(0.30)] + [(0.30)(0.40)] + [(0.45)(0.23)] + [(0.05)(0.12)]}$$

$$= \frac{0.1035}{0.06 + 0.12 + 0.1035 + 0.006}$$

$$= \frac{0.1035}{0.2895}$$

$$= 0.3575$$

d. Analyzing the results of Baye's theorem, Smith realizes she must scale ABC Widget management's prior probability of 0.45 down to 0.36 because of the evaluation of the Super X Widget by 300 key customers.

11. Smith now sets up a table of *prior* and *posterior* probabilities (Table 19.11). However, she must first compute the *posterior* probabilities for the re-

Table 19.11. Prior and Posterior Probabilities for Super X Widget Using Evaluated Demand 1 ($E.D._1$).

Evaluated Demand Levels (Units)		Prior Probabilities	Posterior Probabilities
20,000		0.200	0.207
25,000		0.300	0.414
30,000		0.450	0.358
35,000		0.050	0.021
	Total	1.000	1.000

maining three production levels, $P.L._1$, $P.L._2$, and $P.L._4$, given the evaluated demand level of $E.D._1$. Note that the denominator stays the same with the evaluated demand of $E.D._1$.

  a. Smith determines the posterior probability for production level 1 $(P.L._1)$ and evaluated demand 1 $(E.D._1)$.

$$P(PL_1/ED_1) =$$

$$\frac{P(PL_1)\,P(ED_1/PL_1)}{P(PL_1)P(ED_1/PL_1) + P(PL_2)P(ED_1/PL_2) + P(PL_3)P(ED_1/PL_3) + P(PL_4)P(ED_1/PL_4)}$$

$$= \frac{(0.20)(0.30)}{0.2895}$$

$$= \frac{0.0600}{0.2895}$$

$$= 0.2073$$

  b. Smith determines the posterior probability for production level 2 $(P.L._2)$ and evaluated demand 1 $(E.D._1)$.

$$P(PL_2/ED_1) =$$

$$\frac{P(PL_2)\,P(ED_1/PL_2)}{P(PL_1)P(ED_1/PL_1) + P(PL_2)P(ED_1/PL_2) + P(PL_3)P(ED_1/PL_3) + P(PL_4)P(ED_1/PL_4)}$$

$$= \frac{(0.30)(0.40)}{0.2895}$$

$$= \frac{0.1200}{0.2895}$$

$$= 0.4145$$

  c. Smith determines the posterior probability for production level 4 $(P.L._4)$ and evaluated demand 1 $(E.D._1)$.

Table 19.12. Expected Payoff for Producing 20,000 Units of Super X Widget (in $ Thousands).

Level of Production	Profit	Probability	Expected Profit[a]
20,000	$120	0.207	$ 24.84
25,000	120	0.414	49.68
30,000	120	0.358	42.96
35,000	120	0.021	2.52
		Total	$120.00

[a]Profit × Probability.

$P(PL/ED) =$

$$\frac{P(PL_4)\,P(ED_1/PL_4)}{P(PL_1)(P(ED_1/PL_1) + P(PL_2)P(ED_1/PL_2) + P(PL_3)P(ED_1/PL_3) + P(PL_4)P(ED_1/PL_4)}$$

$$= \frac{(0.05)(0.12)}{0.2895}$$

$$= \frac{0.0060}{0.2895}$$

$$= 0.0207$$

12. Using the *posterior* probabilities from Table 19.11 and expected payoffs from Table 19.2, Smith calculates a new set of expected payoffs (Tables 19.12-19.15).

    a. Smith calculates expected profits using posterior probabilities at the 20,000, 25,000, 30,000, and 35,000 unit levels of production.

Table 19.13. Expected Payoff for Producing 25,000 Units of Super X Widget (in $ Thousands).

Level of Production (Units)	Profit	Probability	Expected Profit[a]
20,000	$100	0.207	$ 20.70
25,000	150	0.414	62.10
30,000	150	0.358	53.70
35,000	150	0.021	3.15
		Total	$139.65

[a]Profit × Probability.

Comparing the *prior* and *posterior* probabilities, Smith sees that management's first estimate of manufacturing 30,000 Super X Widgets (prior probability) yields a maximum expected profit of $145,000, whereas if the posterior probabilities are applied, a level of 25,000 Super X Widgets will most likely yield the greatest maximum profit of $139,650. (See Table 19.16.)

Table 19.14. Expected Payoff for Producing 30,000 Units of Super X Widget (in $ Thousands).

Level of Production	Profit	Probabilities		Expected Profit[a]
20,000	$ 80.0	0.207		$ 16.57
25,000	130.0	0.414		53.82
30,000	180.0	0.358		64.44
35,000	180.0	0.021		3.78
			Total	$138.61

[a]Profit × Probability.

Table 19.15. Expected Payoff for Producing 35,000 Units of Super X Widget (in $ Thousands).

Level of Production (Units)	Profit	Probability		Expected Profit[a]
20,000	$ 60.00	0.207		$ 12.42
25,000	110.00	0.414		45.54
30,000	160.00	0.358		57.28
35,000	210.00	0.021		4.41
			Total	$119.65

[a]Profit × Probability.

Table 19.16. Comparison Expected Payoffs with Prior and Posterior Probabilities (in $ Thousands).

Level of Production (Units)	Prior Probability	Posterior Probability
20,000	$120.00	$120.00
25,000	140.00	139.65
30,000	145.00	138.60
35,000	127.50	119.65

APPENDIX A
COMMON LOGARITHMS

There are definite relationships between numbers and logarithms as outlined below:

| | | Parts of Logarithm | |
Number	Logarithm	Characteristic	Mantissa
2000	3.3010	3	0.3010
200	2.3010	2	0.3010
20	1.3010	1	0.3010
2	0.3010	0	0.3010
0.2	9.3010-10	9.-10(1)	0.3010
0.02	8.3010-10	8.-10(2)	0.3010

From the above notice the following relationships:
1. All numbers in the first column are positive. There are no logarithms for negative numbers.
2. The characteristic of a logarithm is that portion of the log to the left of the decimal point. It determines where the decimal point will be placed in a number subject to the following rules:
   a. If N=1 the log characteristic is zero or positive. It is also one less than the number of places to the left of the decimal in the number. In the table above it can be seen that the characteristic of 2000 is 3 while that of 2 is 0.
   b. If N<1 then the log characteristic is negative. For example, for 0.2 it is -1 while for 0.02 it is -2. Therefore, it can be seen it is one more than the number of zeros just after the decimal point. A negative characteristic may be written 1 of 9 -10.
3. The mantissa is to the right of the decimal point and is always positive or zero.

The following are some examples of the use of logarithms.
1. Division
   A. Divide 92 by 7.
   1. Log of 92 is   1.9638
      Minus Log of 7   0.8451
                       $\overline{1.1877}$

2. Antilog of 1.1877 is 13.1. Looking at Appendix B you will find 1.1877 is nearer 13.1 than 13.2. However, interpolation may be used for a better approximation. (See below).

2. Multiplication
  A. Multiply 358 by 88.
    1. Characteristic of 353 is 2.
    Characteristic of 88 is 1.
    2. Locate mantissa value in table of common logarithms as follows:
      a. Mantissa of 353.
        1) Go to Appendix B and look under column headed N. 2) Go down to 35 then over to column headed. 3) This will yield a mantissa of 5478.
      b. Mantissa of 88.
        1) Go to Appendix B and look under column N. 2) Go down to 88 then over to column headed 0. 3) Mantissa of 9945 is found.
      c. Add sum of logs.
        Log of 353 is   2.5478
        Plus log of 88   1.9445
                    ————
                    4.4923
      d. Locate antilog of 4.4923.
        1) Enter Appendix B and locate mantissa value closest to 4923 which is 4928. 2) Under Column N read the number which appears beside 4928, which is 31. Going across row 31 find the number above 4928, which is 1. Thus the number is 311. 3) Develop antilog of 4.4923. The number is 31100. A more exact number may be achieved by interpolation.

3. Interpolation
  a. 353 multiplied by 88 via logarithms equals 31100. A closer approximation can be done by interpolation as follows:

$$
\begin{array}{ll}
\textit{Number} & \textit{Logarithm} \\
\left. \begin{array}{l} 31100 \\ \\ 31000 \end{array} \right\} 100 & \left. \begin{array}{l} 4.4928 \\ \left. \begin{array}{l} 4.4923 \\ \\ \\ 4.4914 \end{array} \right\} 9 \end{array} \right\} 14
\end{array}
$$

9/14 of 100 = 64; 31000 + 64 = 31064.

  b. The product of 353 × 88 produced via logarithms is 31100. By interpolation it is 31064. Multiplying 353 × 88 gives a product of 31064. Hence, it can be seen that interpolation is more accurate.

4. Raise a number to a given power. For example raise 7 to the 4th power.
  a. Log of 7 = 0.8451.
  b. 0.8451 × 4 = 3.3804.

c. Antilog of 3.3804 is:

Number	Logarithm
2410 ⎫ 10	3.3820
2400 ⎭	3.3804 ⎫ 2 ⎫ 18
	3.3802 ⎭ ⎭

2/18 × 10 = 1.11 or 2400 + 1 = 2401

d. 7^4 by multiplication gives 2401.
5. Obtain the root of a whole number. For example, 4th root of 14.
   a. log of 14 = 1.1461.
   b. 1.1461/4 = 0.28653.
   c. Antilog of 0.28653 is about 1.93.
   d. 4th root of 14 = 1.93.
6. Obtain 5th root of 1/2.
   a. Log of 1 = 10.0000 –10.
   b. Log of 2 = 0.3010.
   c. Subtracting log of 2 from log of 1 is 9.6990 –10.
   d. Divide 9.6990 –10 by 5 yields 1.9398 –2.
   e. The antilog of 1.9398 –2 (8.9398 –10 or 2.9398) is 0.873 or 873/10000.

APPENDIX B

LOGARITHMS

N	0	1	2	3	4	5	6	7	8	9
10	0000	0043	0086	0128	0170	0212	0253	0294	0334	0374
11	0414	0453	0492	0531	0569	0607	0645	0682	0719	0755
12	0792	0828	0864	0899	0934	0969	1004	1038	1072	1106
13	1139	1173	1206	1239	1271	1303	1335	1367	1399	1430
14	1461	1492	1523	1553	1584	1614	1644	1673	1703	1732
15	1761	1790	1818	1847	1875	1903	1931	1959	1987	2014
16	2041	2068	2095	2122	2148	2175	2201	2227	2253	2279
17	2304	2330	2355	2380	2405	2430	2455	2480	2504	2529
18	2553	2577	2601	2625	2648	2672	2695	2718	2742	2765
19	2788	2810	2833	2856	2878	2900	2923	2945	2967	2989
20	3010	3032	3054	3075	3096	3118	3139	3160	3181	3201
21	3222	3243	3263	3284	3304	3324	3345	3365	3385	3404
22	3424	3444	3464	3483	3502	3522	3541	3560	3579	3598
23	3617	3636	3655	3674	3692	3711	3729	3747	3766	3784
24	3802	3820	3838	3856	3874	3892	3909	3927	3945	3962
25	3979	3997	4014	4031	4048	4065	4082	4099	4116	4133
26	4150	4166	4183	4200	4216	4232	4249	4265	4281	4298
27	4314	4330	4346	4362	4378	4393	4409	4425	4440	4456
28	4472	4487	4502	4518	4533	4548	4564	4579	4594	4609
29	4624	4639	4654	4669	4683	4698	4713	4728	4742	4757
30	4771	4786	4800	4814	4829	4843	4857	4871	4886	4900
31	4914	4928	4942	4955	4969	4983	4997	5011	5024	5038
32	5051	5065	5079	5092	5105	5119	5132	5145	5159	5172
33	5185	5198	5211	5224	5237	5250	5263	5276	5289	5302
34	5315	5328	5340	5353	5366	5378	5391	5403	5416	5428
35	5441	5453	5465	5478	5490	5502	5514	5527	5539	5551
36	5563	5575	5587	5599	5611	5623	5635	5647	5658	5670
37	5682	5694	5705	5717	5729	5740	5752	5763	5775	5786
38	5798	5809	5821	5832	5843	5855	5866	5877	5888	5899
39	5911	5922	5933	5944	5955	5966	5977	5988	5999	6010
40	6021	6031	6042	6053	6064	6075	6085	6096	6107	6117
41	6128	6138	6149	6160	6170	6180	6191	6201	6212	6222
42	6232	6243	6253	6263	6274	6284	6294	6304	6314	6325
43	6336	6345	6355	6365	6375	6385	6395	6405	6415	6425
44	6435	6444	6454	6464	6474	6484	6493	6503	6513	6522
45	6532	6542	6551	6561	6571	6580	6590	6599	6609	6618
46	6628	6637	6646	6656	6665	6675	6684	6693	6702	6712
47	6721	6730	6739	6749	6758	6767	6776	6785	6794	6803
48	6812	6821	6830	6839	6848	6857	6866	6875	6884	6893
49	6902	6911	6920	6928	6937	6946	6955	6964	6972	6981
50	6990	6998	7007	7016	7024	7033	7042	7050	7059	7067
51	7076	7084	7093	7101	7110	7118	7126	7135	7143	7152
52	7160	7168	7177	7185	7193	7202	7210	7218	7226	7235
53	7243	7251	7259	7267	7275	7284	7292	7300	7308	7316
54	7324	7332	7340	7348	7356	7364	7372	7380	7388	7396

Logarithms (*continued*)

N	0	1	2	3	4	5	6	7	8	9
55	7404	7412	7419	7427	7435	7443	7451	7459	7466	7474
56	7482	7490	7497	7505	7513	7520	7528	7536	7543	7551
57	7559	7566	7574	7582	7589	7597	7604	7612	7619	7627
58	7634	7642	7649	7657	7664	7672	7679	7686	7694	7701
59	7709	7716	7723	7731	7738	7745	7752	7760	7767	7774
60	7782	7789	7796	7803	7810	7818	7825	7832	7839	7846
61	7853	7860	7868	7875	7882	7889	7896	7903	7910	7917
62	7924	7931	7938	7945	7952	7959	7966	7973	7980	7987
63	7993	8000	8007	8014	8021	8028	8035	8041	8048	8055
64	8062	8069	8075	8082	8089	8096	8102	8109	8116	8122
65	8129	8136	8142	8149	8156	8162	8169	8176	8182	8189
66	8195	8202	8209	8215	8222	8228	8235	8241	8248	8254
67	8261	8267	8274	8280	8287	8293	8299	8306	8312	8319
68	8325	8331	8338	8344	8351	8357	8363	8370	8376	8382
69	8388	8395	8401	8407	8414	8420	8426	8432	8439	8445
70	8451	8457	8463	8470	8476	8482	8488	8494	8500	8506
71	8513	8519	8525	8531	8537	8543	8549	8555	8561	8567
72	8573	8579	8585	8591	8597	8603	8609	8615	8621	8627
73	8633	8639	8645	8651	8657	8663	8669	8675	8681	8686
74	8692	8698	8704	8710	8716	8722	8727	8733	8739	8745
75	8751	8756	8762	8768	8774	8779	8785	8791	8797	8802
76	8808	8814	8820	8825	8831	8837	8842	8848	8854	8859
77	8865	8871	8876	8882	8887	8893	8899	8904	8910	8915
78	8921	8927	8932	8938	8943	8949	8954	8960	8965	8971
79	8976	8982	8987	8993	8998	9004	9009	9015	9020	9025
80	9031	9036	9042	9047	9053	9058	9063	9069	9074	9079
81	9085	9090	9096	9101	9106	9112	9117	9122	9128	9133
82	9138	9143	9149	9154	9159	9165	9170	9175	9180	9186
83	9191	9196	9201	9206	9212	9217	9222	9227	9232	9238
84	9243	9248	9253	9258	9263	9269	9274	9279	9284	9289
85	9294	9299	9304	9309	9315	9320	9325	9330	9335	9340
86	9345	9350	9355	9360	9365	9370	9375	9380	9385	9390
87	9395	9400	9405	9410	9415	9420	9425	9430	9435	9440
88	9445	9450	9455	9460	9465	9469	9474	9479	9484	9489
89	9494	9499	9504	9509	9513	9518	9523	9528	9533	9538
90	9542	9547	9552	9557	9562	9566	9571	9576	9581	9586
91	9590	9595	9600	9605	9609	9614	9619	9624	9628	9633
92	9638	9643	9647	9652	9657	9661	9666	9671	9675	9680
93	9685	9689	9694	9699	9703	9708	9713	9717	9722	9727
94	9731	9736	9741	9745	9750	9754	9759	9763	9768	9773
95	9777	9782	9786	9791	9795	9800	9805	9809	9814	9818
96	9823	9827	9832	9836	9841	9845	9850	9854	9859	9863
97	9868	9872	9877	9881	9886	9890	9894	9899	9903	9908
98	9912	9917	9921	9926	9930	9934	9939	9943	9948	9952
99	9956	9961	9965	9969	9974	9978	9983	9987	9991	9996

TABLE OF AREAS AND ORDINATES OF THE NORMAL CURVE*

Table of areas column (2) shows		Table of ordinates column (3) shows	

$z = \dfrac{X-\mu}{\sigma}$	Area Under the Curve between μ and X	Ordinate (Y) of the curve at X	$z = \dfrac{X-\mu}{\sigma}$	Area Under the Curve between μ and X	Ordinate (Y) of the curve at X
(1)	(2)	(3)	(1)	(2)	(3)
.00	.00000	.39894	.20	.07926	.39104
.01	.00399	.39892	.21	.08317	.39024
.02	.00798	.39886	.22	.08706	.38940
.03	.01197	.39876	.23	.09095	.38853
.04	.01595	.39862	.24	.09483	.38762
.05	.01994	.39844	.25	.09871	.38667
.06	.02392	.39822	.26	.10257	.38568
.07	.02790	.39797	.27	.10642	.38466
.08	.03188	.39767	.28	.11026	.38361
.09	.03586	.39733	.29	.11409	.38251
.10	.03983	.39695	.30	.11791	.38139
.11	.04380	.39654	.31	.12172	.38023
.12	.04776	.39608	.32	.12552	.37903
.13	.05172	.39559	.33	.12930	.37780
.14	.05567	.39505	.34	.13307	.37654
.15	.05962	.39448	.35	.13683	.37524
.16	.06356	.39387	.36	.14058	.37391
.17	.06749	.39322	.37	.14431	.37255
.18	.07142	.39253	.38	.14803	.37115
.19	.07535	.39181	.39	.15173	.36973

* From: J. F. Kenney and E. S. Keeping, *Mathematics of Statistics* (Princeton, N.J.: D. Van Nostrand Company, Inc., 1954).

Table of areas and ordinates of the normal curve (*continued*)

$z = \dfrac{X-\mu}{\sigma}$	Area Under the Curve between μ and X	Ordinate (Y) of the curve at X	$z = \dfrac{X-\mu}{\sigma}$	Area Under the Curve between μ and X	Ordinate (Y) of the curve at X
(1)	(2)	(3)	(1)	(2)	(3)
.40	.15542	.36827	.90	.31594	.26609
.41	.15910	.36678	.91	.31859	.26369
.42	.16276	.36526	.92	.32121	.26129
.43	.16640	.36371	.93	.32381	.25888
.44	.17003	.36213	.94	.32639	.25647
.45	.17364	.36053	.95	.32894	.25406
.46	.17724	.35889	.96	.33147	.25164
.47	.18082	.35723	.97	.33398	.24923
.48	.18439	.35553	.98	.33646	.24681
.49	.18793	.35381	.99	.33891	.24439
.50	.19146	.35207	1.00	.34134	.24197
.51	.19497	.35029	1.01	.34375	.23955
.52	.19847	.34849	1.02	.34614	.23713
.53	.20194	.34667	1.03	.34850	.23471
.54	.20540	.34482	1.04	.35083	.23230
.55	.20884	.34294	1.05	.35314	.22988
.56	.21226	.34105	1.06	.35543	.22747
.57	.21566	.33912	1.07	.35769	.22506
.58	.21904	.33718	1.08	.35993	.22265
.59	.22240	.33521	1.09	.36214	.22025
.60	.22575	.33322	1.10	.36433	.21785
.61	.22907	.33121	1.11	.36650	.21546
.62	.23237	.32918	1.12	.36864	.21307
.63	.23565	.32713	1.13	.37076	.21069
.64	.23891	.32506	1.14	.37286	.20831
.65	.24215	.32297	1.15	.37493	.20594
.66	.24537	.32086	1.16	.37698	.20357
.67	.24857	.31874	1.17	.37900	.20121
.68	.25175	.31659	1.18	.38100	.19886
.69	.25490	.31443	1.19	.38298	.19652
.70	.25804	.31225	1.20	.38493	.19419
.71	.26115	.31006	1.21	.38686	.19186
.72	.26424	.30785	1.22	.38877	.18954
.73	.26730	.30563	1.23	.39065	.18724
.74	.27035	.30339	1.24	.39251	.18494
.75	.27337	.30114	1.25	.39435	.18265
.76	.27637	.29887	1.26	.39617	.18037
.77	.27935	.29659	1.27	.39796	.17810
.78	.28230	.29431	1.28	.39973	.17585
.79	.28524	.29200	1.29	.40147	.17360
.80	.28814	.28969	1.30	.40320	.17137
.81	.29103	.28737	1.31	.40490	.16915
.82	.29389	.28504	1.32	.40658	.16694
.83	.29673	.28269	1.33	.40824	.16474
.84	.29955	.28034	1.34	.40988	.16256
.85	.30234	.27798	1.35	.41149	.16038
.86	.30511	.27562	1.36	.41309	.15822
.87	.30785	.27324	1.37	.41466	.15608
.88	.31057	.27086	1.38	.41621	.15395
.89	.31327	.26848	1.39	.41774	.15183

Table of areas and ordinates of the normal curve (*continued*)

$z = \dfrac{X-\mu}{\sigma}$	Area Under the Curve between μ and X	Ordinate (Y) of the curve at X	$z = \dfrac{X-\mu}{\sigma}$	Area Under the Curve between μ and X	Ordinate (Y) of the curve at X
(1)	(2)	(3)	(1)	(2)	(3)
1.40	.41924	.14973	1.90	.47128	.06562
1.41	.42073	.14764	1.91	.47193	.06438
1.42	.42220	.14556	1.92	.47257	.06316
1.43	.42364	.14350	1.93	.47320	.06195
1.44	.42507	.14146	1.94	.47381	.06077
1.45	.42647	.13943	1.95	.47441	.05959
1.46	.42786	.13742	1.96	.47500	.05844
1.47	.42922	.13542	1.97	.47558	.05730
1.48	.43056	.13344	1.98	.47615	.05618
1.49	.43189	.13147	1.99	.47670	.05508
1.50	.43319	.12952	2.00	.47725	.05399
1.51	.43448	.12758	2.01	.47778	.05292
1.52	.43574	.1256€	2.02	.47831	.05186
1.53	.43699	.12376	2.03	.47882	.05082
1.54	.43822	.12188	2.04	.47932	.04980
1.55	.43943	.12001	2.05	.47982	.04879
1.56	.44062	.11816	2.06	.48030	.04780
1.57	.44179	.11632	2.07	.48077	.04682
1.58	.44295	.11450	2.08	.48124	.04586
1.59	.44408	.11270	2.09	.48169	.04491
1.60	.44520	.11092	2.10	.48214	.04398
1.61	.44630	.10915	2.11	.48257	.04307
1.62	.44738	.10741	2.12	.48300	.04217
1.63	.44845	.10567	2.13	.48341	.04128
1.64	.44950	.10396	2.14	.48382	.04041
1.65	.45053	.10226	2.15	.48422	.03955
1.66	.45154	.10059	2.16	.484€1	.03871
1.67	.45254	.09893	2.17	.48500	.03788
1.68	.45352	.09728	2.18	.48537	.03706
1.69	.45449	.09566	2.19	.48574	.03626
1.70	.45543	.09405	2.20	.48610	.03547
1.71	.45637	.09246	2.21	.48645	.03470
1.72	.45728	.09089	2.22	.48679	.03394
1.73	.45818	.08933	2.23	.48713	.03319
1.74	.45907	.08780	2.24	.48745	.03246
1.75	.45994	.08628	2.25	.48778	.03174
1.76	.46080	.08478	2.26	.48809	.03103
1.77	.46164	.08329	2.27	.48840	.03034
1.78	.46246	.08183	2.28	.48870	.02965
1.79	.46327	.08038	2.29	.48899	.02898
1.80	.46407	.07895	2.30	.48928	.02833
1.81	.46485	.07754	2.31	.48956	.02768
1.82	.46562	.07614	2.32	.48983	.02705
1.83	.46638	.07477	2.33	.49010	.02643
1.84	.46712	.07341	2.34	.49036	.02582
1.85	.46784	.07206	2.35	.49064	.02522
1.86	.46856	.07074	2.36	.49086	.02463
1.87	.46926	.06943	2.37	.49111	.02406
1.88	.46995	.06814	2.38	.49134	.02349
1.89	.47062	.06687	2.39	.49158	.02294

Table of areas and ordinates of the normal curve (*continued*)

$z = \dfrac{X-\mu}{\sigma}$	Area Under the Curve between μ and X	Ordinate (Y) of the curve at X	$z = \dfrac{X-\mu}{\sigma}$	Area Under the Curve between μ and X	Ordinate (Y) of the curve at X
(1)	(2)	(3)	(1)	(2)	(3)
2.40	.49180	.02239	2.90	.49813	.00595
2.41	.49202	.02186	2.91	.49819	.00578
2.42	.49224	.02134	2.92	.49825	.00562
2.43	.49245	.02083	2.93	.49831	.00545
2.44	.49266	.02033	2.94	.49836	.00530
2.45	.49286	.01984	2.95	.49841	.00514
2.46	.49305	.01936	2.96	.49846	.00499
2.47	.49324	.01889	2.97	.49851	.00485
2.48	.49343	.01842	2.98	.49856	.00471
2.49	.49361	.01797	2.99	.49861	.00457
2.50	.49379	.01753	3.00	.49865	.00443
2.51	.49396	.01709	3.01	.49869	.00430
2.52	.49413	.01667	3.02	.49874	.00417
2.53	.49430	.01625	3.03	.49878	.00405
2.54	.49446	.01585	3.04	.49882	.00393
2.55	.49461	.01545	3.05	.49886	.00381
2.56	.49477	.01506	3.06	.49889	.00370
2.57	.49492	.01468	3.07	.49893	.00358
2.58	.49506	.01431	3.08	.49897	.00348
2.59	.49520	.01394	3.09	.49900	.00337
2.60	.49534	.01358	3.10	.49903	.00327
2.61	.49547	.01323	3.11	.49906	.00317
2.62	.49560	.01289	3.12	.49910	.00307
2.63	.49573	.01256	3.13	.49913	.00298
2.64	.49585	.01223	3.14	.49916	.00288
2.65	.49598	.01191	3.15	.49918	.00279
2.66	.49609	.01160	3.16	.49921	.00271
2.67	.49621	.01130	3.17	.49924	.00262
2.68	.49632	.01100	3.18	.49926	.00254
2.69	.49643	.01071	3.19	.49929	.00246
2.70	.49653	.01042	3.20	.49931	.00238
2.71	.49664	.01014	3.21	.49934	.00231
2.72	.49674	.00987	3.22	.49936	.00224
2.73	.49683	.00961	3.23	.49938	.00216
2.74	.49693	.00935	3.24	.49940	.00210
2.75	.49702	.00909	3.25	.49942	.00203
2.76	.49711	.00885	3.26	.49944	.00196
2.77	.49720	.00861	3.27	.49946	.00190
2.78	.49728	.00837	3.28	.49948	.00184
2.79	.49736	.00814	3.29	.49950	.00178
2.80	.49744	.00792	3.30	.49952	.00172
2.81	.49752	.00770	3.31	.49953	.00167
2.82	.49760	.00748	3.32	.49955	.00161
2.83	.49767	.00727	3.33	.49957	.00156
2.84	.49774	.00707	3.34	.49958	.00151
2.85	.49781	.00687	3.35	.43960	.00146
2.86	.49788	.00668	3.36	.49961	.00141
2.87	.49795	.00649	3.37	.49962	.00136
2.88	.49801	.00631	3.38	.49964	.00132
2.89	.49807	.00613	3.39	.49965	.00127

Table of areas and ordinates of the normal curve (concluded)

$z = \dfrac{X-\mu}{\sigma}$	Area Under the Curve between μ and X	Ordinate (Y) of the curve at X	$z = \dfrac{X-\mu}{\sigma}$	Area Under the Curve between μ and X	Ordinate (Y) of the curve at X
(1)	(2)	(3)	(1)	(2)	(3)
3.40	.49966	.00123	3.70	.49989	.00042
3.41	.49968	.00119	3.71	.49990	.00041
3.42	.49969	.00115	3.72	.49990	.00039
3.43	.49970	.00111	3.73	.49990	.00038
3.44	.49971	.00107	3.74	.49991	.00037
3.45	.49972	.00104	3.75	.49991	.00035
3.46	.49973	.00100	3.76	.49992	.00034
3.47	.49974	.00097	3.77	.49992	.00033
3.48	.49975	.00094	3.78	.49992	.00031
3.49	.49976	.00090	3.79	.49992	.00030
3.50	.49977	.00087	3.80	.49993	.00029
3.51	.49978	.00084	3.81	.49993	.00028
3.52	.49978	.00081	3.82	.49993	.00027
3.53	.49979	.00079	3.83	.49994	.00026
3.54	.49980	.00076	3.84	.49994	.00025
3.55	.49981	.00073	3.85	.49994	.00024
3.56	.49981	.00071	3.86	.49994	.00023
3.57	.49982	.00068	3.87	.49995	.00022
3.58	.49983	.00066	3.88	.49995	.00021
3.59	.49983	.00063	3.89	.49995	.00021
3.60	.49984	.00061	3.90	.49995	.00020
3.61	.49985	.00059	3.91	.49995	.00019
3.62	.49985	.00057	3.92	.49996	.00018
3.63	.49986	.00055	3.93	.49996	.00018
3.64	.49986	.00053	3.94	.49996	.00017
3.65	.49987	.00051	3.95	.49996	.00016
3.66	.49987	.00049	3.96	.49996	.00016
3.67	.49988	.00047	3.97	.49996	.00015
3.68	.49988	.00046	3.98	.49997	.00014
3.69	.49989	.00044	3.99	.49997	.00014

BINOMIAL DISTRIBUTION

$$P\{r\} = \frac{n!}{r! \, (n-r)!} \, p^r q^{n-r}$$

n	r	.05	.10	.15	.20	.25	P .30	.35	.40	.45	.50
1	0	.9500	.9000	.8500	.8000	.7500	.7000	.6500	.6000	.5500	.5000
	1	.0500	.1000	.1500	.2000	.2500	.3000	.3500	.4000	.4500	.5000
2	0	.9025	.8100	.7225	.6400	.5625	.4900	.4225	.3600	.3025	.2500
	1	.0950	.1800	.2550	.3200	.3750	.4200	.4550	.4800	.4950	.5000
	2	.0025	.0100	.0225	.0400	.0625	.0900	.1225	.1600	.2025	.2500
3	0	.8574	.7290	.6141	.5120	.4219	.3430	.2746	.2160	.1664	.1250
	1	.1354	.2430	.3251	.3840	.4219	.4410	.4436	.4320	.4084	.3750
	2	.0071	.0270	.0574	.0960	.1406	.1890	.2389	.2880	.3341	.3750
	3	.0001	.0010	.0034	.0080	.0156	.0270	.0429	.0640	.0911	.1250
4	0	.8145	.6561	.5220	.4096	.3164	.2401	.1785	.1296	.0915	.0625
	1	.1715	.2916	.3685	.4096	.4219	.4116	.3845	.3456	.2995	.2500
	2	.0135	.0486	.0975	.1536	.2109	.2646	.3105	.3456	.3675	.3750
	3	.0005	.0036	.0115	.0256	.0469	.0756	.1115	.1536	.2005	.2500
	4	.0000	.0001	.0005	.0016	.0039	.0081	.0150	.0256	.0410	.0625
5	0	.7738	.5905	.4437	.3277	.2373	.1681	.1160	.0778	.0503	.0312
	1	.2036	.3280	.3915	.4096	.3955	.3602	.3124	.2592	.2059	.1562
	2	.0214	.0729	.1382	.2048	.2637	.3087	.3364	.3456	.3369	.3125
	3	.0011	.0081	.0244	.0512	.0879	.1323	.1811	.2304	.2757	.3125
	4	.0000	.0004	.0022	.0064	.0146	.0284	.0488	.0768	.1128	.1562
	5	.0000	.0000	.0001	.0003	.0010	.0024	.0053	.0102	.0185	.0312
6	0	.7351	.5314	.3771	.2621	.1780	.1176	.0754	.0467	.0277	.0156
	1	.2321	.3543	.3993	.3932	.3560	.3025	.2437	.1866	.1359	.0938
	2	.0305	.0984	.1762	.2458	.2966	.3241	.3280	.3110	.2780	.2344
	3	.0021	.0146	.0415	.0819	.1318	.1852	.2355	.2765	.3032	.3125
	4	.0001	.0012	.0055	.0154	.0330	.0595	.0951	.1382	.1861	.2344
	5	.0000	.0001	.0004	.0015	.0044	.0102	.0205	.0369	.0609	.0938
	6	.0000	.0000	.0000	.0001	.0002	.0007	.0018	.0041	.0083	.0156
7	0	.6983	.4783	.3206	.2097	.1335	.0824	.0490	.0280	.0152	.0078
	1	.2573	.3720	.3960	.3670	.3115	.2471	.1848	.1306	.0872	.0547
	2	.0406	.1240	.2097	.2753	.3115	.3177	.2985	.2613	.2140	.1641
	3	.0036	.0230	.0617	.1147	.1730	.2269	.2679	.2903	.2918	.2734
	4	.0002	.0026	.0109	.0287	.0577	.0972	.1442	.1935	.2388	.2734
	5	.0000	.0002	.0012	.0043	.0115	.0250	.0466	.0774	.1172	.1641
	6	.0000	.0000	.0001	.0004	.0013	.0036	.0084	.0172	.0320	.0547
	7	.0000	.0000	.0000	.0000	.0001	.0002	.0006	.0016	.0037	.0078
8	0	.6634	.4305	.2725	.1678	.1002	.0576	.0319	.0168	.0084	.0039
	1	.2793	.3826	.3847	.3355	.2670	.1977	.1373	.0896	.0548	.0312
	2	.0515	.1488	.2376	.2936	.3115	.2065	.2587	.2090	.1569	.1094

Source: Extracted from "Tables of the Binomial Probability Distribution," U.S. Department of Commerce, National Bureau of Standards, Applied Mathematics Series 6, 1952.

Binomial distribution (*continued*)

n	r	.05	.10	.15	.20	.25	P .30	.35	.40	.45	.50
8	3	.0054	.0331	.0839	.1468	.2076	.2541	.2786	.2787	.2568	.2188
	4	.0004	.0046	.0185	.0459	.0865	.1361	.1875	.2322	.2627	.2734
	5	.0000	.0004	.0026	.0092	.0231	.0467	.0808	.1239	.1719	.2188
	6	.0000	.0000	.0002	.0011	.0038	.0100	.0217	.0413	.0403	.1094
	7	.0000	.0000	.0000	.0001	.0004	.0012	.0033	.0079	.0164	.0312
	8	.0000	.0000	.0000	.0000	.0000	.0001	.0002	.0007	.0017	.0039
9	0	.6302	.3874	.2316	.1342	.0751	.0404	.0207	.0101	.0046	.0020
	1	.2985	.3874	.3679	.3020	.2253	.1556	.1004	.0605	.0339	.0176
	2	.0629	.1722	.2597	.3020	.3003	.2668	.2162	.1612	.1110	.0703
	3	.0077	.0446	.1069	.1762	.2336	.2668	.2716	.2508	.2119	.1641
	4	.0006	.0074	.0283	.0661	.1168	.1715	.2194	.2508	.2600	.2461
	5	.0000	.0008	.0050	.0165	.0389	.0735	.1181	.1672	.2128	.2461
	6	.0000	.0001	.0006	.0028	.0087	.0210	.0424	.0743	.1160	.1641
	7	.0000	.0000	.0000	.0003	.0012	.0039	.0098	.0212	.0407	.0703
	8	.0000	.0000	.0000	.0000	.0001	.0004	.0013	.0035	.0083	.0176
	9	.0000	0000	0000	0000	0000	0000	0001	.0003	.0008	.0020
10	0	.5987	.3487	.1969	.1074	.0563	.0282	.0135	.0060	.0025	.0010
	1	.3151	.3874	.3474	.2684	.1877	.1211	.0725	.0403	.0207	.0098
	2	.0746	.1937	.2759	.3020	.2816	.2335	.1757	.1209	.0763	.0439
	3	.0105	.0574	.1298	.2013	.2503	.2668	.2522	.2150	.1665	.1172
	4	.0010	.0112	.0401	.0881	.1460	.2001	.2377	.2508	.2384	.2051
	5	.0001	.0015	.0085	.0264	.0584	.1029	.1536	.2007	.2340	.2461
	6	.0000	.0001	.0012	.0055	.0162	.0368	.0689	.1115	.1596	.2051
	7	.0000	.0000	.0001	.0008	.0031	.0090	.0212	.0425	.0746	.1172
	8	.0000	.0000	.0000	.0001	.0004	.0014	.0043	.0106	.0229	.0439
	9	.0000	.0000	.0000	.0000	.0000	.0001	.0005	.0016	.0042	.0098
	10	.0000	.0000	.0000	.0000	.0000	.0000	.0000	.0001	.0003	.0010
11	0	.5688	.3138	.1673	.0859	.0422	.0198	.0088	.0036	.0014	.0005
	1	.3293	.3835	.3248	.2362	.1549	.0932	.0518	.0266	.0125	.0054
	2	.0867	.2131	.2866	.2953	.2581	.1998	.1395	.0887	.0513	.0269
	3	.0137	.0710	.1517	.2215	.2581	.2568	.2254	.1774	.1259	.0806
	4	.0014	.0158	.0536	.1107	.1721	.2201	.2428	.2365	.2060	.1611
	5	.0001	.0025	.0132	.0388	.0803	.1321	.1830	.2207	.2360	.2256
	6	.0000	.0003	.0023	.0097	.0268	.0566	.0985	.1471	.1931	.2256
	7	.0000	.0000	.0003	.0017	.0064	.0173	.0379	.0701	.1128	.1611
	8	.0000	.0000	.0000	.0002	.0011	.0037	.0102	.0234	.0462	.0806
	9	.0000	.0000	.0000	.0000	.0001	.0005	.0018	.0052	.0126	.0269
	10	.0000	.0000	.0000	.0000	.0000	.0000	.0002	.0007	.0021	.0054
	11	.0000	.0000	.0000	.0000	.0000	.0000	.0000	.0000	.0002	.0005
12	0	.5404	.2824	.1422	.0687	.0317	.0138	.0057	.0022	.0008	.0002
	1	.3413	.3766	.3012	.2062	.1267	.0712	.0368	.0174	.0075	.0029

Binomial distribution (*continued*)

n	r	.05	.10	.15	.20	.25	.30	.35	.40	.45	.50
12	2	.0988	.2301	.2924	.2835	.2323	.1678	.1088	.0639	.0339	.0161
	3	.0173	.0852	.1720	.2362	.2581	.2397	.1954	.1419	.0923	.0537
	4	.0021	.0213	.0683	.1329	.1936	.2311	.2367	.2128	.1700	.1208
	5	.0002	.0038	.0193	.0532	.1032	.1585	.2039	.2270	.2225	.1934
	6	.0000	.0005	.0040	.0155	.0401	.0792	.1281	.1766	.2124	.2256
	7	.0000	.0000	.0006	.0033	.0115	.0291	.0591	.1009	.1489	.1934
	8	.0000	.0000	.0001	.0005	.0024	.0078	.0199	.0420	.0762	.1208
	9	.0000	.0000	.0000	.0001	.0004	.0015	.0048	.0125	.0277	.0537
	10	.0000	.0000	.0000	.0000	.0000	.0002	.0008	.0025	.0068	.0161
	11	.0000	.0000	.0000	.0000	.0000	.0000	.0001	.0003	.0010	.0029
	12	.0000	.0000	.0000	.0000	.0000	.0000	.0000	.0000	.0001	.0002
13	0	.5133	.2542	.1209	.0550	.0238	.0097	.0037	.0013	.0004	.0001
	1	.3512	.3672	.2774	.1787	.1029	.0540	.0259	.0113	.0045	.0016
	2	.1109	.2448	.2937	.2680	.2059	.1388	.0836	.0453	.0220	.0095
	3	.0214	.0997	.1900	.2457	.2517	.2181	.1651	.1107	.0660	.0349
	4	.0028	.0277	.0838	.1535	.2097	.2337	.2222	.1845	.1350	.0873
	5	.0003	.0055	.0266	.0691	.1258	.1803	.2154	.2214	.1989	.1571
	6	.0000	.0008	.0063	.0230	.0559	.1030	.1546	.1968	.2169	.2095
	7	.0000	.0001	.0011	.0058	.0186	.0442	.0833	.1312	.1775	.2095
	8	.0000	.0001	.0001	.0011	.0047	.0142	.0336	.0656	.1089	.1571
	9	.0000	.0000	.0000	.0001	.0009	.0034	.0101	.0243	.0495	.0873
	10	.0000	.0000	.0000	.0000	.0001	.0006	.0022	.0065	.0162	.0349
	11	.0000	.0000	.0000	.0000	.0000	.0001	.0003	.0012	.0036	.0095
	12	.0000	.0000	.0000	.0000	.0000	.0000	.0000	.0001	.0005	.0016
	13	.0000	.0000	.0000	.0000	.0000	.0000	.0000	.0000	.0000	.0001
14	0	.4877	.2288	.1028	.0440	.0178	.0068	.0024	.0008	.0002	.0001
	1	.3593	.3559	.2539	.1539	.0832	.0407	.0181	.0073	.0027	.0009
	2	.1229	.2570	.2912	.2501	.1802	.1134	.0634	.0317	.0141	.0056
	3	.0259	.1142	.2056	.2501	.2402	.1943	.1366	.0845	.0462	.0222
	4	.0037	.0349	.0998	.1720	.2202	.2290	.2022	.1549	.1040	.0611
	5	.0004	.0078	.0352	.0860	.1468	.1963	.2178	.2066	.1701	.1222
	6	.0000	.0013	.0093	.0322	.0734	.1262	.1759	.2086	.2088	.1833
	7	.0000	.0002	.0019	.0092	.0280	.0618	.1082	.1574	.1952	.2095
	8	.0000	.0000	.0003	.0020	.0082	.0232	.0510	.0918	.1398	.1833
	9	.0000	.0000	.0000	.0003	.0018	.0066	.0183	.0408	.0762	.1222
	10	.0000	.0000	.0000	.0000	.0003	.0014	.0049	.0136	.0312	.0611
	11	.0000	.0000	.0000	.0000	.0000	.0002	.0010	.0033	.0093	.0222
	12	.0000	.0000	.0000	.0000	.0000	.0000	.0001	.0005	.0019	.0056
	13	.0000	.0000	.0000	.0000	.0000	.0000	.0000	.0001	.0002	.0009
	14	.0000	.0000	.0000	.0000	.0000	.0000	.0000	.0000	.0000	.0001
15	0	.4633	.2059	.0874	.0352	.0134	.0047	.0016	.0005	.0001	.0000
	1	.3658	.3432	.2312	.1319	.0668	.0305	.0126	.0047	.0016	.0005
	2	.1348	.2669	.2856	.2309	.1559	.0916	.0476	.0219	.0090	.0032

Binomial distribution (*continued*)

n	r	.05	.10	.15	.20	.25	p .30	.35	.40	.45	.50
15	3	.0307	.1285	.2184	.2501	.2252	.1700	.1110	.0634	.0318	.0139
	4	.0049	.0428	.1156	.1876	.2252	.2186	.1792	.1268	.0780	.0417
	5	.0006	.0105	.0449	.1032	.1651	.2061	.2123	.1859	.1404	.0916
	6	.0000	.0019	.0132	.0430	.0917	.1472	.1906	.2066	.1914	.1527
	7	.0000	.0003	.0030	.0138	.0393	.0811	.1319	.1771	.2013	.1964
	8	.0000	.0000	.0005	.0035	.0131	.0348	.0710	.1181	.1647	.1964
	9	.0000	.0000	.0001	.0007	.0034	.0116	.0298	.0612	.1048	.1527
	10	.0000	.0000	.0000	.0001	.0007	.0030	.0096	.0245	.0515	.0916
	11	.0000	.0000	.0000	.0000	.0001	.0006	.0024	.0074	.0191	.0417
	12	.0000	.0000	.0000	.0000	.0000	.0001	.0004	.0016	.0052	.0139
	13	.0000	.0000	.0000	.0000	.0000	.0000	.0001	.0003	.0010	.0032
	14	.0000	.0000	.0000	.0000	.0000	.0000	.0000	.0000	.0001	.0005
	15	.0000	.0000	.0000	.0000	.0000	.0000	.0000	.0000	.0000	.0000
16	0	.4401	.1853	.0743	.0281	.0100	.0033	.0010	.0003	.0001	.0000
	1	.3706	.3294	.2097	.1126	.0535	.0228	.0087	.0030	.0009	.0002
	2	.1463	.2745	.2775	.2111	.1336	.0732	.0353	.0150	.0056	.0018
	3	.0359	.1423	.2285	.2463	.2079	.1465	.0888	.0468	.0215	.0085
	4	.0061	.0514	.1311	.2001	.2252	.2040	.1553	.1014	.0572	.0278
	5	.0008	.0137	.0555	.1201	.1802	.2099	.2008	.1623	.1123	.0667
	6	.0001	.0028	.0180	.0550	.1101	.1649	.1982	.1983	.1684	.1222
	7	.0000	.0004	.0045	.0197	.0524	.1010	.1524	.1889	.1969	.1746
	8	.0000	.0001	.0009	.0055	.0197	.0487	.0923	.1417	.1812	.1964
	9	.0000	.0000	.0001	.0012	.0058	.0185	.0442	.0840	.1318	.1746
	10	.0000	.0000	.0000	.0002	.0014	.0056	.0167	.0392	.0755	.1222
	11	.0000	.0000	.0000	.0000	.0002	.0013	.0049	.0142	.0337	.0667
	12	.0000	.0000	.0000	.0000	.0000	.0002	.0011	.0040	.0115	.0278
	13	.0000	.0000	.0000	.0000	.0000	.0000	.0002	.0008	.0029	.0085
	14	.0000	.0000	.0000	.0000	.0000	.0000	.0000	.0001	.0005	.0018
	15	.0000	.0000	.0000	.0000	.0000	.0000	.0000	.0000	.0001	.0002
	16	.0000	.0000	.0000	.0000	.0000	.0000	.0000	.0000	.0000	.0000
17	0	.4181	.1668	.0631	.0225	.0075	.0023	.0007	.0002	.0000	.0000
	1	.3741	.3150	.1893	.0957	.0426	.0169	.0060	.0019	.0005	.0001
	2	.1575	.2800	.2673	.1914	.1136	.0581	.0260	.0102	.0035	.0010
	3	.0415	.1556	.2359	.2393	.1893	.1245	.0701	.0341	.0144	.0052
	4	.0076	.0605	.1457	.2093	.2209	.1868	.1320	.0796	.0411	.0182
	5	.0010	.0175	.0668	.1361	.1914	.2081	.1849	.1379	.0875	.0472
	6	.0001	.0039	.0236	.0680	.1276	.1784	.1991	.1839	.1432	.0944
	7	.0000	.0007	.0065	.0267	.0668	.1201	.1685	.1927	.1841	.1484
	8	.0000	.0001	.0014	.0084	.0279	.0644	.1134	.1606	.1883	.1855
	9	.0000	.0000	.0003	.0021	.0093	.0276	.0611	.1070	.1540	.1855

Binomial distribution (*continued*)

n	r	.05	.10	.15	.20	.25	.30	.35	.40	.45	.50
17	10	.0000	.0000	.0000	.0004	.0025	.0095	.0263	.0571	.1008	.1484
	11	.0000	.0000	.0000	.0001	.0005	.0026	.0090	.0242	.0525	.0944
	12	.0000	.0000	.0000	.0000	.0001	.0006	.0024	.0081	.0215	.0472
	13	.0000	.0000	.0000	.0000	.0000	.0001	.0005	.002₁	.0066	.0182
	14	.0000	.0000	.0000	.0000	.0000	.0000	.0001	.0004	.0016	.0052
	15	.0000	.0000	.0000	.0000	.0000	.0000	.0000	.0001	.0003	.0010
	16	.0000	.0000	.0000	.0000	.0000	.0000	.0000	.0000	.0000	.0001
	17	.0000	.0000	.0000	.0000	.0000	.0000	.0000	.0000	.0000	.0000
18	0	.3972	.1501	.0536	.0180	.0056	.0016	.0004	.0001	.0000	.0000
	1	.3763	.3002	.1704	.0811	.0338	.0126	.0042	.0012	.0003	.0001
	2	.1683	.2835	.2556	.1723	.0958	.0458	.0190	.0069	.0022	.0006
	3	.0473	.1680	.2406	.2297	.1704	.1046	.0547	.0246	.0095	.0031
	4	.0093	.0700	.1592	.2153	.2130	.1681	.1104	.0614	.0291	.0117
	5	.0014	.0218	.0787	.1507	.1988	.2017	.1664	.1146	.0666	.0327
	6	.0002	.0052	.0301	.0816	.1436	.1873	.1941	.1655	.1181	.0708
	7	.0000	.0010	.0091	.0350	.0820	.1376	.1792	.1892	.1657	.1214
	8	.0000	.0002	.0022	.0120	.0376	.0811	.1327	.1734	.1864	.1669
	9	.0000	.0000	.0004	.0033	.0139	.0386	.0794	.1284	.1694	.1855
	10	.0000	.0000	.0001	.0008	.0042	.0149	.0385	.0771	.1248	.1669
	11	.0000	.0000	.0000	.0001	.0010	.0046	.0151	.0374	.0742	.1214
	12	.0000	.0000	.0000	.0000	.0002	.0012	.0047	.0145	.0354	.0708
	13	.0000	.0000	.0000	.0000	.0000	.0002	.0012	.0045	.0134	.0327
	14	.0000	.0000	.0000	.0000	.0000	.0000	.0002	.0011	.0039	.0117
	15	.0000	.0000	.0000	.0000	.0000	.0000	.0000	.0002	.0009	.0031
	16	.0000	.0000	.0000	.0000	.0000	.0000	.0000	.0000	.0001	.0006
	17	.0000	.0000	.0000	.0000	.0000	.0000	.0000	.0000	.0000	.0001
	18	.0000	.0000	.0000	.0000	.0000	.0000	.0000	.0000	.0000	.0000
19	0	.3774	.1351	.0456	.0144	.0042	.0011	.0003	.0001	.0000	.0000
	1	.3774	.2852	.1529	.0685	.0268	.0093	.0029	.0008	.0002	.0000
	2	.1787	.2852	.2428	.1540	.0803	.0358	.0138	.0046	.0013	.0003
	3	.0533	.1796	.2428	.2182	.1517	.0869	.0422	.0175	.0062	.0018
	4	.0112	.0798	.1714	.2182	.2023	.1491	.0909	.0467	.0203	.0074
	5	.0018	.0266	.0907	.1636	.2023	.1916	.1468	.0933	.0497	.0222
	6	.0002	.0069	.0374	.0955	.1574	.1916	.1844	.1451	.0949	.0518
	7	.0000	.0014	.0122	.0443	.0974	.1525	.1844	.1797	.1443	.0961
	8	.0000	.0002	.0032	.0166	.0487	.0981	.1489	.1797	.1771	.1442
	9	.0000	.0000	.0007	.0051	.0198	.0514	.0980	.1464	.1771	.1762
	10	.0000	.0000	.0001	.0013	.0066	.0220	.0528	.0976	.1449	.1762
	11	.0000	.0000	.0000	.0003	.0018	.0077	.0233	.0532	.0970	.1442
	12	.0000	.0000	.0000	.0000	.0004	.0022	.0083	.0237	.0529	.0961
	13	.0000	.0000	.0000	.0000	.0001	.0005	.0024	.0085	.0233	.0518
	14	.0000	.0000	.0000	.0000	.0000	.0001	.0006	.0024	.0082	.0222

Binomial distribution (*concluded*)

n	r	.05	.10	.15	.20	.25	p .30	.35	.40	.45	.50
19	15	.0000	.0000	.0000	.0000	.0000	.0000	.0001	.0005	.0022	.0074
	16	.0000	.0000	.0000	.0000	.0000	.0000	.0000	.0001	.0005	.0018
	17	.0000	.0000	.0000	.0000	.0000	.0000	.0000	.0000	.0001	.0003
	18	.0000	.0000	.0000	.0000	.0000	.0000	.0000	.0000	.0000	.0000
	19	.0000	.0000	.0000	.0000	.0000	.0000	.0000	.0000	.0000	.0000
20	0	.3585	.1216	.0388	.0115	.0032	.0008	.0002	.0000	.0000	.0000
	1	.3774	.2702	.1368	.0576	.0211	.0068	.0020	.0005	.0001	.0000
	2	.1887	.2852	.2293	.1369	.0669	.0278	.0100	.0031	.0008	.0002
	3	.0596	.1901	.2428	.2054	.1339	.0718	.0323	.0123	.0040	.0011
	4	.0133	.0898	.1821	.2182	.1897	.1304	.0738	.0350	.0139	.0046
	5	.0022	.0319	.1028	.1746	.2023	.1789	.1272	.0746	.0365	.0148
	6	.0003	.0089	.0454	.1091	.1686	.1916	.1712	.1244	.0746	.0370
	7	.0000	.0020	.0160	.0545	.1124	.1643	.1844	.1659	.1221	.0739
	8	.0000	.0004	.0046	.0222	.0609	.1144	.1614	.1797	.1623	.1201
	9	.0000	.0001	.0011	.0074	.0271	.0654	.1158	.1597	.1771	.1602
	10	.0000	.0000	.0002	.0020	.0099	.0308	.0686	.1171	.1593	.1762
	11	.0000	.0000	.0000	.0005	.0030	.0120	.0336	.0710	.1185	.1602
	12	.0000	.0000	.0000	.0001	.0008	.0039	.0136	.0355	.0727	.1201
	13	.0000	.0000	.0000	.0000	.0002	.0010	.0045	.0146	.0366	.0739
	14	.0000	.0000	.0000	.0000	.0000	.0002	.0012	.0049	.0150	.0370
	15	.0000	.0000	.0000	.0000	.0000	.0000	.0003	.0013	.0049	.0148
	16	.0000	.0000	.0000	.0000	.0000	.0000	.0000	.0003	.0013	.0046
	17	.0000	.0000	.0000	.0000	.0000	.0000	.0000	.0000	.0002	.0011
	18	.0000	.0000	.0000	.0000	.0000	.0000	.0000	.0000	.0000	.0002
	19	.0000	.0000	.0000	.0000	.0000	.0000	.0000	.0000	.0000	.0000
	20	.0000	.0000	.0000	.0000	.0000	.0000	.0000	.0000	.0000	.0000

APPENDIX E

POISSON DISTRIBUTION FOR SELECTED VALUES OF MU

Values in the table are for the function:

$$P(x) = \frac{\mu^x e^{-\mu}}{x(x-1)(x-2)\text{---}\,1}$$

x	\multicolumn{10}{c	}{$P(x)$ for specified values of μ}
	$\mu = 0.1$	$\mu = 0.2$	$\mu = 0.3$	$\mu = 0.4$	$\mu = 0.5$	$\mu = 0.6$	$\mu = 0.7$	$\mu = 0.8$	$\mu = 0.9$	$\mu = 1.0$
0	.9048374	.8187308	.7408182	.6703200	.606531	.548812	.496585	.449329	.406570	.367879
1	.0904837	.1637462	.2222455	.2681280	.303265	.329287	347610	.359463	.365913	.367879
2	.0045242	.0163746	.0333368	.0536256	.075816	.098786	.121663	.143785	.164661	.183940
3	.0001508	.0010916	.0033337	.0071501	.012636	.019757	.028388	.038343	.049398	.061313
4	.0000038	.0000546	.0002500	.0007150	.001580	.002964	004968	.007669	.011115	.015328
5	.0000001	.0000022	.0000150	.0000572	.000158	.000356	000696	.001227	.002001	.003066
6		.0000001	.0000008	.0000038	.000013	.000036	.000081	.000164	.000300	.000511
7				.0000002	.000001	.000003	.000008	.000019	.000039	.000073
8							.000001	.000002	.000004	.000009
9										.000001

x	$\mu = 2.0$	$\mu = 3.0$	$\mu = 4.0$	$\mu = 5.0$	$\mu = 6.0$	$\mu = 7.0$	$\mu = 8.0$	$\mu = 9.0$	$\mu = 10.0$
0	.135335	.049787	.018316	.006738	.002479	.000912	.000335	.000123	.000045
1	.270671	.149361	.073263	.033690	.014873	.006383	.002684	.001111	.000454
2	.270671	.224042	.146525	.084224	.044618	.022341	.010735	.004998	.002270
3	.180447	.224042	.195367	.140374	.089235	.052129	.028626	.014994	.007567
4	.090224	.168031	.195367	.175467	.133853	.091226	.057252	.033737	.018917
5	.036089	.100819	.156293	.175467	.160623	.127717	.091604	.060727	.037833
6	.012030	.050409	.104196	.146223	.160623	.149003	.122138	.091090	.063055
7	.003437	.021604	.059540	.104445	.137677	.149003	.139587	.117116	.090079
8	000859	.008102	.029770	.065278	.103258	.130377	.139587	.131756	.112599
9	.000191	.002701	.013231	.036266	.068838	.101405	.124077	.131756	.125110
10	.000038	.000810	.005292	.018133	.041303	.070983	.099262	.118580	.125110
11	.000007	.000221	.001925	.008242	.022529	.045171	.072190	.097020	.113736
12	.000001	.000055	.000642	.003434	.011264	.026350	.048127	.072765	.094780
13		.000013	.000197	.001321	.005199	.014188	.029616	.050376	.072908
14		.000003	.000056	.000472	.002228	.007094	.016924	.032384	.052077
15		.000001	.000015	.000157	.000891	.003311	.009026	.019431	.034718
16			.000004	.000049	.000334	.001448	.004513	.010930	.021699
17			.000001	.000014	.000118	.000596	.002124	.005786	.012764
18				.000004	.000039	.000232	.000944	.002893	.007091
19				.000001	.000012	.000085	.000397	.001370	.003732
20					.000004	.000030	.000159	.000617	.001866
21					.000001	.000010	.000061	.000264	.000889
22						.000003	.000022	.000108	.000404
23						.000001	.000008	.000042	.000176
24							.000003	.000016	.000073
25							.000001	.000006	.000029
26								.000002	.000011
27								.000001	.000004
28									.000001
29									.000001

Source: E. C. Molina, *Poisson's Exponential Binomial Limit* (Princeton, N.J.: D. Van Nostrand Co., Inc., 1942). Reprinted by permission.

FACTORS FOR CONTROL CHARTS

Number of Items in Sample, n	Chart for Averages — Factors for Control Limits A_2	Chart for Ranges — Factors for Central Line d_2	Chart for Ranges — Factors for Control Limits D_3	Chart for Ranges — Factors for Control Limits D_4
2	1.880	1.128	0	3.267
3	1.023	1.693	0	2.575
4	.729	2.059	0	2.282
5	.577	2.326	0	2.115
6	.483	2.534	0	2.004
7	.419	2.704	.076	1.924
8	.373	2.847	.136	1.864
9	.337	2.970	.184	1.816
10	.308	3.078	.223	1.777
11	.285	3.173	.256	1.744
12	.266	3.258	.284	1.716-
13	.249	3.336	.308	1.692
14	.235	3.407	.329	1.671
15	.223	3.472	.348	1.652

Source: Adapted from American Society for Testing and Materials, *Manual on Quality Control of Materials,* 1951, table B2, p. 115. For a more detailed table and explanation, see Acheson J. Duncan, *Quality Control and Industrial Statistics,* 3d ed. (Homewood, Ill.: Richard D. Irwin, 1974), table M, p. 927.

APPENDIX G

SQUARES AND SQUARE ROOTS

N	N²	√N	√10N	1/N
1	1	1.000 000	3.162 278	1.0000000
2	4	1.414 214	4.472 136	.5000000
3	9	1.732 051	5.477 226	.3333333
4	16	2.000 000	6.324 555	.2500000
5	25	2.236 068	7.071 068	.2000000
6	36	2.449 490	7.745 967	.1666667
7	49	2.645 751	8.366 600	.1428571
8	64	2.828 427	8.944 272	.1250000
9	81	3.000 000	9.486 833	.1111111
10	100	3.162 278	10.00000	.1000000
11	121	3.316 625	10.48809	.09090909
12	144	3.464 102	10.95445	.08333333
13	169	3.605 551	11.40175	.07692308
14	196	3.741 657	11.83216	.07142857
15	225	3.872 983	12.24745	.06666667
16	256	4.000 000	12.64911	.06250000
17	289	4.123 106	13.03840	.05882353
18	324	4.242 641	13.41641	.05555556
19	361	4.358 899	13.78405	.05263158
20	400	4.472 136	14.14214	.05000000
21	441	4.582 576	14.49138	.04761905
22	484	4.690 416	14.83240	.04545455
23	529	4.795 832	15.16575	.04347826
24	576	4.898 979	15.49193	.04166667
25	625	5.000 000	15.81139	.04000000
26	676	5.099 020	16.12452	.03846154
27	729	5.196 152	16.43168	.03703704
28	784	5.291 503	16.73320	.03571429
29	841	5.385 165	17.02939	.03448276
30	900	5.477 226	17.32051	.03333333
31	961	5.567 764	17.60682	.03225806
32	1 024	5.656 854	17.88854	.03125000
33	1 089	5.744 563	18.16590	.03030303
34	1 156	5.830 952	18.43909	.02941176
35	1 225	5.916 080	18.70829	.02857143
36	1 296	6.000 000	18.97367	.02777778
37	1 369	6.082 763	19.23538	.02702703
38	1 444	6.164 414	19.49359	.02631579
39	1 521	6.244 998	19.74842	.02564103
40	1 600	6.324 555	20.00000	.02500000
41	1 681	6.403 124	20.24846	.02439024
42	1 764	6.480 741	20.49390	.02380952
43	1 849	6.557 439	20.73644	.02325581
44	1 936	6.633 250	20.97618	.02272727
45	2 025	6.708 204	21.21320	.02222222
46	2 116	6.782 330	21.44761	.02173913
47	2 209	6.855 655	21.67948	.02127660
48	2 304	6.928 203	21.90890	.02083333
49	2 401	7.000 000	22.13594	.02040816
50	2 500	7.071 068	22.36068	.02000000

N	N²	√N	√10N	1/N .0
50	2 500	7.071 068	22.36068	2000000
51	2 601	7.141 428	22.58318	1960784
52	2 704	7.211 103	22.80351	1923077
53	2 809	7.280 110	23.02173	1886792
54	2 916	7.348 469	23.23790	1851852
55	3 025	7.416 198	23.45208	1818182
56	3 136	7.483 315	23.66432	1785714
57	3 249	7.549 834	23.87467	1754386
58	3 364	7.615 773	24.08319	1724138
59	3 481	7.681 146	24.28992	1694915
60	3 600	7.745 967	24.49490	1666667
61	3 721	7.810 250	24.69818	1639344
62	3 844	7.874 008	24.89980	1612903
63	3 969	7.937 254	25.09980	1587302
64	4 096	8.000 000	25.29822	1562500
65	4 225	8.062 258	25.49510	1538462
66	4 356	8.124 038	25.69047	1515152
67	4 489	8.185 353	25.88436	1492537
68	4 624	8.246 211	26.07681	1470588
69	4 761	8.306 624	26.26785	1449275
70	4 900	8.366 600	26.45751	1428571
71	5 041	8.426 150	26.64583	1408451
72	5 184	8.485 281	26.83282	1388889
73	5 329	8.544 004	27.01851	1369863
74	5 476	8.602 325	27.20294	1351351
75	5 625	8.660 254	27.38613	1333333
76	5 776	8.717 798	27.56810	1315789
77	5 929	8.774 964	27.74887	1298701
78	6 084	8.831 761	27.92848	1282051
79	6 241	8.888 194	28.10694	1265823
80	6 400	8.944 272	28.28427	1250000
81	6 561	9.000 000	28.46050	1234568
82	6 724	9.055 385	28.63564	1219512
83	6 889	9.110 434	28.80972	1204819
84	7 056	9.165 151	28.98275	1190476
85	7 225	9.219 544	29.15476	1176471
86	7 396	9.273 618	29.32576	1162791
87	7 569	9.327 379	29.49576	1149425
88	7 744	9.380 832	29.66479	1136364
89	7 921	9.433 981	29.83287	1123596
90	8 100	9.486 833	30.00000	1111111
91	8 281	9.539 392	30.16621	1098901
92	8 464	9.591 663	30.33150	1086957
93	8 649	9.643 651	30.49590	1075269
94	8 836	9.695 360	30.65942	1063830
95	9 025	9.746 794	30.82207	1052632
96	9 216	9.797 959	30.98387	1041667
97	9 409	9.848 858	31.14482	1030928
98	9 604	9.899 495	31.30495	1020408
99	9 801	9.949 874	31.46427	1010101
100	10 000	10.00000	31.62278	1000000

Squares and square roots (*continued*)

N	N^2	$\sqrt{N}$	$\sqrt{10N}$	$1/N$ .0	N	N^2	$\sqrt{N}$	$\sqrt{10N}$	$1/N$ .00
100	10 000	10.00000	31.62278	10000000	150	22 500	12.24745	38.72983	6666667
101	10 201	10.04988	31.78050	09900990	151	22 801	12.28821	38.85872	6622517
102	10 404	10.09950	31.93744	09803922	152	23 104	12.32883	38.98718	6578947
103	10 609	10.14889	32.09361	09708738	153	23 409	12.36932	39.11521	6535948
104	10 816	10.19804	32.24903	09615385	154	23 716	12.40967	39.24283	6493506
105	11 025	10.24695	32.40370	09523810	155	24 025	12.44990	39.37004	6451613
106	11 236	10.29563	32.55764	09433962	156	24 336	12.49000	39.49684	6410256
107	11 449	10.34408	32.71085	09345794	157	24 649	12.52996	39.62323	6369427
108	11 664	10.39230	32.86335	09259259	158	24 964	12.56981	39.74921	6329114
109	11 881	10.44031	33.01515	09174312	159	25 281	12.60952	39.87480	6289308
110	12 100	10.48809	33.16625	09090909	160	25 600	12.64911	40.00000	6250000
111	12 321	10.53565	33.31666	09009009	161	25 921	12.68858	40.12481	6211180
112	12 544	10.58301	33.46640	08928571	162	26 244	12.72792	40.24922	6172840
113	12 769	10.63015	33.61547	08849558	163	26 569	12.76715	40.37326	6134969
114	12 996	10.67708	33.76389	08771930	164	26 896	12.80625	40.49691	6097561
115	13 225	10.72381	33.91165	08695652	165	27 225	12.84523	40.62019	6060606
116	13 456	10.77033	34.05877	08620690	166	27 556	12.88410	40.74310	6024096
117	13 689	10.81665	34.20526	08547009	167	27 889	12.92285	40.86563	5988024
118	13 924	10.86278	34.35113	08474576	168	28 224	12.96148	40.98780	5952381
119	14 161	10.90871	34.49638	08403361	169	28 561	13.00000	41.10961	5917160
120	14 400	10.95445	34.64102	08333333	170	28 900	13.03840	41.23106	5882353
121	14 641	11.00000	34.78505	08264463	171	29 241	13.07670	41.35215	5847953
122	14 884	11.04536	34.92850	08196721	172	29 584	13.11488	41.47288	5813953
123	15 129	11.09054	35.07136	08130081	1/3	29 929	13.15295	41.59327	5780347
124	15 376	11.13553	35.21363	08064516	174	30 276	13.19091	41.71331	5747126
125	15 625	11.18034	35.35534	08000000	175	30 625	13.22876	41.83300	5714286
126	15 876	11.22497	35.49648	07936508	176	30 976	13.26650	41.95235	5681818
127	16 129	11.26943	35.63706	07874016	177	31 329	13.30413	42.07137	5649718
128	16 384	11.31371	35.77709	07812500	178	31 684	13.34166	42.19005	5617978
129	16 641	11.35782	35.91657	07751938	179	32 041	13.37909	42.30839	5586592
130	16 900	11.40175	36.05551	07692308	180	32 400	13.41641	42.42641	5555556
131	17 161	11.44552	36.19392	07633588	181	32 761	13.45362	42.54409	5524862
132	17 424	11.48913	36.33180	07575758	182	33 124	13.49074	42.66146	5494505
133	17 689	11.53256	36.46917	07518797	183	33 489	13.52775	42.77850	5464481
134	17 956	11.57584	36.60601	07462687	184	33 856	13.56466	42.89522	5434783
135	18 225	11.61895	36.74235	07407407	185	34 225	13.60147	43.01163	5405405
136	18 496	11.66190	36.87818	07352941	186	34 596	13.63818	43.12772	5376344
137	18 769	11.70470	37.01351	07299270	187	34 969	13.67479	43.24350	5347594
138	19 044	11.74734	37.14835	07246377	188	35 344	13.71131	43.35897	5319149
139	19 321	11.78983	37.28270	07194245	189	35 721	13.74773	43.47413	5291005
140	19 600	11.83216	37.41657	07142857	190	36 100	13.78405	43.58899	5263158
141	19 881	11.87434	37.54997	07092199	191	36 481	13.82027	43.70355	5235602
142	20 164	11.91638	37.68289	07042254	192	36 864	13.85641	43.81780	5208333
143	20 449	11.95826	37.81534	06993007	193	37 249	13.89244	43.93177	5181347
144	20 736	12.00000	37.94733	06944444	194	37 636	13.92839	44.04543	5154639
145	21 025	12.04159	38.07887	06896552	195	38 025	13.96424	44.15880	5128205
146	21 316	12.08305	38.20995	06849315	196	38 416	14.00000	44.27189	5102041
147	21 609	12.12436	38.34058	06802721	197	38 809	14.03567	44.38468	5076142
148	21 904	12.16553	38.47077	06756757	198	39 204	14.07125	44.49719	5050505
149	22 201	12.20656	38.60052	06711409	199	39 601	14.10674	44.60942	5025126
150	22 500	12.24745	38.72983	06666667	200	40 000	14.14214	44.72136	5000000

Squares and square roots (*continued*)

N	N²	√N	√10N	1/N .00	N	N²	√N	√10N	1/N .00
200	40 000	14.14214	44.72136	5000000	250	62 500	15.81139	50.00000	4000000
201	40 401	14.17745	44.83302	4975124	251	63 001	15.84298	50.09990	3984064
202	40 804	14.21267	44.94441	4950495	252	63 504	15.87451	50.19960	3968254
203	41 209	14.24781	45.05552	4926108	253	64 009	15.90597	50.29911	3952569
204	41 616	14.28286	45.16636	4901961	254	64 516	15.93738	50.39841	3937008
205	42 025	14.31782	45.27693	4878049	255	65 025	15.96872	50.49752	3921569
206	42 436	14.35270	45.38722	4854369	256	65 536	16.00000	50.59644	3906250
207	42 849	14.38749	45.49725	4830918	257	66 049	16.03122	50.69517	3891051
208	43 264	14.42221	45.60702	4807692	258	66 564	16.06238	50.79370	3875969
209	43 681	14.45683	45.71652	4784689	259	67 081	16.09348	50.89204	3861004
210	44 100	14.49138	45.82576	4761905	260	67 600	16.12452	50.99020	3846154
211	44 521	14.52584	45.93474	4739336	261	68 121	16.15549	51.08816	3831418
212	44 944	14.56022	46.04346	4716981	262	68 644	16.18641	51.18594	3816794
213	45 369	14.59452	46.15192	4694836	263	69 169	16.21727	51.28353	3802281
214	45 796	14.62874	46.26013	4672897	264	69 696	16.24808	51.38093	3787879
215	46 225	14.66288	46.36809	4651163	265	70 225	16.27882	51.47815	3773585
216	46 656	14.69694	46.47580	4629630	266	70 756	16.30951	51.57519	3759398
217	47 089	14.73092	46.58326	4608295	267	71 289	16.34013	51.67204	3745318
218	47 524	14.76482	46.69047	4587156	268	71 824	16.37071	51.76872	3731343
219	47 961	14.79865	46.79744	4566210	269	72 361	16.40122	51.86521	3717472
220	48 400	14.83240	46.90416	4545455	270	72 900	16.43168	51.96152	3703704
221	48 841	14.86607	47.01064	4524887	271	73 441	16.46208	52.05766	3690037
222	49 284	14.89966	47.11688	4504505	272	73 984	16.49242	52.15362	3676471
223	49 729	14.93318	47.22288	4484305	273	74 529	16.52271	52.24940	3663004
224	50 176	14.96663	47.32864	4464286	274	75 076	16.55295	52.34501	3649635
225	50 625	15.00000	47.43416	4444444	275	75 625	16.58312	52.44044	3636364
226	51 076	15.03330	47.53946	4424779	276	76 176	16.61325	52.53570	3623188
227	51 529	15.06652	47.64452	4405286	277	76 729	16.64332	52.63079	3610108
228	51 984	15.09967	47.74935	4385965	278	77 284	16.67333	52.72571	3597122
229	52 441	15.13275	47.85394	4366812	279	77 841	16.70329	52.82045	3584229
230	52 900	15.16575	47.95832	4347826	280	78 400	16.73320	52.91503	3571429
231	53 361	15.19868	48.06246	4329004	281	78 961	16.76305	53.00943	3558719
232	53 824	15.23155	48.16638	4310345	282	79 524	16.79286	53.10367	3546099
233	54 289	15.26434	48.27007	4291845	283	80 089	16.82260	53.19774	3533569
234	54 756	15.29706	48.37355	4273504	284	80 656	16.85230	53.29165	3521127
235	55 225	15.32971	48.47680	4255319	285	81 225	16.88194	53.38539	3508772
236	55 696	15.36229	48.57983	4237288	286	81 796	16.91153	53.47897	3496503
237	56 169	15.39480	48.68265	4219409	287	82 369	16.94107	53.57238	3484321
238	56 644	15.42725	48.78524	4201681	288	82 944	16.97056	53.66563	3472222
239	57 121	15.45962	48.88763	4184100	289	83 521	17.00000	53.75872	3460208
240	57 600	15.49193	48.98979	4166667	290	84 100	17.02939	53.85165	3448276
241	58 081	15.52417	49.09175	4149378	291	84 681	17.05872	53.94442	3436426
242	58 564	15.55635	49.19350	4132231	292	85 264	17.08801	54.03702	3424658
243	59 049	15.58846	49.29503	4115226	293	85 849	17.11724	54.12947	3412969
244	59 536	15.62050	49.39636	4098361	294	86 436	17.14643	54.22177	3401361
245	60 025	15.65248	49.49747	4081633	295	87 025	17.17556	54.31390	3389831
246	60 516	15.68439	49.59839	4065041	296	87 616	17.20465	54.40588	3378378
247	61 009	15.71623	49.69909	4048583	297	88 209	17.23369	54.49771	3367003
248	61 504	15.74802	49.79960	4032258	298	88 804	17.26268	54.58938	3355705
249	62 001	15.77973	49.89990	4016064	299	89 401	17.29162	54.68089	3344482
250	62 500	15.81139	50.00000	4000000	300	90 000	17.32051	54.77226	3333333

Squares and square roots (*continued*)

N	N²	√N	√10N	1/N .00	N	N²	√N	√10N	1/N .00
300	90 000	17.32051	54.77226	3333333	350	122 500	18.70829	59.16080	2857143
301	90 601	17.34935	54.86347	3322259	351	123 201	18.73499	59.24525	2849003
302	91 204	17.37815	54.95453	3311258	352	123 904	18.76166	59.32959	2840909
303	91 809	17.40690	55.04544	3300330	353	124 609	18.78829	59.41380	2832861
304	92 416	17.43560	55.13620	3289474	354	125 316	18.81489	59.49790	2824859
305	93 025	17.46425	55.22681	3278689	355	126 025	18.84144	59.58188	2816901
306	93 636	17.49286	55.31727	3267974	356	126 736	18.86796	59.66574	2808989
307	94 249	17.52142	55.40758	3257329	357	127 449	18.89444	59.74948	2801120
308	94 864	17.54993	55.49775	3246753	358	128 164	18.92089	59.83310	2793296
309	95 481	17.57840	55.58777	3236246	359	128 881	18.94730	59.91661	2785515
310	96 100	17.60682	55.67764	3225806	360	129 600	18.97367	60.00000	2777778
311	96 721	17.63519	55.76737	3215434	361	130 321	19.00000	60.08328	2770083
312	97 344	17.66352	55.85696	3205128	362	131 044	19.02630	60.16644	2762431
313	97 969	17.69181	55.94640	3194888	363	131 769	19.05256	60.24948	2754821
314	98 596	17.72005	56.03570	3184713	364	132 496	19.07878	60.33241	2747253
315	99 225	17.74824	56.12486	3174603	365	133 225	19.10497	60.41523	2739726
316	99 856	17.77639	56.21388	3164557	366	133 956	19.13113	60.49793	2732240
317	100 489	17.80449	56.30275	3154574	367	134 689	19.15724	60.58052	2724796
318	101 124	17.83255	56.39149	3144654	368	135 424	19.18333	60.66300	2717391
319	101 761	17.86057	56.48008	3134796	369	136 161	19.20937	60.74537	2710027
320	102 400	17.88854	56.56854	3125000	370	136 900	19.23538	60.82763	2702703
321	103 041	17.91647	56.65686	3115265	371	137 641	19.26136	60.90977	2695418
322	103 684	17.94436	56.74504	3105590	372	138 384	19.28730	60.99180	2688172
323	104 329	17.97220	56.83309	3095975	373	139 129	19.31321	61.07373	2680965
324	104 976	18.00000	56.92100	3086420	374	139 876	19.33908	61.15554	2673797
325	105 625	18.02776	57.00877	3076923	375	140 625	19.36492	61.23724	2666667
326	106 276	18.05547	57.09641	3067485	376	141 376	19.39072	61.31884	2659574
327	106 929	18.08314	57.18391	3058104	377	142 129	19.41649	61.40033	2652520
328	107 584	18.11077	57.27128	3048780	378	142 884	19.44222	61.48170	2645503
329	108 241	18.13836	57.35852	3039514	379	143 641	19.46792	61.56298	2638522
330	108 900	18.16590	57.44563	3030303	380	144 400	19.49359	61.64414	2631579
331	109 561	18.19341	57.53260	3021148	381	145 161	19.51922	61.72520	2624672
332	110 224	18.22087	57.61944	3012048	382	145 924	19.54483	61.80615	2617801
333	110 889	18.24829	57.70615	3003003	383	146 689	19.57039	61.88699	2610966
334	111 556	18.27567	57.79273	2994012	384	147 456	19.59592	61.96773	2604167
335	112 225	18.30301	57.87918	2985075	385	148 225	19.62142	62.04837	2597403
336	112 896	18.33030	57.96551	2976190	386	148 996	19.64688	62.12890	2590674
337	113 569	18.35756	58.05170	2967359	387	149 769	19.67232	62.20932	2583979
338	114 244	18.38478	58.13777	2958580	388	150 544	19.69772	62.28965	2577320
339	114 921	18.41195	58.22371	2949853	389	151 321	19.72308	62.36986	2570694
340	115 600	18.43909	58.30952	2941176	390	152 100	19.74842	62.44998	2564103
341	116 281	18.46619	58.39521	2932551	391	152 881	19.77372	62.52999	2557545
342	116 964	18.49324	58.48077	2923977	392	153 664	19.79899	62.60990	2551020
343	117 649	18.52026	58.56620	2915452	393	154 449	19.82423	62.68971	2544529
344	118 336	18.54724	58.65151	2906977	394	155 236	19.84943	62.76942	2538071
345	119 025	18.57418	58.73670	2898551	395	156 025	19.87461	62.84903	2531646
346	119 716	18.60108	58.82176	2890173	296	156 816	19.89975	62.92853	2525253
347	120 409	18.62794	58.90671	2881844	397	157 609	19.92486	63.00794	2518892
348	121 104	18.65476	58.99152	2873563	398	158 404	19.94994	63.08724	2512563
349	121 801	18.68154	59.07622	2865330	299	159 201	19.97498	63.16645	2506266
350	122 500	18.70829	59.16080	2857143	400	160 000	20.00000	63.24555	2500000

Squares and square roots (*continued*)

N	N^2	$\sqrt{N}$	$\sqrt{10N}$	$1/N$ .00	N	N^2	$\sqrt{N}$	$\sqrt{10N}$	$1/N$ .00
400	160 000	20.00000	63.24555	2500000	450	202 500	21.21320	67.08204	2222222
401	160 801	20.02498	63.32456	2493766	451	203 401	21.23676	67.15653	2217295
402	161 604	20.04994	63.40347	2487562	452	204 304	21.26029	67.23095	2212389
403	162 409	20.07486	63.48228	2481390	453	205 209	21.28380	67.30527	2207506
404	163 216	20.09975	63.56099	2475248	454	206 116	21.30728	67.37952	2202643
405	164 025	20.12461	63.63961	2469136	455	207 025	21.33073	67.45369	2197802
406	164 836	20.14944	63.71813	2463054	456	207 936	21.35416	67.52777	2192982
407	165 649	20.17424	63.79655	2457002	457	208 849	21.37756	67.60178	2188184
408	166 464	20.19901	63.87488	2450980	458	209 764	21.40093	67.67570	2183406
409	167 281	20.22375	63.95311	2444988	459	210 681	21.42429	67.74954	2178649
410	168 100	20.24846	64.03124	2439024	460	211 600	21.44761	67.82330	2173913
411	168 921	20.27313	64.10928	2433090	461	212 521	21.47091	67.89698	2169197
412	169 744	20.29778	64.18723	2427184	462	213 444	21.49419	67.97058	2164502
413	170 569	20.32240	64.26508	2421308	463	214 369	21.51743	68.04410	2159827
414	171 396	20.34699	64.34283	2415459	464	215 296	21.54066	68.11755	2155172
415	172 225	20.37155	64.42049	2409639	465	216 225	21.56386	68.19091	2150538
416	173 056	20.39608	64.49806	2403846	466	217 156	21.58703	68.26419	2145923
417	173 889	20.42058	64.57554	2398082	467	218 089	21.61018	68.33740	2141328
418	174 724	20.44505	64.65292	2392344	468	219 024	21.63331	68.41053	2136752
419	175 561	20.46949	64.73021	2386635	469	219 961	21.65641	68.48357	2132196
420	176 400	20.49390	64.80741	2380952	470	220 900	21.67948	68.55655	2127660
421	177 241	20.51828	64.88451	2375297	471	221 841	21.70253	68.62944	2123142
422	178 084	20.54264	64.96153	2369668	472	222 784	21.72556	68.70226	2118644
423	178 929	20.56696	65.03845	2364066	473	223 729	21.74856	68.77500	2114165
424	179 776	20.59126	65.11528	2358491	474	224 676	21.77154	68.84766	2109705
425	180 625	20.61553	65.19202	2352941	475	225 625	21.79449	68.92024	2105263
426	181 476	20.63977	65.26868	2347418	476	226 576	21.81742	68.99275	2100840
427	182 329	20.66398	65.34524	2341920	477	227 529	21.84033	69.06519	2096436
428	183 184	20.68816	65.42171	2336449	478	228 484	21.86321	69.13754	2092050
429	184 041	20.71232	65.49809	2331002	479	229 441	21.88607	69.20983	2087683
430	184 900	20.73644	65.57439	2325581	480	230 400	21.90890	69.28203	2083333
431	185 761	20.76054	65.65059	2320186	481	231 361	21.93171	69.35416	2079002
432	186 624	20.78461	65.72671	2314815	482	232 324	21.95450	69.42622	2074689
433	187 489	20.80865	65.80274	2309469	483	233 289	21.97726	69.49820	2070393
434	188 356	20.83267	65.87868	2304147	484	234 256	22.00000	69.57011	2066116
435	189 225	20.85665	65.95453	2298851	485	235 225	22.02272	69.64194	2061856
436	190 096	20.88061	66.03030	2293578	486	236 196	22.04541	69.71370	2057613
437	190 969	20.90454	66.10598	2288330	487	237 169	22.06808	69.78539	2053388
438	191 844	20.92845	66.18157	2283105	488	238 144	22.09072	69.85700	2049180
439	192 721	20.95233	66.25708	2277904	489	239 121	22.11334	69.92853	2044990
440	193 600	20.97618	66.33250	2272727	490	240 100	22.13594	70.00000	2040816
441	194 481	21.00000	66.40783	2267574	491	241 081	22.15852	70.07139	2036660
442	195 364	21.02380	66.48308	2262443	492	242 064	22.18107	70.14271	2032520
443	196 249	21.04757	66.55825	2257336	493	243 049	22.20360	70.21396	2028398
444	197 136	21.07131	66.63332	2252252	494	244 036	22.22611	70.28513	2024291
445	198 025	21.09502	66.70832	2247191	495	245 025	22.24860	70.35624	2020202
446	198 916	21.11871	66.78323	2242152	496	246 016	22.27106	70.42727	2016129
447	199 809	21.14237	66.85806	2237136	497	247 009	22.29350	70.49823	2012072
448	200 704	21.16601	66.93280	2232143	498	248 004	22.31591	70.56912	2008032
449	201 601	21.18962	67.00746	2227171	499	249 001	22.33831	70.63993	2004008
450	202 500	21.21320	67.08204	2222222	500	250 000	22.36066	70.71068	2000000

Squares and square roots (*continued*)

N	N^2	$\sqrt{N}$	$\sqrt{10N}$	$1/N$ .00	N	N^2	$\sqrt{N}$	$\sqrt{10N}$	$1/N$ .00
500	250 000	22.36068	70.71068	2000000	550	302 500	23.45208	74.16198	1818182
501	251 001	22.38303	70.78135	1996008	551	303 601	23.47339	74.22937	1814882
502	252 004	22.40536	70.85196	1992032	552	304 704	23.49468	74.29670	1811594
503	253 009	22.42766	70.92249	1988072	553	305 809	23.51595	74.36397	1808318
504	254 016	22.44994	70.99296	1984127	554	306 916	23.53720	74.43118	1805054
505	255 025	22.47221	71.06335	1980198	555	308 025	23.55844	74.49832	1801802
506	256 036	22.49444	71.13368	1976285	556	309 136	23.57965	74.56541	1798561
507	257 049	22.51666	71.20393	1972387	557	310 249	23.60085	74.63243	1795332
508	258 064	22.53886	71.27412	1968504	558	311 364	23.62202	74.69940	1792115
509	259 081	22.56103	71.34424	1964637	559	312 481	23.64318	74.76630	1788909
510	260 100	22.58318	71.41428	1960784	560	313 600	23.66432	74.83315	1785714
511	261 121	22.60531	71.48426	1956947	561	314 721	23.68544	74.89993	1782531
512	262 144	22.62742	71.55418	1953125	562	315 844	23.70654	74.96666	1779359
513	263 169	22.64950	71.62402	1949318	563	316 969	23.72762	75.03333	1776199
514	264 196	22.67157	71.69379	1945525	564	318 096	23.74868	75.09993	1773050
515	265 225	22.69361	71.76350	1941748	565	319 225	23.76973	75.16648	1769912
516	266 256	22.71563	71.83314	1937984	566	320 356	23.79075	75.23297	1766784
517	267 289	22.73763	71.90271	1934236	567	321 489	23.81176	75.29940	1763668
518	268 324	22.75961	71.97222	1930502	568	322 624	23.83275	75.36577	1760563
519	269 361	22.78157	72.04165	1926782	569	323 761	23.85372	75.43209	1757469
520	270 400	22.80351	72.11103	1923077	570	324 900	23.87467	75.49834	1754386
521	271 441	22.82542	72.18033	1919386	571	326 041	23.89561	75.56454	1751313
522	272 484	22.84732	72.24957	1915709	572	327 184	23.91652	75.63068	1748252
523	273 529	22.86919	72.31874	1912046	573	328 329	23.93742	75.69676	1745201
524	274 576	22.89105	72.38784	1908397	574	329 476	23.95830	75.76279	1742160
525	275 625	22.91288	72.45688	1904762	575	330 625	23.97916	75.82875	1739130
526	276 676	22.93469	72.52586	1901141	576	331 776	24.00000	75.89466	1736111
527	277 729	22.95648	72.59477	1897533	577	332 929	24.02082	75.96052	1733102
528	278 784	22.97825	72.66361	1893939	578	334 084	24.04163	76.02631	1730104
529	279 841	23.00000	72.73239	1890359	579	335 241	24.06242	76.09205	1727116
530	280 900	23.02173	72.80110	1886792	580	336 400	24.08319	76.15773	1724138
531	281 961	23.04344	72.86975	1883239	581	337 561	24.10394	76.22336	1721170
532	283 024	23.06513	72.93833	1879699	582	338 724	24.12468	76.28892	1718213
533	284 089	23.08679	73.00685	1876173	583	339 889	24.14539	76.35444	1715266
534	285 156	23.10844	73.07530	1872659	584	341 056	24.16609	76.41989	1712329
535	286 225	23.13007	73.14369	1869159	585	342 225	24.18677	76.48529	1709402
536	287 296	23.15167	73.21202	1865672	586	343 396	24.20744	76.55064	1706485
537	288 369	23.17326	73.28028	1862197	587	344 569	24.22808	76.61593	1703578
538	289 444	23.19483	73.34848	1858736	588	345 744	24.24871	76.68116	1700680
539	290 521	23.21637	73.41662	1855288	589	346 921	24.26932	76.74634	1697793
540	291 600	23.23790	73.48469	1851852	590	348 100	24.28992	76.81146	1694915
541	292 681	23.25941	73.55270	1848429	591	349 281	24.31049	76.87652	1692047
542	293 764	23.28089	73.62065	1845018	592	350 464	24.33105	76.94154	1689189
543	294 849	23.30236	73.68853	1841621	593	351 649	24.35159	77.00649	1686341
544	295 936	23.32381	73.75636	1838235	594	352 836	24.37212	77.07140	1683502
545	297 025	23.34524	73.82412	1834862	595	354 025	24.39262	77.13624	1680672
546	298 116	23.36664	73.89181	1831502	596	355 216	24.41311	77.20104	1677852
547	299 209	23.38803	73.95945	1828154	597	356 409	24.43358	77.26578	1675042
548	300 304	23.40940	74.02702	1824818	598	357 604	24.45404	77.33046	1672241
549	301 401	23.43075	74.09453	1821494	599	358 801	24.47448	77.39509	1669449
550	302 500	23.45208	74.16198	1818182	600	360 000	24.49490	77.45967	1666667

Squares and square roots (*continued*)

N	N^2	$\sqrt{N}$	$\sqrt{10N}$	$1/N$ .00	N	N^2	$\sqrt{N}$	$\sqrt{10N}$	$1/N$ .00
600	360 000	24.49490	77.45967	1666667	650	422 500	25.49510	80.62258	1538462
601	361 201	24.51530	77.52419	1663894	651	423 801	25.51470	80.68457	1536098
602	362 404	24.53569	77.58866	1661130	652	425 104	25.53429	80.74652	1533742
603	363 609	24.55606	77.65307	1658375	653	426 409	25.55386	80.80842	1531394
604	364 816	24.57641	77.71744	1655629	654	427 716	25.57342	80.87027	1529052
605	366 025	24.59675	77.78175	1652893	655	429 025	25.59297	80.93207	1526718
606	367 236	24.61707	77.84600	1650165	656	430 336	25.61250	80.99383	1524390
607	368 449	24.63737	77.91020	1647446	657	431 649	25.63201	81.05554	1522070
608	369 664	24.65766	77.97435	1644737	658	432 964	25.65151	81.11720	1519757
609	370 881	24.67793	78.03845	1642036	659	434 281	25.67100	81.17881	1517451
610	372 100	24.69818	78.10250	1639344	660	435 600	25.69047	81.24038	1515152
611	373 321	24.71841	78.16649	1636661	661	436 921	25.70992	81.30191	1512859
612	374 544	24.73863	78.23043	1633987	662	438 244	25.72936	81.36338	1510574
613	375 769	24.75884	78.29432	1631321	663	439 569	25.74879	81.42481	1508296
614	376 996	24.77902	78.35815	1628664	664	440 896	25.76820	81.48620	1506024
615	378 225	24.79919	78.42194	1626016	665	442 225	25.78759	81.54753	1503759
616	379 456	24.81935	78.48567	1623377	666	443 556	25.80698	81.60882	1501502
617	380 689	24.83948	78.54935	1620746	667	444 889	25.82634	81.67007	1499250
618	381 924	24.85961	78.61298	1618123	668	446 224	25.84570	81.73127	1497006
619	383 161	24.87971	78.67655	1615509	669	447 561	25.86503	81.79242	1494768
620	384 400	24.89980	78.74008	1612903	670	448 900	25.88436	81.85353	1492537
621	385 641	24.91987	78.80355	1610306	671	450 241	25.90367	81.91459	1490313
622	386 884	24.93993	78.86698	1607717	672	451 584	25.92296	81.97561	1488095
623	388 129	24.95997	78.93035	1605136	673	452 929	25.94224	82.03658	1485884
624	389 376	24.97999	78.99367	1602564	674	454 276	25.96151	82.09750	1483680
625	390 625	25.00000	79.05694	1600000	675	455 625	25.98076	82.15838	1481481
626	391 876	25.01999	79.12016	1597444	676	456 976	26.00000	82.21922	1479290
627	393 129	25.03997	79.18333	1594896	677	458 329	26.01922	82.28001	1477105
628	394 384	25.05993	79.24645	1592357	678	459 684	26.03843	82.34076	1474926
629	395 641	25.07987	79.30952	1589825	679	461 041	26.05763	82.40146	1472754
630	396 900	25.09980	79.37254	1587302	680	462 400	26.07681	82.46211	1470588
631	398 161	25.11971	79.43551	1584786	681	463 761	26.09598	82.52272	1468429
632	399 424	25.13961	79.49843	1582278	682	465 124	26.11513	82.58329	1466276
633	400 689	25.15949	79.56130	1579779	683	466 489	26.13427	82.64381	1464129
634	401 956	25.17936	79.62412	1577287	684	467 856	26.15339	82.70429	1461988
635	403 225	25.19921	79.68689	1574803	685	469 225	26.17250	82.76473	1459854
636	404 496	25.21904	79.74961	1572327	686	470 596	26.19160	82.82512	1457726
637	405 769	25.23886	79.81228	1569859	687	471 969	26.21068	82.88546	1455604
638	407 044	25.25866	79.87490	1567398	688	473 344	26.22975	82.94577	1453488
639	408 321	25.27845	79.93748	1564945	689	474 721	26.24881	83.00602	1451379
640	409 600	25.29822	80.00000	1562500	690	476 100	26.26785	83.06624	1449275
641	410 881	25.31798	80.06248	1560062	691	477 481	26.28688	83.12641	1447178
642	412 164	25.33772	80.12490	1557632	692	478 864	26.30589	83.18654	1445087
643	413 449	25.35744	80.18728	1555210	693	480 249	26.32489	83.24662	1443001
644	414 736	25.37716	80.24961	1552795	694	481 636	26.34388	83.30666	1440922
645	416 025	25.39685	80.31189	1550388	695	483 025	26.36285	83.36666	1438849
646	417 316	25.41653	80.37413	1547988	696	484 416	26.38181	83.42661	1436782
647	418 609	25.43619	80.43631	1545595	697	485 809	26.40076	83.48653	1434720
648	419 904	25.45584	80.49845	1543210	698	487 204	26.41969	83.54639	1432665
649	421 201	25.47548	80.56054	1540832	699	488 601	26.43861	83.60622	1430615
650	422 500	25.49510	80.62258	1538462	700	490 000	26.45751	83.66600	1428571

Squares and square roots (*continued*)

N	N^2	$\sqrt{N}$	$\sqrt{10N}$	$1/N$ .00	N	N^2	$\sqrt{N}$	$\sqrt{10N}$	$1/N$ .00
700	490 000	26.45751	83.66600	1428571	750	562 500	27.38613	86.60254	1333333
701	491 401	26.47640	83.72574	1426534	751	564 001	27.40438	86.66026	1331558
702	492 804	26.49528	83.78544	1424501	752	565 504	27.42262	86.71793	1329787
703	494 209	26.51415	83.84510	1422475	753	567 009	27.44085	86.77557	1328021
704	495 616	26.53300	83.90471	1420455	754	568 516	27.45906	86.83317	1326260
705	497 025	26.55184	83.96428	1418440	755	570 025	27.47726	86.89074	1324503
706	498 436	26.57066	84.02381	1416431	756	571 536	27.49545	86.94826	1322751
707	499 849	26.58947	84.08329	1414427	757	573 049	27.51363	87.00575	1321004
708	501 264	26.60827	84.14274	1412429	758	574 564	27.53180	87.06320	1319261
709	502 681	26.62705	84.20214	1410437	759	576 081	27.54995	87.12061	1317523
710	504 100	26.64583	84.26150	1408451	760	577 600	27.56810	87.17798	1315789
711	505 521	26.66458	84.32082	1406470	761	579 121	27.58623	87.23531	1314060
712	506 944	26.68333	84.38009	1404494	762	580 644	27.60435	87.29261	1312336
713	508 369	26.70206	84.43933	1402525	763	582 169	27.62245	87.34987	1310616
714	509 796	26.72078	84.49852	1400560	764	583 696	27.64055	87.40709	1308901
715	511 225	26.73948	84.55767	1398601	765	585 225	27.65863	87.46428	1307190
716	512 656	26.75818	84.61678	1396648	766	586 756	27.67671	87.52143	1305483
717	514 089	26.77686	84.67585	1394700	767	588 289	27.69476	87.57854	1303781
718	515 524	26.79552	84.73488	1392758	768	589 824	27.71281	87.63561	1302083
719	516 961	26.81418	84.79387	1390821	769	591 361	27.73085	87.69265	1300390
720	518 400	26.83282	84.85281	1388889	770	592 900	27.74887	87.74964	1298701
721	519 841	26.85144	84.91172	1386963	771	594 441	27.76689	87.80661	1297017
722	521 284	26.87006	84.97058	1385042	772	595 984	27.78489	87.86353	1295337
723	522 729	26.88866	85.02941	1383126	773	597 529	27.80288	87.92042	1293661
724	524 176	26.90725	85.08819	1381215	774	599 076	27.82086	87.97727	1291990
725	525 625	26.92582	85.14693	1379310	775	600 625	27.83882	88.03408	1290323
726	527 076	26.94439	85.20563	1377410	776	602 176	27.85678	88.09086	1288660
727	528 529	26.96294	85.26429	1375516	777	603 729	27.87472	88.14760	1287001
728	529 984	26.98148	85.32292	1373626	778	605 284	27.89265	88.20431	1285347
729	531 441	27.00000	85.38150	1371742	779	606 841	27.91057	88.26098	1283697
730	532 900	27.01851	85.44004	1369863	780	608 400	27.92848	88.31761	1282051
731	534 361	27.03701	85.49854	1367989	781	609 961	27.94638	88.37420	1280410
732	535 824	27.05550	85.55700	1366120	782	611 524	27.96426	88.43076	1278772
733	537 289	27.07397	85.61542	1364256	783	613 089	27.98214	88.48729	1277139
734	538 756	27.09243	85.67380	1362398	784	614 656	28.00000	88.54377	1275510
735	540 225	27.11088	85.73214	1360544	785	616 225	28.01785	88.60023	1273885
736	541 696	27.12932	85.79044	1358696	786	617 796	28.03569	88.65664	1272265
737	543 169	27.14774	85.84870	1356852	787	619 369	28.05352	88.71302	1270648
738	544 644	27.16616	85.90693	1355014	788	620 944	28.07134	88.76936	1269036
739	546 121	27.18455	85.96511	1353180	789	622 521	28.08914	88.82567	1267427
740	547 600	27.20294	86.02325	1351351	790	624 100	28.10694	88.88194	1265823
741	549 081	27.22132	86.08136	1349528	791	625 681	28.12472	88.93818	1264223
742	550 564	27.23968	86.13942	1347709	792	627 264	28.14249	88.99438	1262626
743	552 049	27.25803	86.19745	1345895	793	628 849	28.16026	89.05055	1261034
744	553 536	27.27636	86.25543	1344086	794	630 436	28.17801	89.10668	1259446
745	555 025	27.29469	86.31338	1342282	795	632 025	28.19574	89.16277	1257862
746	556 516	27.31300	86.37129	1340483	796	633 616	28.21347	89.21883	1256281
747	558 009	27.33130	86.42916	1338688	797	635 209	28.23119	89.27486	1254705
748	559 504	27.34959	86.48699	1336898	798	636 804	28.24889	89.33085	1253133
749	561 001	27.36786	86.54479	1335113	799	638 401	28.26659	89.38680	1251564
750	562 500	27.38613	86.60254	1333333	800	640 000	28.28427	89.44272	1250000

Squares and square roots (*continued*)

N	N²	√N	√10N	1/N .00	N	N²	√N	√10N	1/N .00
800	640 000	28.28427	89.44272	1250000	850	722 500	29.15476	92.19544	1176471
801	641 601	28.30194	89.49860	1248439	851	724 201	29.17190	92.24966	1175088
802	643 204	28.31960	89.55445	1246883	852	725 904	29.18904	92.30385	1173709
803	644 809	28.33725	89.61027	1245330	853	727 609	29.20616	92.35800	1172333
804	646 416	28.35489	89.66605	1243781	854	729 316	29.22328	92.41212	1170960
805	648 025	28.37252	89.72179	1242236	855	731 025	29.24038	92.46621	1169591
806	649 636	28.39014	89.77750	1240695	856	732 736	29.25748	92.52027	1168224
807	651 249	28.40775	89.83318	1239157	857	734 449	29.27456	92.57429	1166861
808	652 864	28.42534	89.88882	1237624	858	736 164	29.29164	92.62829	1165501
809	654 481	28.44293	89.94443	1236094	859	737 881	29.30870	92.68225	1164144
810	656 100	28.46050	90.00000	1234568	860	739 600	29.32576	92.73618	1162791
811	657 721	28.47806	90.05554	1233046	861	741 321	29.34280	92.79009	1161440
812	659 344	28.49561	90.11104	1231527	862	743 044	29.35984	92.84396	1160093
813	660 969	28.51315	90.16651	1230012	863	744 769	29.37686	92.89779	1158749
814	662 596	28.53069	90.22195	1228501	864	746 496	29.39388	92.95160	1157407
815	664 225	28.54820	90.27735	1226994	865	748 225	29.41088	93.00538	1156069
816	665 856	28.56571	90.33272	1225490	866	749 956	29.42788	93.05912	1154734
817	667 489	28.58321	90.38805	1223990	867	751 689	29.44486	93.11283	1153403
818	669 124	28.60070	90.44335	1222494	868	753 424	29.46184	93.16652	1152074
819	670 761	28.61818	90.49862	1221001	869	755 161	29.47881	93.22017	1150748
820	672 400	28.63564	90.55385	1219512	870	756 900	29.49576	93.27379	1149425
821	674 041	28.65310	90.60905	1218027	871	758 641	29.51271	93.32738	1148106
822	675 684	28.67054	90.66422	1216545	872	760 384	29.52965	93.38094	1146789
823	677 329	28.68798	90.71935	1215067	873	762 129	29.54657	93.43447	1145475
824	678 976	28.70540	90.77445	1213592	874	763 876	29.56349	93.48797	1144165
825	680 625	28.72281	90.82951	1212121	875	765 625	29.58040	93.54143	1142857
826	682 276	28.74022	90.88454	1210654	876	767 376	29.59730	93.59487	1141553
827	683 929	28.75761	90.93954	1209190	877	769 129	29.61419	93.64828	1140251
828	685 584	28.77499	90.99451	1207729	878	770 884	29.63106	93.70165	1138952
829	687 241	28.79236	91.04944	1206273	879	772 641	29.64793	93.75500	1137656
830	688 900	28.80972	91.10434	1204819	880	774 400	29.66479	93.80832	1136364
831	690 561	28.82707	91.15920	1203369	881	776 161	29.68164	93.86160	1135074
832	692 224	28.84441	91.21403	1201923	882	777 924	29.69848	93.91486	1133787
833	693 889	28.86174	91.26883	1200480	883	779 689	29.71532	93.96808	1132503
834	695 556	28.87906	91.32360	1199041	884	781 456	29.73214	94.02127	1131222
835	697 225	28.89637	91.37833	1197605	885	783 225	29.74895	94.07444	1129944
836	698 896	28.91366	91.43304	1196172	886	784 996	29.76575	94.12757	1128668
837	700 569	28.93095	91.48770	1194743	887	786 769	29.78255	94.18068	1127396
838	702 244	28.94823	91.54234	1193317	888	788 544	29.79933	94.23375	1126126
839	703 921	28.96550	91.59694	1191895	889	790 321	29.81610	94.28680	1124859
840	705 600	28.98275	91.65151	1190476	890	792 100	29.83287	94.33981	1123596
841	707 281	29.00000	91.70605	1189061	891	793 881	29.84962	94.39280	1122334
842	708 964	29.01724	91.76056	1187648	892	795 664	29.86637	94.44575	1121076
843	710 649	29.03446	91.81503	1186240	893	797 449	29.88311	94.49868	1119821
844	712 336	29.05168	91.86947	1184834	894	799 236	29.89983	94.55157	1118568
845	714 025	29.06888	91.92388	1183432	895	801 025	29.91655	94.60444	1117318
846	715 716	29.08608	91.97826	1182033	896	802 816	29.93326	94.65728	1116071
847	717 409	29.10326	92.03260	1180638	897	804 609	29.94996	94.71008	1114827
848	719 104	29.12044	92.08692	1179245	898	806 404	29.96665	94.76286	1113586
849	720 801	29.13760	92.14120	1177856	899	808 201	29.98333	94.81561	1112347
850	722 500	29.15476	92.19544	1176471	900	810 000	30.00000	94.86833	1111111

Squares and square roots (concluded)

N	N²	√N	√10N	1/N .00	N	N²	√N	√10N	1/N .00
900	810 000	30.00000	94.86833	1111111	950	902 500	30.82207	97.46794	1052632
901	811 801	30.01666	94.92102	1109878	951	904 401	30.83829	97.51923	1051525
902	813 604	30.03331	94.97368	1108647	952	906 304	30.85450	97.57049	1050420
903	815 409	30.04996	95.02631	1107420	953	908 209	30.87070	97.62172	1049318
904	817 216	30.06659	95.07891	1106195	954	910.116	30.88689	97.67292	1048218
905	819 025	30.08322	95.13149	1104972	955	912 025	30.90307	97.72410	1047120
906	820 836	30.09983	95.18403	1103753	956	913 936	30.91925	97.77525	1046025
907	822 649	30.11644	95.23655	1102536	957	915 849	30.93542	97.82638	1044932
908	824 464	30.13304	95.28903	1101322	958	917 764	30.95158	97.87747	1043841
909	826 281	30.14963	95.34149	1100110	959	919 681	30.96773	97.92855	1042753
910	828 100	30.16621	95.39392	1098901	960	921 600	30.98387	97.97959	1041667
911	829 921	30.18278	95.44632	1097695	961	923 521	31.00000	98.03061	1040583
912	831 744	30.19934	95.49869	1096491	962	925 444	31.01612	98.08160	1039501
913	833 569	30.21589	95.55103	1095290	963	927 369	31.03224	98.13256	1038422
914	835 396	30.23243	95.60335	1094092	964	929 296	31.04835	98.18350	1037344
915	837 225	30.24897	95.65563	1092896	965	931 225	31.06445	98.23441	1036269
916	839 056	30.26549	95.70789	1091703	966	933 156	31.08054	98.28530	1035197
917	840 889	30.28201	95.76012	1090513	967	935 089	31.09662	98.33616	1034126
918	842 724	30.29851	95.81232	1089325	968	937 024	31.11270	98.38699	1033058
919	844 561	30.31501	95.86449	1088139	969	938 961	31.12876	98.43780	1031992
920	846 400	30.33150	95.91663	1086957	970	940 900	31.14482	98.48858	1030928
921	848 241	30.34798	95.96874	1085776	971	942 841	31.16087	98.53933	1029866
922	850 084	30.36445	96.02083	1084599	972	944 784	31.17691	98.59006	1028807
923	851 929	30.38092	96.07289	1083424	973	946 729	31.19295	98.64076	1027749
924	853 776	30.39737	96.12492	1082251	974	948 676	31.20897	98.69144	1026694
925	855 625	30.41381	96.17692	1081081	975	950 625	31.22499	98.74209	1025641
926	857 476	30.43025	96.22889	1079914	976	952 576	31.24100	98.79271	1024590
927	859 329	30.44667	96.28084	1078749	977	954 529	31.25700	98.84331	1023541
928	861 184	30.46309	96.33276	1077586	978	956 484	31.27299	98.89388	1022495
929	863 041	30.47950	96.38465	1076426	979	958 441	31.28898	98.94443	1021450
930	864 900	30.49590	96.43651	1075269	980	960 400	31.30495	98.99495	1020408
931	866 761	30.51229	96.48834	1074114	981	962 361	31.32092	99.04544	1019368
932	868 624	30.52868	96.54015	1072961	982	964 324	31.33688	99.09591	1018330
933	870 489	30.54505	96.59193	1071811	983	966 289	31.35283	99.14636	1017294
934	872 356	30.56141	96.64368	1070664	984	968 256	31.36877	99.19677	1016260
935	874 225	30.57777	96.69540	1069519	985	970 225	31.38471	99.24717	1015228
936	876 096	30.59412	96.74709	1068376	986	972 196	31.40064	99.29753	1014199
937	877 969	30.61046	96.79876	1067236	987	974 169	31.41656	99.34787	1013171
938	879 844	30.62679	96.85040	1066098	988	976 144	31.43247	99.39819	1012146
939	881 721	30.64311	96.90201	1064963	989	978 121	31.44837	99.44848	1011129
940	883 600	30.65942	96.95360	1063830	990	980 100	31.46427	99.49874	1010101
941	885 481	30.67572	97.00515	1062699	991	982 081	31.48015	99.54898	1009082
942	887 364	30.69202	97.05668	1061571	992	984 064	31.49603	99.59920	1008065
943	889 249	30.70831	97.10819	1060445	993	986 049	31.51190	99.64939	1007049
944	391 136	30.72458	97.15966	1059322	994	988 036	31.52777	99.69955	1006036
945	893 025	30.74085	97.21111	1058201	995	990 025	31.54362	99.74969	1005025
946	894 916	30.75711	97.26253	1057082	996	992 016	31.55947	99.79980	1004016
947	896 809	30.77337	97.31393	1055966	997	994 009	31.57531	99.84989	1003009
948	898 704	30.78961	97.36529	1054852	998	996 004	31.59114	99.89995	1002004
949	900 601	30.80584	97.41663	1053741	999	998 001	31.60696	99.94999	1001001
950	902 500	30.82207	97.46794	1052632	1000	1 000 000	31.62278	100.00000	1000000

APPENDIX H

CRITICAL VALUES OF t^*

df	Level of significance for one-tailed test					
	.10	.05	.025	.01	.005	.0005
	Level of significance for two-tailed test					
	.20	.10	.05	.02	.01	.001
1	3.078	6.314	12.706	31.821	63.657	636.619
2	1.886	2.920	4.303	6.965	9.925	31.598
3	1.638	2.353	3.182	4.541	5.841	12.941
4	1.533	2.132	2.776	3.747	4.604	8.610
5	1.476	2.015	2.571	3.365	4.032	6.859
6	1.440	1.943	2.447	3.143	3.707	5.959
7	1.415	1.895	2.365	2.998	3.499	5.405
8	1.397	1.860	2.306	2.896	3.355	5.041
9	1.383	1.833	2.262	2.821	3.250	4.781
10	1.372	1.812	2.228	2.764	3.169	4.587
11	1.363	1.796	2.201	2.718	3.106	4.437
12	1.356	1.782	2.179	2.681	3.055	4.318
13	1.350	1.771	2.160	2.650	3.012	4.221
14	1.345	1.761	2.145	2.624	2.977	4.140
15	1.341	1.753	2.131	2.602	2.947	4.073
16	1.337	1.746	2.120	2.583	2.921	4.015
17	1.333	1.740	2.110	2.567	2.898	3.965
18	1.330	1.734	2.101	2.552	2.878	3.922
19	1.328	1.729	2.093	2.539	2.861	3.883
20	1.325	1.725	2.086	2.528	2.845	3.850
21	1.323	1.721	2.080	2.518	2.831	3.819
22	1.321	1.717	2.074	2.508	2.819	3.792
23	1.319	1.714	2.069	2.500	2.807	3.767
24	1.318	1.711	2.064	2.492	2.797	3.745
25	1.316	1.708	2.060	2.485	2.787	3.725
26	1.315	1.706	2.056	2.479	2.779	3.707
27	1.314	1.703	2.052	2.473	2.771	3.690
28	1.313	1.701	2.048	2.467	2.763	3.674
29	1.311	1.699	2.045	2.462	2.756	3.659
30	1.310	1.697	2.042	2.457	2.750	3.646
40	1.303	1.684	2.021	2.423	2.704	3.551
60	1.296	1.671	2.000	2.390	2.660	3.460
120	1.289	1.658	1.980	2.358	2.617	3.373
∞	1.282	1.645	1.960	2.326	2.576	3.291

*This table is abridged from Table III of Fisher and Yates: *Statistical Tables for Biological, Agricultural, and Medical Research*, published by Longman Group Ltd., (1974) 6th ed., by permission of the authors and publishers.

APPENDIX I
TABLE OF RANDOM NUMBERS

```
READY
RUNNH:PROBE*FIN
***VERSION 5.80***    JOB NO. 037

COMMAND ?RANNUM = RND(2000)*1000


COMMAND ?REPORT RANNUM NOC DIGIT3


NON-PRINTING CHARACTER IN INPUT LINE
COMMAND ?REPORT RANNUM NOC DIGIT 3
```

RANNUM	UNDATED									
1	732.	609.	323.	108.	188.	62.	713.	638.	49.	671.
11	392.	379.	538.	884.	409.	800.	436.	20.	134.	679.
21	391.	298.	182.	366.	136.	686.	306.	457.	369.	956.
31	117.	432.	267.	37.	470.	362.	439.	555.	747.	38.
41	109.	574.	873.	883.	405.	665.	305.	288.	352.	145.
51	235.	999.	100.	374.	831.	413.	233.	589.	828.	13.
61	557.	170.	131.	33.	571.	566.	44.	226.	735.	557.
71	660.	522.	236.	663.	849.	294.	6.	802.	430.	185.
81	523.	932.	56.	884.	511.	427.	923.	664.	453.	57.
91	985.	278.	715.	148.	956.	862.	999.	966.	901.	697.
101	776.	778.	28.	979.	451.	694.	109.	788.	429.	856.
111	158.	770.	266.	677.	127.	850.	857.	804.	175.	19.
121	16.	82.	798.	631.	575.	639.	145.	309.	252.	736.
131	912.	681.	484.	953.	120.	176.	927.	442.	187.	609.
141	342.	463.	780.	982.	210.	109.	985.	302.	465.	77.
151	772.	174.	146.	68.	391.	898.	486.	220.	206.	656.
161	217.	32.	910.	669.	974.	902.	848.	829.	16.	342.
171	235.	860.	705.	535.	952.	923.	954.	784.	67.	496.
181	797.	633.	719.	791.	755.	448.	220.	515.	649.	13.
191	372.	533.	244.	766.	787.	30.	171.	959.	221.	885.
201	497.	368.	543.	16.	880.	543.	328.	635.	2.	29.
211	685.	256.	574.	192.	955.	534.	729.	33.	753.	928.
221	314.	232.	428.	744.	0.	469.	336.	927.	966.	449.
231	800.	898.	753.	117.	160.	885.	56.	915.	383.	782.
241	699.	203.	286.	813.	738.	587.	780.	372.	980.	212.
251	244.	465.	44.	582.	350.	901.	273.	652.	205.	654.
261	424.	274.	955.	638.	938.	331.	565.	945.	226.	643.
271	148.	907.	385.	792.	486.	481.	158.	740.	985.	45.
281	415.	988.	493.	982.	19.	383.	111.	328.	890.	784.
291	549.	226.	54.	848.	120.	305.	995.	719.	461.	142.
301	651.	993.	248.	230.	968.	145.	591.	113.	3.	797.
311	402.	57.	528.	987.	405.	844.	186.	13.	227.	941.
321	709.	314.	634.	703.	450.	822.	408.	740.	723.	772.
331	71.	875.	649.	658.	379.	605.	611.	211.	306.	848.
341	59.	385.	473.	126.	17.	462.	33.	178.	969.	834.
351	263.	647.	750.	286.	252.	969.	97.	752.	29.	766.
361	335.	945.	242.	697.	470.	924.	757.	411.	811.	142.
371	312.	929.	975.	210.	739.	178.	311.	78.	513.	850.
381	922.	110.	23.	351.	751.	532.	389.	566.	75.	715.
391	376.	537.	368.	590.	1000.	491.	461.	463.	39.	24.

Table of Random Numbers (*continued*)

401	454.	761.	903.	238.	468.	550.	846.	569.	175.	986.
411	304.	384.	0.	192.	999.	979.	46.	582.	354.	760.
421	416.	932.	862.	475.	654.	752.	392.	753.	626.	214.
431	277.	654.	8.	628.	726.	613.	997.	834.	3.	674.
441	324.	661.	696.	691.	513.	314.	293.	904.	573.	641.
451	992.	549.	745.	918.	197.	349.	699.	601.	805.	138.
461	378.	419.	876.	713.	956.	758.	258.	109.	67.	679.
471	188.	286.	348.	720.	978.	760.	765.	584.	788.	523.
481	493.	100.	381.	349.	232.	228.	2.	338.	255.	199.
491	880.	185.	528.	775.	994.	841.	35.	962.	758.	321.
501	328.	194.	587.	758.	412.	84.	251.	262.	438.	653.
511	781.	564.	14.	761.	708.	561.	452.	572.	629.	375.
521	602.	720.	113.	902.	638.	355.	392.	209.	933.	730.
531	904.	557.	143.	795.	572.	366.	356.	61.	482.	268.
541	253.	190.	236.	216.	547.	403.	449.	692.	896.	14.
551	402.	776.	153.	47.	892.	92.	391.	744.	886.	427.
561	89.	551.	112.	462.	628.	664.	563.	829.	582.	521.
571	137.	942.	921.	588.	462.	620.	853.	459.	554.	368.
581	274.	569.	487.	131.	524.	403.	579.	708.	313.	801.
591	747.	239.	122.	372.	154.	867.	741.	622.	527.	471.
601	315.	414.	994.	358.	192.	178.	74.	806.	868.	525.
611	857.	456.	825.	324.	628.	693.	96.	634.	943.	556.
621	361.	46.	133.	33.	64.	722.	564.	632.	942.	45.
631	583.	398.	553.	607.	225.	654.	422.	537.	356.	356.
641	252.	724.	902.	481.	838.	873.	105.	784.	658.	719.
651	416.	241.	128.	783.	622.	589.	982.	59.	131.	864.
661	199.	727.	911.	527.	458.	831.	145.	530.	122.	908.
671	83.	54.	574.	993.	713.	0.	531.	293.	432.	904.
681	945.	850.	668.	399.	649.	16.	313.	729.	867.	759.
691	781.	712.	337.	613.	263.	78.	13.	657.	438.	134.
701	961.	50.	514.	696.	896.	379.	125.	76.	139.	476.
711	26.	305.	66.	726.	605.	9.	854.	298.	892.	937.
721	587.	238.	687.	634.	865.	387.	834.	991.	988.	282.
731	219.	400.	907.	332.	66.	130.	497.	95.	263.	449.
741	884.	780.	995.	33.	832.	480.	998.	5.	783.	806.
751	399.	518.	716.	531.	316.	702.	726.	672.	143.	30.
761	3.	173.	478.	979.	319.	615.	967.	388.	956.	398.
771	988.	148.	369.	994.	424.	615.	593.	27.	21.	398.
781	377.	822.	241.	610.	148.	272.	68.	139.	123.	698.
791	149.	441.	662.	93.	92.	999.	698.	519.	324.	672.
801	429.	630.	195.	641.	382.	354.	509.	99.	417.	720.
811	440.	213.	947.	888.	415.	530.	469.	889.	36.	171.
821	310.	758.	165.	547.	519.	670.	753.	804.	64.	148.
831	962.	158.	986.	691.	704.	177.	89.	957.	504.	930.
841	208.	502.	116.	911.	289.	247.	905.	64.	262.	100.
851	967.	535.	484.	590.	851.	179.	864.	583.	833.	355.
861	937.	371.	353.	264.	249.	821.	842.	956.	230.	205.
871	877.	407.	226.	751.	417.	809.	282.	364.	119.	269.
881	960.	512.	43.	83.	37.	566.	497.	789.	454.	857.
891	766.	53.	502.	608.	564.	430.	361.	926.	606.	981.
901	32.	347.	665.	11.	729.	713.	118.	200.	775.	271.
911	78.	691.	730.	484.	334.	70.	727.	591.	490.	303.
921	863.	636.	457.	720.	397.	262.	223.	23.	597.	216.
931	346.	203.	514.	549.	29.	413.	300.	419.	555.	267.
941	268.	820.	633.	53.	83.	661.	753.	327.	133.	977.
951	494.	116.	450.	883.	330.	736.	140.	128.	448.	906.
961	664.	114.	71.	797.	475.	165.	197.	803.	704.	39.
971	173.	505.	986.	89.	161.	281.	547.	743.	660.	997.

Table of Random Numbers (*continued*)

```
 981   27.  997.  371.  191>  920.  678.  153.  138.  803.  598.
 991  892.  909.  988.  428.   25.  980.   20.  693.  995.  554.
1001  166.  116.  805.  484.  595.  312.  712.  318.  936.  585.
1011  100.  938.  314.  760.  886.  872.  155.  379.  960.  488.
1021  235.  907.  923.  868.  798.  809.  328.  283.  690.  522.
1031  304.  705.  892.  231.  723.  522.  741.  789.  779.  648.
1041  830.  259.  708.  908.   44.  926.   78.  331.  203.  880.
1051  921.  303.  640.  294.  190.  616.  529.  291.  876.  203.
1061  942.  900.  325.  687.  416.  257.  592.  726.  233.  118.
1071  706.  936.  115.  508.  863.  814.  479.  839.  296.  824.
1081  774.  710.  981.    5.  225.  493.  372.  185.  190.  579.
1091  839.  893.  814.  131.  316.  854.  784.  224.  122.  280.
1101  758.   31.  990.  987.   31.  128.  497.  275.  979.  719.
1111  535.  569.  935.  921.  716.  217.  318.  409.  186.  971.
1121  296.  832.  214.  667.  307.  861.  197.  575.  946.  247.
1131  717.  196.  684.  807.  964.  182.  987.  524.  535.  534.
1141  499.  361.  893.  316.  957.  138.  954.  232.  927.  264.
1151  609.  776.  839.  616.  741.  118.  538.  223.   14.  989.
1161  293.  607.  256.  720.   44.  953.  184.  708.  954.  999.
1171  728.  459.  686.  240.  418.  830.  450.  482.  766.  883.
1181  573.  797.  794.  654.  145.  506.  700.  606.  537.  435.
1191  123.  446.  733.  543.  863.  374.  481.  793.  219.  126.
1201  507.  547.  374.  893.  145.  877.  232.  684.  497.  581.
1211  309.  276.  709.  483.    2.  318.  422.   71.   77.  624.
1221  323.  793.  123.   75.  554.  650.  434.  911.  140.  557.
1231  877.  565.  546.   37.  755.   12.  680.  276.  926.  967.
1241  939.  256.   46.  128.  148.  268.  799.  873.  309.  634.
1251  916.  642.  183.  668.  598.    1.  418.  148.  588.  960.
1261  790.   64.  232.  448.  509.  806.  429.  783.  549.  477.
1271  252.  734.  131.  158.  847.  896.  597.  640.  298.  436.
1281  792.  148.  274.  425.  307.  787.  874.  363.  409.  992.
1291  227.  523.  338.  337.  325.  682.  899.  223.  298.   25.
1301  225.  888.  428.  420.  297.  438.  728.   49.  590.  762.
1311  332.  157.  721.  502.  223.  641.  493.   98.  238.  786.
1321  187.  382.  463.  547.   11.  242.  245.  252.  454.  856.
1331  170.  196.  782.   23.  225.  659.   21.  155.  540.  814.
1341   98.  937.  485.  120.  340.  164.  466.  640.  190.  301.
1351    5.  976.  648.  115.  626.  399.  116.  817.  193.  723.
1361   70.  589.  169.  777.  111.  718.  993.  642.  855.  488.
1371  583.  710.  596.  878.  260.   96.  332.   31.  830.  954.
1381  734.  763.  439.  647.   80.  404.  402.  373.  210.  505.
1391  673.  459.  891.  282.  129.  280.   91.  519.  227.  321.
1401  630.  392.  172.  972.  792.   98.  932.  891.  631.  933.
1411  113.  873.  229.  996.  766.  599.  953.  117.  824.  295.
1421  111.  624.  604.  153.  672.  378.  587.   67.  264.  733.
1431  351.   78.  407.  610.  748.  494.  521.  328.  421.  247.
1441  750.   19. 1000.  579.   61.  441.   82.  253.  196.  548.
1451   93.  543.  675.  999.  428.  916.  296.  547.  553.  444.
1461  423.  999.  590.  191.  358.  485.  556.  922.  538.  546.
1471  984.  242.  102.  543.  295.  642.  167.  644.  378.  336.
1481  652.  118.  150.  673.  995.  664.  201.  146.  251.  891.
1491  755.  163.  269.  795.  482.  423.  325.  173.  668.  860.
1501  887.  319.  486.  398.  985.  543.  970.  570.  895.  705.
1511   99.  331.  439.  243.  813.  137.  651.  502.   43.  413.
1521  523.  703.   77.   13. 1000.  547.  119.  916.  863.  515.
1531  897.  817.  676.  742.  824.   86.  297.  731.  327.  977.
1541  378.   10.  293.    7.  760.  662.  723.  898.  881.  588.
1551  584.  319.  506.  500.  177.  267.  173.  705.  582.  472.
1561  480.  703.  118.  854.  918.  672.  192.  838.  471.  519.
```

Table of Random Numbers (*concluded*)

1571	749.	393.	764.	340.	290.	804.	852.	637.	260.	298.
1581	587.	836.	710.	841.	159.	405.	113.	306.	705.	344.
1591	346.	268.	676.	683.	793.	888.	711.	757.	199.	468.
1601	57.	327.	286.	752.	119.	631.	257.	380.	539.	94.
1611	139.	796.	650.	276.	990.	125.	755.	476.	27.	576.
1621	605.	470.	158.	635.	972.	395.	683.	126.	442.	891.
1631	494.	45.	971.	830.	418.	624.	47.	223.	212.	198.
1641	980.	995.	353.	157.	787.	590.	408.	723.	699.	979.
1651	320.	652.	951.	732.	8.	769.	140.	979.	621.	453.
1661	147.	790.	703.	576.	269.	583.	207.	844.	192.	729.
1671	504.	251.	189.	977.	115.	487.	247.	190.	153.	561.
1681	179.	909.	752.	260.	713.	959.	461.	603.	26.	903.
1691	449.	592.	867.	950.	806.	495.	550.	643.	622.	378.
1701	127.	437.	52.	598.	240.	813.	428.	415.	539.	396.
1711	834.	445.	493.	849.	603.	164.	241.	760.	903.	341.
1721	231.	647.	397.	82.	949.	635.	665.	437.	581.	194.
1731	547.	82.	487.	488.	609.	774.	858.	629.	419.	662.
1741	500.	503.	425.	817.	531.	692.	612.	27.	709.	514.
1751	344.	609.	359.	858.	309.	246.	83.	512.	386.	47.
1761	404.	337.	93.	104.	442.	13.	632.	349.	813.	11.
1771	651.	491.	473.	624.	651.	223.	156.	122.	803.	914.
1781	638.	965.	982.	584.	633.	404.	522.	923.	164.	966.
1791	41.	333.	127.	75.	173.	271.	992.	940.	598.	923.
1801	276.	434.	948.	97.	23.	738.	781.	717.	823.	549.
1811	85.	675.	48.	34.	698.	288.	799.	589.	774.	736.
1821	268.	821.	854.	132.	138.	231.	255.	793.	526.	419.
1831	22.	358.	364.	826.	933.	876.	363.	488.	59.	86.
1841	864.	976.	930.	435.	883.	63.	435.	880.	968.	446.
1851	264.	486.	764.	701.	239.	355.	682.	78.	703.	185.
1861	35.	765.	69.	382.	206.	166.	479.	89.	116.	774.
1871	349.	301.	514.	436.	193.	242.	968.	283.	268.	564.
1881	293.	66.	723.	538.	464.	758.	425.	626.	837.	170.
1891	266.	848.	224.	623.	161.	169.	597.	827.	68.	628.
1901	549.	966.	841.	486.	42.	52.	988.	921.	977.	472.
1911	294.	548.	148.	910.	65.	213.	737.	485.	957.	961.
1921	864.	608.	175.	502.	998.	608.	45.	248.	302.	200.
1931	999.	229.	543.	373.	725.	567.	718.	150.	808.	664.
1941	885.	961.	634.	601.	586.	959.	882.	175.	819.	314.
1951	705.	465.	206.	649.	842.	613.	310.	354.	905.	976.
1961	873.	659.	275.	932.	673.	544.	697.	505.	96.	978.
1971	414.	770.	490.	737.	857.	569.	653.	708.	351.	426.
1981	956.	113.	988.	285.	566.	84.	469.	575.	293.	528.
1991	243.	141.	874.	44.	986.	149.	577.	522.	109.	546.

COMMAND ?END

USED: 154.7 UNITS

READY
BYE

OFF AT 09:48

APPENDIX J

CRITICAL VALUES OF CHI-SQUARE

Percentages represent areas in right-hand
end of distribution. Example:

For 9 degrees of freedom:
$P[x^2 > 16.92] = 0.05$

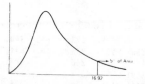

Degrees of freedom	Probability that chi-square value will be exceeded									
	0.995	0.990	0.975	0.950	0.900	0.100	0.050	0.025	0.010	0.005
1	0.0⁴393	0.0³157	0.0³982	0.0²393	0.0158	2.71	3.84	5.02	6.63	7.88
2	0.0100	0.0201	0.0506	0.103	0.211	4.61	5.99	7.38	9.21	10.60
3	0.072	0.115	0.216	0.352	0.584	6.25	7.81	9.35	11.34	12.84
4	0.207	0.297	0.484	0.711	1.064	7.78	9.49	11.14	13.28	14.86
5	0.412	0.554	0.831	1.145	1.61	9.24	11.07	12.83	15.09	16.75
6	0.676	0.872	1.24	1.64	2.20	10.64	12.59	14.45	16.81	18.55
7	0.989	1.24	1.69	2.17	2.83	12.02	14.07	16.01	18.48	20.28
8	1.34	1.65	2.18	2.73	3.49	13.36	15.51	17.53	20.09	21.96
9	1.73	2.09	2.70	3.33	4.17	14.68	16.92	19.02	21.67	23.59
10	2.16	2.56	3.25	3.94	4.87	15.99	18.31	20.48	23.21	25.19
11	2.60	3.05	3.82	4.57	5.58	17.28	19.68	21.92	24.72	26.76
12	3.07	3.57	4.40	5.23	6.30	18.55	21.03	23.34	26.22	28.30
13	3.57	4.11	5.01	5.89	7.04	19.81	22.36	24.74	27.69	29.82
14	4.07	4.66	5.63	6.57	7.79	21.06	23.68	26.12	29.14	31.32
15	4.60	5.23	6.26	7.26	8.55	22.31	25.00	27.49	30.58	32.80
16	5.14	5.81	6.91	7.96	9.31	23.54	26.30	28.85	32.00	34.27
17	5.70	6.41	7.56	8.67	10.09	24.77	27.59	30.19	33.41	35.72
18	6.26	7.01	8.23	9.39	10.86	25.99	28.87	31.53	34.81	37.16
19	6.84	7.63	8.91	10.12	11.65	27.20	30.14	32.85	36.19	38.58
20	7.43	8.26	9.59	10.85	12.44	28.41	31.41	34.17	37.57	40.00
21	8.03	8.90	10.28	11.59	13.24	29.62	32.67	35.48	38.93	41.40
22	8.64	9.54	10.98	12.34	14.04	30.81	33.92	36.78	40.29	42.80
23	9.26	10.20	11.69	13.09	14.85	32.01	35.17	38.08	41.64	44.18
24	9.89	10.86	12.40	13.85	15.66	33.20	36.42	39.36	42.98	45.56
25	10.52	11.52	13.12	14.61	16.47	34.38	37.65	40.65	44.31	46.93
26	11.16	12.20	13.84	15.38	17.29	35.56	38.89	41.92	45.64	48.29
27	11.81	12.88	14.57	16.15	18.11	36.74	40.11	43.19	46.96	49.64
28	12.46	13.56	15.31	16.93	18.94	37.92	41.34	44.46	48.28	50.99
29	13.12	14.26	16.05	17.71	19.77	39.09	42.56	45.72	49.59	52.34
30	13.79	14.95	16.79	18.49	20.60	40.26	43.77	46.98	50.89	53.67
40	20.71	22.16	24.43	26.51	29.05	51.80	55.76	59.34	63.69	66.77
50	27.99	29.71	32.36	34.76	37.69	63.17	67.50	71.42	76.15	79.49
60	35.53	37.48	40.48	43.19	46.46	74.40	79.08	83.30	88.38	91.95
70	43.28	45.44	48.76	51.74	55.33	85.53	90.53	95.02	100.4	104.22
80	51.17	53.54	57.15	60.39	64.28	96.58	101.9	106.6	112.3	116.32
90	59.20	61.75	65.65	69.13	73.29	107.6	113.1	118.1	124.1	128.3
100	67.33	70.06	74.22	77.93	82.36	118.5	124.3	129.6	135.8	140.2
z_α	−2.58	−2.33	−1.96	−1.64	−1.28	+1.28	+1.64	+1.96	+2.33	+2.58

Source: Adapted from E. S. Pearson and H. O. Hartley, eds., *Biometrika Tables for Statisticians*, vol. I, Table 18, pp. 160–63, published for the Biometrika trustees by Cambridge University, 1954, by permission of Professor Pearson and the trustees of Biometrika.

APPENDIX K

CRITICAL VALUES OF U IN THE MANN-WHITNEY TEST

In the first table the entries are the critical values of U for a one-tailed test at 0.025 or for a two-tailed test at 0.05; in the second, for a one-tailed test at 0.05 or for a two-tailed test at 0.10.

n_2 \ n_1	1	2	3	4	5	6	7	8	9	10	11	12	13	14	15	16	17	18	19	20
1																				
2								0	0	0	0	1	1	1	1	1	2	2	2	2
3					0	1	1	2	2	3	3	4	4	5	5	6	6	7	7	8
4				0	1	2	3	4	4	5	6	7	8	9	10	11	11	12	13	13
5			0	1	2	3	5	6	7	8	9	11	12	13	14	15	17	18	19	20
6			1	2	3	5	6	8	10	11	13	14	16	17	19	21	22	24	25	27
7			1	3	5	6	8	10	12	14	16	18	20	22	24	26	28	30	32	34
8		0	2	4	6	8	10	13	15	17	19	22	24	26	29	31	34	36	38	41
9		0	2	4	7	10	12	15	17	20	23	26	28	31	34	37	39	42	45	48
10		0	3	5	8	11	14	17	20	23	26	29	33	36	39	42	45	48	52	55
11		0	3	6	9	13	16	19	23	26	30	33	37	40	44	47	51	55	58	62
12		1	4	7	11	14	18	22	26	29	33	37	41	45	49	53	57	61	65	69
13		1	4	8	12	16	20	24	28	33	37	41	45	50	54	59	63	67	72	76
14		1	5	9	13	17	22	26	31	36	40	45	50	55	59	64	67	74	78	83
15		1	5	10	14	19	24	29	34	39	44	49	54	59	64	70	75	80	85	90
16		1	6	11	15	21	26	31	37	42	47	53	59	64	70	75	81	86	92	98
17		2	6	11	17	22	28	34	39	45	51	57	63	67	75	81	87	93	99	105
18		2	7	12	18	24	30	36	42	48	55	61	67	74	80	86	93	99	106	112
19		2	7	13	19	25	32	38	45	52	58	65	72	78	85	92	99	106	113	119
20		2	8	13	20	27	34	41	48	55	62	69	76	83	90	98	105	112	119	127

n_2 \ n_1	1	2	3	4	5	6	7	8	9	10	11	12	13	14	15	16	17	18	19	20
1																			0	0
2					0	0	0	1	1	1	1	2	2	2	3	3	3	4	4	4
3			0	0	1	2	2	3	3	4	5	5	6	7	7	8	9	9	10	11
4			0	1	2	3	4	5	6	7	8	9	10	11	12	14	15	16	17	18
5		0	1	2	4	5	6	8	9	11	12	13	15	16	18	19	20	22	23	25
6		0	2	3	5	7	8	10	12	14	16	17	19	21	23	25	26	28	30	32
7		0	2	4	6	8	11	13	15	17	19	21	24	26	28	30	33	35	37	39
8		1	3	5	8	10	13	15	18	20	23	26	28	31	33	36	39	41	44	47
9		1	3	6	9	12	15	18	21	24	27	30	33	36	39	42	45	48	51	54
10		1	4	7	11	14	17	20	24	27	31	34	37	41	44	48	51	55	58	62
11		1	5	8	12	16	19	23	27	31	34	38	42	46	50	54	57	61	65	69
12		2	5	9	13	17	21	26	30	34	38	42	47	51	55	60	64	68	72	77
13		2	6	10	15	19	24	28	33	37	42	47	51	56	61	65	70	75	80	84
14		2	7	11	16	21	26	31	36	41	46	51	56	61	66	71	77	82	87	92
15		3	7	12	18	23	28	33	39	44	50	55	61	66	72	77	83	88	94	100
16		3	8	14	19	25	30	36	42	48	54	60	65	71	77	83	89	95	101	107
17		3	9	15	20	26	33	39	45	51	57	64	70	77	83	89	96	102	109	115
18		4	9	16	22	28	35	41	48	55	61	68	75	82	88	95	102	109	116	123
19	0	4	10	17	23	30	37	44	51	58	65	72	80	87	94	101	109	116	123	130
20	0	4	11	18	25	32	39	47	54	62	69	77	84	92	100	107	115	123	130	138

Reproduced from the *Bulletin of the Institute of Educational Research at Indiana University*, vol. 1, no. 2; with the permission of the author D. Auble, and the publisher.

CRITICAL VALUES OF D IN THE KOLMOGOROV-SMIRNOV TWO-SAMPLE TEST (large samples: two-tailed test)*

Level of significance	Value of D so large as to call for rejection of H_0 at the indicated level of significance, where $D = \text{maximum } \lvert S_{n_1}(X) - S_{n_2}(X) \rvert$
.10	$1.22 \sqrt{\dfrac{n_1 + n_2}{n_1 n_2}}$
.05	$1.36 \sqrt{\dfrac{n_1 + n_2}{n_1 n_2}}$
.025	$1.48 \sqrt{\dfrac{n_1 + n_2}{n_1 n_2}}$
.01	$1.63 \sqrt{\dfrac{n_1 + n_2}{n_1 n_2}}$
.005	$1.73 \sqrt{\dfrac{n_1 + n_2}{n_1 n_2}}$
.001	$1.95 \sqrt{\dfrac{n_1 + n_2}{n_1 n_2}}$

* Adapted from N. Smirnov, "Tables for Estimating the Goodness of Fit of Empirical Distributions," *Annals of Mathematical Statistics* 19 (1948), pp. 280–81, with the kind permission of the publisher.

APPENDIX M

WILCOXON T VALUES
Critical values of T, the Wilcoxon signed rank statistic, where T
is the largest integer such that $Pr(T \leq t/N) \leq \alpha$
the cumulative one-tail probability

N	2α .15 α.075	.10 .050	.05 .025	.04 .020	.03 .015	.02 .010	.01 .005
4	0						
5	1	0					
6	2	2	0	0			
7	4	3	2	1	0	0	
8	7	5	3	3	2	1	0
9	9	8	5	5	4	3	1
10	12	10	8	7	6	5	3
11	16	13	10	9	8	7	5
12	19	17	13	12	11	9	7
13	24	21	17	16	14	12	9
14	28	25	21	19	18	15	12
15	33	30	25	23	21	19	15
16	39	35	29	28	26	23	19
17	45	41	34	33	30	27	23
18	51	47	40	38	35	32	27
19	58	53	46	43	41	37	32
20	65	60	52	50	47	43	37
21	73	67	58	56	53	49	42
22	81	75	65	63	59	55	48
23	89	83	73	70	66	62	54
24	98	91	81	78	74	69	61
25	108	100	89	86	82	76	68
26	118	110	98	94	90	84	75
27	128	119	107	103	99	92	83
28	138	130	116	112	108	101	91
29	150	140	126	122	117	110	100
30	161	151	137	132	127	120	109
31	173	163	147	143	137	130	118
32	186	175	159	154	148	140	128
33	199	187	170	165	159	151	138
34	212	200	182	177	171	162	148
35	226	213	195	189	182	173	159
40	302	286	264	257	249	238	220
50	487	466	434	425	413	397	373
60	718	690	648	636	620	600	567
70	995	960	907	891	872	846	805
80	1318	1276	1211	1192	1168	1136	1086
90	1688	1638	1560	1537	1509	1471	1410
100	2105	2045	1955	1928	1894	1850	1779

Source: Abridged from Robert L. McCormack, "Extended Tables of the Wilcoxon Matched Pair Signed Rank Statistic," *Journal of the American Statistical Association*, September 1965, pp. 866–67.

APPENDIX N

CRITICAL VALUES OF THE F DISTRIBUTION AT A 5 PERCENT LEVEL AND A 1 PERCENT LEVEL OF SIGNIFICANCE

Degrees of freedom for numerator

	1	2	3	4	5	6	7	8	9	10	12	15	20	24	30	40	60	120	∞
1	161	200	216	225	230	234	237	239	241	242	244	246	248	249	250	251	252	253	254
2	18.5	19.0	19.2	19.2	19.3	19.3	19.4	19.4	19.4	19.4	19.4	19.4	19.4	19.5	19.5	19.5	19.5	19.5	19.5
3	10.1	9.55	9.28	9.12	9.01	8.94	8.89	8.85	8.81	8.79	8.74	8.70	8.66	8.64	8.62	8.59	8.57	8.55	8.53
4	7.71	6.94	6.59	6.39	6.26	6.16	6.09	6.04	6.00	5.96	5.91	5.86	5.80	5.77	5.75	5.72	5.69	5.66	5.63
5	6.61	5.79	5.41	5.19	5.05	4.95	4.88	4.82	4.77	4.74	4.68	4.62	4.56	4.53	4.50	4.46	4.43	4.40	4.37
6	5.99	5.14	4.76	4.53	4.39	4.28	4.21	4.15	4.10	4.06	4.00	3.94	3.87	3.84	3.81	3.77	3.74	3.70	3.67
7	5.59	4.74	4.35	4.12	3.97	3.87	3.79	3.73	3.68	3.64	3.57	3.51	3.44	3.41	3.38	3.34	3.30	3.27	3.23
8	5.32	4.46	4.07	3.84	3.69	3.58	3.50	3.44	3.39	3.35	3.28	3.22	3.15	3.12	3.08	3.04	3.01	2.97	2.93
9	5.12	4.26	3.86	3.63	3.48	3.37	3.29	3.23	3.18	3.14	3.07	3.01	2.94	2.90	2.86	2.83	2.79	2.75	2.71
10	4.96	4.10	3.71	3.48	3.33	3.22	3.14	3.07	3.02	2.98	2.91	2.85	2.77	2.74	2.70	2.66	2.62	2.58	2.54
11	4.84	3.98	3.59	3.36	3.20	3.09	3.01	2.95	2.90	2.85	2.79	2.72	2.65	2.61	2.57	2.53	2.49	2.45	2.40
12	4.75	3.89	3.49	3.26	3.11	3.00	2.91	2.85	2.80	2.75	2.69	2.62	2.54	2.51	2.47	2.43	2.38	2.34	2.30
13	4.67	3.81	3.41	3.18	3.03	2.92	2.83	2.77	2.71	2.67	2.60	2.53	2.46	2.42	2.38	2.34	2.30	2.25	2.21
14	4.60	3.74	3.34	3.11	2.96	2.85	2.76	2.70	2.65	2.60	2.53	2.46	2.39	2.35	2.31	2.27	2.22	2.18	2.13
15	4.54	3.68	3.29	3.06	2.90	2.79	2.71	2.64	2.59	2.54	2.48	2.40	2.33	2.29	2.25	2.20	2.16	2.11	2.07
16	4.49	3.63	3.24	3.01	2.85	2.74	2.66	2.59	2.54	2.49	2.42	2.35	2.28	2.24	2.19	2.15	2.11	2.06	2.01
17	4.45	3.59	3.20	2.96	2.81	2.70	2.61	2.55	2.49	2.45	2.38	2.31	2.23	2.19	2.15	2.10	2.06	2.01	1.96
18	4.41	3.55	3.16	2.93	2.77	2.66	2.58	2.51	2.46	2.41	2.34	2.27	2.19	2.15	2.11	2.06	2.02	1.97	1.92
19	4.38	3.52	3.13	2.90	2.74	2.63	2.54	2.48	2.42	2.38	2.31	2.23	2.16	2.11	2.07	2.03	1.98	1.93	1.88
20	4.35	3.49	3.10	2.87	2.71	2.60	2.51	2.45	2.39	2.35	2.28	2.20	2.12	2.08	2.04	1.99	1.95	1.90	1.84
21	4.32	3.47	3.07	2.84	2.68	2.57	2.49	2.42	2.37	2.32	2.25	2.18	2.10	2.05	2.01	1.96	1.92	1.87	1.81
22	4.30	3.44	3.05	2.82	2.66	2.55	2.46	2.40	2.34	2.30	2.23	2.15	2.07	2.03	1.98	1.94	1.89	1.84	1.78
23	4.28	3.42	3.03	2.80	2.64	2.53	2.44	2.37	2.32	2.27	2.20	2.13	2.05	2.01	1.96	1.91	1.86	1.81	1.76
24	4.26	3.40	3.01	2.78	2.62	2.51	2.42	2.36	2.30	2.25	2.18	2.11	2.03	1.98	1.94	1.89	1.84	1.79	1.73
25	4.24	3.39	2.99	2.76	2.60	2.49	2.40	2.34	2.28	2.24	2.16	2.09	2.01	1.96	1.92	1.87	1.82	1.77	1.71
30	4.17	3.32	2.92	2.69	2.53	2.42	2.33	2.27	2.21	2.16	2.09	2.01	1.93	1.89	1.84	1.79	1.74	1.68	1.62
40	4.08	3.23	2.84	2.61	2.45	2.34	2.25	2.18	2.12	2.08	2.00	1.92	1.84	1.79	1.74	1.69	1.64	1.58	1.51
60	4.00	3.15	2.76	2.53	2.37	2.25	2.17	2.10	2.04	1.99	1.92	1.84	1.75	1.70	1.65	1.59	1.53	1.47	1.39
120	3.92	3.07	2.68	2.45	2.29	2.18	2.09	2.02	1.96	1.91	1.83	1.75	1.66	1.61	1.55	1.50	1.43	1.35	1.25
∞	3.84	3.00	2.60	2.37	2.21	2.10	2.01	1.94	1.88	1.83	1.75	1.67	1.57	1.52	1.46	1.39	1.32	1.22	1.00

Degrees of freedom for denominator

Critical values of the F distribution at a 1 percent level of significance, $\alpha = 0.01$ (concluded)

Degrees of freedom for numerator

Degrees of freedom for denominator	1	2	3	4	5	6	7	8	9	10	12	15	20	24	30	40	60	120	∞
1	4,052	5,000	5,403	5,625	5,764	5,859	5,928	5,982	6,023	6,056	6,106	6,157	6,209	6,235	6,261	6,287	6,313	6,339	6,366
2	98.5	99.0	99.2	99.2	99.3	99.3	99.4	99.4	99.4	99.4	99.4	99.4	99.4	99.5	99.5	99.5	99.5	99.5	99.5
3	34.1	30.8	29.5	28.7	28.2	27.9	27.7	27.5	27.3	27.2	27.1	26.9	26.7	26.6	26.5	26.4	26.3	26.2	26.1
4	21.2	18.0	16.7	16.0	15.5	15.2	15.0	14.8	14.7	14.5	14.4	14.2	14.0	13.9	13.8	13.7	13.7	13.6	13.5
5	16.3	13.3	12.1	11.4	11.0	10.7	10.5	10.3	10.2	10.1	9.89	9.72	9.55	9.47	9.38	9.29	9.20	9.11	9.02
6	13.7	10.9	9.78	9.15	8.75	8.47	8.26	8.10	7.98	7.87	7.72	7.56	7.40	7.31	7.23	7.14	7.06	6.97	6.88
7	12.2	9.55	8.45	7.85	7.46	7.19	6.99	6.84	6.72	6.62	6.47	6.31	6.16	6.07	5.99	5.91	5.82	5.74	5.65
8	11.3	8.65	7.59	7.01	6.63	6.37	6.18	6.03	5.91	5.81	5.67	5.52	5.36	5.28	5.20	5.12	5.03	4.95	4.86
9	10.6	8.02	6.99	6.42	6.06	5.80	5.61	5.47	5.35	5.26	5.11	4.96	4.81	4.73	4.65	4.57	4.48	4.40	4.31
10	10.0	7.56	6.55	5.99	5.64	5.39	5.20	5.06	4.94	4.85	4.71	4.56	4.41	4.33	4.25	4.17	4.08	4.00	3.91
11	9.65	7.21	6.22	5.67	5.32	5.07	4.89	4.74	4.63	4.54	4.40	4.25	4.10	4.02	3.94	3.86	3.78	3.69	3.60
12	9.33	6.93	5.95	5.41	5.06	4.82	4.64	4.50	4.39	4.30	4.16	4.01	3.86	3.78	3.70	3.62	3.54	3.45	3.36
13	9.07	6.70	5.74	5.21	4.86	4.62	4.44	4.30	4.19	4.10	3.96	3.82	3.66	3.59	3.51	3.43	3.34	3.25	3.17
14	8.86	6.51	5.56	5.04	4.70	4.46	4.28	4.14	4.03	3.94	3.80	3.66	3.51	3.43	3.35	3.27	3.18	3.09	3.00
15	8.68	6.36	5.42	4.89	4.56	4.32	4.14	4.00	3.89	3.80	3.67	3.52	3.37	3.29	3.21	3.13	3.05	2.96	2.87
16	8.53	6.23	5.29	4.77	4.44	4.20	4.03	3.89	3.78	3.69	3.55	3.41	3.26	3.18	3.10	3.02	2.93	2.84	2.75
17	8.40	6.11	5.19	4.67	4.34	4.10	3.93	3.79	3.68	3.59	3.46	3.31	3.16	3.08	3.00	2.92	2.83	2.75	2.65
18	8.29	6.01	5.09	4.58	4.25	4.01	3.84	3.71	3.60	3.51	3.37	3.23	3.08	3.00	2.92	2.84	2.75	2.66	2.57
19	8.19	5.93	5.01	4.50	4.17	3.94	3.77	3.63	3.52	3.43	3.30	3.15	3.00	2.92	2.84	2.76	2.67	2.58	2.49
20	8.10	5.85	4.94	4.43	4.10	3.87	3.70	3.56	3.46	3.37	3.23	3.09	2.94	2.86	2.78	2.69	2.61	2.52	2.42
21	8.02	5.78	4.87	4.37	4.04	3.81	3.64	3.51	3.40	3.31	3.17	3.03	2.88	2.80	2.72	2.64	2.55	2.46	2.36
22	7.95	5.72	4.82	4.31	3.99	3.76	3.59	3.45	3.35	3.26	3.12	2.98	2.83	2.75	2.67	2.58	2.50	2.40	2.31
23	7.88	5.66	4.76	4.26	3.94	3.71	3.54	3.41	3.30	3.21	3.07	2.93	2.78	2.70	2.62	2.54	2.45	2.35	2.26
24	7.82	5.61	4.72	4.22	3.90	3.67	3.50	3.36	3.26	3.17	3.03	2.89	2.74	2.66	2.58	2.49	2.40	2.31	2.21
25	7.77	5.57	4.68	4.18	3.86	3.63	3.46	3.32	3.22	3.13	2.99	2.85	2.70	2.62	2.53	2.45	2.36	2.27	2.17
30	7.56	5.39	4.51	4.02	3.70	3.47	3.30	3.17	3.07	2.98	2.84	2.70	2.55	2.47	2.39	2.30	2.21	2.11	2.01
40	7.31	5.18	4.31	3.83	3.51	3.29	3.12	2.99	2.89	2.80	2.66	2.52	2.37	2.29	2.20	2.11	2.02	1.92	1.80
60	7.08	4.98	4.13	3.65	3.34	3.12	2.95	2.82	2.72	2.63	2.50	2.35	2.20	2.12	2.03	1.94	1.84	1.73	1.60
120	6.85	4.79	3.95	3.48	3.17	2.96	2.79	2.66	2.56	2.47	2.34	2.19	2.03	1.95	1.86	1.76	1.66	1.53	1.38
∞	6.63	4.61	3.78	3.32	3.02	2.80	2.64	2.51	2.41	2.32	2.18	2.04	1.88	1.79	1.70	1.59	1.47	1.32	1.00

Source: This table is reproduced from M. Merrington and C. M. Thompson, "Tables of Percentage Points of the Inverted Beta (F) Distribution," Biometrika, vol. 33 (1943), by permission of the Biometrika trustees.

Index